AF531197

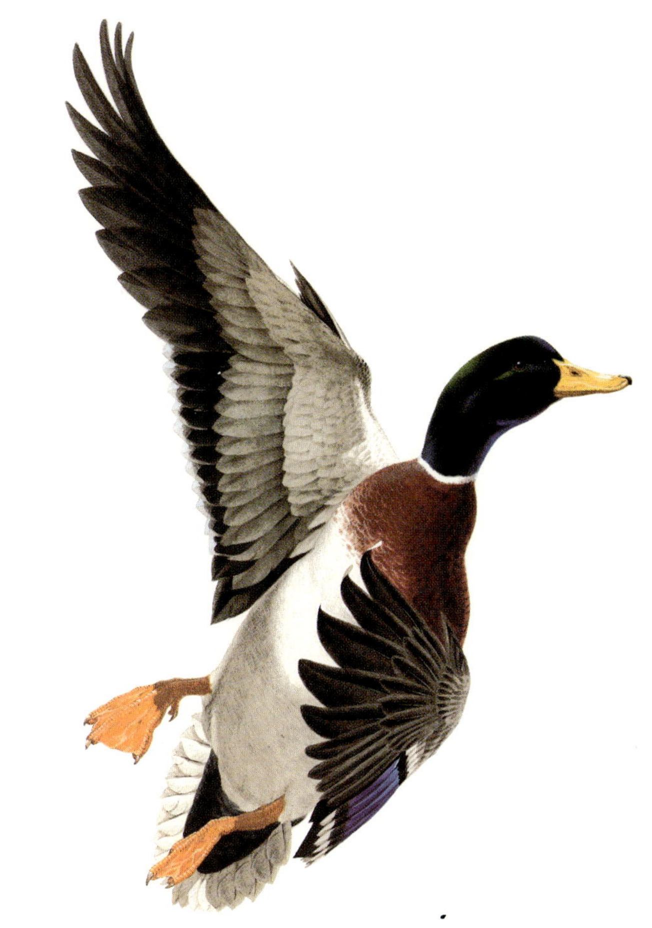

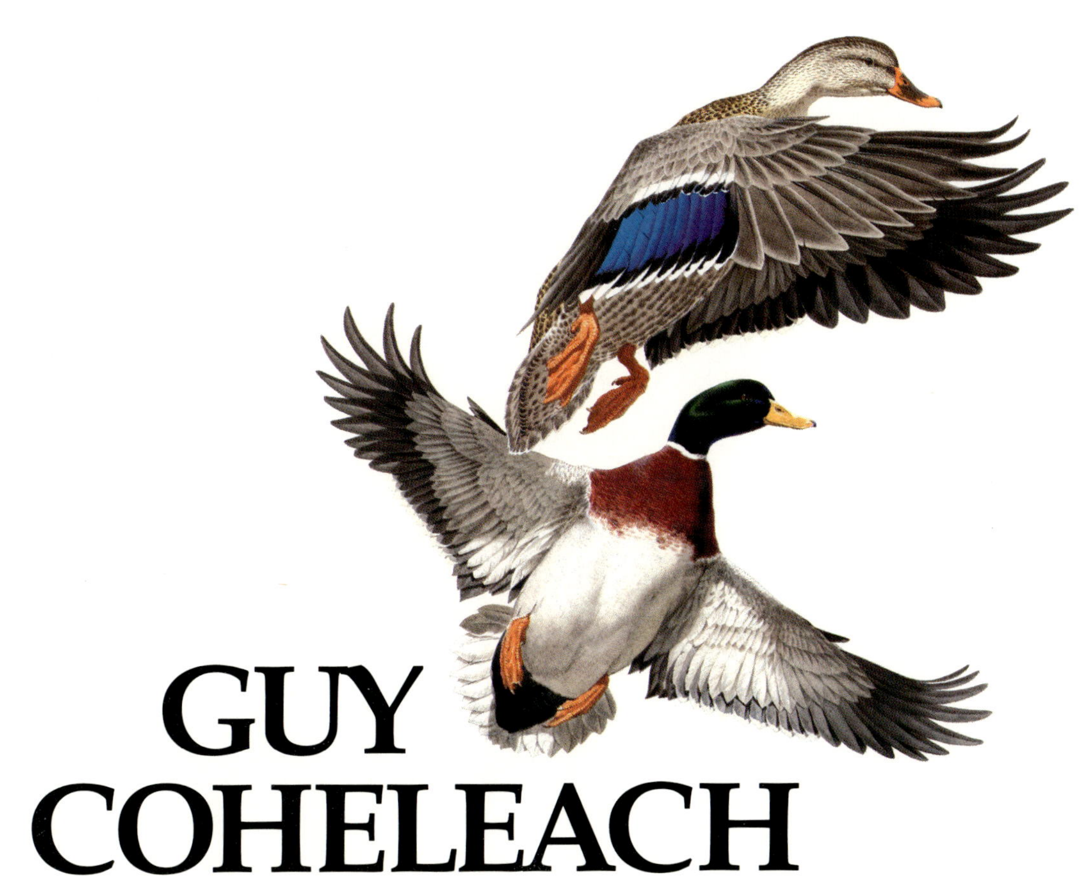

GUY COHELEACH

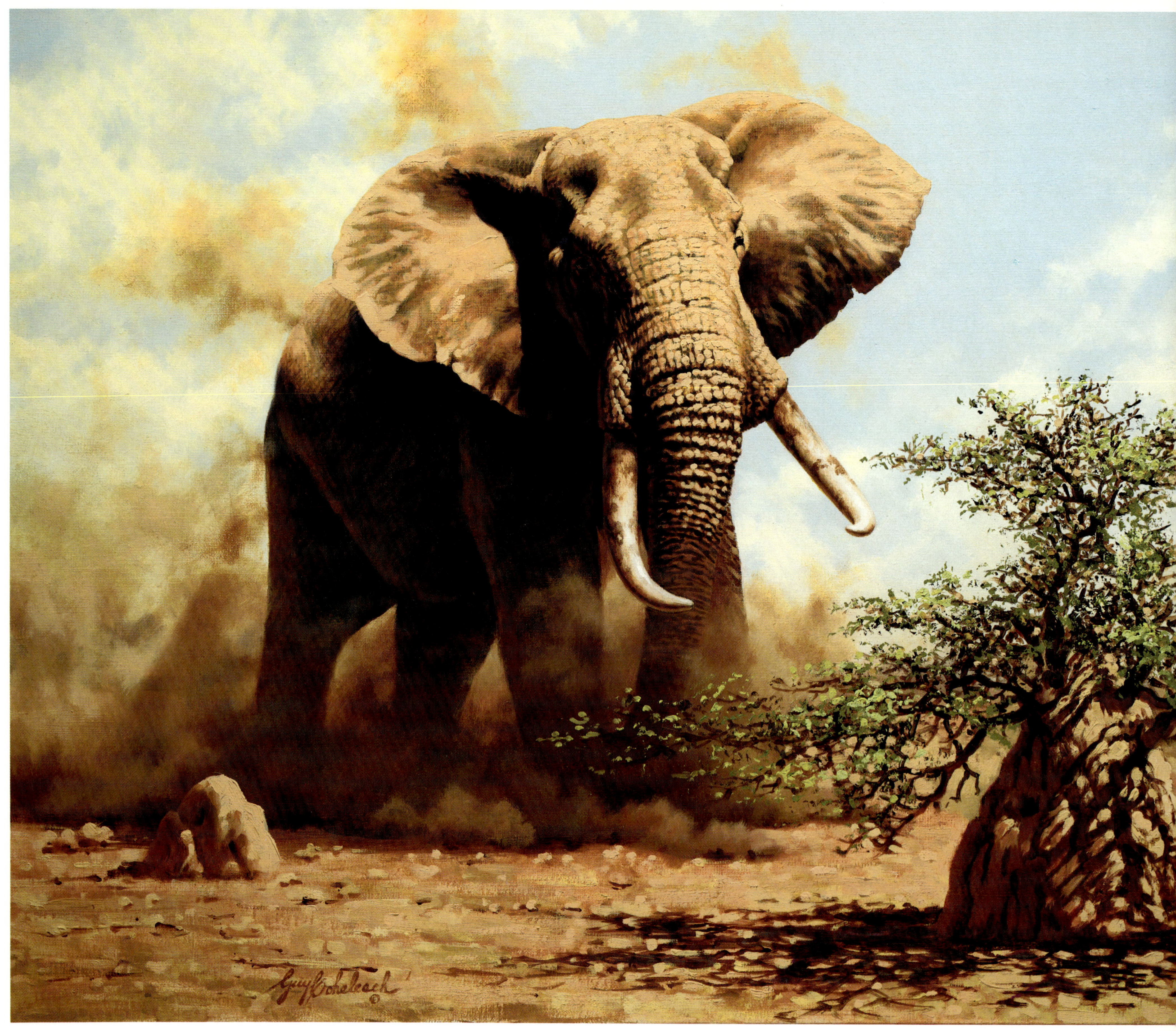

Bull Elephant, 30 X 22, Oil on Canvas

MASTERS OF THE WILD

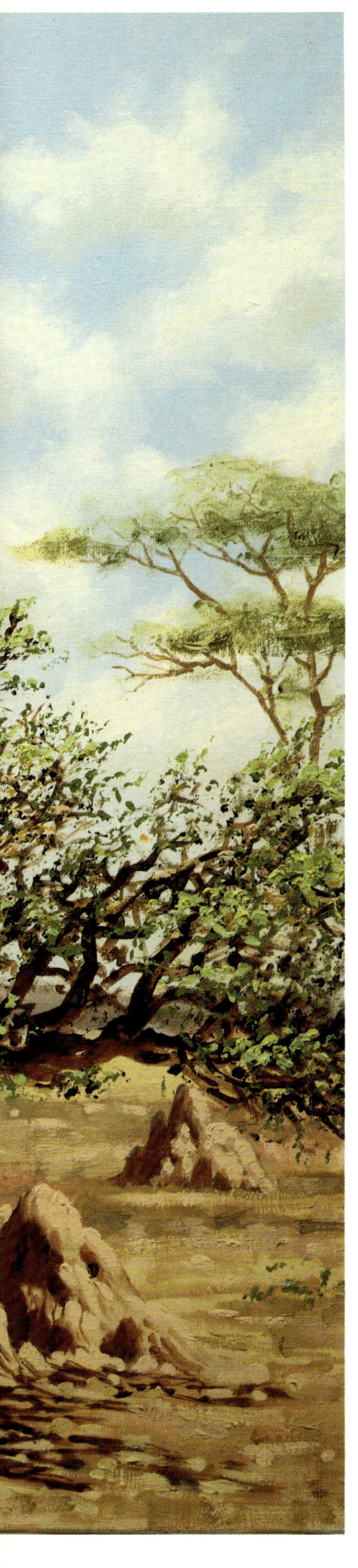

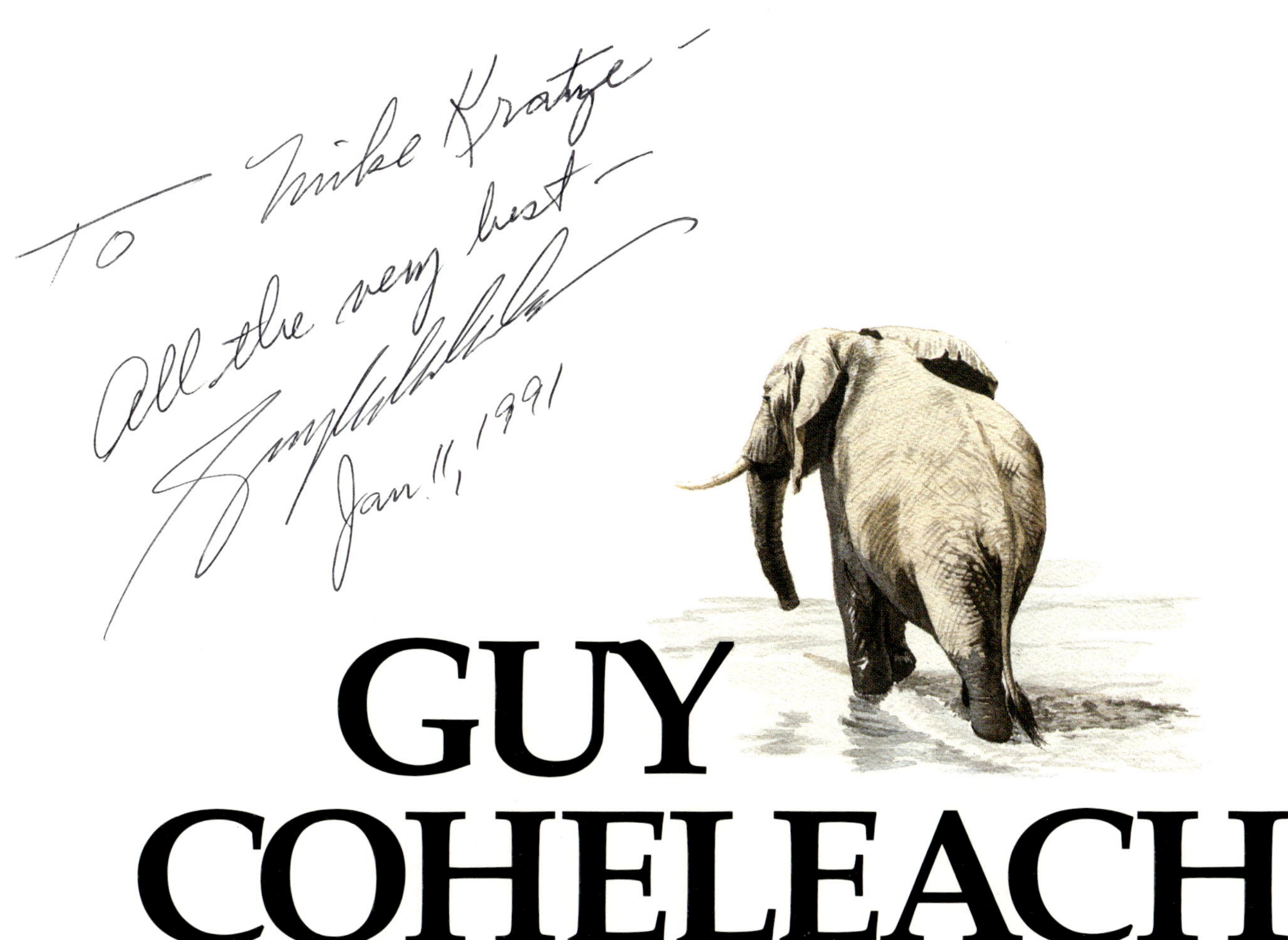

GUY COHELEACH

TEXT BY
TERRY WIELAND

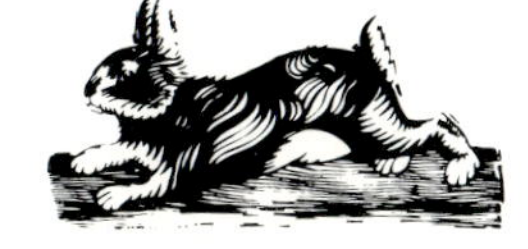

BRIAR PATCH PRESS
CAMDEN, SOUTH CAROLINA

Briar Patch Press, Inc.
John Culler, *Publisher*
Charles A. Wechsler, *Editor*
Kay K. Jackson, *Art Director/Designer*

Copyright © by Briar Patch Press, Inc.

This book and other volumes in *Masters of the Wild* are produced by Briar Patch Press, Inc., P.O. Box 1017, Camden, South Carolina 29020.

All rights reserved. No part of this book may be reproduced, stored or introduced into a retrieval system, or transmitted in any form by any means without prior written permission of the publisher, and by Guy Coheleach, except by a reviewer who may quote brief passages in a review.

ISBN 0-922724-00-8

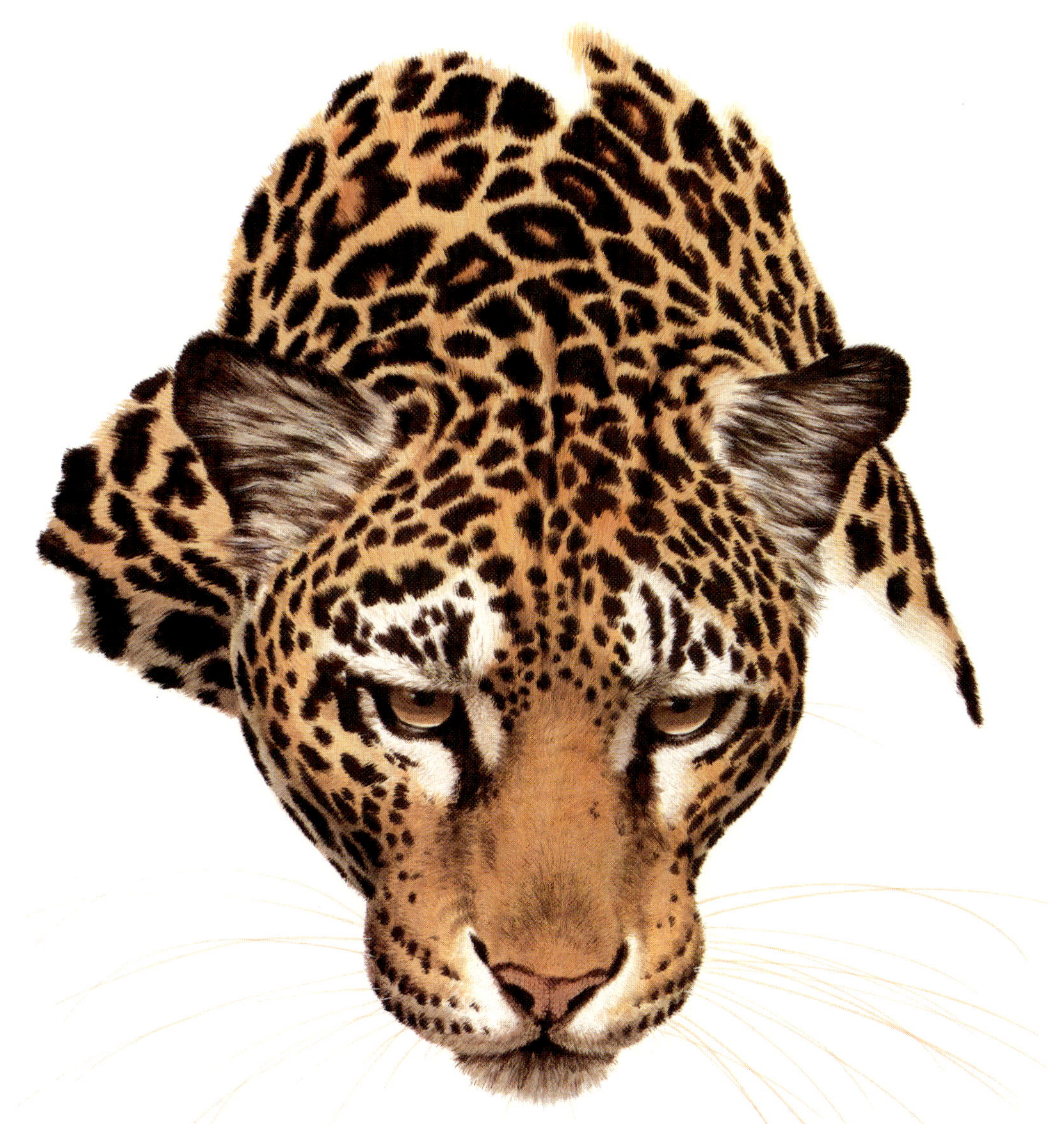

DEDICATION

*To Don Eckelberry,
whose unselfish genius
is responsible for
whatever is good
in this book.*

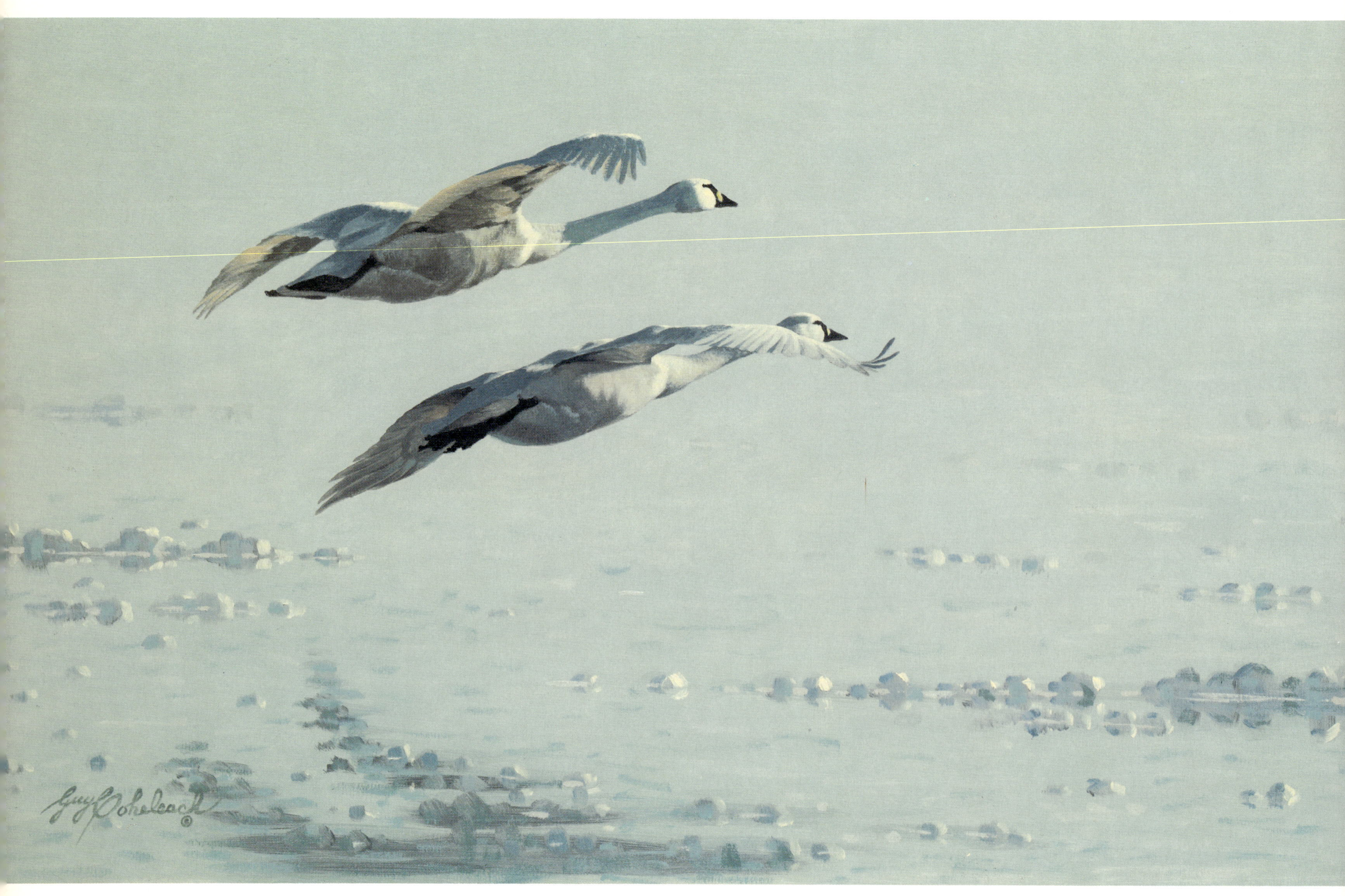

Whistling Swans, 30 x 15, Oil on Canvas

FOREWORD

I don't know how many artists have been asked if they want a book written about themselves and their work, but I can tell you it is a wonderful, heady experience.

When the people at Briar Patch Press first approached me on doing a book, I jumped at it. Their reputation for quality is well known, and it would be a great opportunity to present a large body of my work, including many commissioned pieces that have never been seen by the art community. The clincher, of course, was the company I would be keeping in *Masters of the Wild:* Liljefors, Kuhnert, Rungius, etc. ... whew!

My only problem was that of identity. I don't think there is a "typical" Coheleach style — my work is simply all over the spectrum. When Roger Tory Peterson first saw one of my exhibitions, he thought it was a group show! Although I try to finish one piece at a time, it is not uncommon to see in my studio a huge, painterly oil-on-canvas — with paint a half-inch thick and four-inch wide brushstrokes — next to a detailed portrait showing every hair and feather. While my penchant for working in all kinds of styles and media may pose some problems from a recognition standpoint, it has certainly prevented me from getting bored.

Then came the awesome responsibility of selecting drawings and paintings that would stand up to discerning eyes over a long period of time. Somehow, what I once regarded as pretty good portraits faded quickly in the glare of permanent exposure. My publishers, however, assured me that whatever I chose would add to the evolutionary value of such a book.

If there is a commonality to my work, I hope it is the life that is so painstakingly put into it. Whether it be a tight rendering or an impressionistic piece, it must smack of life. The subject, design, and colors, no matter how subtle, should live! Accomplishing that goal is quite another matter, of course, and I suppose objective judgment is now at hand.

What follows is the first retrospective of my work. I am very grateful for the opportunity and pray that you will enjoy seeing wildlife as I have interpreted it through these years.

GUY COHELEACH

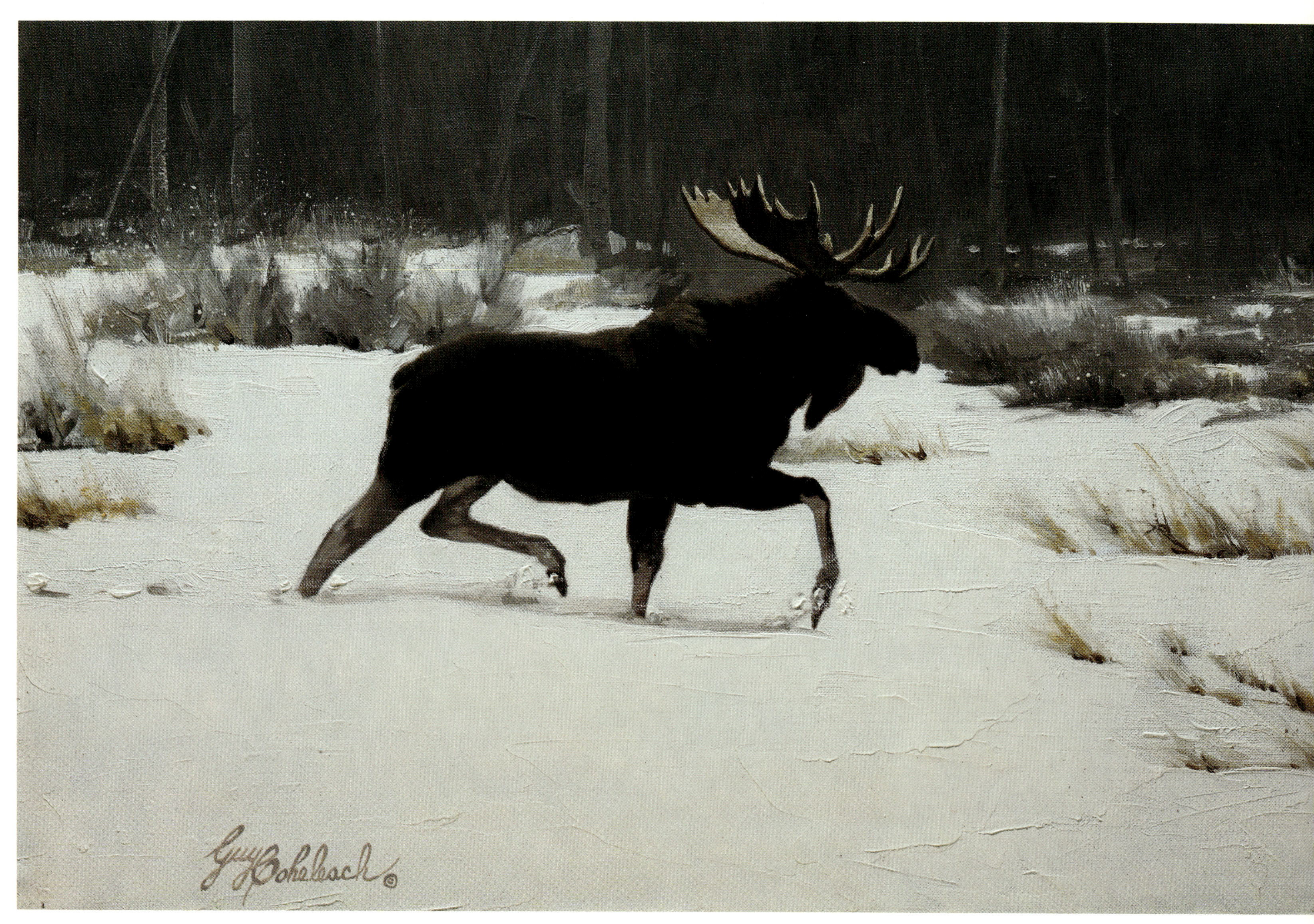

Lone Moose, 24 X 12, Oil on Canvas

INTRODUCTION

Families, especially those involving two daughters, rarely find unanimity on controversial subjects like decor, yet in my home the whole of one hallway is covered with Guy Coheleach prints. The girls had a lot of other art to choose from, since I'm some sort of a collector of outdoor-related art, so why Coheleach?

I don't have either the courage or insight to speak for the girls, but I think I know why Coheleach's art appealed to them so strongly. To me, he has an immense evocative power, the ability to create a piece of art that is continually bringing to both the mind and the eye something new and arresting.

One of our favorites is a leopard that I never pass without pausing to wonder at this essential primitive being. Here is the very rawest of vigilance, the edge of survival; a creature crouched between two stones that symbolize the total indifference of nature. I see a painting that tells me more about life than I'm sometimes comfortable with. If life goes well, the stones are a home, a refuge; if not, they will serve equally well as a grave.

I like my passageway of Coheleach's for another, personal reason — that Guy is an old and very treasured friend. He is witty, intelligent, generous, and kind (I see a lot of these qualities in his work as well.) We've fished together, shot together, and pleasured ourselves in each other's company. We've talked and often argued about art, what we like, who we like and why. I can assure you that is a rare treat. Having known many writers and artists, I know too that introspective, challenging, and enriching conversations are not common. And while I agree that it is not right or fair to equate quality of work with the morality or intelligence of the artist, it is a great pleasure to find an artist who is as articulate in his objective analysis of his field of interest as he is in his own creations.

Guy is a man who brings to his art the insight of an extremely experienced sportsman and an educated naturalist. These, combined with his near limitless technical abilities, create works that contain an aura that frequently involve time, environment, circumstance, and what I choose to call myth.

An example of what I mean by myth can be seen in his fascination with the cats. His leopards are not only animals to see, they are animals to think about. If you have hunted leopard, you know that you do so for many reasons; to be there with this ultimate hunter, to be a part of his world for a time, to try to understand the taste of blood, to understand the continuum of survival at its most elemental level.

These factors are not accidental in a Coheleach leopard. He is not merely painting what he sees, he is painting what he knows, what he is in a surrealistic sense. His leopard is not only a leopard, it is a magic piece of the Great Puzzle. And that, my friends, is what good art is supposed to be.

It's easy to see that, because Guy is a hunter, he understands the consequences of success and failure in the wild. Perhaps his feeling for danger is so evident because he has endangered himself to a high degree in almost all of the activities a man can involve himself in that virtually promise getting scared or hurt or worse. He understands this environmental "edge" to an uncanny degree.

This is strongly evident in another of my favorite Coheleach's: *Lone Moose*. Here we have what seems at first a certainly majestic animal, an elemental lordliness. But then we study the surround, we feel the cold, we take in the forbidding touches of the North. Our awe of this forest giant slides thoughtfully into something else that we are helpless to do much more about than "watch." Here is a painting of cold and hunger, of uncertainty and fear. Here is an animal, like one of us, who fears the coming of the storm, the tolling of the Northern wind. Guy has painted the

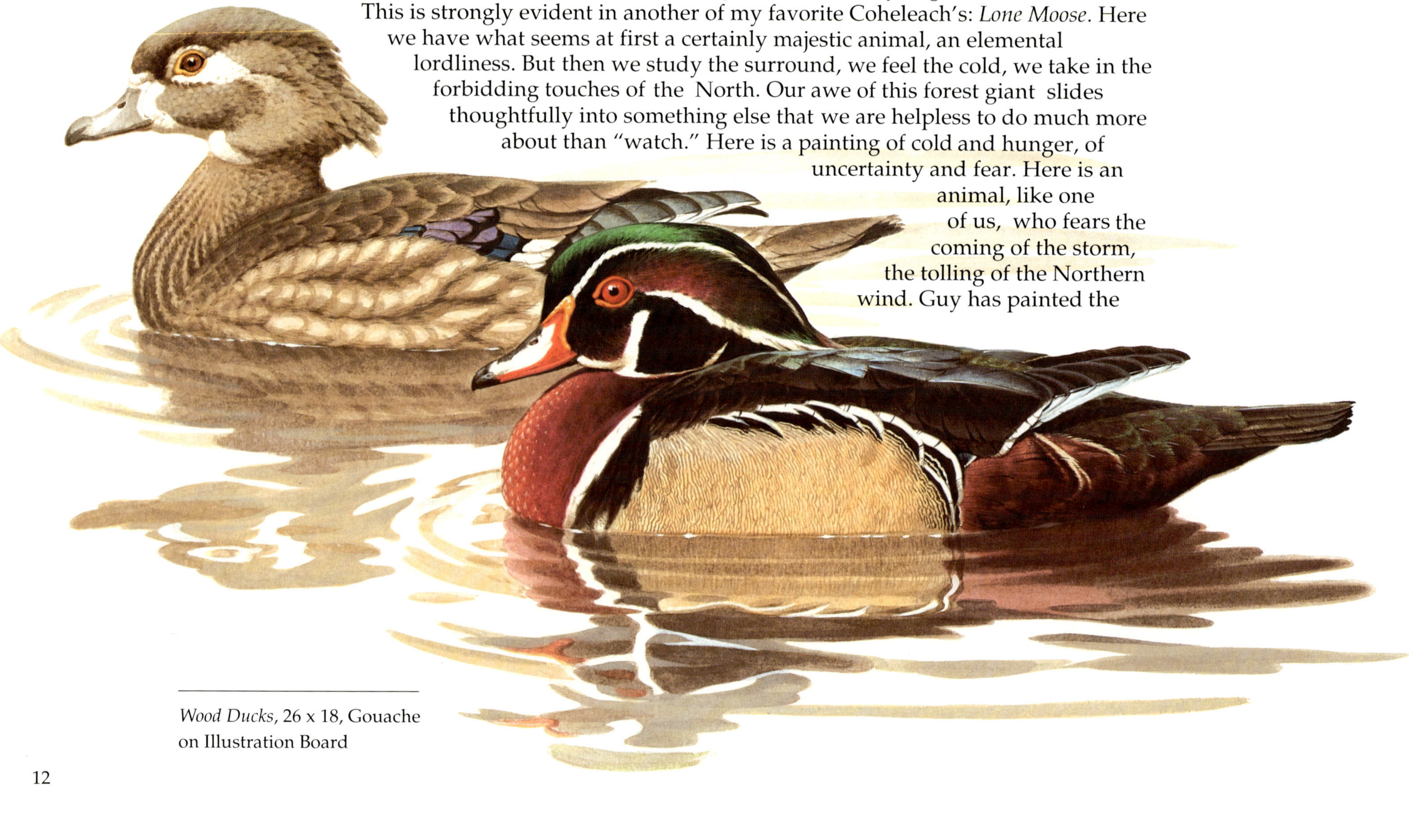

Wood Ducks, 26 x 18, Gouache on Illustration Board

urgent thought, I allow myself to imagine, of every wild and not-so-wild animal when every corner holds the final threat ... if it is not now, it might never be.

Because of his tremendous scope, technically and intellectually, Coheleach forces himself to take chances. He is constantly experimenting with method and subject matter and point of view. He is a serious student, continuing to increase his knowledge of his subject matter as well as his studies in fine art. I have rarely known him to be completely satisfied with a painting; his integrity and pride continuing to be restless demons tormenting him toward the impossibility of his version of perfection. I remember him discussing another painter with great admiration and when I interrupted him saying "Guy, you're ten times the artist he is" and Guy replying "I know I am overall, but his skies have a coloration that I just can't seem to match." Guy works in a league where he thinks it's wrong or at least unfair that you can't bat a thousand!

I wonder, with pleasurable expectation, what next from him? What will he show us in a curving line or phrase of color that we have never seen quite that way before? I know he's searching for it, that elusive something, that eclectic vision that we have never seen — until Guy Coheleach shows it to us. But whatever it is, I know it will penetrate our minds, it will watch us and captivate us. It will dare you to come closer ... or frighten you deep inside like life does when we ask the hard questions and get an answer.

GENE HILL

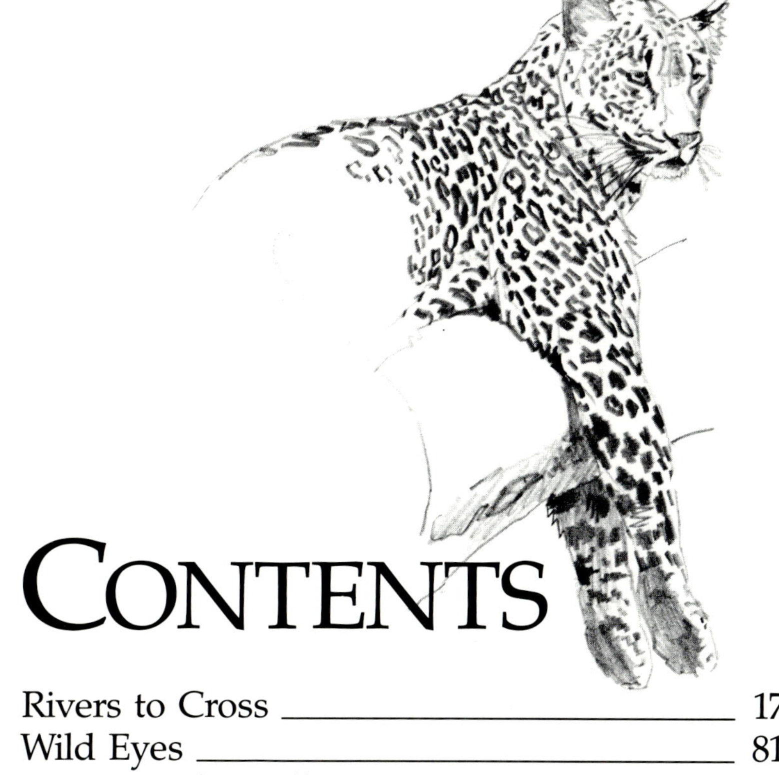

CONTENTS

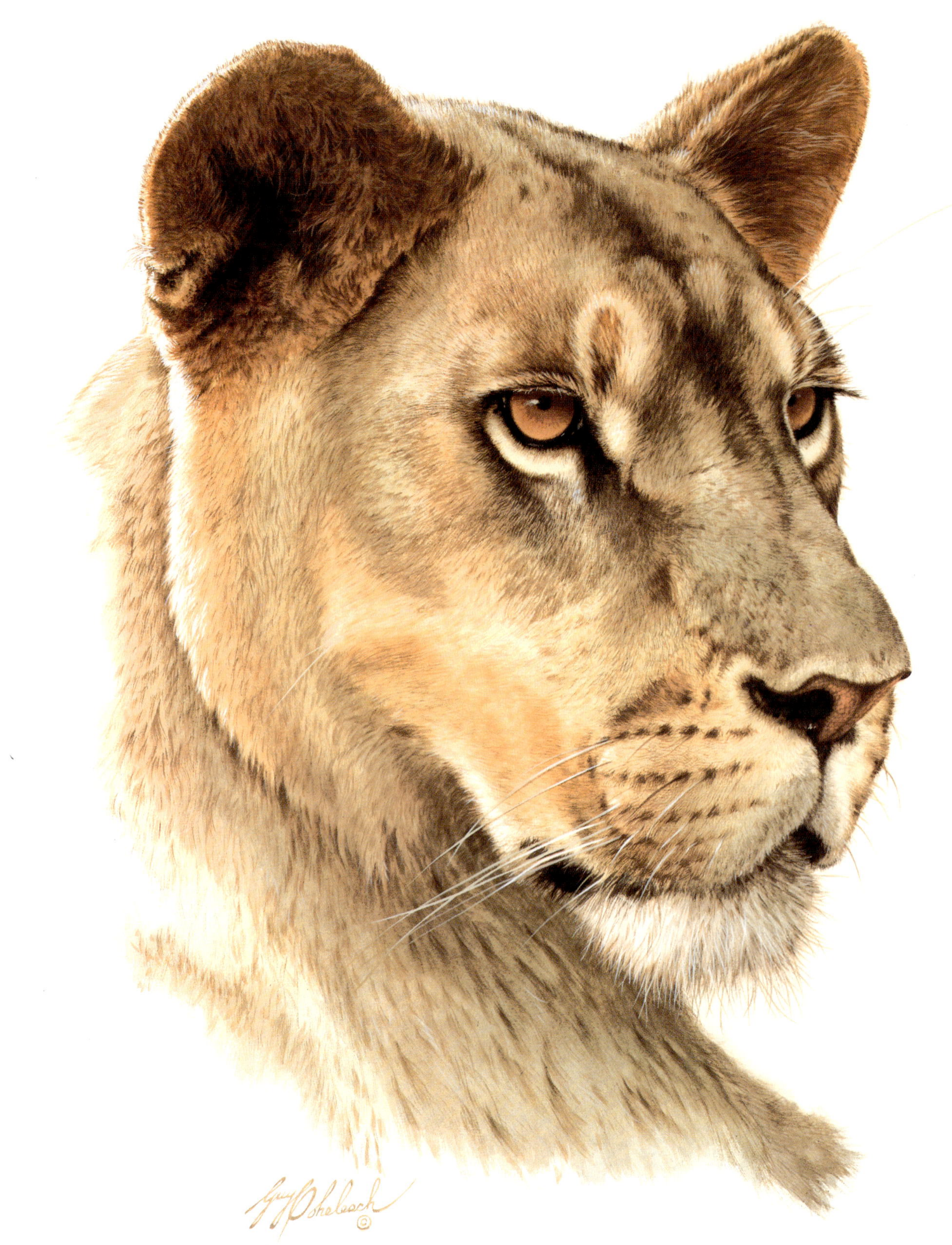

Lioness Head, 20 X 26,
Gouache on Illustration
Board

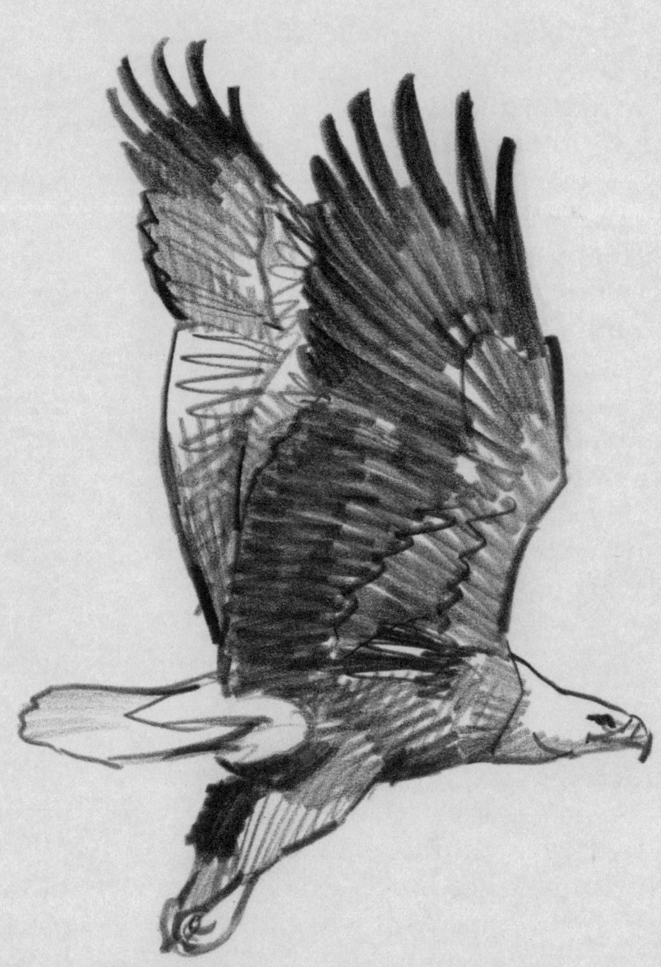

RIVERS TO CROSS

When you go looking for a man with Guy Coheleach's reputation, you half expect to catch up to him just as he is about to jump out of an airplane, jump into a racing car, or jump out of the way of a charging elephant. Over the years, tales of his daredevil lifestyle have grown to the point where they begin to eclipse his reputation as an artist, a point that Coheleach himself regards with suspicion and (I think) no small amount of regret. He enjoys his reputation as a *bon vivant;* he treasures his reputation as an artist. There's a difference.

Even so, he is a man who moves around. He moves around a lot. It was a stroke of luck to find him at home at all, much less at home with time to spare. Well, a little time. Just back from a short vacation in Salzburg with his wife, Pam, he was about to jump on another plane for Cincinnati for the auction of a painting he had donated to the Cincinnati Zoo. If I could meet him in Philadelphia, we would take it from there...

I found Coheleach in a small knot of people in the center of the old Bank of the United States building on 3rd Street between Walnut and Chestnut. Old Philadelphia. The historic section was in the middle of its 200th Anniversary-of-the-Constitution year-long birthday bash, the narrow streets decked in flags and banners, squeaky clean with groups of tourists being shepherded along by guides in the haberdashery of 1787.

Coheleach was standing in the emptiness of the bank's great hall with other members of the Society of Animal Artists, discussing arrangements for a coming exhibition. Their voices floated to the glass dome ceiling and bounced softly back to earth.

Waiting, I wandered around the empty hall, reading the words carved into the stone. The Bank of the United States was founded in 1791 to raise money to pay off the country's war debts. During its 20-year history, it succeeded in stabilizing the currency and prevented abuses by state banks, and even compiled a good record in handling public funds. Obviously, such a state of affairs in government could not be allowed to continue, and Andrew Jackson pulled the plug on the bank in 1811.

The First Bank of the United States died, but the First Bank of the United States Building in Philadelphia lived on, first as headquarters for the Bank of Stephen Girard, and after a refurbishing in the early 1900s, as a center for exhibitions. Now, it was to host an exhibition of wildlife art, including the paintings of Guy Coheleach.

Slowly, the informal meeting ended and the people drifted out one at a time, until only Coheleach was left, talking with the organizers of the coming exhibition. His voice drifted across the room, through the sunlight that streamed in through the big old windows, his New Yorker's inflections as strangely out of place as the Forest Service uniform of the bank's attendant.

"The bank has the same status as a national park, so that's why we have the forest rangers," Coheleach told me as we made our way out of the old section, crawling through the streets in search of I-95, the Delaware River, and the beginning of the two-hour drive to his home in rural New Jersey.

"That bank's a great old building, isn't it? You like history, like old things?" he asked. "Philadelphia's full of history. Lotta jokes about it, how people come here to die. Really like it, myself."

We find ourselves in what is obviously a housing project, clean and neat, the chainlink fences only moderately battered, the row houses devoid of soul.

"'Scuse me, ma'am," Coheleach calls out the window. "Can you tell me how to get to Route 95?"

The woman pauses and stares.

"Got no idea."

"Well, thank you very much anyway," he calls after her, nary a trace of sarcasm in a situation where a touch would be richly deserved. We resume our meandering, Coheleach steering, reading a road map, negotiating road repair crews and torn-up pavement, and talking all the time.

"Two ways we can go. We can take the interstate up to Jersey, or we can take an older road that runs along the Delaware. Which do you want? The river road's slower, but it's a lot more scenic. Nice little towns. We can stop in one of them for lunch."

The Delaware road it is. If we can find it.

"What made you leave Long Island?"

"Taxes. Bastards wanted me to pay six and a half per cent of the market value of my house every damn year."

"Who was going to determine market value?"

"Not me, that's for sure."

And so Long Island lost one of its resident artists, a man who had been made practically an artistic institution by the local press. Long Island's cultural loss was a financial loss for a few of the local saloons — Popeye's, Vinny's, and Codfish Bob's. According to Coheleach, his wife Pam was not sorry to see him deprived of the waterfront company he loved, and so they fled to Florida.

"Great place to work, Florida. Impossible to take it seriously. How can you be serious when you go to work every morning in shorts and sandals? Like California, only not so weird."

So why the move back to New Jersey?

"The kids. We've buried two kids. Still got three, and they're all in the New York area. Pam wanted to be close to them, so she told me one day she was moving back here, and was I coming?"

Back to sons George and Hugh, and daughter Coleen. George, married with a couple of kids himself. Hugh, the youngest remaining, in his early twenties and starting out a career on the floor of the New York Stock Exchange. Coleen, with a masters degree in education and a career as a teacher of handicapped children.

An infant daughter died shortly after birth, and their youngest son was killed by a hit-and-run driver when he was 10 years old. The memories of these events are evident not only in Coheleach's words, but in what he doesn't say.

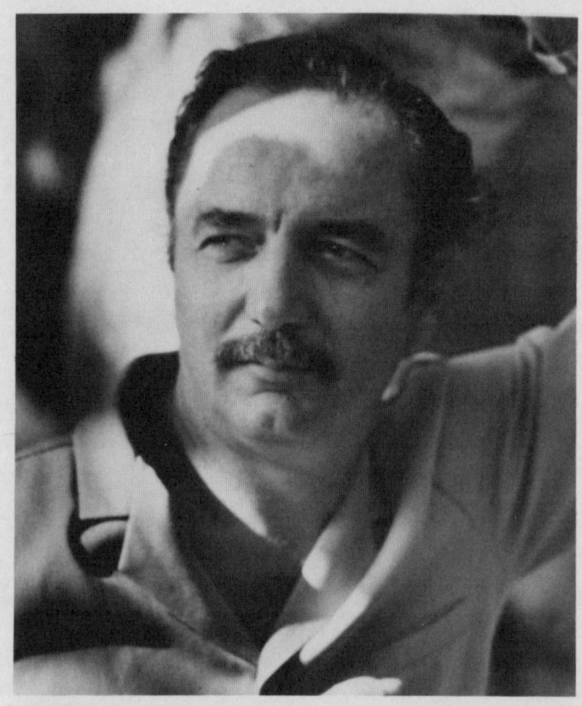

Guy Coheleach in the early '80s.

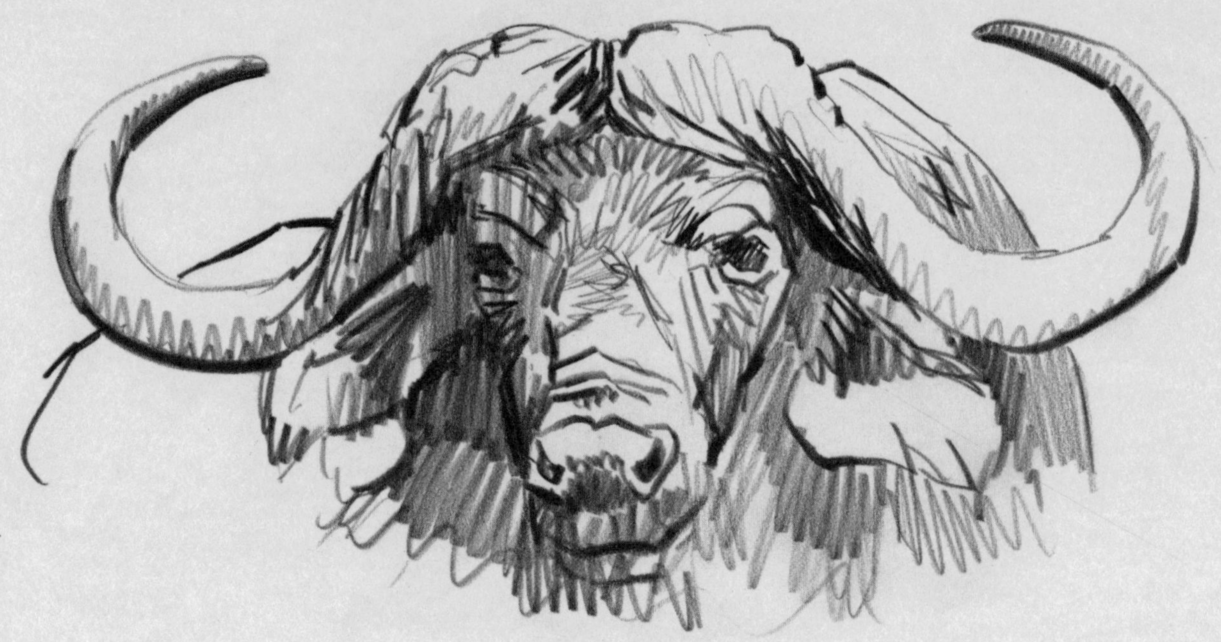

"A thing like that, it changes your way of thinking completely. Things that used to matter to you don't matter at all. Things you took for granted become unbelievably precious. So we moved back here. Now we get to see our grandchildren, and we get to see Hughie and Coleen all the time. On top of which, I really like the country up here."

"Up here" is Bernardsville, New Jersey, a quiet and well-bred little town in the affluence belt that surrounds New York City. At one time, it was farming country. Today, because it is only an hour's drive from Manhattan, the farms are gone, divided and subdivided into building lots — if you can call five acres of real estate selling for better than half a million dollars a "building lot." The country is heavily treed, the highways narrow and twisting, well kept but not expressways, little more really than extensions of driveways that lead, ultimately, to Manhattan skyscrapers, and the source of the incomes that finance the huge rural Jersey houses that change hands at two or three million dollars a crack.

But Bernardsville might as well have been on the moon. We still had to get out of Philadelphia. Finally, we reach I-95 and head north, Coheleach negotiating the expressway as he had the torn-up streets, road map on his knee, one eye on the road, one hand on the wheel. Immediate destination: Lambertsville, astride the Delaware River and, according to Coheleach, possessed of several excellent eateries.

Time to discuss the book.

"Okay, so how do you want to handle it? You tell me." I suggest splitting the text into three parts: a general introduction to Guy Coheleach, another to his hunting, the third to his work in conservation.

"Why so much about hunting? Hunting's a very small part of my life. If I didn't have it, I wouldn't miss it. There's so much more I'm concerned with than that."

"But you've shot 93 (at last count) Cape buffalo and 19 elephants — how can you say hunting's a small part of your life?"

"Most of those were a long time ago. Look. I love hunting buffalo, but it's not something that possesses me. Sure, I'm weird for buffalo. But I never shot an elephant that I didn't feel sick about afterwards. Most of those were shot on control, anyway. Thing is, there are a lot more important things in life..."

Like what?

"Like leaving the place a little better than you found it. I'll tell you a story. You know I paint a lot of baby animals. Don Eckelberry, who is a great artist and a really dear friend of mine, used to kid me a lot. He'd say 'There goes Coheleach, painting the cute little animals and laughing all the way to the bank.' Don't I wish! Don used to ask me when I was going to stop painting that stuff and produce some real art. So I decided that was what I was going to do — stop painting baby animal pictures and turn out art.

"I swear it wasn't two days later I got a letter in the mail from a nurse in Wisconsin. She was caring for a little girl, who she said was 'seriously ill,' which in nurse's parlance means she was terminally ill. In all the time she'd been nursing this little girl, she'd never seen her smile. I'd donated a lot of prints to this hospital — basically, I'll donate as many as they'll have framed and hung — and they had hung a print of a baby polar bear in this little girl's room.

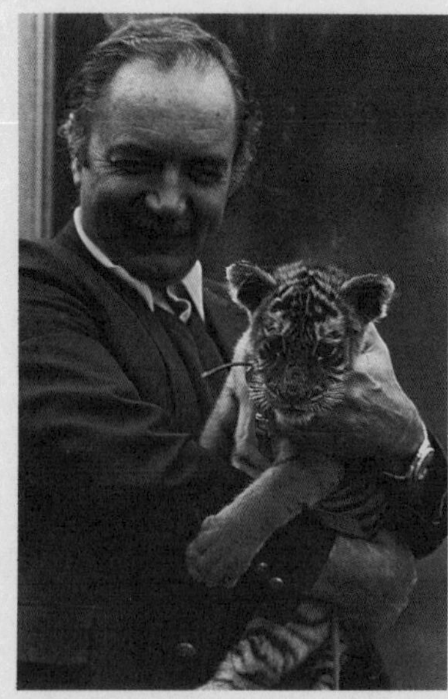

Coheleach enjoys the company of a Bengal tiger cub while on a 1986 visit to the Cincinnati zoo.

"The next day, when the nurse went into the room, the little girl was sitting there smiling at the picture, for the first time.

"And I thought, Christ, how can I stop painting pictures that will do that? That's what it's all about: producing something that will make people feel a little better."

We pull into Lambertville, New Jersey, across the muddy Delaware, 30 miles and about 100 light years away from Philadelphia. How would one describe Lambertville? Prim? Yes, prim's a good word. We wander down the main street towards the bridge. The restaurant Coheleach had in mind is gone, but the Lambertville Station remains, converted, as so many historic railway stations have been, into upscale public houses with dark polished bars and dark polished bartenders, wallpaper music wafting from hidden speakers, the biting fragrance of hops and malt greeting you at the door.

Coheleach sounds almost anxious as he inquires whether this would suit me. Devoted as I am to sleazy saloons, I was more inclined to wonder whether I would suit it. But anyplace that has Heineken on tap gets my vote — and Coheleach's, too, as it turns out.

"In Salzburg (Austria) I think I spent about 50 percent of the time drinking their draught beer," he said. "It shows, too — but what the hell? They've got the best beer in the world."

One of the better-known Guy Coheleach stories takes place in a saloon — New York's celebrated speakeasy, '21'. Seems he went in for dinner one time feeling particularly peckish and in a mood for lamb. Knowing '21' is famous for the quality of its lambchops, if not for their size, Coheleach ordered eight.

The waiter, snotty to a fault: "Eight orders, sirrrrr?"

"Eight lambchops," Coheleach replied.

"Yes sirrrrr, lambchops. Eight orders?"

After going through this about three times, Coheleach finally had enough and said, all right, goddammit, bring me eight orders.

"I thought there were two chops to an order. Turned out there were three. So there I was with 24 lambchops sitting in front of me. Ate every damned one. Frankly, it says more about the size of their lambchops than it does about the size of my stomach."

Today, with no waiter to cut down to size, we settle for less. French onion soup, seafood chowder, a buffalo burger very rare, all washed down with the rich and bitter Heineken, so cold the glasses sweat and water gathers in pools around the stems. After two, Coheleach switches to diet cola, determined to replenish his caffein supply so he can stay awake driving the rest of the way to Bernardsville.

"I have a tendency to fall asleep at the wheel. Since I don't drink coffee or tea, this is the only thing keeps me awake."

He's been on the road since 7:00 in the morning, up at dawn and on his way to Philadelphia to check on lighting arrangements for the exhibition — a two-hour drive each way for a one-hour meeting. Work on behalf of the Society of Animal Artists. Coheleach does not begrudge them the time, or at least, he says he doesn't.

"Well, maybe I do spend too much time on this kind of stuff when I should be working, but I guess it's all part of giving something back. That's something that concerns me more and more as I get older. Sometimes I think that's really the only thing there is."

My glass is almost empty.

"You want another? Sir, would you bring this man another Heineken? I'll have another Tab, or whatever."

I protest. Then I drink the beer. Coheleach nurses his diet cola and kibitzes with the bartender, admiring the cut of the old station and the layout of the bar. Time slows down and merges with the hum of the music from the wall, and then Coheleach gathers in the bill as a croupier gathers chips and we pour back out into the sunshine and onto the road to Bernardsville...

For Guy Coheleach, the road to Bernardsville, New Jersey and the subtle incidentals of assumed affluence (the land where an unpaved driveway is a status symbol) has been anything like our sunwashed, pokey procession up the road along the Delaware. There are many rivers to cross between Baldwin, Long Island, and Bernardsville. More than just the Hudson and Passaic and Long Island Sound.

One of nine children, Coheleach was born in 1933 in New York City, was raised in Baldwin, Long Island and went to school in Brooklyn. Like the country, you can take the boy out of Brooklyn, and Coheleach retains his Brooklyn boyhood in his speech and street kid mannerisms which slip only occasionally.

As the magazine articles never tire of pointing out, Coheleach's father, Gaetan, was a test pilot of Franco-Swiss origin (the name is pronounced CO-lee-ack), but Guy says that calling him a test pilot is an exaggeration.

"He worked for the phone company, but he did a lot of crazy things before he was married. I've got pictures of him in airplane crashes up at the Great Lakes naval station. I don't know if he was involved in all of them, but he loved flying and all kinds of crazy things like that. Once he got married and the children came along, my mother said 'Enough of that, get yourself a job.'

"Which he did. He faced his responsibilities, got a job with the phone company, and he stayed with them until he died (in 1963). He was on medical leave, and he went around to see all the kids. We were spread out all over the country at that time — Virginia, Florida, California. And he was on his way back, there was a wind storm, turned the trailer over, and he was in it.

"When I realize the sacrifices the man gave for his responsibilities; coming out of that generation, he never did have a lot of money. Worked days and nights and weekends to support us, and he was just one of those people never had anything brand new for himself. It's a shame he died before I could do a couple of nice things for him."

"Did you get along well with him?"

"Oh, God ... yeah ... I guess I was in high school before I realized he wasn't God. He was so fair. If he ever had a favorite with the nine children, none of us ever knew."

While phonetically and physically close to Brooklyn, the village of Baldwin was not in the same league in other ways.

"I remember we left our doors unlocked when I was a kid. My mother always said, 'there's nothing there for anybody to steal except food, and if they're hungry, they're welcome to it.' They never had a lot of material things to give us, which probably bothered them a little, but there was never any doubt in any of our minds that they loved us dearly. I mean when you realize that I came home with rattlesnakes and cobras and kept them in the cellar, and all they demanded was that they be kept in clean cages, with fresh water, and well fed..."

Another bit of Coheleach folklore: the basement full of deadly reptiles...

Who knows at what point a person takes a passion for living creatures and a deep talent for painting, and combines them and turns them into wildlife art? Coheleach doesn't. He does know that he pursued a career as an amateur herpetologist early in life, keeping his snake collection in the basement of the family home. He fed them mice, collected from laboratories at Columbia University, where he cultivated friendships with doctorate students, even going so far as to do field work for them.

But a basement full of serpents?

"I don't think I ever had more than five or six snakes at home, and then generally because they were sick and I wanted to keep an eye on them," he says. "But no, I didn't just have a whole bunch of goddamned snakes home. I had all kinds home — God, I had a 12-foot king cobra! But I only had that one because it had a respiratory ailment. But let me tell you something, when you're injecting a 12-foot king cobra you do it with great care!"

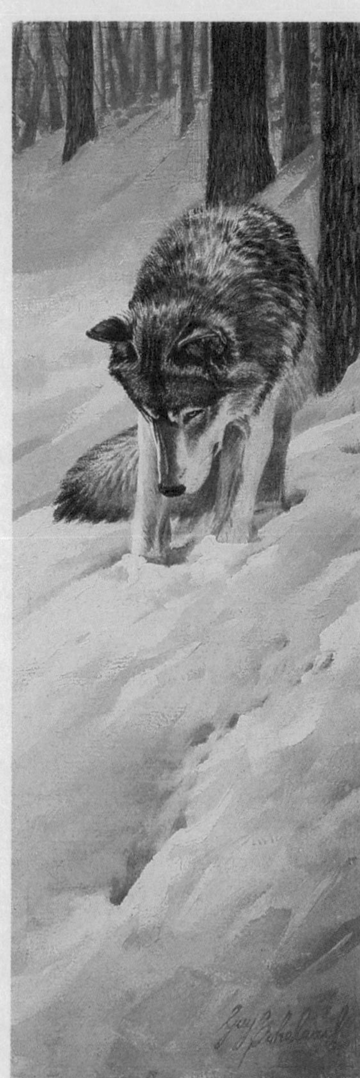

Timber Wolf in Snow, Oil on Canvas, 1987.

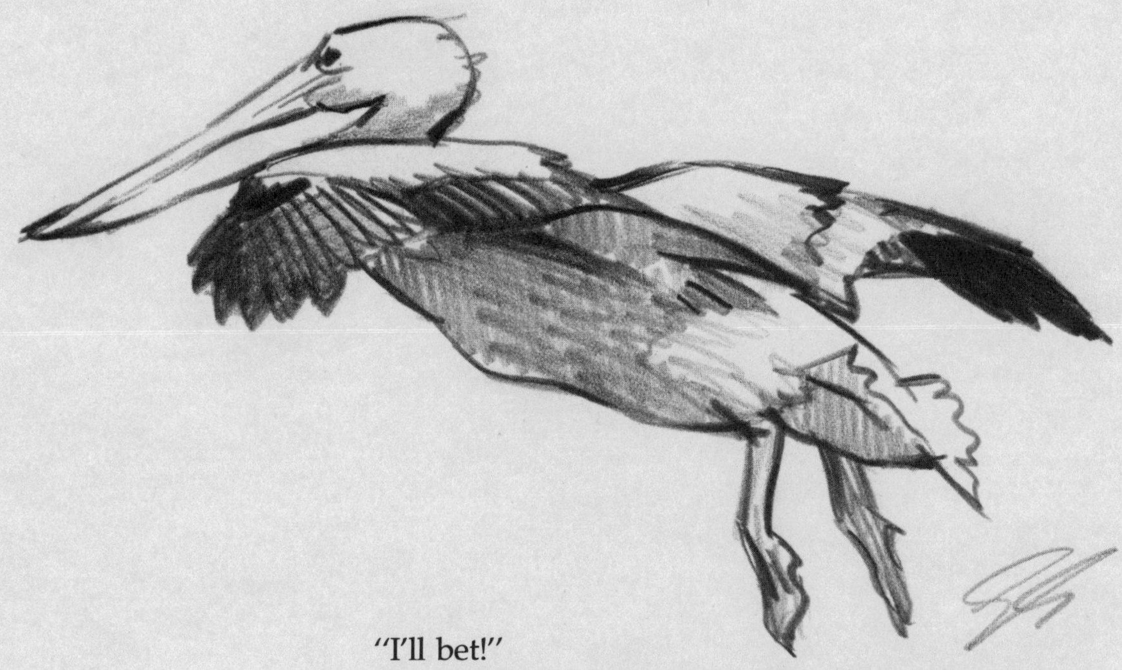

"I'll bet!"

"And when I think of how serious it could have been ... I mean, my mother went down one time and there was a six-foot Indian cobra loose. She got the broom, swept it aside, did the wash and came up and told me, 'Those snakes are goin' if that ever happens again!'

"Now that's understanding parents. You know? They just thought that what I was doing at least was constructive. Had them fooled..."

Between field work and trips to Columbia, the Bronx Zoo, and the American Museum of Natural History, Coheleach picked up an immense mount of knowledge about wildlife.

On a bird-watching trip, he discovered Roger Tory Peterson's *A Field Guide To The Birds,* and became hooked on birds-of-prey. Within two weeks, he says, he knew the Latin name for every bird-of-prey in the United States. Years later, in 1983, when Coheleach received the Master Artist Award at the Birds in Art Exhibition, he was introduced by Peterson himself as "a Renaissance man .. the most professional and versatile artist (I) have ever known..."

Young Coheleach was a natural academic in the only good sense of the word — a kid with an overwhelming curiosity about life around him, combined with an ability to absorb information, file it, and go looking for more. Instead of writing about what he learned, he translated it graphically, filling notebooks with sketches and drawings of birds, animals, and reptiles, and earning a scholarship to the Cooper Union School of Art, near the corner of Third Avenue and 8th Street in New York City.

It was not a match made in heaven. The wise-cracking Brooklynite realist with the strong interest in birds and animals did not mesh well with the avant garde radical communist New York East Village atmosphere of Cooper Union. Cooper Union taught only abstract art, and the discussion in the halls was of socialism; Coheleach retaliated by admiring the Republicans and sorting out what was useful to him, and today concedes that much of what he knows of design originated at Cooper Union.

He was also strategically located, geographically, to frequent some of the great centers of New York culture. The nearby Institute of Fine Arts at NYU, for one. McSorley's Old Ale House, for another...

"Did I hang out at McSorley's?! One-half inch slabs of liverwurst, one-half inch slabs of onion, tons of mustard that would peel your lips, and the greatest ale in the world.

"I go to a lot of fancy bars in New York when I'm entertaining people, but if you really want to enjoy yourself, you gotta go to McSorley's. I offered — well, an obscene amount of money — for one of their oak tables that'd been there for a hundred years, where my initials are, from when I was back in school..."

McSorley's, the previously males-only preserve on Eighth Street, a stronghold of pickled eggs and woodsmoke and dark brown ale, has been serving beer since 1837, 22 years longer than Cooper Union has been serving education. In fact, as the oldest continuously operating alehouse in the U.S., it is only six years younger than NYU, and with many more alumni.

"Oh, yeah, McSorley's. I saw Bobby Thompson's famous home run there. Right during school hours. The teacher

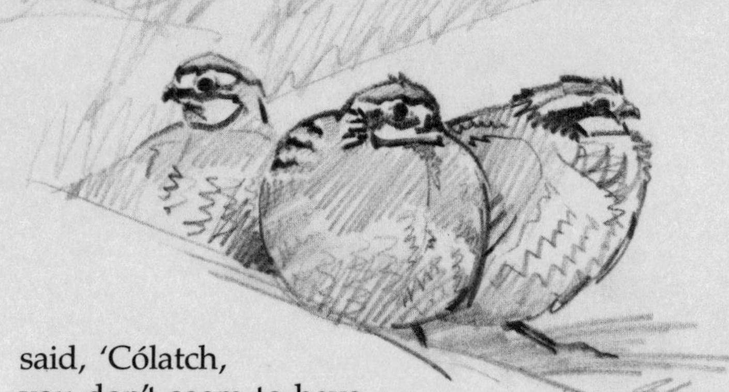

said, 'Cólatch, you don't seem to have your heart in it this afternoon. Why don't you just go down to McSorley's and keep an eye on that ballgame for us and let us know how it comes out when it's over?' Now that guy was a communist. He really was; he led the Young Socialist Party in the school.

"But God bless him, I always loved him for that, lettin' me go down and see that game, cuz that was about as dramatic a hit as you'll ever get in baseball. If you like baseball. I'm not crazy about baseball, but I was then. Mainly because I didn't like school. Even art school."

It was a relief to both Cooper Union and Coheleach himself when the army reached down and plucked him away to serve his country.

At Camp Kilmer, New Jersey, Coheleach was subjected to the usual battery of tests as Uncle Sam sought to find some military skill for which he might be suited. One of these was a test called "pattern analysis."

"What they do, they show you five patterns. Then they show you a house. You have to tell them which pattern built the house. Then they show you five houses and one pattern, and you have to pick out the house. That sort of thing."

Coheleach was the first in the history of Camp Kilmer even to finish the test, or so they told him. Worse still, he got 100 per cent. Next thing he knew, he was en route to Korea in charge of intelligence for a battalion of combat engineers.

1953. The students at Cooper Union argued painting and politics. Guy Coheleach fretted with his unit in an almost peaceful Korea. Meanwhile, French forces in Indochina planned a daring coup against the Viet Minh. In November, six battalions of French paratroops seized the valley of Dien Bien Phu, 500 miles northwest of Hanoi, and prepared for the decisive battle of the war.

In early 1954 Vice President Nixon toured the new fortress; in May, the Viet Minh launched their attack. Coincidentally, Guy Coheleach's unit was ordered back to Hawaii. Coheleach himself, however, having made the mistake of displaying an aptitude for his work, went to Saigon to help assess the strength of bridges between Hanoi and Saigon.

For Guy Coheleach, the notorious Red River of Indochina was one more stream lying between Baldwin, N.Y., and Bernardsville, N.J. One year and nine months after answering the call, the veteran of Korea and Indochina returned to Cooper Union to complete his course.

From the East Village, Coheleach paddled uptown, 22 years old and on his way to a job on Madison Avenue, applying his hard-won artistic expertise to the drawing of brassieres and can openers (says one writer) and candy boxes (says another) or in fact anything they wanted him to (says Coheleach himself) for a catalogue house at the munificent salary of $55 a week. In truth, looking back, it is easy to trivialize both the job and the salary, but in 1955 it was a good job at decent money. Like Hemingway and Ruark crediting their early experience in journalism for their discipline and ability to meet deadlines, Coheleach credits Madison Avenue with teaching him a lot about design and a lot more about the realities of painting for a living: the need to sit down, day after day, and produce.

Offered a $10 raise, Coheleach declined and took a job as a magazine illustrator at $150 a week, which he says he thought was "all the money in the world." However, it set in motion a train of events. Coheleach was admitted to the Adventurer's Club of New York, the youngest member ever, and then elected a fellow of the much more prestige-ridden Explorer's Club. He went one day in 1962 to hear a talk by Don Eckelberry, one of North America's foremost painters of wild birds. It ignited a friendship which has lasted to this day, and

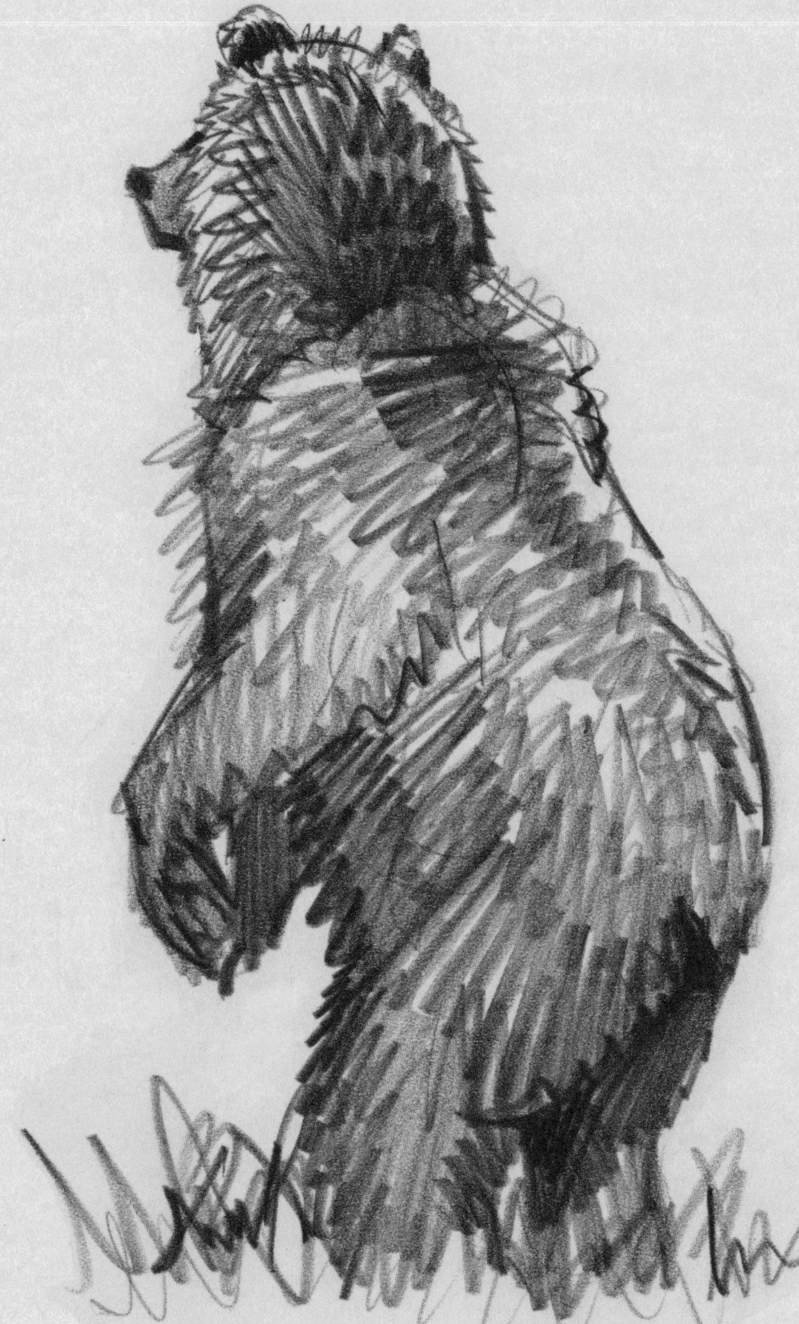

Pencil sketch of Alaska brown bear, the foundation for a future Coheleach painting.

propelled Coheleach a giant step closer to leaving the world of commercial art and becoming an artist — a wildlife artist.

One thing he learned from Eckelberry was, there was money in wildlife art. One thing he did not learn immediately is that the money was not just there for the taking. Having quit his illustrator's job at $15,000, he watched his income return to its former level of $5,000 — a tough drop to take, given Coheleach's self-admitted superhuman ability to live beyond his means, any means — and was soon scrambling for work as Ma Bell moved in to disconnect his telephone and everyone except bill collectors steadfastly refused to beat a path to his door.

Enter, once again, Don Eckelberry. Almost as if laying down lessons in life, one by one — teaching first that wildlife art could be a career, and second that one had to earn it — he returned to give lesson number three: the helping hand up the ladder that every artist receives, and later, every artist owes, in some measure, to those coming after. Approached to do paintings of birds for a calendar, Eckelberry pled overwork and suggested Coheleach do it instead. In fact, he said that if Coheleach's work was not good enough, he would do the calendar for them himself, for free. "I am," Coheleach said, "forever indebted to him for that." Needless, perhaps, to say, Eckelberry was not called upon to fulfill his promise. Coheleach's work was perfect. His career was launched.

Well, sort of launched. Perhaps it was some deep racial instinct; perhaps it was an attitude picked up from his French buddies in Hanoi. Whatever, Coheleach borrowed from Danton's famous admonition of 1792, *"De l'audace, et encore de l'audace, et toujours de l'audace,"* and instead of taking his $1,680 in cash, he took it in calendars and mailed one to every art studio in New York City!

Audacity, and again, audacity, and always audacity, has led the French to Waterloo, and later Dien Bien Phu,

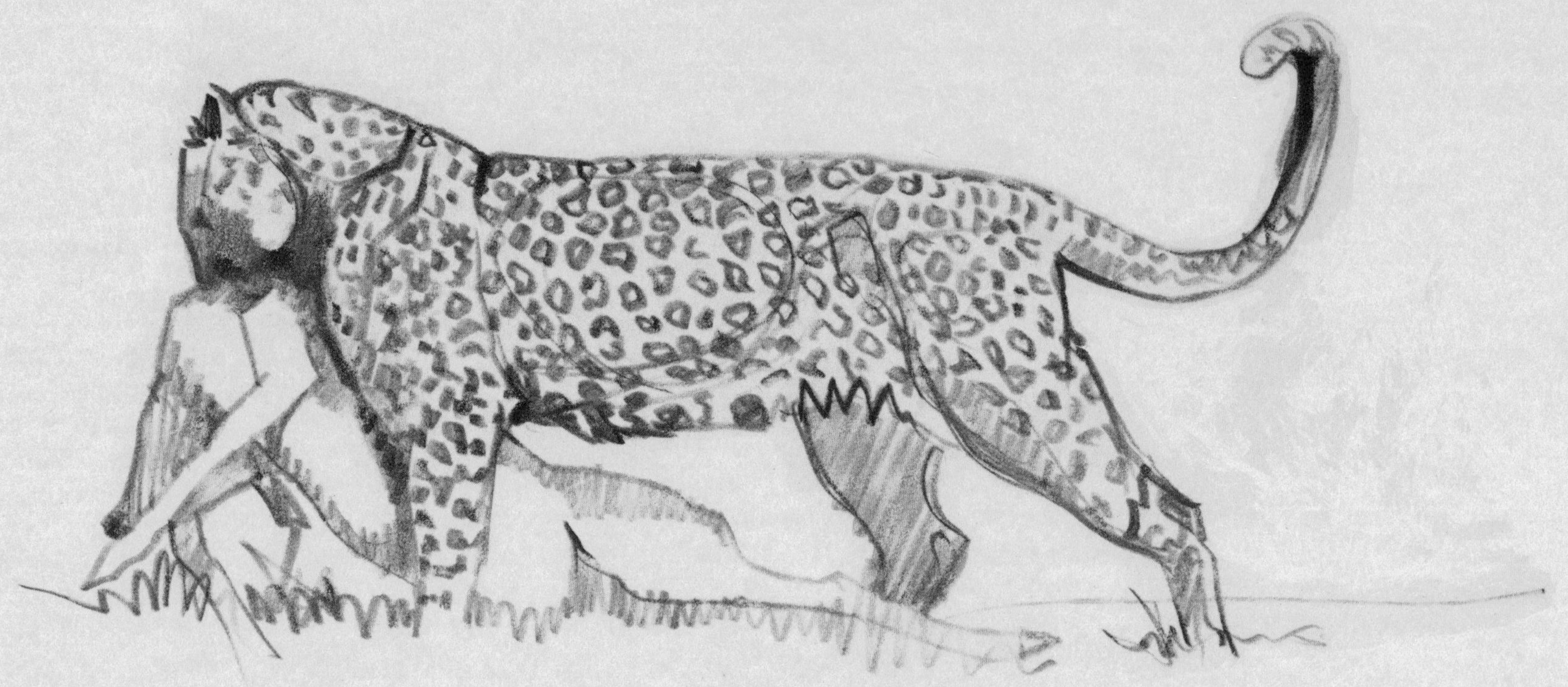

and still later to allowing a McDonald's on the Champs Elysees; and while the policy has, in later life, led Coheleach to near disaster at the trunk-and-tusks of a charging elephant, in this instance it paid off. Art directors looked at the calendar, liked what they saw, and Coheleach was in demand.

For the next ten or so years, he pursued his career and enlarged his following, noting several milestones: his work appeared in *Audubon, National Wildlife,* and *The Saturday Evening Post*, among others; his originals were shown in private and public collections, among them the White House, the National Collection of Fine Arts, and the Corcoran Gallery. A commission for a poster led to a burgeoning print career, and the founding of Regency House Art, his own company to market his prints. He exhibited in Peking, one of the first post-war American artists to do so.

His private life burgeoned as well. He acquired reputations in various fields — jumping out of airplanes, playing tournament chess, shooting championship-level trap and skeet. He married Patricia Arlene (Pam) McGauley, a Long Islander of Irish descent (and Irish temper) and had five children.

In 1966 an event of seemingly trivial importance in his long train of accomplishments occurred: Coheleach won the Novice Division of the Winchester National Trap and Skeet Championships. The prize was a trip to London, England. Having had enough of London after just a few days, he hopped a plane to Africa. What he saw there changed his life and his career. It was the beginning of his African period, and his blooming as an artist.

He was hooked by the Dark Continent in more ways than one. His passion for animals, expressed by the painting thereof, gained further expression in the hunting thereof. Particularly, he was bitten by a bug that has enslaved hunters for hundreds of years: the Cape buffalo, regarded by Robert Ruark (among others) as the most dangerous of Africa's "Big Five."

The big cats — the lion, the leopard — he preferred to paint. In 1982 he published his masterpiece: *The Big Cats*. More than a collection of first-rate wildlife art, *The Big Cats* is a textbook on the world's great feline predators. The text is a scientific treatise on the natural history of cats, from the mechanical workings of their retractable claws to their antecedents in the dawn of time, to their present day range, mating habits, and prospects for survival. Published by Abrams of New York, *The Big Cats: The Paintings of Guy Coheleach* was a Book-of-the-Month Club selection, sold out quickly in first edition, and has since come out in a second edition.

His African work led to academic recognition: In 1975 he received an honorary doctorate in arts from the College of William and Mary and a scholarly analysis of his work by Dr. Scott C. Whitney in the William and Mary Review. In 1983 came his Master Artist award and introduction by Roger Tory Peterson; in 1985 Coheleach was named Wildlife Artist of the Year by the National Wildlife & Western Art Collectors Society.

Behind the scenes, however, Coheleach's life was rocky. In 1975, the year of his honorary doctorate, Guy Jr., was killed by a hit-and-run driver on Long Island. It was, Coheleach says, *the* turning point in his life — one of the times that makes you realize what is important, and what isn't.

In the early 1980s, life in the Coheleach abode in Bay Shore, Long Island, received a shock of a different kind. The tax man cameth, and the Coheleachs wenteth — to Stuart, Florida, where Guy could go to work in shorts and sandals, and pursue another passion: deep-sea fishing for shark. But his absence from New York was shortlived. After two years, Pam Coheleach was tired of Florida, tired of being away from the amenities of New York they had grown up with and come to take for granted, like the ballet and the galleries, and tired of being unable to see her remaining children and just-arrived grandchildren without making a full-scale journey north. They packed up and headed home. At age 52, many years and many rivers later, Guy Coheleach embarked on the last lap of his journey from Baldwin, Long Island to Bernardsville, New Jersey — from the streets of Brooklyn to a wooded hillside sanctuary "just an hour's drive from Manhattan."

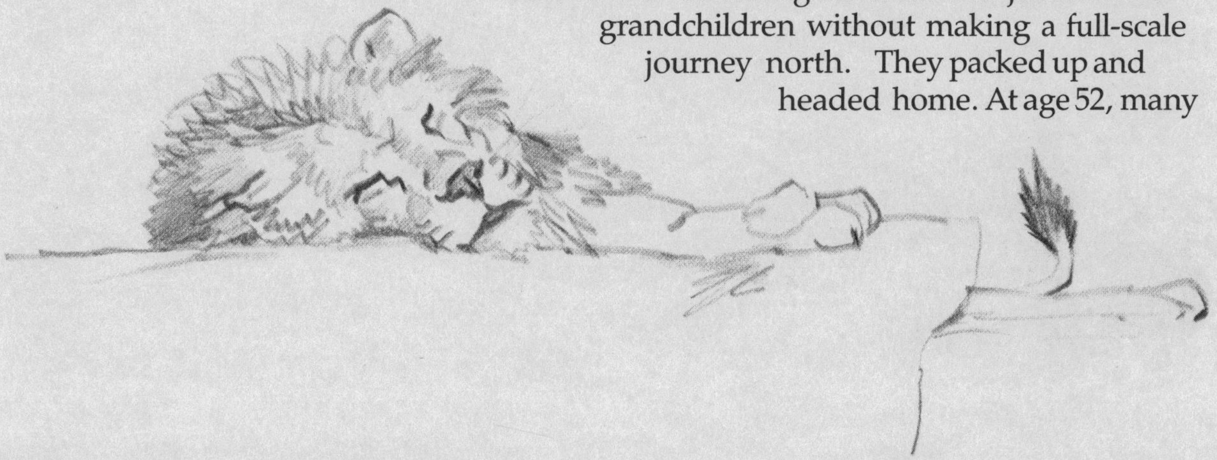

We pulled onto the unpaved, twin-tracked, fine gravel driveway in early afternoon, the lulling effects of lunch in Lambertville all but gone, the necessity of running a few errands before dinner becoming all the more urgent with the realization that the refrigerator was empty and that no self-respecting interview could possibly continue without a visit to the Bernardsville suds emporium.

Coheleach's Jersey house is one of those deceptively shaped buildings that seems small when you first see it, as you come around a bend in the drive, its twin garage door staring, fronting for the rest of the house like the eyes of a cubist tadpole. You never see how large it really is because there is no vantage point from which you can look at the whole. In front and behind, the trees come in thick and close. There are no neighbors visible through the mixed hardwoods rising on the hillside behind and descending the hill in front, and the view from the long terrace is of endless trees.

As the door opens, the Coheleach dogs emerge, large golden retrievers almost the color of Irish setters, the old one, Lucky, well into his teens, the younger, Kir, a fat seven-year-old with a passion for retrieving. Both, it would appear, have a passion for Coheleach.

They are around when he goes to work, in the newly-built studio building off to one side, built to match the house but not be part of it. To go to work in the morning, Coheleach must leave his house and walk through the weather of the day before he can begin. It is a type of discipline, although what type we are not sure. If the weather is good, he leaves the doors open and the dogs come and go.

"I'll be working away, and one of them will come in and just stand there, behind me. After a bit, he'll come up and touch me with his nose, just like he's saying 'I'm here.' I'm more attached to them than I ever realized."

Lucky got his name the hard way: he survived being hit by a car — not once, but twice. Now he is too old to climb stairs well, and Coheleach carefully avoids staircases when Lucky is out and following him around.

Coheleach's *Noo Yawk* street kid persona is contradicted by his house, by the James Clarke bronze rhino in the vestibule, the Wilhelm Kuhnert lion over the mantelpiece, the Dennis Anderson bronze Cape buffalo head by the window staring down his nose at you as you enter, looking like William F. Buckley about to address a liberal, looking, as Robert Ruark once said, "Like you owe him money." The buffalo almost manages to dominate the room even when Coheleach himself is in it. This house is a long way from Brooklyn.

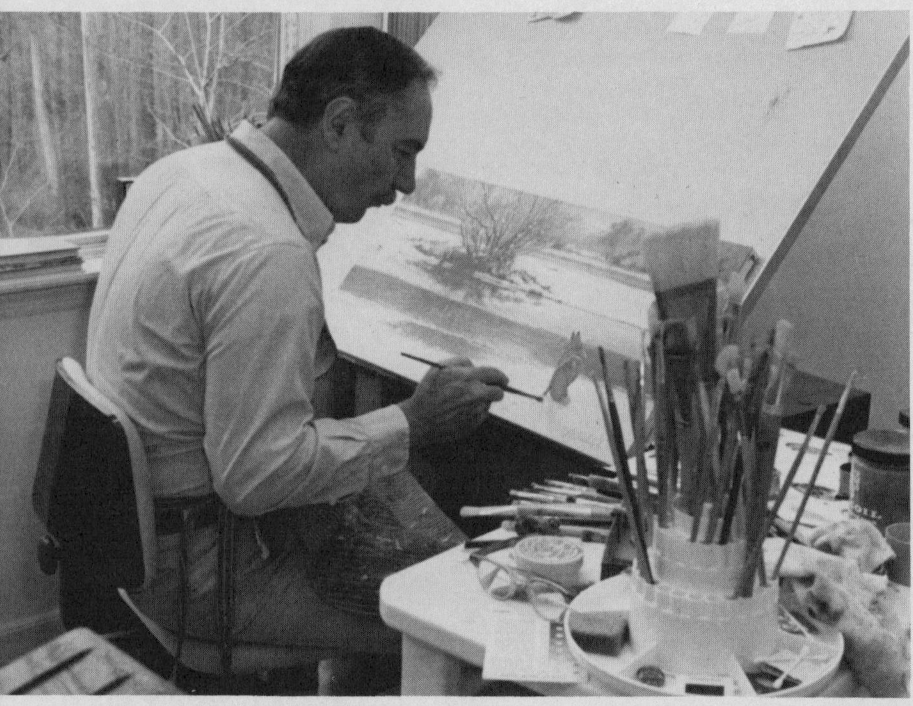

Coheleach at his studio in Bernardsville. He built the studio apart from his house so that to go to work each morning, he would have to walk through the weather of the day.

Unlike many wildlife artists who seem to consciously seek out pretentious and melodramatic names for their works, Coheleach tends towards simplicity and even, on occasion, playfulness.

One work I particularly like is a rendition of vultures feeding, fighting over a carcass unseen in the grass, surrounded as it is by flapping tearing birds, with more drifting in every moment to grab their piece of the action. The painting is entitled *Attorneys and Bankers.*

"Want to see the original?" Coheleach asked, and I said sure. By coincidence, it happens to be hanging right here in Bernardsville in what may just be the ultimate status symbol. It seems that shortly after Coheleach moved to Bernardsville, the old and revered gunsmithing firm of Griffin & Howe announced they would be opening their second outlet there. The first (and since 1923, the only one) has always been in midtown Manhattan, most recently on 44th Street just west of Fifth Avenue, their gunsmithing shop housed on the premises. Now, the shop and a second showroom would be opened in Bernardsville. Having your very own Griffin & Howe — my God!

Attorneys & Bankers, all three-by-six feet of it, is one of a half-dozen Coheleach originals that grace the dark-panelled-walnut-and-linseed smelling G&H showroom in Bernardsville, not yet open for business when we visit, but getting perilously close, an ancient church that has been relocated out of harm's way and is awaiting the blessing of the altar. Coheleach breezes in, on first name terms with everyone, through the showroom, through the shop, down to the basement where the artifacts are stored, a treasure house of half-finished masterpieces and semi-discarded rifle actions, boxes packed and half unpacked, sawdust on the floor, and a few beers in the fridge.

Introductions, a fast beer, poking through the rack of dusty actions and walnut stock blanks that look out of this world even in the rough, a fit of uncontrollable drooling in the showroom and back out to the car.

"I don't see how you ever get any work done, with them in town," I say.

"It's tough. Particularly since they sell paintings for me. I can always argue that I'm going down there on business."

Hanging around a custom gunshop on a rainy afternoon. Heaven. Pure heaven.

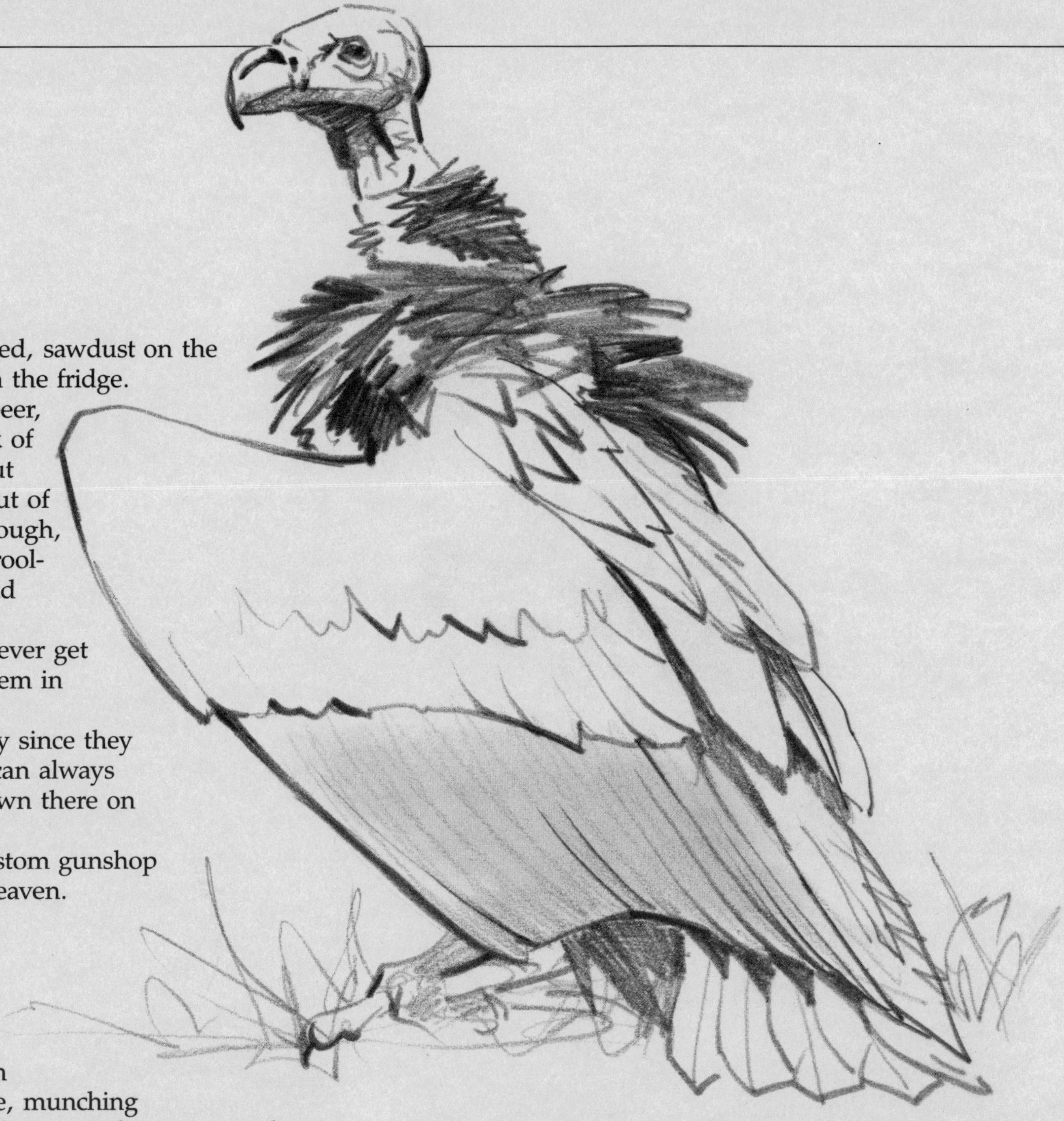

The skies have cleared now, and we are out on the balcony of the house, munching pieces of shaved smoked venison from a mound on a piece of waxed paper. The venison is like Serrano ham, but lean and less salty. Fresh from the Coheleach freezer, the pieces are rimmed with frost and stick together, and we warm them in our mouths before chewing and washing them down with Heineken from cans.

"You really like this stuff?"

"I love it. Never had it before, but it's wonderful."

"Well, I got a freezer full of it. If you've got room in your bag, I'll pack some up for you to take home. Can't eat it all myself."

The venison came from Texas. The woods around the house in New Jersey are full of deer, and they frequently wander down out of the woods to investigate the goings on, but they aren't hunted. They probably should be, there's so many of them, Coheleach says, but they aren't.

Morning arrives with a strange request.

"Ever drive a Jaguar E-type?"

"No. Used to dream about it, but I never drove one."

"You can drive, though, huh?"

"Sure."

"Well, my problem is this. I have a Jaguar that was in for some work and I have to go pick it up. Mind coming with me and driving it back? We got time?"

"Sure, we can talk in the car just as well as here."

The repair shop is somewhere beyond the Great Swamp Refuge, a wildlife sanctuary just outside Bernardsville.

"I bought this thing (the Jag) about 10 years ago," Coheleach says. "I saw a picture of it and just had to have one. So I go into the dealer and I buy one. It had a manual transmission, which we weren't used to. Well, the very first day we have it, it gets banged up, $800 worth. Put it into reverse instead of forward and bang, so I call the dealer and I say, 'I want a red E-type with an automatic. You got one?'

"Dealer says he has a white one. 'Paint it red and I'll be down to pick it up,' I said. 'You can't be serious,' he said. 'Damn right I am. Paint the damn thing red, I want a red Jaguar. So he did."

That particular Jaguar obviously preferred to remain white, and it has been taking its revenge on Coheleach for the paint job ever since — doing its best to see that his bank account is also in the red.

"Damn thing's got about 28,000 miles on it, and most of them were put on by mechanics trying to get it to run right.

"Most beautiful sports car anybody ever designed, engine's fantastic, and the wiring's done by a two-year old," Coheleach says. "Gonna sell it."

The Jaguar is crouched in the corner outside the garage, hemmed in by lesser beings — MGs and such, but flanked by a shabby genteel Bentley that sits embarrassed by the rust around its edges and the dashboard tossed onto its leather back seat. Coheleach collects the key and walks over. The Jaguar eyes him. He slides into the front seat, pulls the choke, turns the key. The engine turns once, turns again more slowly, and dies. For the one thousand, three hundred and eighty-second time, the Jaguar requires help getting started.

The mechanic has done his work, however; a quick boost later the Jaguar is purring away, smoke curling out from under the engine cowling ("I just can't find that oil leak, Mr. Coheleach, but don't worry — it's just a drop or two onto the manifold, and only when it's not running.") I am shepherded carefully home, Coheleach leading the way in his less elegant but more reliable Japanese sedan, the Jag's fuel gauge reading Empty all the way, the warning light on, the choke out to keep it running. Acceleration to burn, though, and wonderful on the corners: A red E-type convertible on back roads on a sunny day in summer when the air is just starting to feel a touch of fall and you could use a sweater but would rather shiver a little and watch the girls walking down the street.

Later, we go driving through the countryside (NOT in the Jaguar), looking for nothing, just driving to look. The roads follow the contours of the land, over streams, around lakes and hills, connecting myriad towns each like the last, surprisingly uniform in the front they present, small and not getting larger, providing amenities for the people around — a well-bred bar, gasoline, a liquor store, books, antiques, clean family restaurants. They have no aspirations to big citydom. New York is the city. But this is where people come to live.

We stop at a smalltown pub, in Gladstone or maybe it was in Peapack, New Jersey. The Brass Penny, it was called. We park beside a Jersey Jeep: a four-wheel drive Mercedes adventure car. The ultimate Yuppie 4X4. Migawd! The Brass Penny has dress regulations: all gentleman must be wearing "shirts with collars." Fortunately, I am. Shoes, too. There is a lineup for tables but there's room at the bar.

The piano player is getting draught beer in a goblet the size of a chamber pot, before sitting down and striking up some Scott Joplin. Coheleach is transported.

"Goddamn, I love this music," he says, ordering me a beer in a goblet like the piano player's.

"Wish we had time to take a run up to Long Island and I'd show you some real good places. There were some saloons I used to hang out in up there. Waterfront

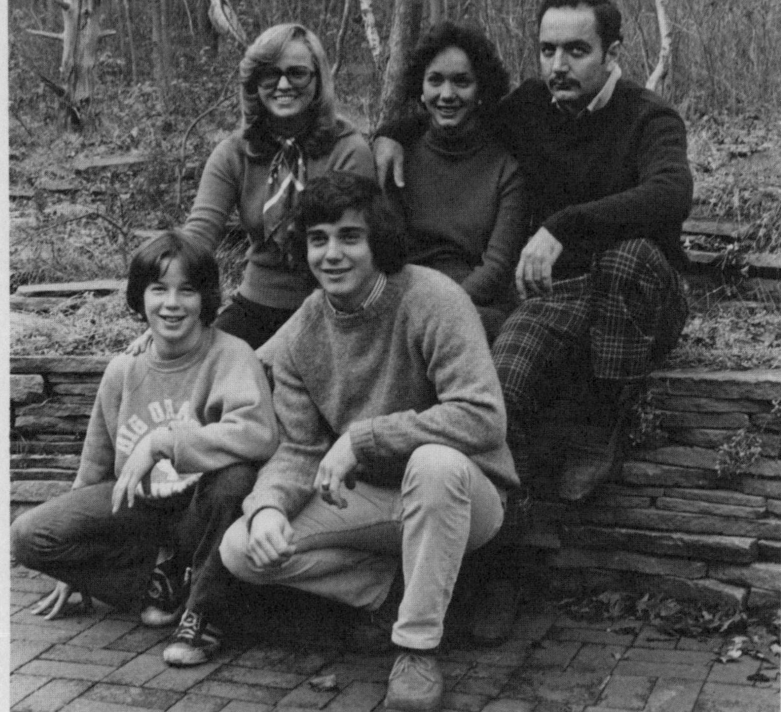

The Coheleach family in spring, 1976. L-R: Hugh, Pam, George, Coleen and Guy.

places. Really rough. Popeye's. Vinny's. Codfish Bob's. Used to go over there in the afternoon after I finished working. Never got home until late, and somebody always drove me.

"I know if we went up today we'd never get back tonight. Five minutes after we walked in we'd have drinks lined up for us from here to the wall."

His wife hated him going there, and wondered what possessed him to hang out in those places.

"I felt at home there. There's no pretension at all. None. You are who you are. Period."

One of Coheleach's pet hates is wearing a tie. At '21', a tie is required.

"I always wore the worst, ugliest tie I could find when I went there," he says. "If I was going alone; if I had someone with me who would be embarrassed, I wouldn't do it, but who the hell are they to tell me I have to wear a tie?"

We decide to lunch elsewhere. There is a mill in the next town, dating back a hundred years but now converted to a restaurant and a little more to our taste, although the Brass Penny is nice and the piano player is good. Coheleach buys him a beer and thanks him on the way out.

As we leave Gladstone-Peapack, Coheleach points out a car dealership.

"The only car dealer in town. Rolls-Royce."

Later, drifting along the back roads in the sunshine, we pass the Jacqueline Onassis estate where her horses are kept and she comes to ride. Or rather, he drives past a stretch of deep woods, behind which and over the hill, safe from passersby, lie the house and the barns and the paddocks. The trees maintain a stiff silence, refusing to acknowledge our presence, and we drive on.

Down the road, around a bend, alongside a pond and across a bridge, a gate with a firm black PRIVATE protects more estates from our idle gaze. Coheleach calmly drives through, occasionally pausing to point out the abode of this or that notable, most of them unknown to me but presumably luminaries in the Big Apple spectrum. Privacy, it seems, is a valued commodity — perhaps the most valued of all, after the seamier necessities, like money.

"Wish I was driving the Mercedes," Coheleach says. "When you drive a Mercedes, nobody tries to throw you out. They naturally assume you belong."

Already, Coheleach has a sense of belonging in his adopted New Jersey home, or at least "as much here as anywhere else in North America."

"But nowhere feels as much like home as Africa," he says. "When I got off the plane in Nairobi the second time, I felt more at home than when I go to Long Island. There was this tremendous feeling — all the pressure, all the nonsense, just disappeared."

In Africa, Coheleach's life changes. He can go to bed at 3 a.m., be up before dawn, and not even need to rest during the day; more than just invigoration, Africa makes him feel like a different person.

"If there is reincarnation, I must have spent a number of lifetimes there."

Back at the Jersey house, on the deck with the dogs and some smoked venison and cold beer, shielded from the highway by his own five acres of maple and beech, ash, and the odd evergreen, his Mercedes now parked by the back door, we await the arrival of his family for dinner: Hugh, from the floor of the NYSE, where the clouds that preceded the storm of October 19 are gathering already; Coleen, with her boyfriend.

Hugh is the acknowledged burger master in the Coheleach household. As he grills ground filet on the barbecue, Guy grills him on the state of the stock market. Suddenly concerned about his prospects for retirement in a world of changing tastes and the onset of a little self-doubt, Coheleach has ventured into the market for the first time seeking a haven where some capital can live, grow, prosper, and succor his old age — and he is as nervous about it as a new mother cat.

"It's something I never really gave a lot of thought to before. I was always too busy, painting, going to Africa, selling prints, running here, running there. Then I had a few problems, legal problems, and that cost a lot of money, and moving here cost money, and I began to think, how am I going to pay the bills if people stop buying my paintings, or I can't paint anymore, or something. What am I supposed to do? At my age, I can't mortgage the house..."

As we devour the cheeseburgers, complimenting Hugh with our mouths full, he regales us with tales from the floor of the NYSE, describing this trader and that broker and his first full day as acting senior clerk, encouraged with his insider's knowledge of a unique and ghastly world about which the rest of us really can know nothing.

"George (the eldest) is like me, I guess. You could give him $20,000 a week, and he'd need $21,000," Coheleach told me. "Coleen — you could give her $10 a week, and she'd manage to save $9.50. Hughie? I don't really know.

"I'm so proud of all of them. That's why it's great living here, close to them. We can all get together like tonight, not just once or twice a year. It's so important."

We are sitting at an iron lawn table out behind the studio, in the glare of the *de rigeur* outside spotlights of modern rural life, in steel chairs that never warm up, attended by two golden retrievers and surrounded by a welter of paving stones, wheelbarrows, bags of cement, half-finished rock walls, drainpipe and drainage tiles, an elaborate system of pools and fountains, in pieces in September when they were supposed to be in operation by July. Tough to get good help these days.

The old dog, Lucky, becomes overly persistent and draws a threat. He retreats a few feet and settles lightly on his belly, his chin on his paws, watching Coheleach.

"You gotta come down and see this once I get it finished. This is going to be a pool, here, and another one over there. They'll have fish in them, and I am putting in a system of indirect lighting. You'll be able to look right through the glass into the tank, and the fish can come and look out at you — big fish, I'm talking about, trout and bass — and the lights over the tank will attract bugs, and the bugs will hit the lights and fall into the tank and feed the fish.

"Efficient, no work, and it costs you nothing. Neat, huh?"

Neat, indeed.

The conversation meanders, taking with it my concentration, and soon Coheleach suggests we retire — I to the spare bedroom, he and Lucky to the solace of late-night television and his books and a drink and insomnia. We have to be up at five and on our way to Newark Airport in the predawn — for Coheleach, the fund raising in Cincinnati in aid of the Cincinnati Zoo. He has painted *Angel's Chase,* an imaginary rendering of the zoo's star cheetah Angel, in pursuit of a fleeing lunch, as she might have been on the Serengeti Plain.

Hours later, rising in the darkness, I open the door to find a cup of coffee steaming and a large box, neatly wrapped and taped and insulated with layer after layer of newspaper: the promised smoked venison, carefully packaged sometime in the solitary hours when commitments assume their greatest importance and even the dogs are asleep.

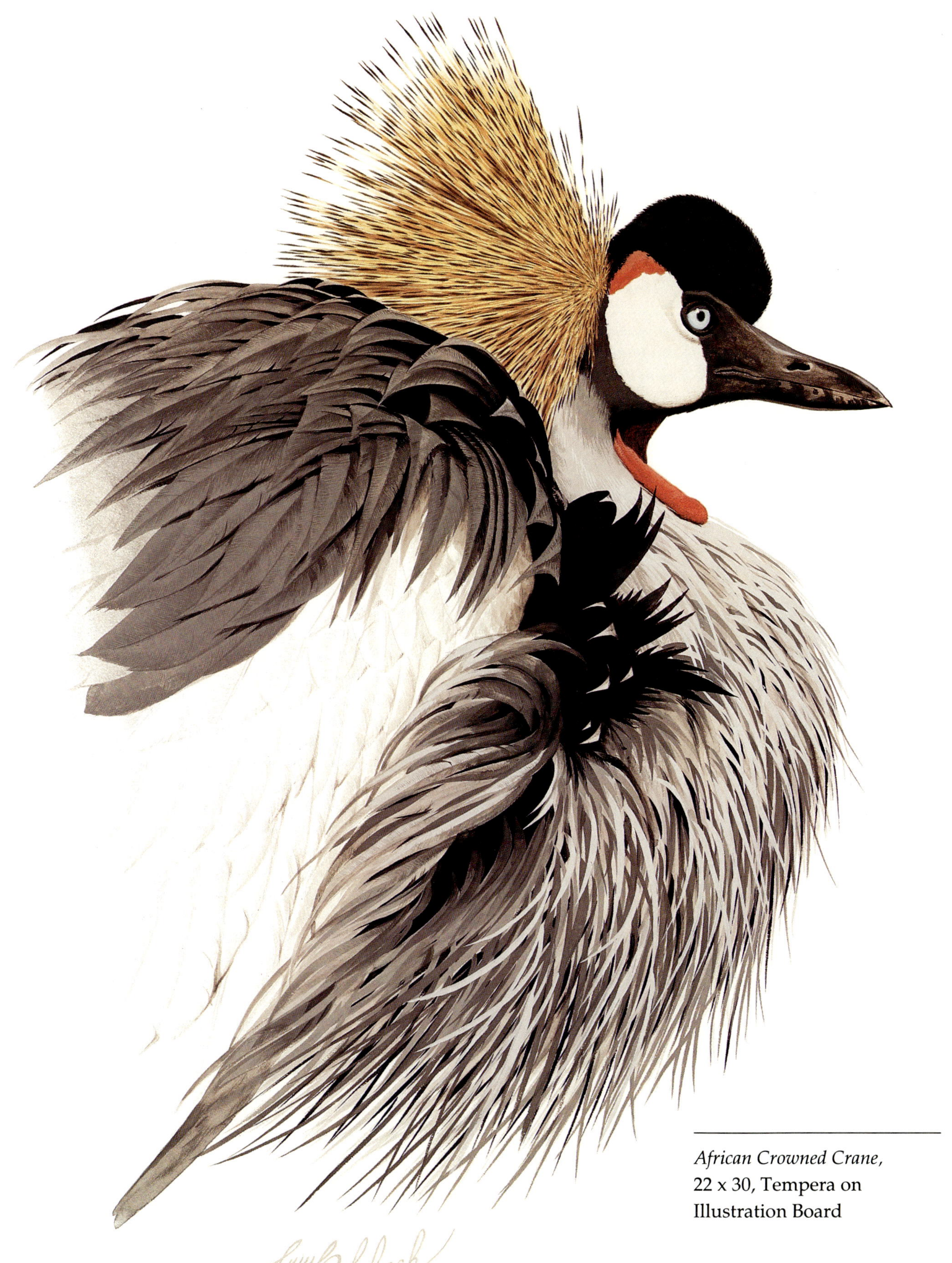

African Crowned Crane,
22 x 30, Tempera on
Illustration Board

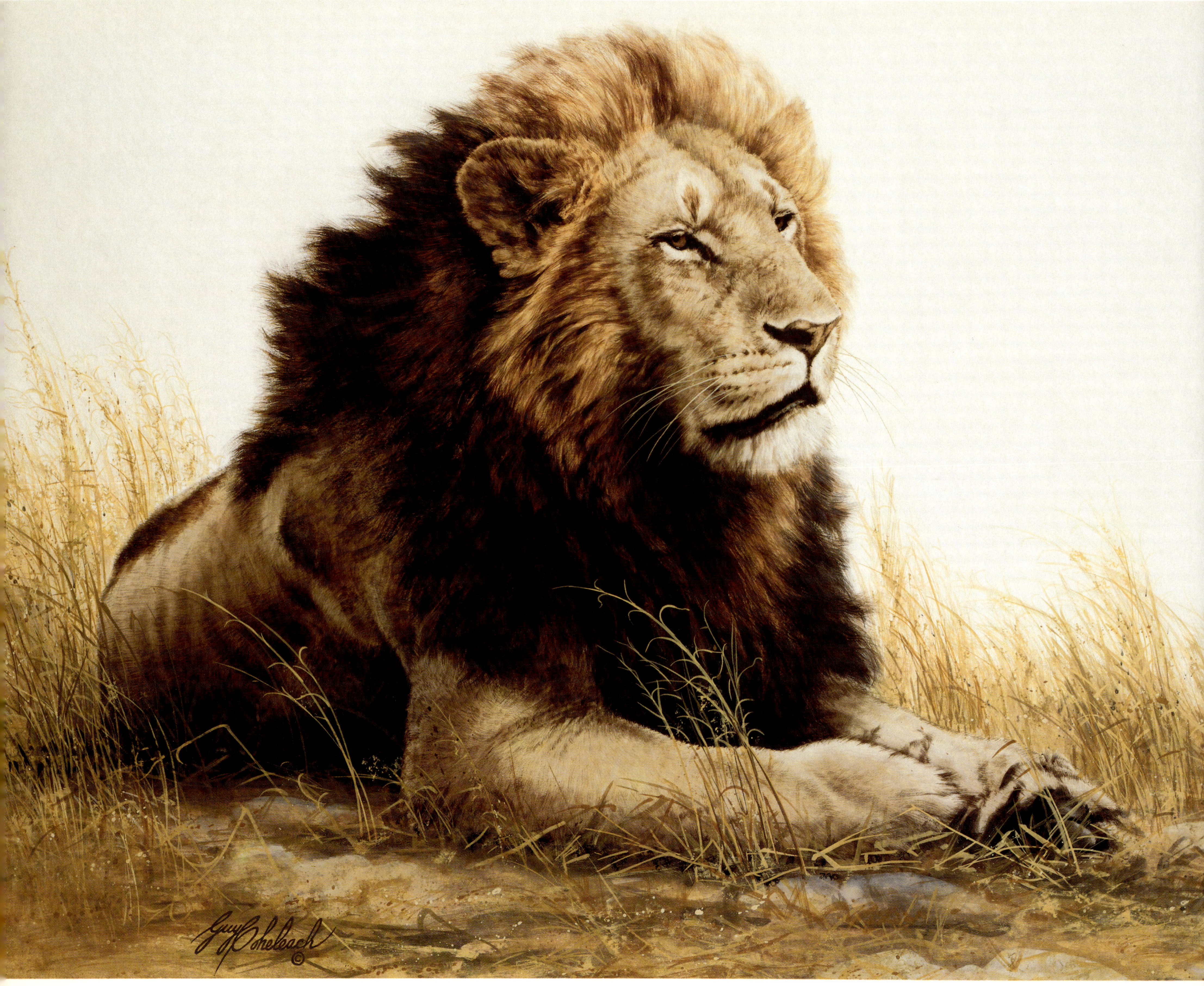
Guy Coheleach ©

The greatest lion painter of all time, Coheleach insists, is Germany's Wilhelm Kuhnert. A Kuhnert original—of a lion, naturally—hangs above the mantlepiece at Coheleach's home in Bernardsville, New Jersey. *Ngorongoro Lion*, however, demonstrates that Guy Coheleach himself is in the same class.

I painted this in 1972. It is very detailed, very hairy and grassy—the kind of painting I was doing at that time. Africa was still relatively new to me and I felt a need to reproduce African animals as realistically as possible, almost as a record of them.

I love painting lions—hell, I love lions!—and particularly black-maned lions. A dark mane adds so much in the way of contrast and drama. They are just, quite simply, prettier than the lighter-maned males.

Ngorongoro Lion, 40 X 30, Gouache and Acrylic on Illustration Board.

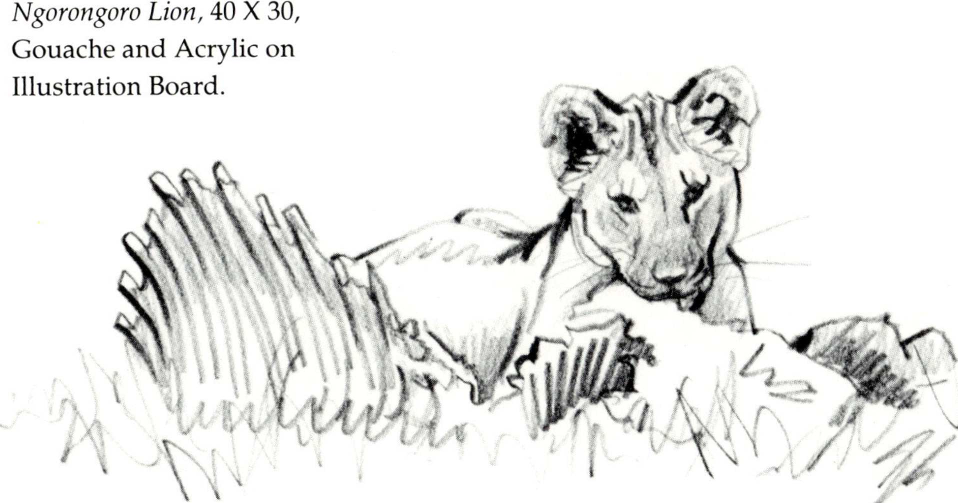

At some time or another, every artist uses photos for reference, especially when painting an animal which is so inaccessible that firsthand observation is impossible or highly impractical. This painting of musk oxen is one such case.

I cheated a little on this one, because I don't know the musk ox well and you should not paint animals you don't know. I worked from photographs and magazine illustrations, mainly; the problem was getting them running. There are very few pictures of galloping musk ox. Still, the animal's skeletal structure and musculature are basic enough that I felt confident painting them from photographs.

Also, I like painting snow and I like a lot of action. This has both, and I think that makes up, in terms of art, for anything that may be missing in terms of accuracy.

Musk Ox, 24 X 12, Oil on Canvas

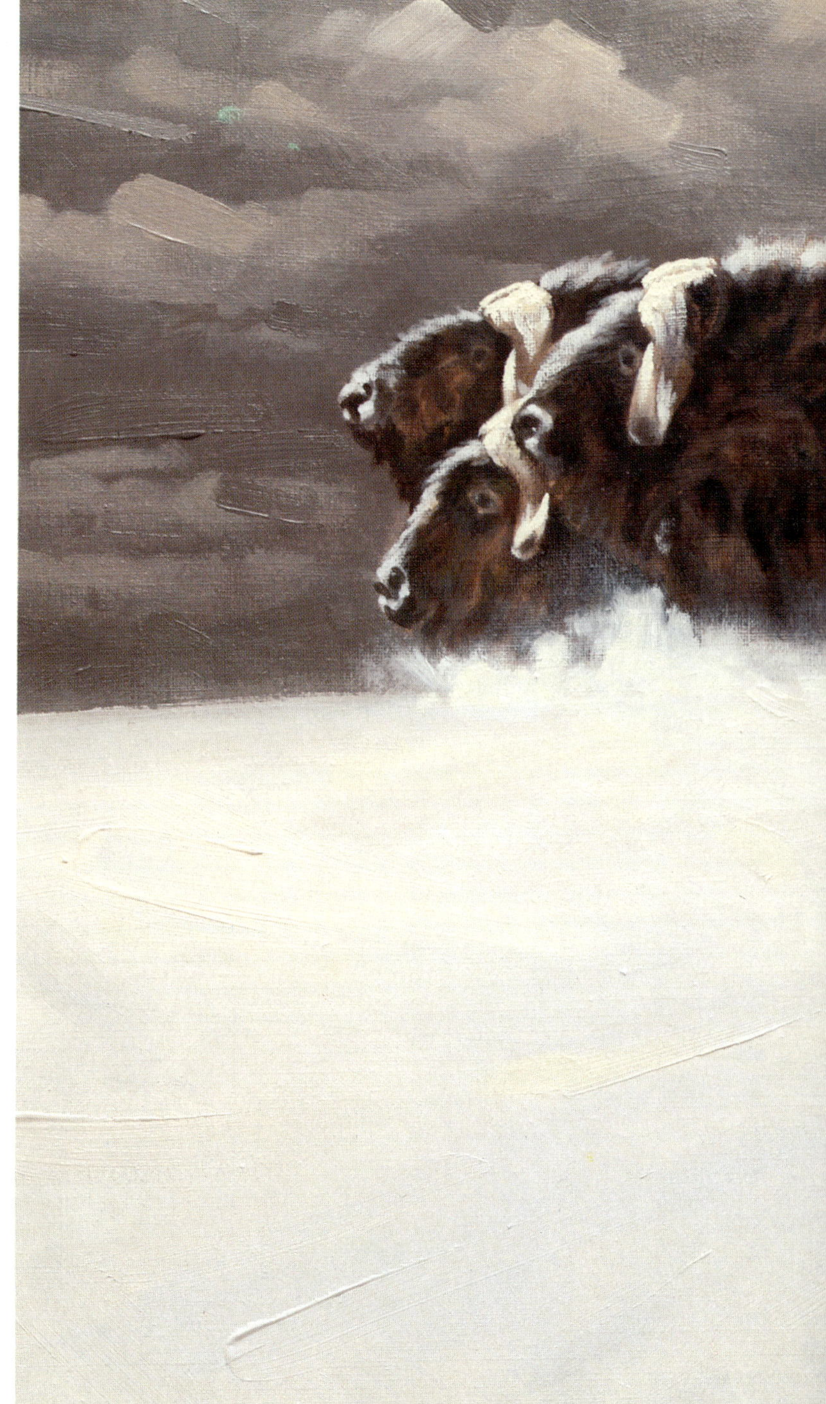

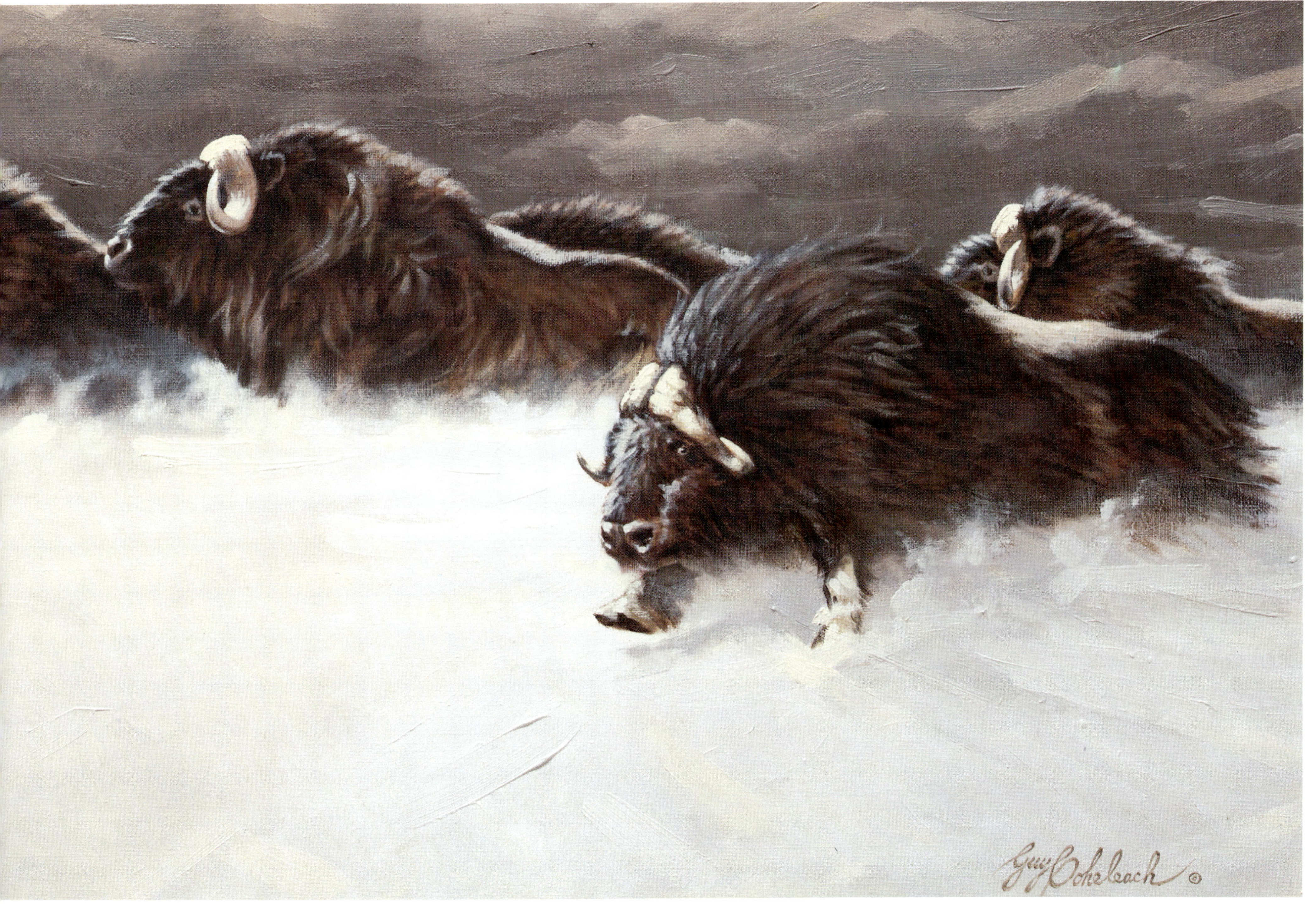
Guy Coheleach ©

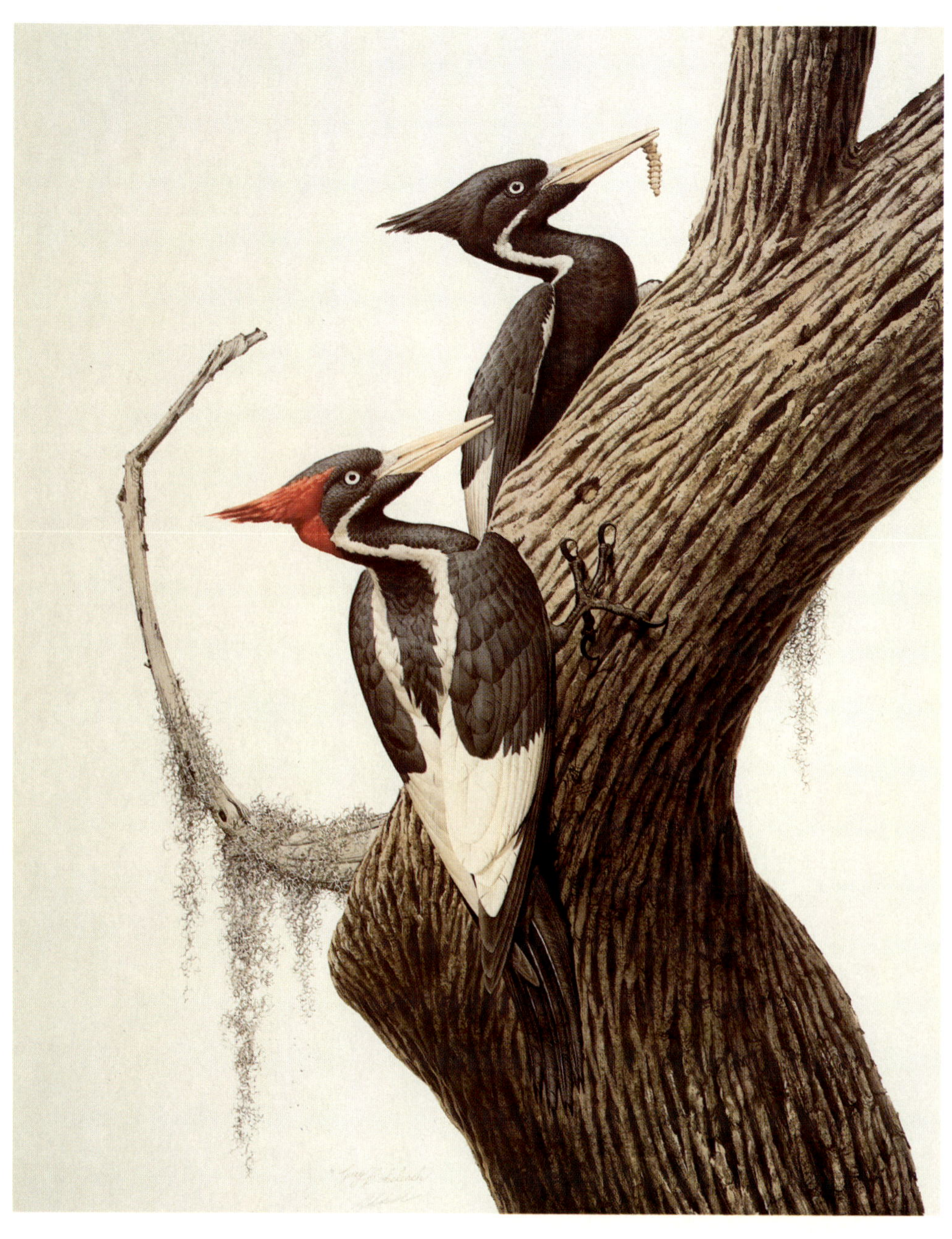

I got a call from Les Line, editor of Audubon magazine. Someone had claimed to have rediscovered the ivory-billed woodpecker in the swamps of Louisiana. He got permission for me to take the best study skin of an ivory-billed woodpecker from the American Museum of Natural History in New York City. I took it home and worked round the clock for four days to meet the magazine's deadline.

The painting was done back in 1966. Typical Coheleach back then: white background, very detailed, incredibly scientific approach to it. Still, it is very design-y, I like to think, which is the reason for including it here.

Ivory-billed Woodpeckers, 30 X 40, Watercolor and Tempera on Illustration Board.

Some subjects are difficult to paint in their natural surroundings, because they go out of their way not to be seen and showing them in plain view is quite unnatural. Nocturnal creatures such as owls, which are only rarely observed at night and almost never during the daylight hours—and then only in dark, shadowy places—are good examples.

Here, Coheleach paints the barred owl in its daytime haunt, away from the sunlight which just dapples one shoulder, hidden among the Spanish moss.

I like to paint birds and animals in hiding places. The owl is not worried about jays or crows coming from behind him. He is secure and he likes it. So do I.

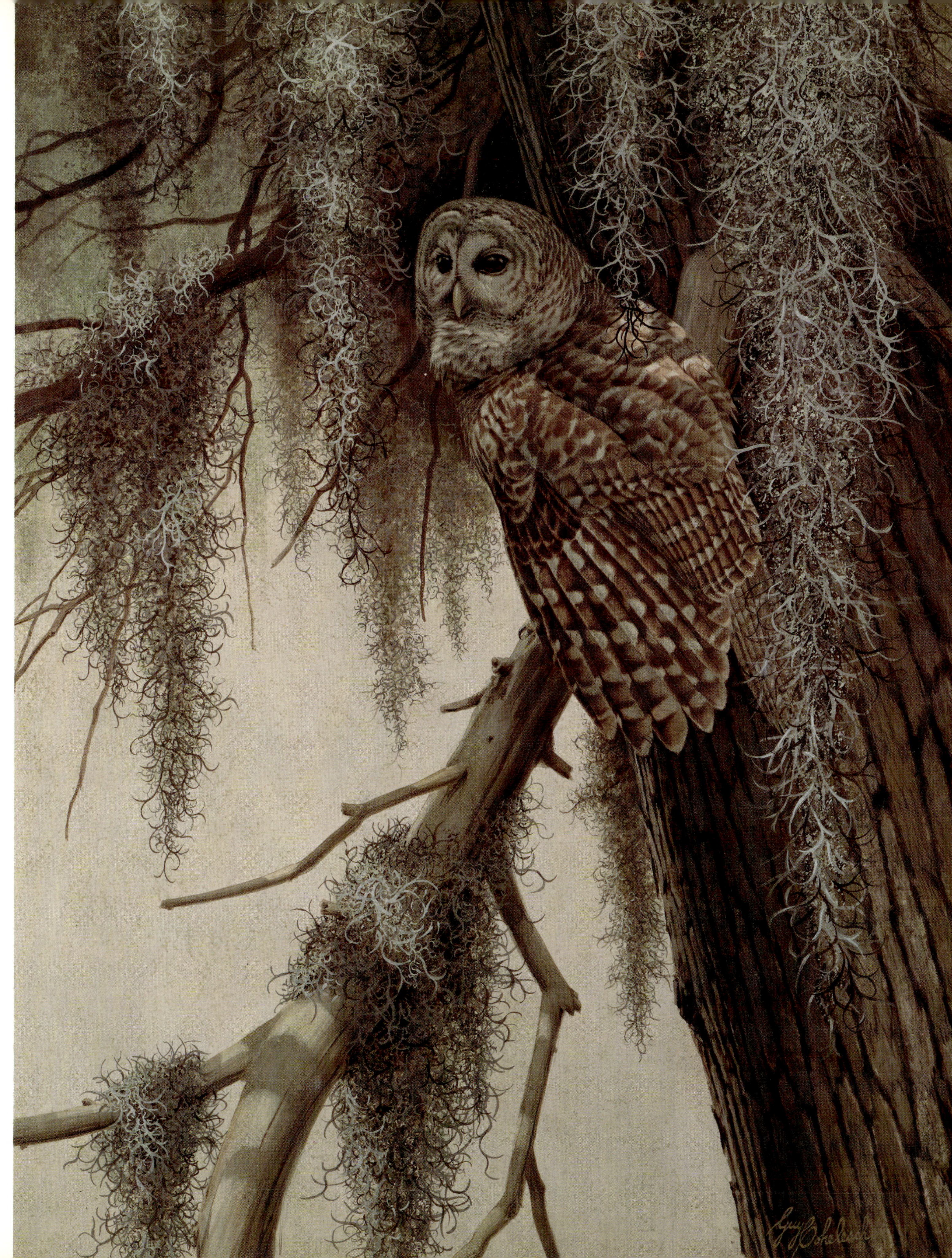

Barred Owl, 30 X 40, Gouache and Acrylic on Illustration Board.

A typical scene from the beaches of Long Island where Coheleach was raised, when the northwest winds would come through, carrying big black clouds after breaking up a front.

One thing that impresses me about the peregrine falcon is its incredible speed and maneuverability. The greater yellowlegs is also a very fast bird. The peregrine has just come around the sand dune, and he's banking, with the tail making the turn.

Leaving the far-side wing out—which is hidden—implies much more action than putting the wing in.

Barrier Beach Chase, 72 X 36, Oil on Canvas

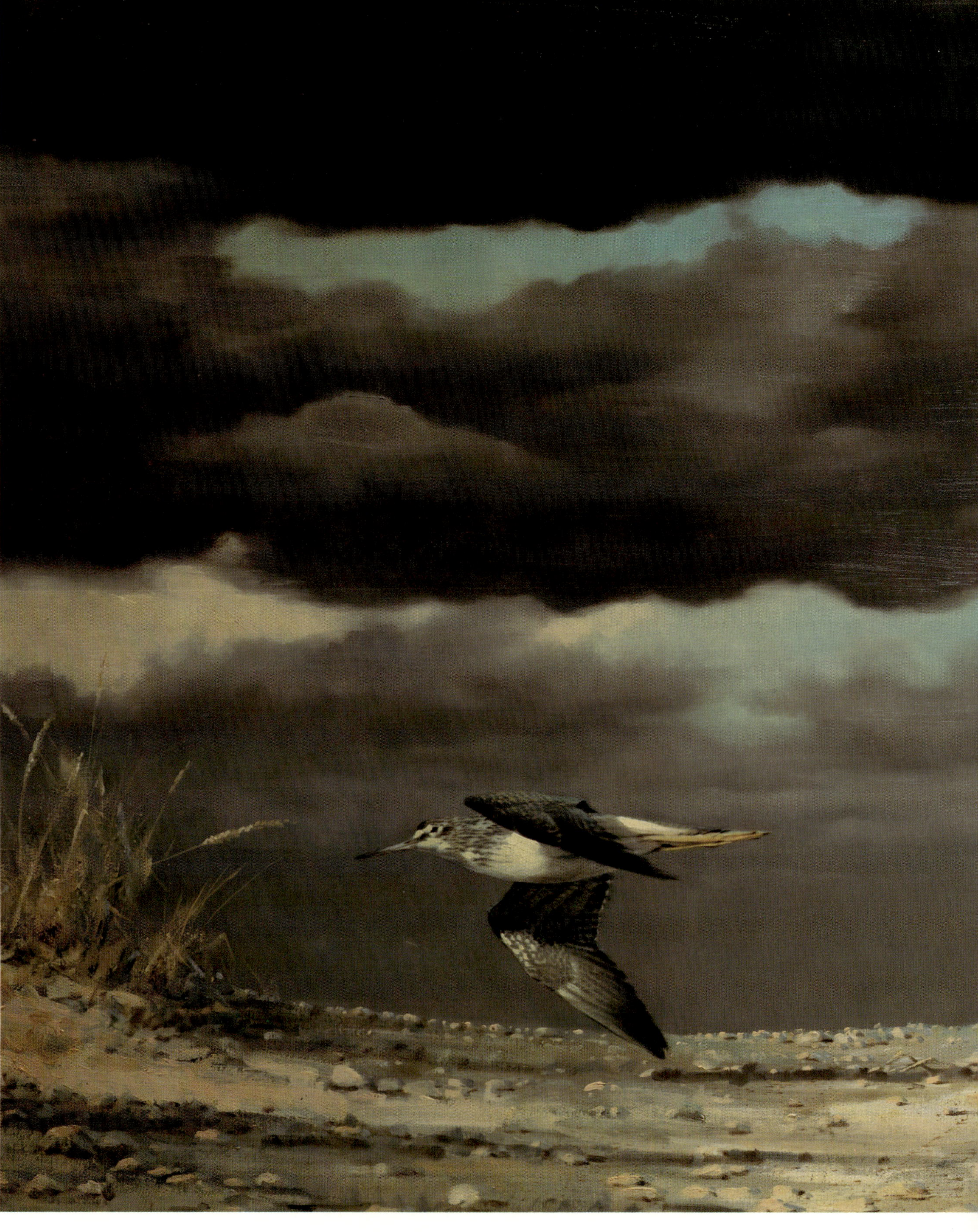

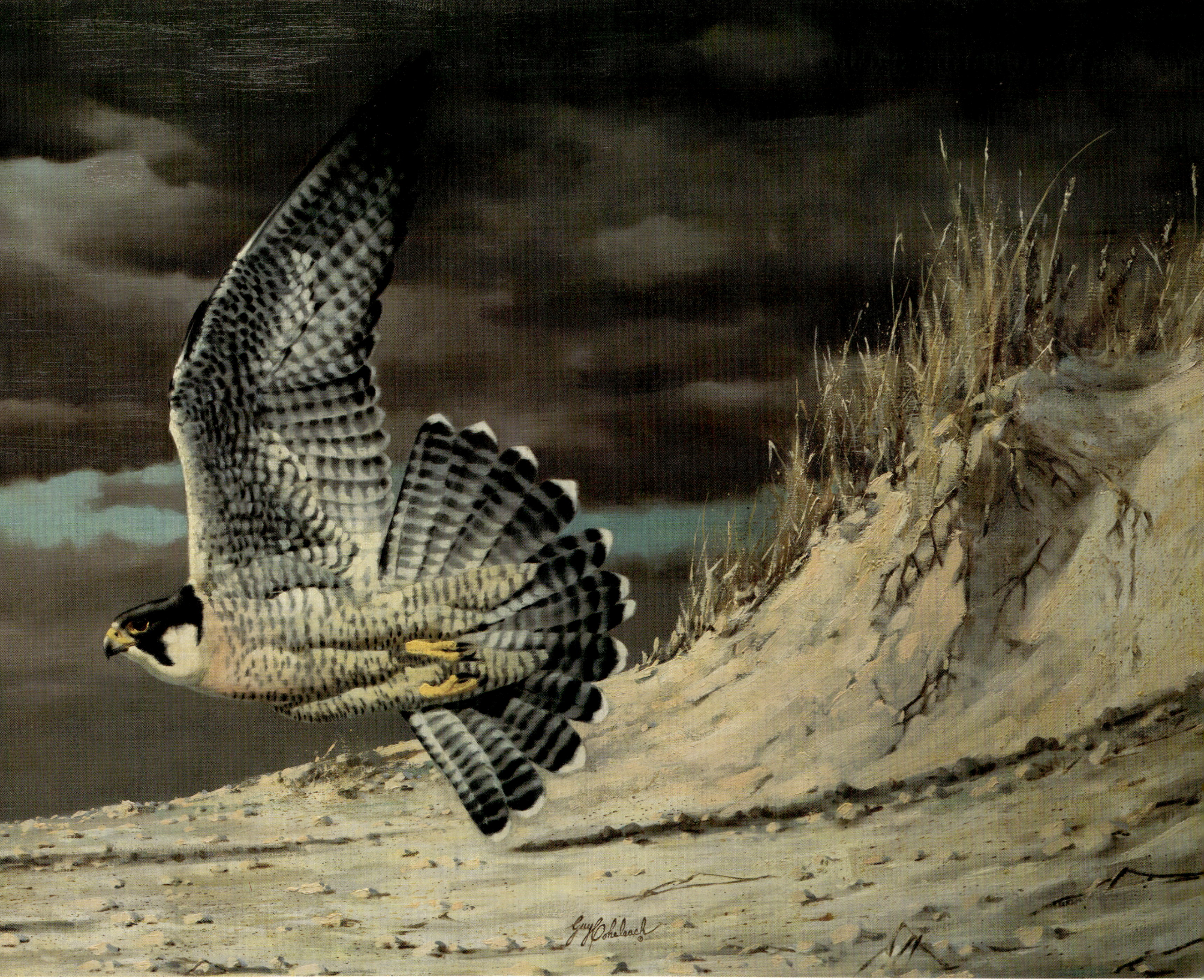
Guy Coheleach

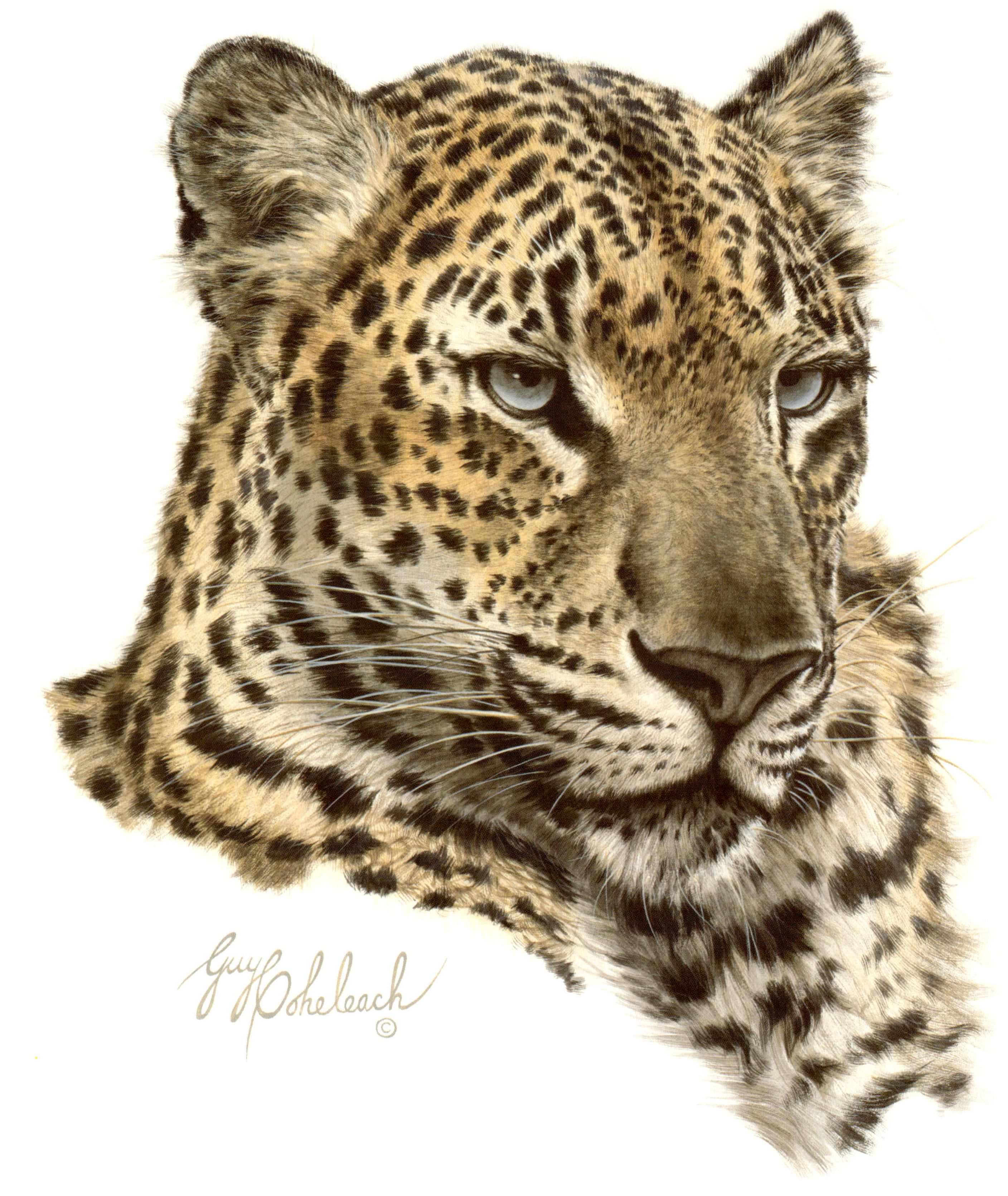
Guy Coheleach ©

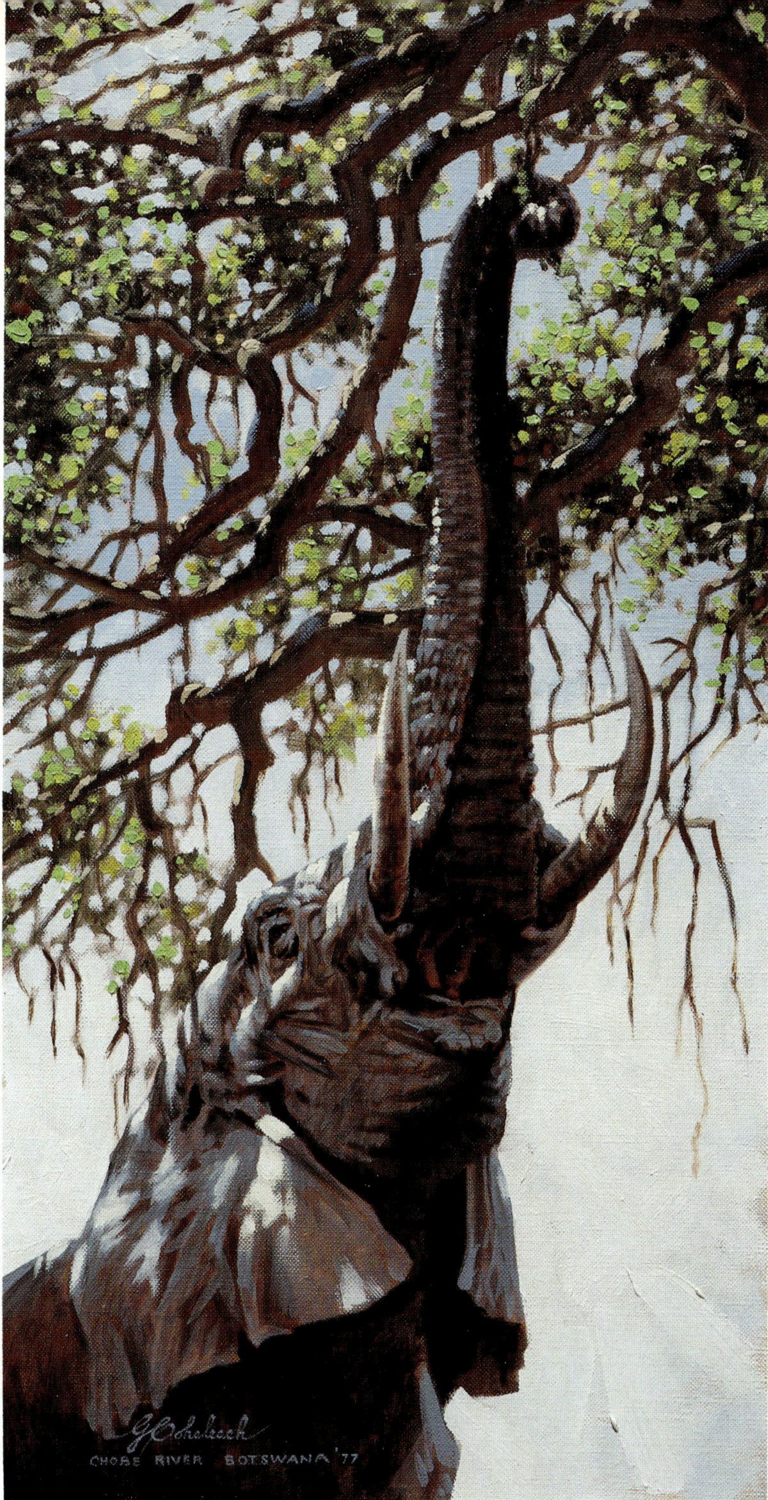

This is a small sketch I did in Botswana, at Chobe Game Park in 1977. The Chobe has thousands and thousands of elephants and Cape buffalo. I stayed at the park's game lodge, which is shaped like a huge boomerang with a concrete swimming pool in the center. About 11 o'clock one night I went out for a swim and there was an elephant they called Charlie in the swimming pool. I understand that old Charlie even ventured into the open-air lobby on several occasions.

On the page opposite is a striking portrait of a Chinese leopard. Many individuals in this race have blue eyes, different from the yellowish-green eyes of most leopards. And because they live farther north and in cooler temperatures, Chinese leopards have longer hair than their African cousins.

Bull Elephant, 10 X 20, Oil on Canvas

Chinese Leopard, 20 X 28, Gouache on Illustration Board.

This was originally painted with just the bighorn sheep, but when I needed more puma paintings for the cat book, I went back in and added the cougar.

I like the explosive quality in the painting, the spontaneity, the 'boom' look that the brushstrokes give to it...like a flock of quail exploding into the air. This is really the way I like to paint. I could have put in every little hair and left the background as it is, but it all ties together better by conveying the animals with loose, painterly strokes.

Rocky Mountain Chase,
40 x 30, Oil on Canvas

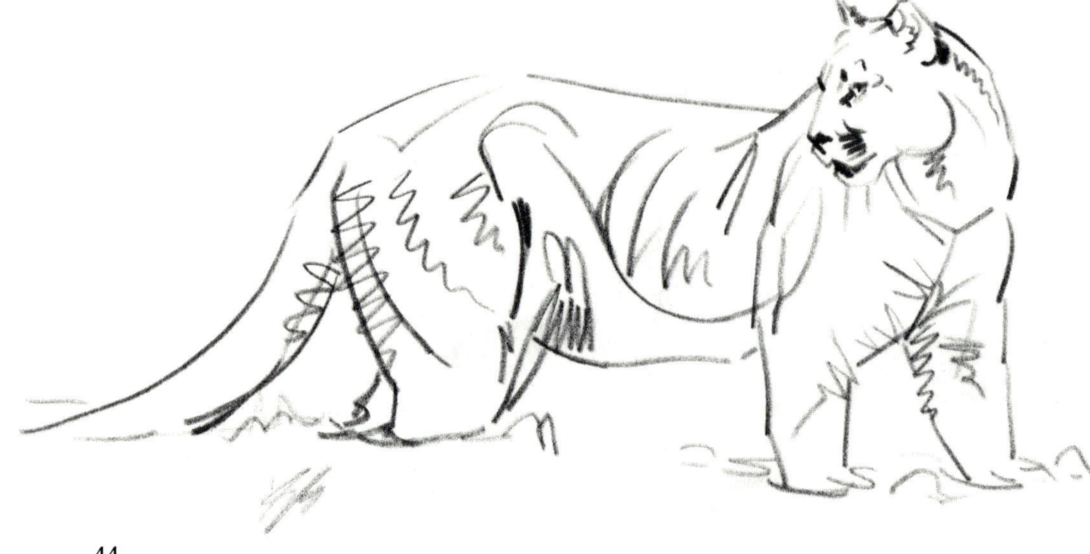

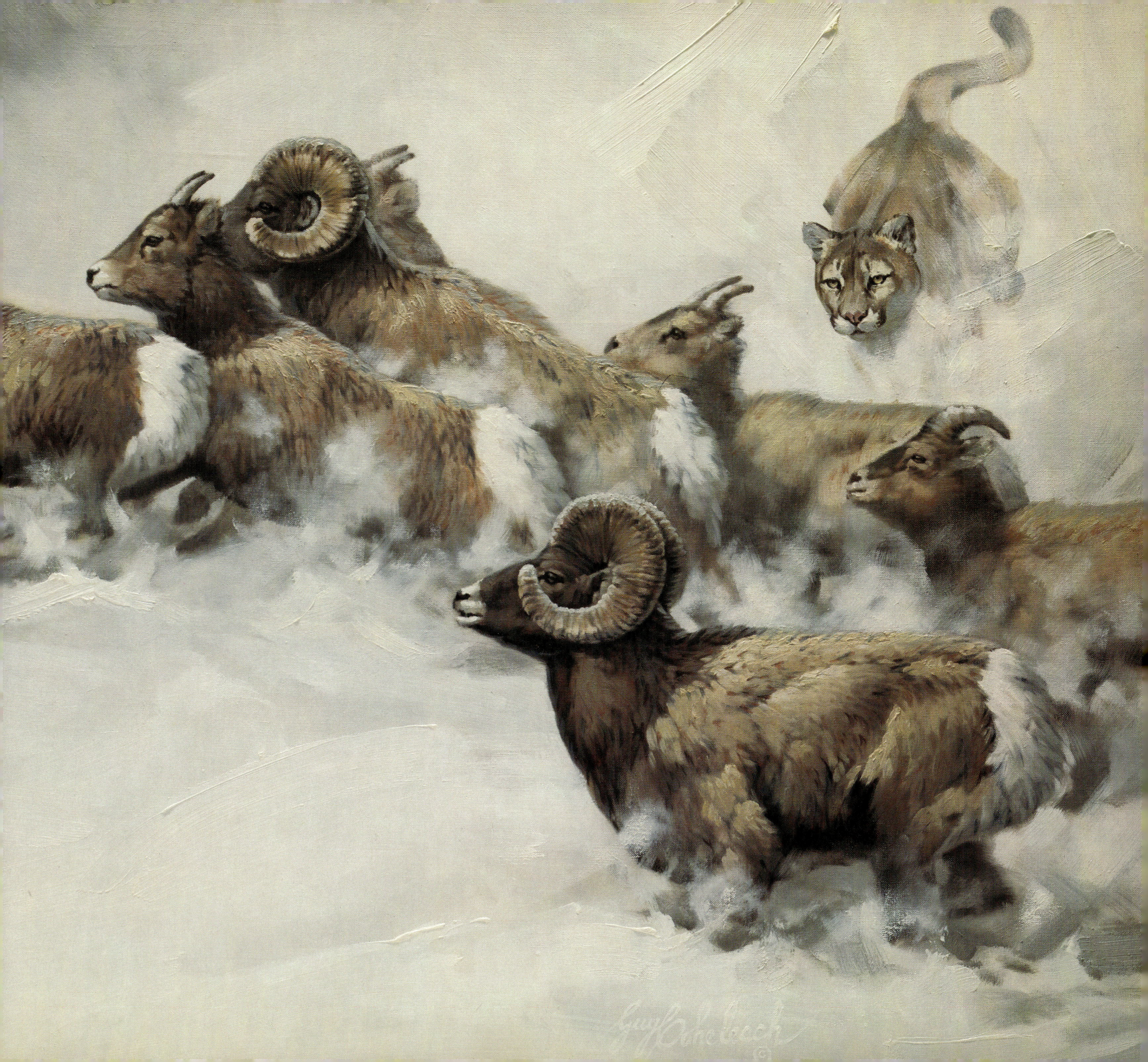

One of Coheleach's most celebrated paintings, *Brightwaters Creek* has won a number of awards and now hangs in Leigh Yawkey Woodson Art Museum where, in 1983, he was honored as a "Master Artist" at the prestigious Birds in Art exhibition.

Oil (on linen canvas) is Coheleach's favorite medium, its only drawback being a rather lengthy drying time. Oil is perfect for the effect he wanted in *Brightwaters Creek*—water that shimmers and sparkles before the eye. The secret of the scintillating water, he says, is "vibration."

Up close, you can see the strokes from my brush and palette knife. It looks like a palette covered with paint. But when you move back, all of the colors fall into place. Rather than blending them in and starting to look gray, the blue against the light brown really vibrates...it just looks much more alive from a distance.

Brightwaters Creek, 72 X 36, Oil on Canvas

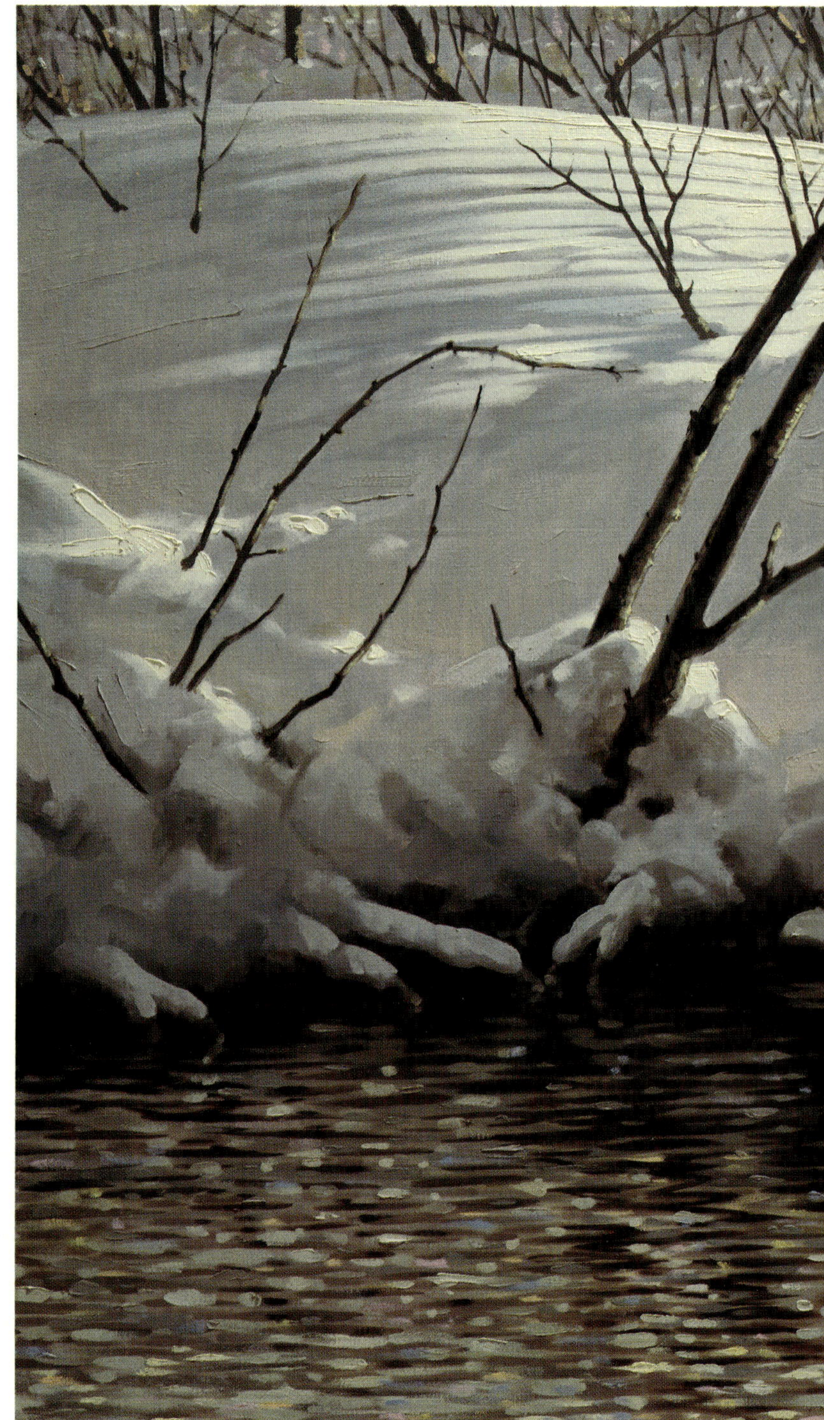

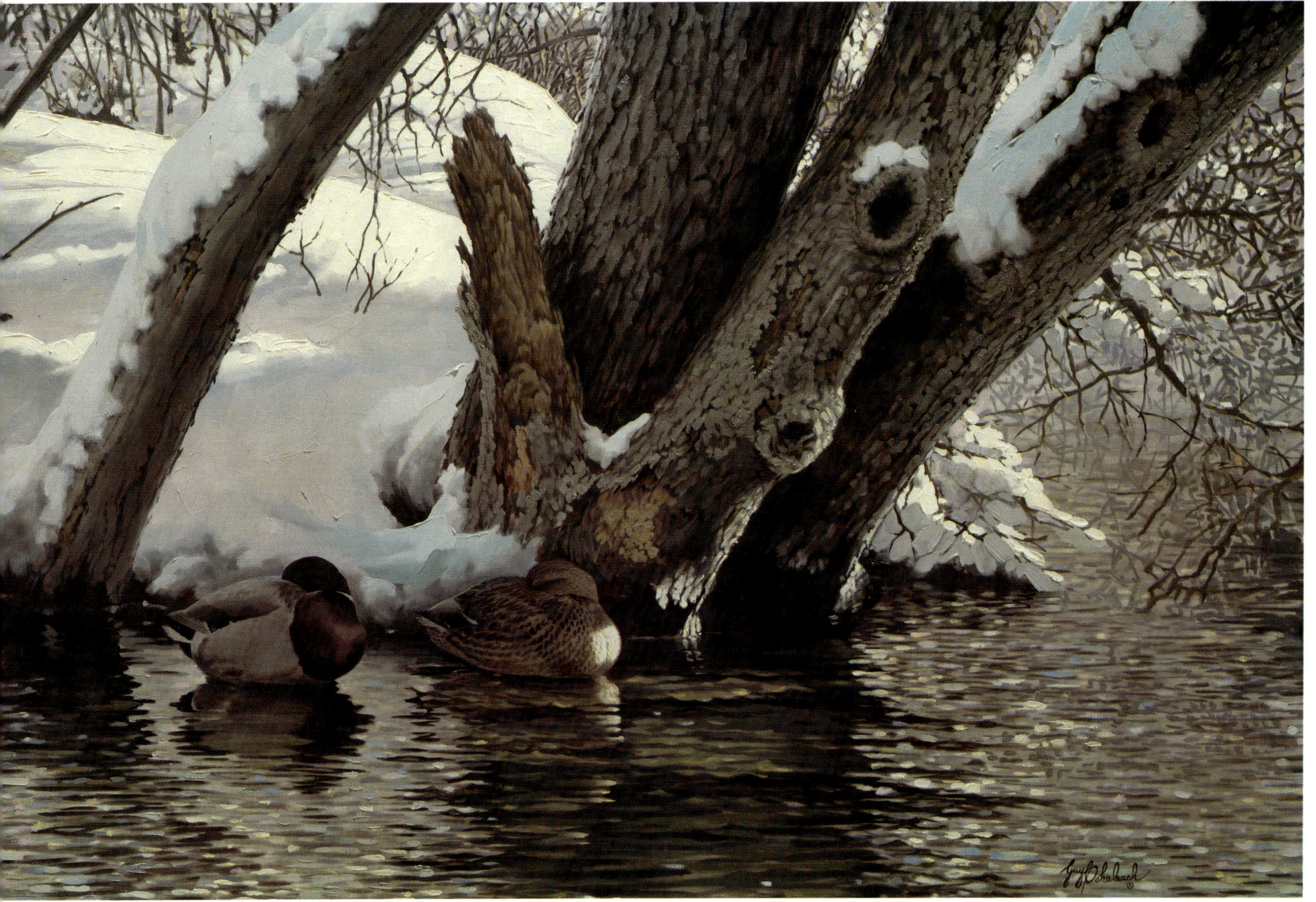

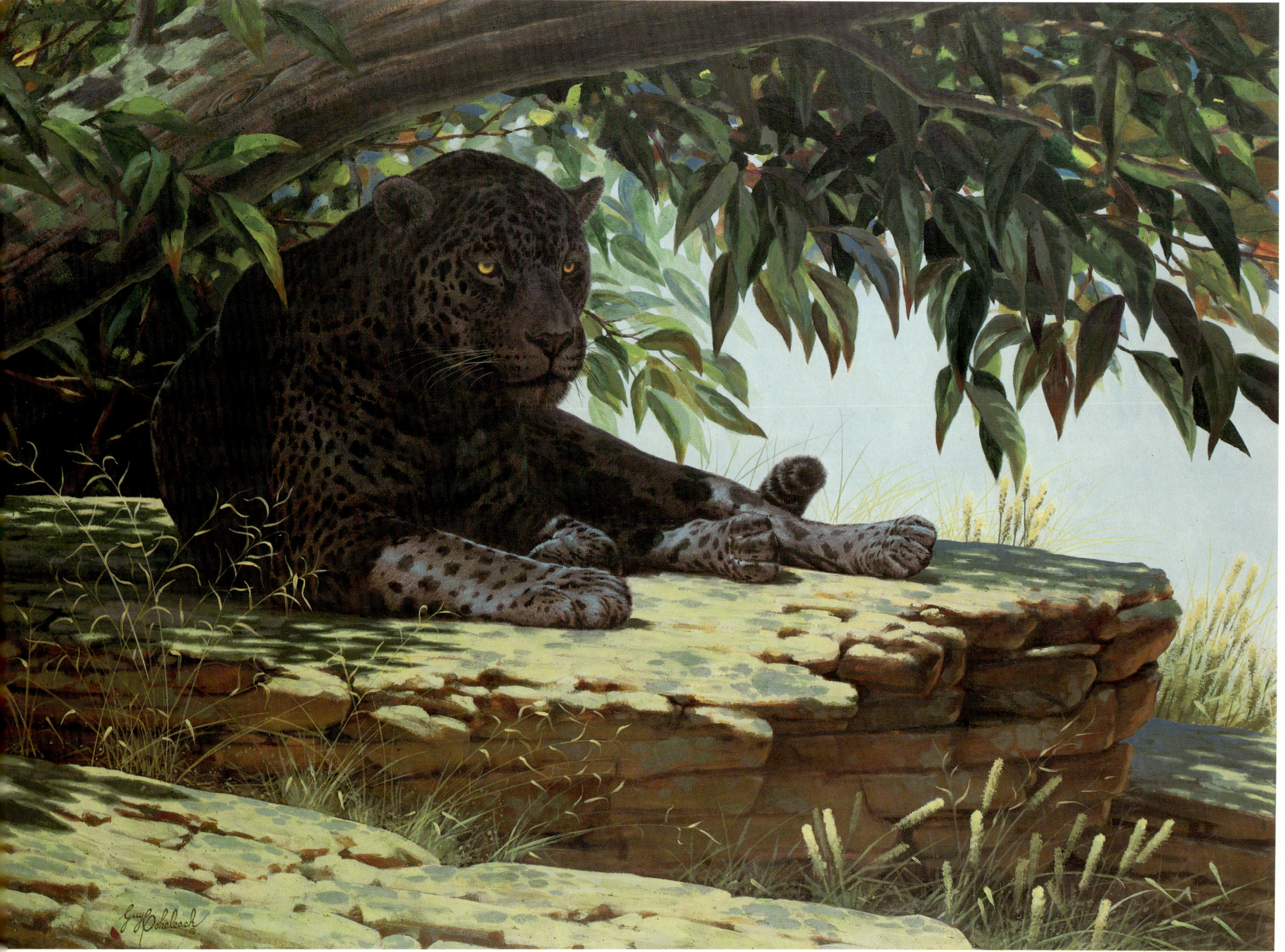

*B*razilian Noon combines realism and drama. It is the middle of the day; the sun is directly overhead. On a rock in the shade, a black jaguar rests.

Here is a case where I did exaggerate a little. A couple of his paws are out in the sunlight, and you can see the sun hitting them. The reason I brought the sunlight so close to him is so it would light up his eyes, but without hitting him directly.

The yellow-orange eyes are glowing, reflecting the light striking in front of the cat, in a way that could not have happened with direct light, and yet the scene remains natural and unforced.

Brazilian Noon, 40 X 30, Gouache and Acrylic on Illustration Board.

This portrait of a great horned owl is a simple little sketch, but it is pure watercolor—there is no white paint anywhere. The advantage of watercolor is that it dries very quickly, which gives the medium a feeling of great spontaneity.

Acrylic is another good medium for imparting spontaneity. It dries almost as fast as watercolor, yet it is as permanent and opaque as oil. Acrylic looks a little too plastic to be used thickly; if I am going to use acrylic, I like to use it thin, for background.

Great Horned Owl, 8 X 10, Watercolor on Paper

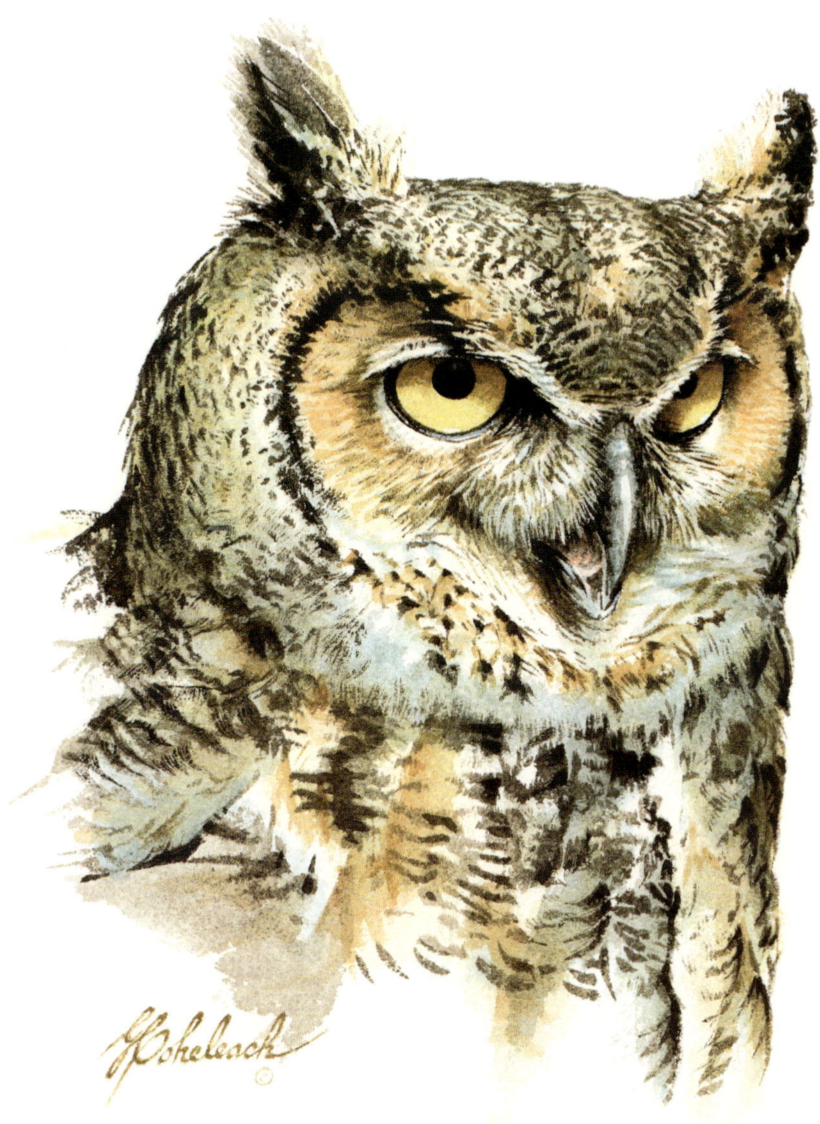

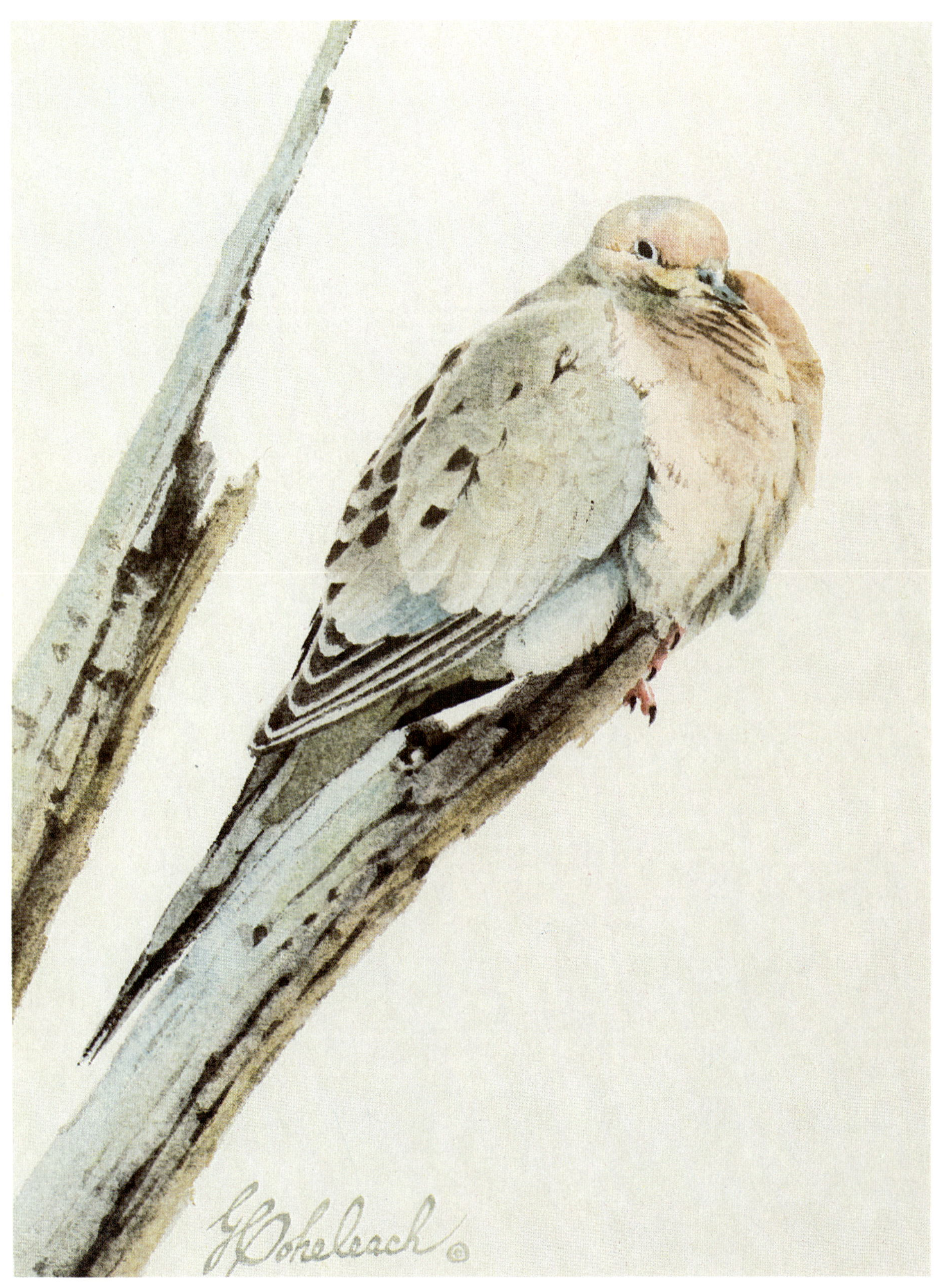

I like doing studies; if all of a sudden I see an interesting bird outside my studio window, I may drop what I'm doing and record the scene. In this case, it was the shape of the dove on a branch—like an upside-down drop of water or a small balloon growing out of a straw.

Studies are ways to experiment with ideas and concepts. Sometimes I do them just because I feel like doodling. I've done several studies on matchbook covers...I didn't have anything else to draw on at the time.

Mourning Dove, 8 X 10, Watercolor on Illustration Board

When painting a detailed portrait such as this, Coheleach prefers to work from study skins rather than taxidermy mounts or photographs.

There's a danger in working with mounted birds and mammals because the taxidermist may have arranged the creature in a shape that is inaccurate. You don't want to be influenced by someone else's interpretation of how an animal should look.

The red-shafted flicker is a common bird in the West; the fact that it is common and that many people have seen it and know its characteristics, makes it even more important to be absolutely certain of your facts. And the way to be certain of its colors and plumage is to get the actual bird and study it.

Red-shafted Flicker, 22 X 30, Gouache on Illustration Board

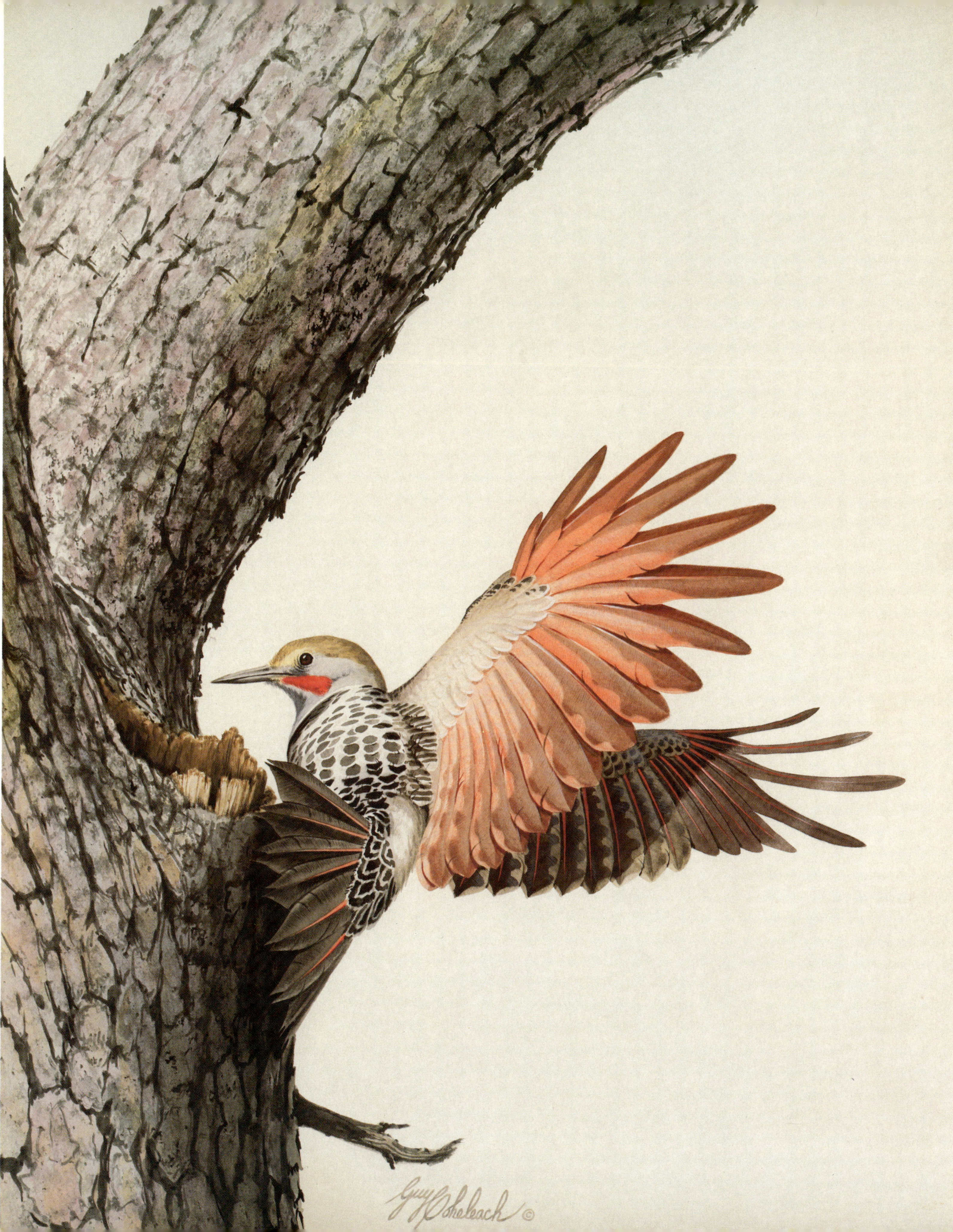

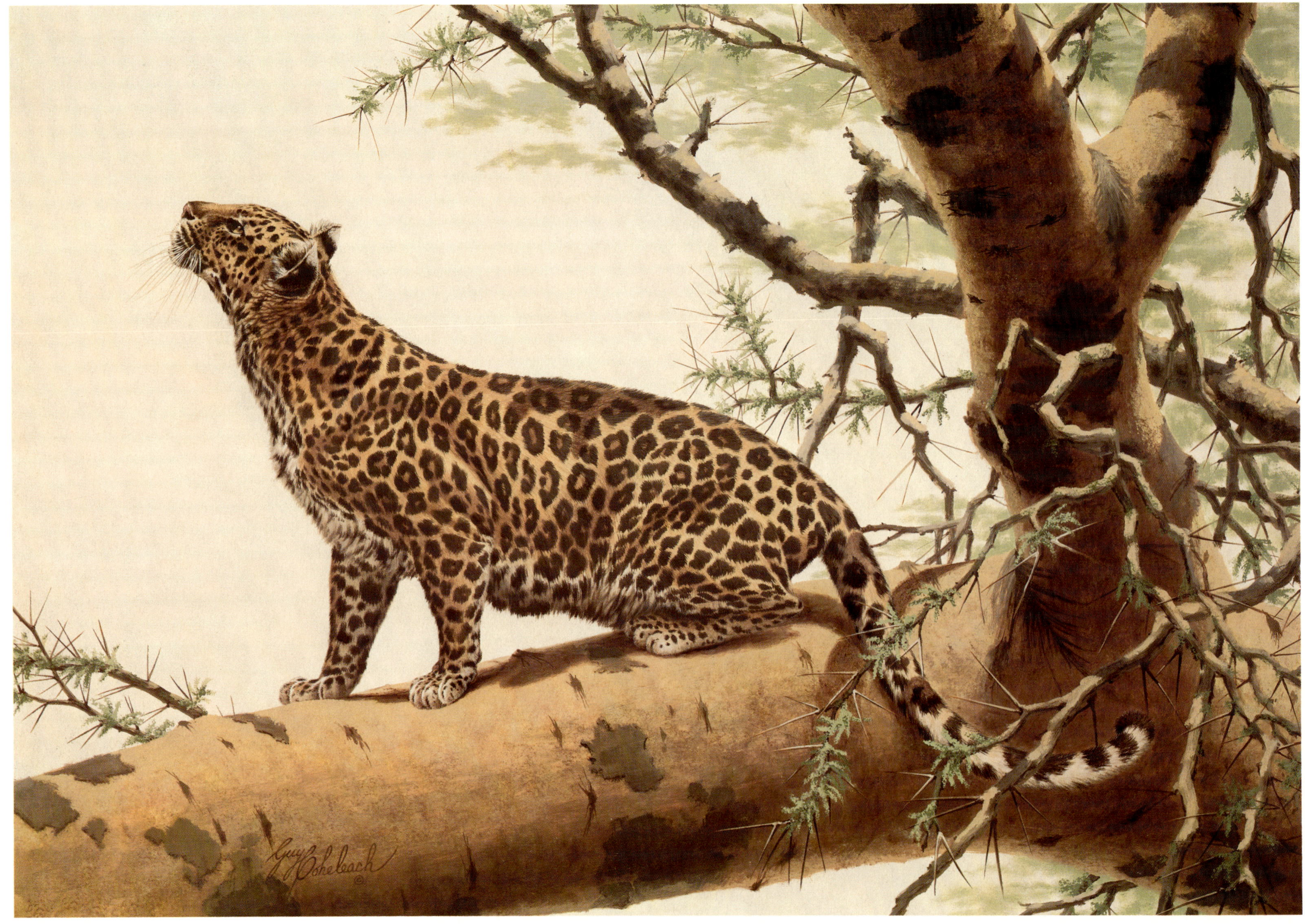
Guy Coheleach ©

The concept of portraying an animal looking out of the painting was a radical approach when *Monkeys Above* was painted in 1972. Coheleach uses the massive limbs of the acacia tree to prevent the leopard's gaze from pulling your eye off the page.

Normally, I would not have the leopard's head—which is the focal point—so close to the edge and looking off. For instance, if I painted the cat on a white rock with nothing else around, I would put him much farther back and down. But there is so much happening with the acacia over at the right and down at the bottom, that I can justify it. Your imagination sees the tree continuing; you know there is more tree up there, and probably a monkey or something that he's interested in. It's almost as if you are looking at a much greater picture, and this is just one corner of it—a detail, if you will.

Monkeys Above — Leopard, 40 X 30, Gouache on Illustration Board

---

Cape Buffalo, 10 X 8, Watercolor on Paper

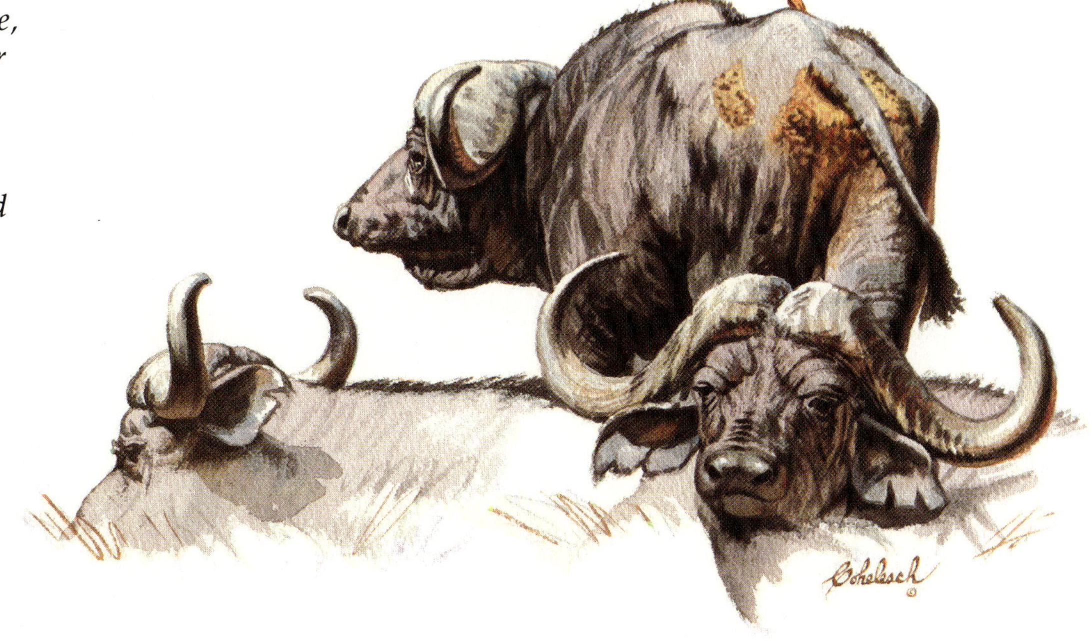

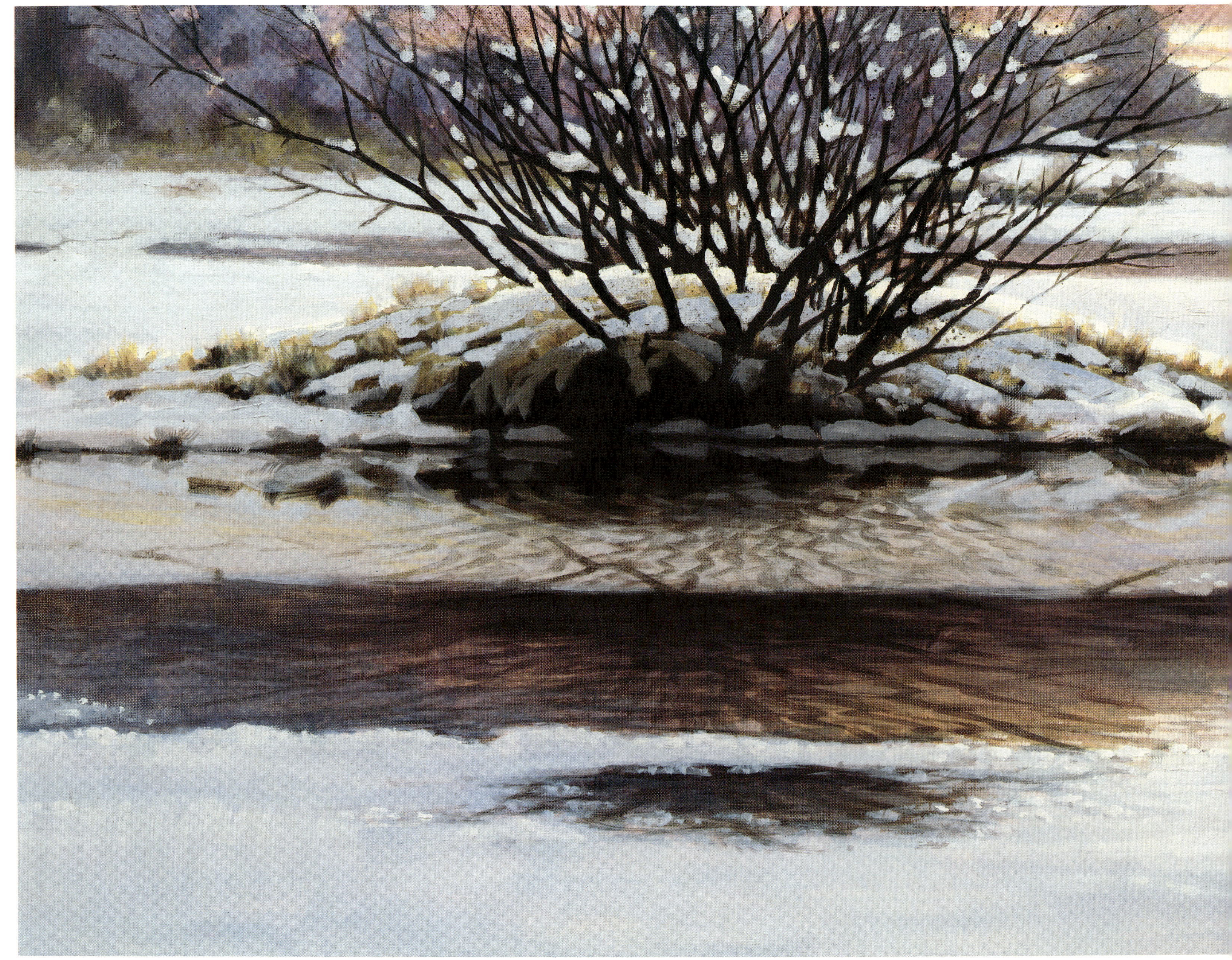

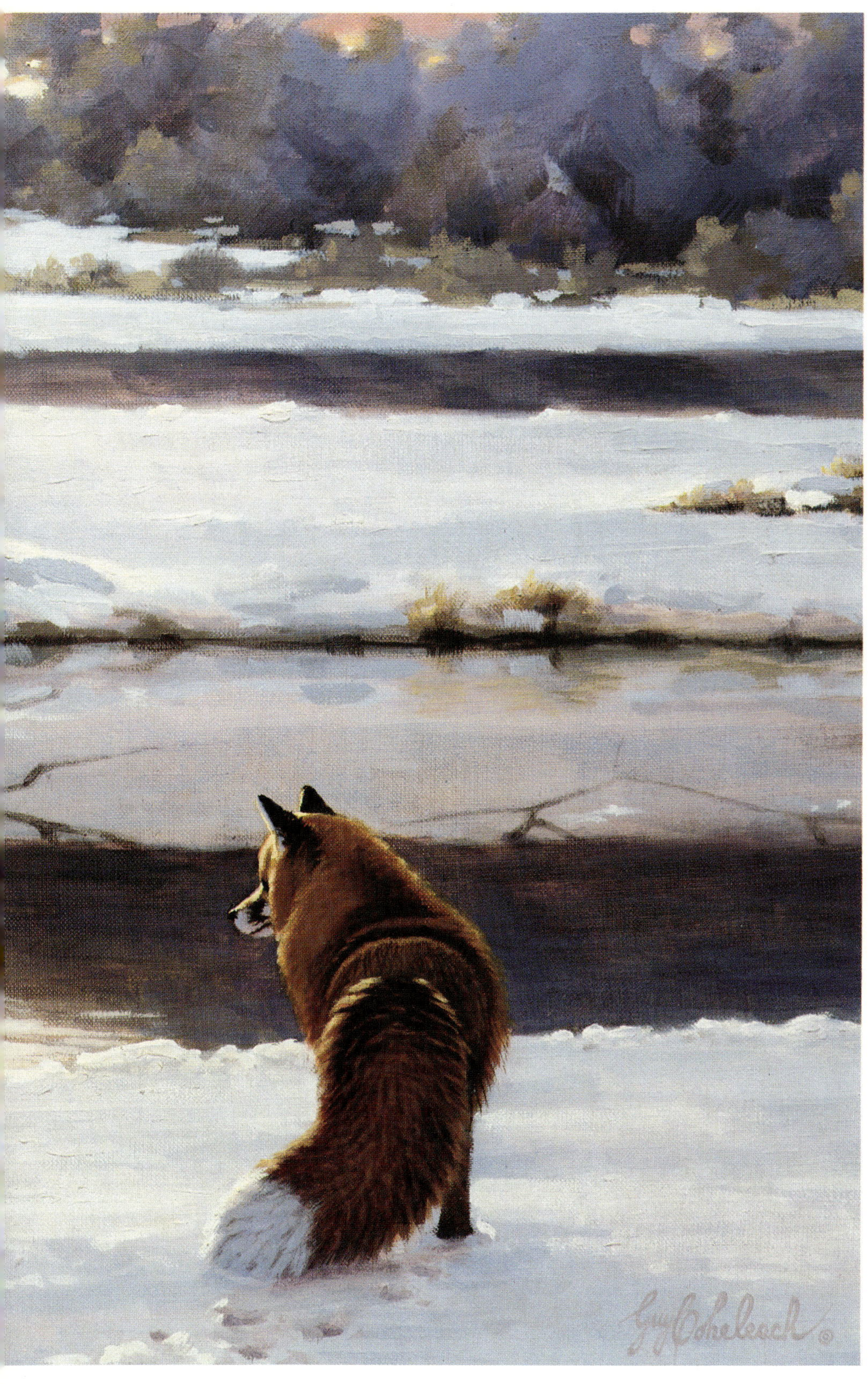

Coheleach entered the original version of this painting in the 1988 Society of Animal Artists exhibition at the Rochester Museum of Art. Museum officials liked the painting so well that they reproduced it on their exhibition poster. Later, the decision was made to reproduce the image as a fine-art print. For that, Coheleach created this version, essentially the same composition but with much brighter colors.

It's a gray day, with a little sunlight coming underneath the clouds, just enough to enhance the colors of the landscape, like the purplish trees way back in the distance. Interesting colors like these make for interesting paintings.

Captree Fox, 30 X 15, Oil on Canvas

The low perspective in this painting heightens the drama and emphasizes the pugnacious nature of Cape buffalo.

Normally you show something from about eye-level, about five or five and a half feet above ground. Otherwise, it looks disproportionate. If you show it from above, it looks like you are in a tree; if you show it from below, you can make it look huge.

Here, it's as if you are kneeling down and looking up. Cape buffalo are big animals—big in every way, including their well-deserved reputation, and one way of conveying that bigness is the proper use of perspective.

Spooked, 44 X 24, Oil on Canvas

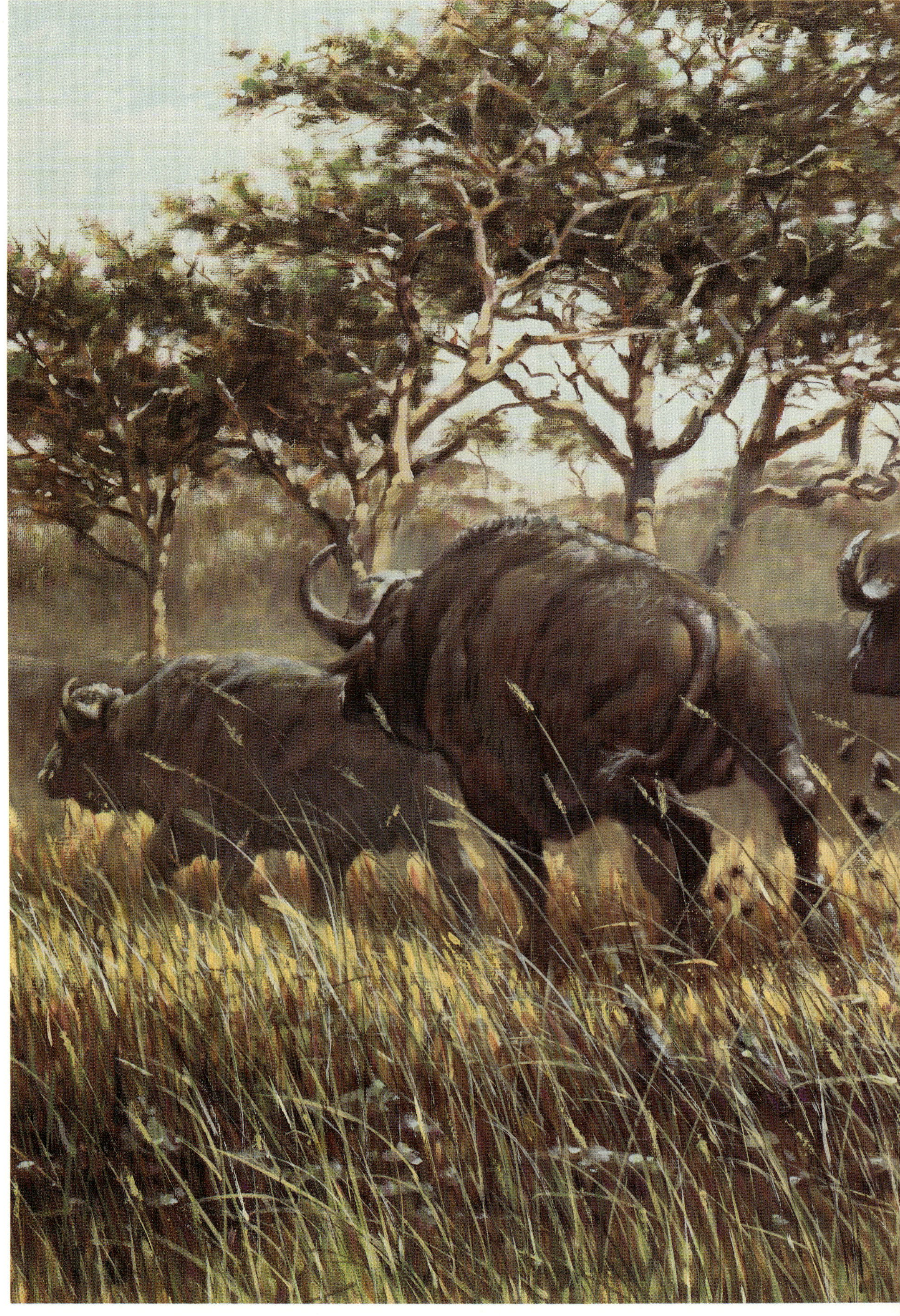

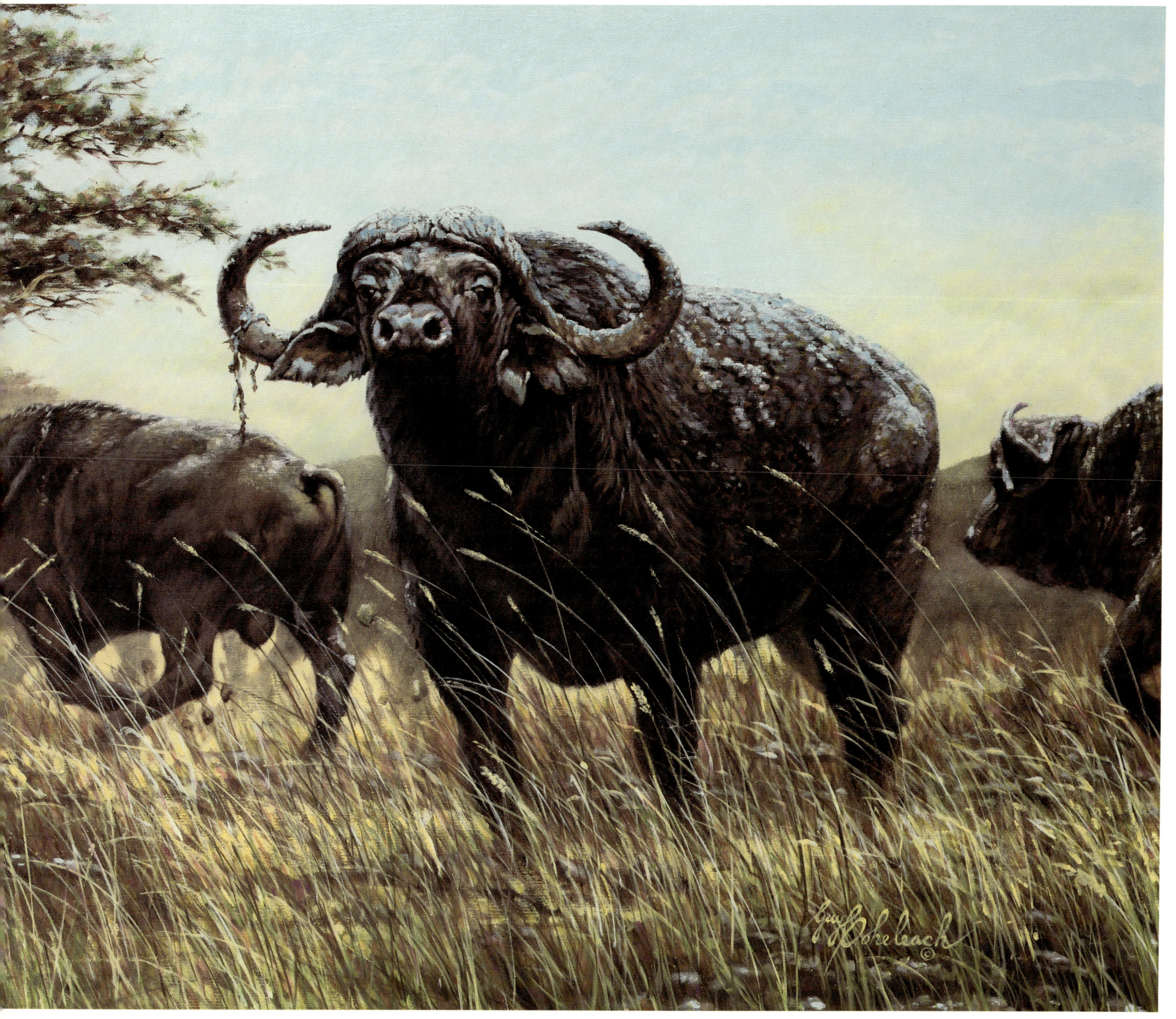

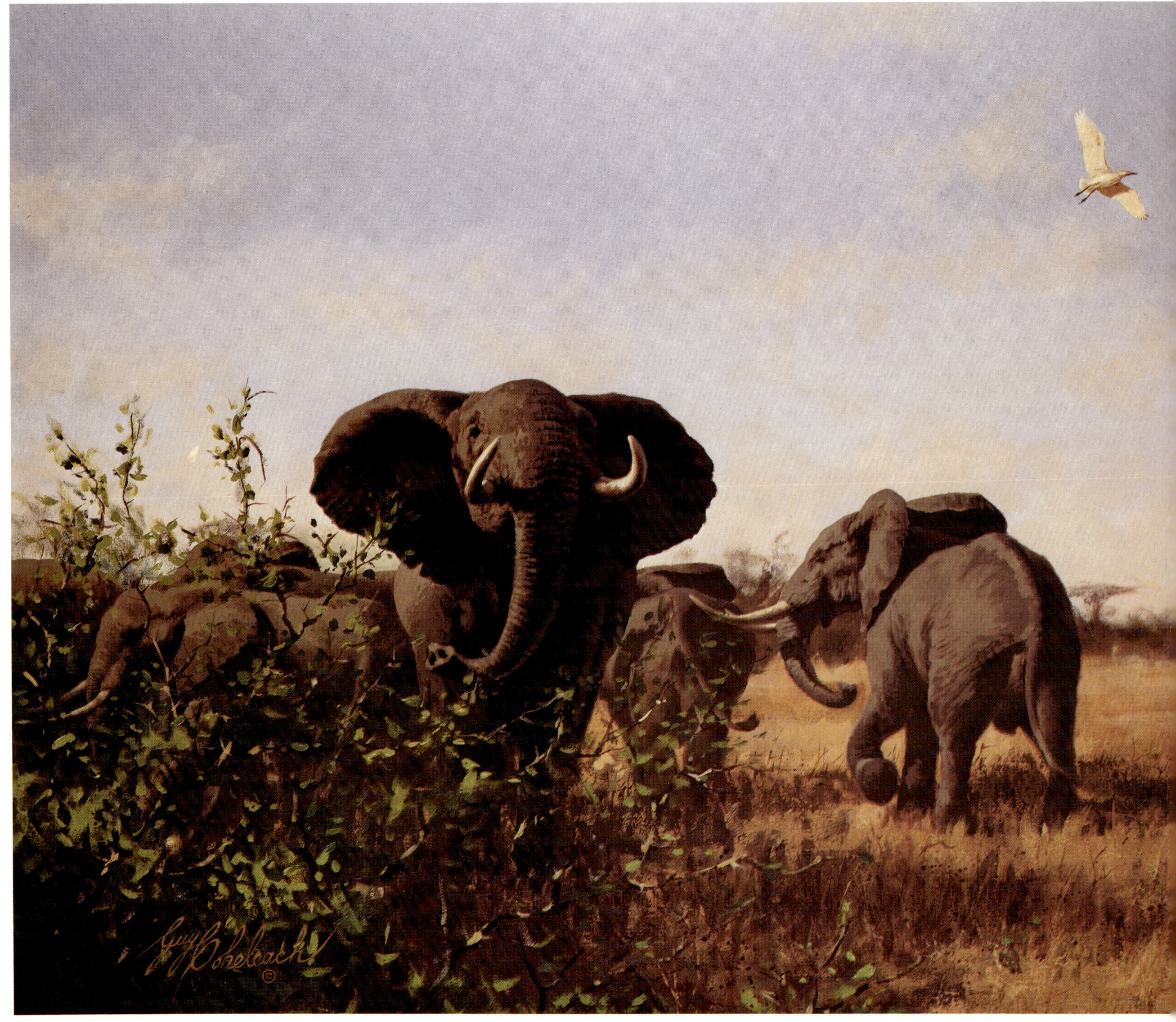

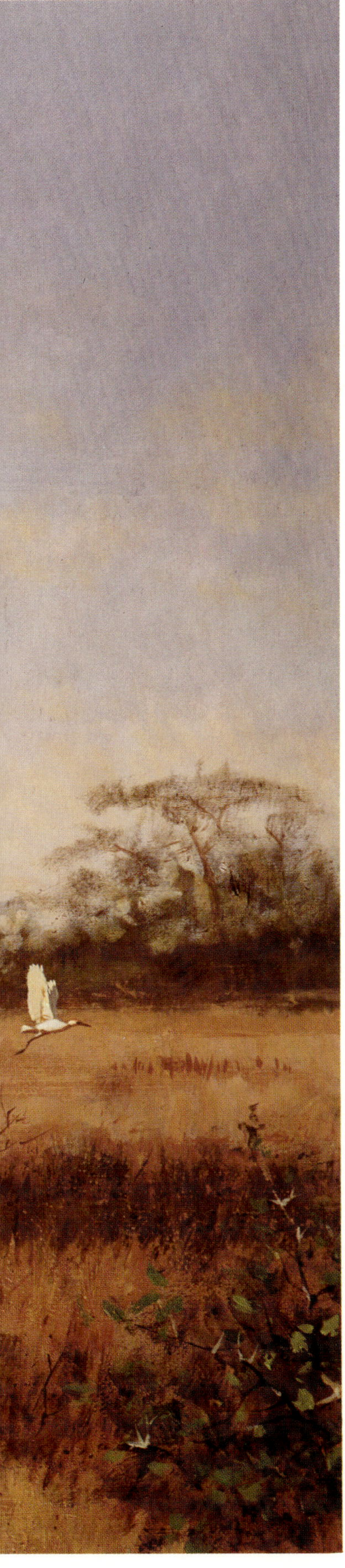

Elephants and Cattle Egrets portrays the sere landscape of Botswana, home of the sprawling Kalahari. Coheleach added the egrets to heighten the feeling of excitement in the air. You can almost hear the elephants' shrill trumpeting and feel the ground shaking beneath your feet as the huge animals stomp about, their way of intimidating the intruder.

Elephants and Cattle Egrets, 40 X 30, Oil on Canvas

The most beautiful and elegant of Africa's antelope, the giant sable is noted for its harlequin markings and long, scimitar horns that make it a formidable adversary to a hungry lion or leopard. The gouache painting was among a series of animal portraits created for *Audubon* magazine in the 1960s.

Giant Sable, 20 X 28, Gouache on Illustration Board

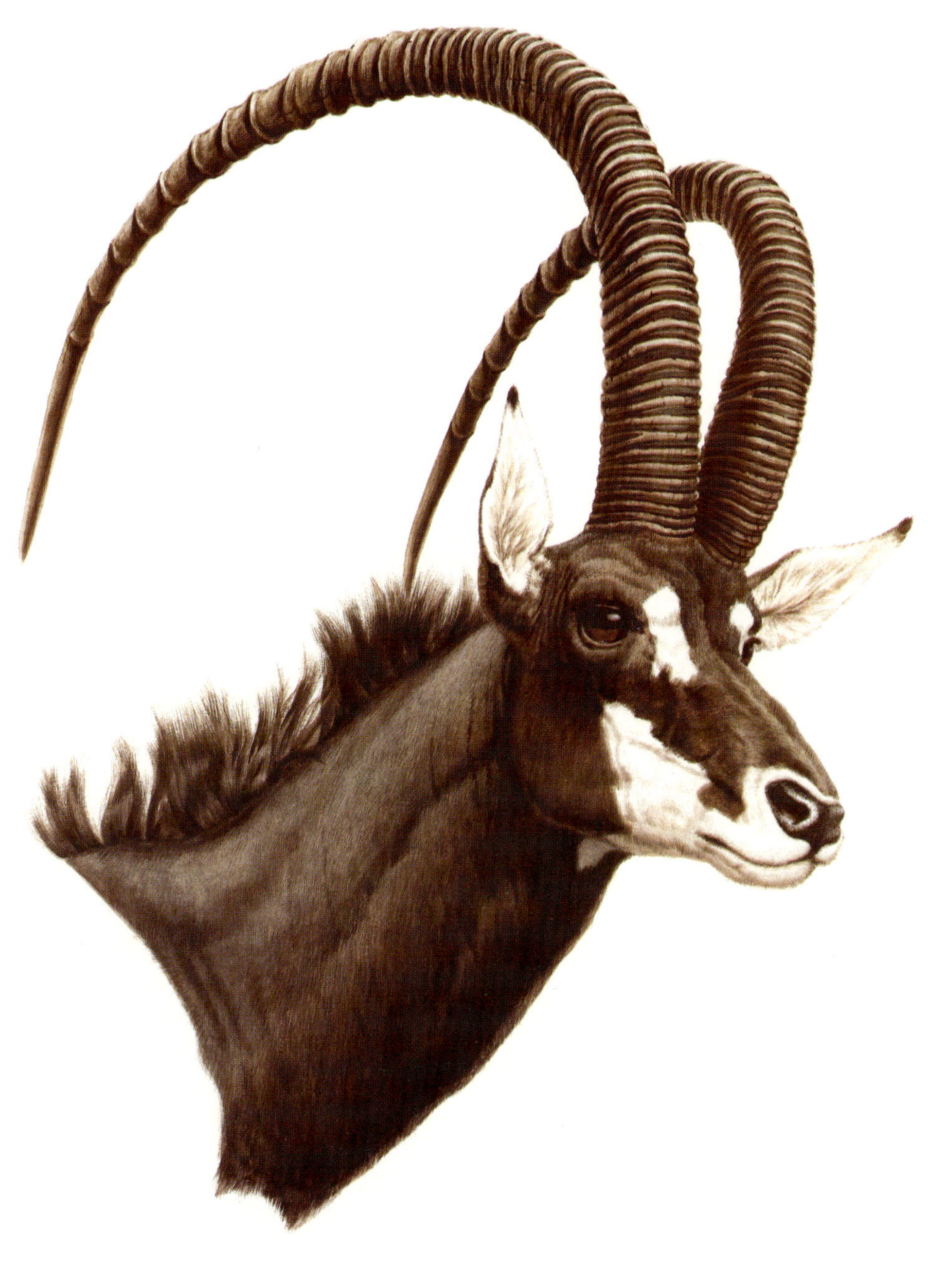

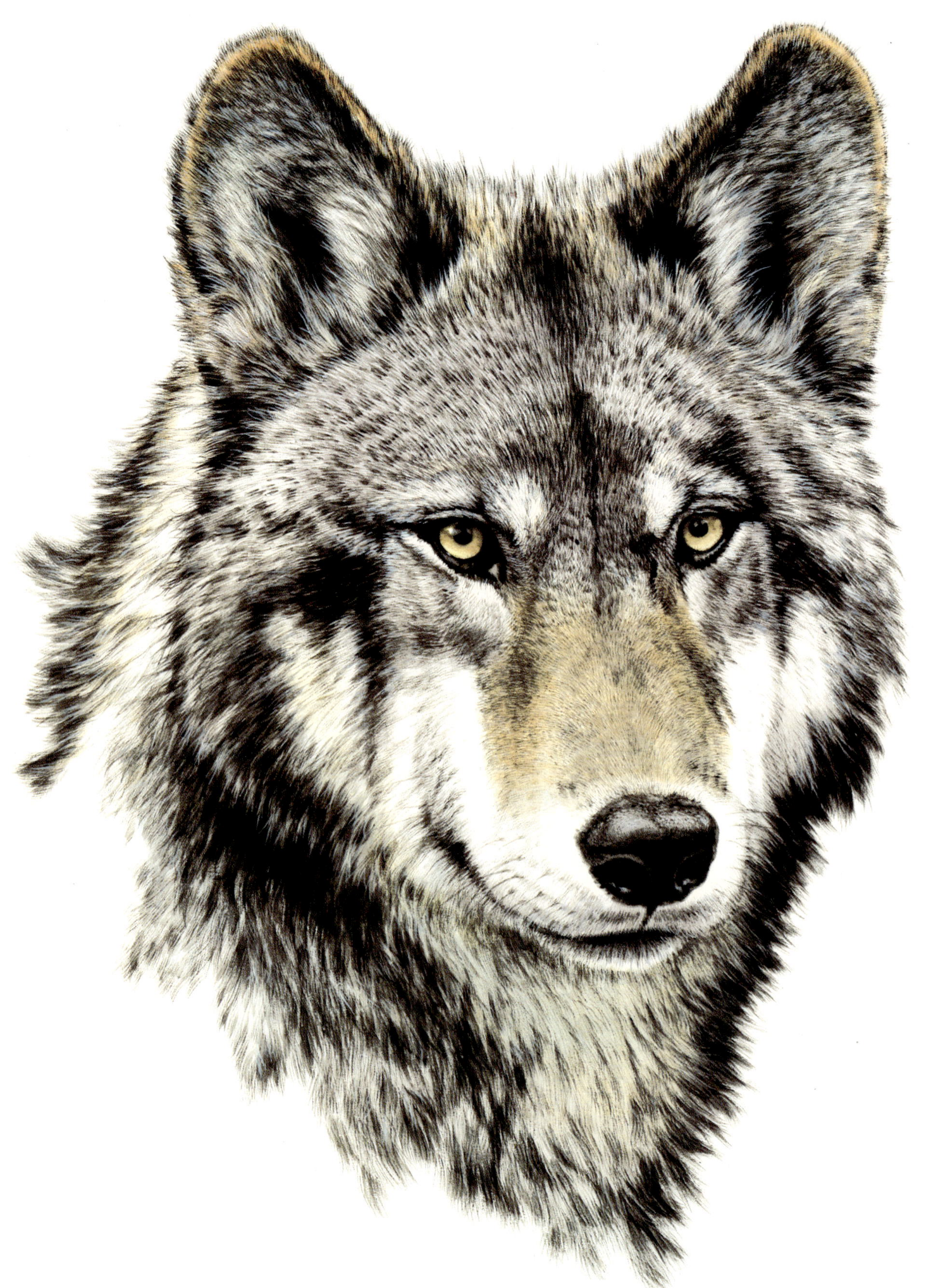

There are two good reasons for artists to paint vignettes like this one:

They sell very well and they are a very good exercise in painting detail and getting it exactly right. It is a discipline, like five-finger exercises on the piano. And that discipline carries over into looser paintings.

I like doing detail, but it gets boring if you do it all over the canvas. A vignette allows me to detail the things I want to paint in detail, and leave the rest.

Timber Wolf, 22 X 30, Gouache on Illustration Board.

A fleeting moment of wolves on the move, pausing to glance, and then gone again. Their condensed breath combined with the looseness of the painting convey the ephemeral quality of their existence.

The design, the color, the mood, the frosted breath—they all seem to work well. I am getting to like wolves and foxes and coyotes. This miniature will be the basis for a larger painting sometime in the future.

Timber Wolves, 9 X 12, Oil on Illustration Board

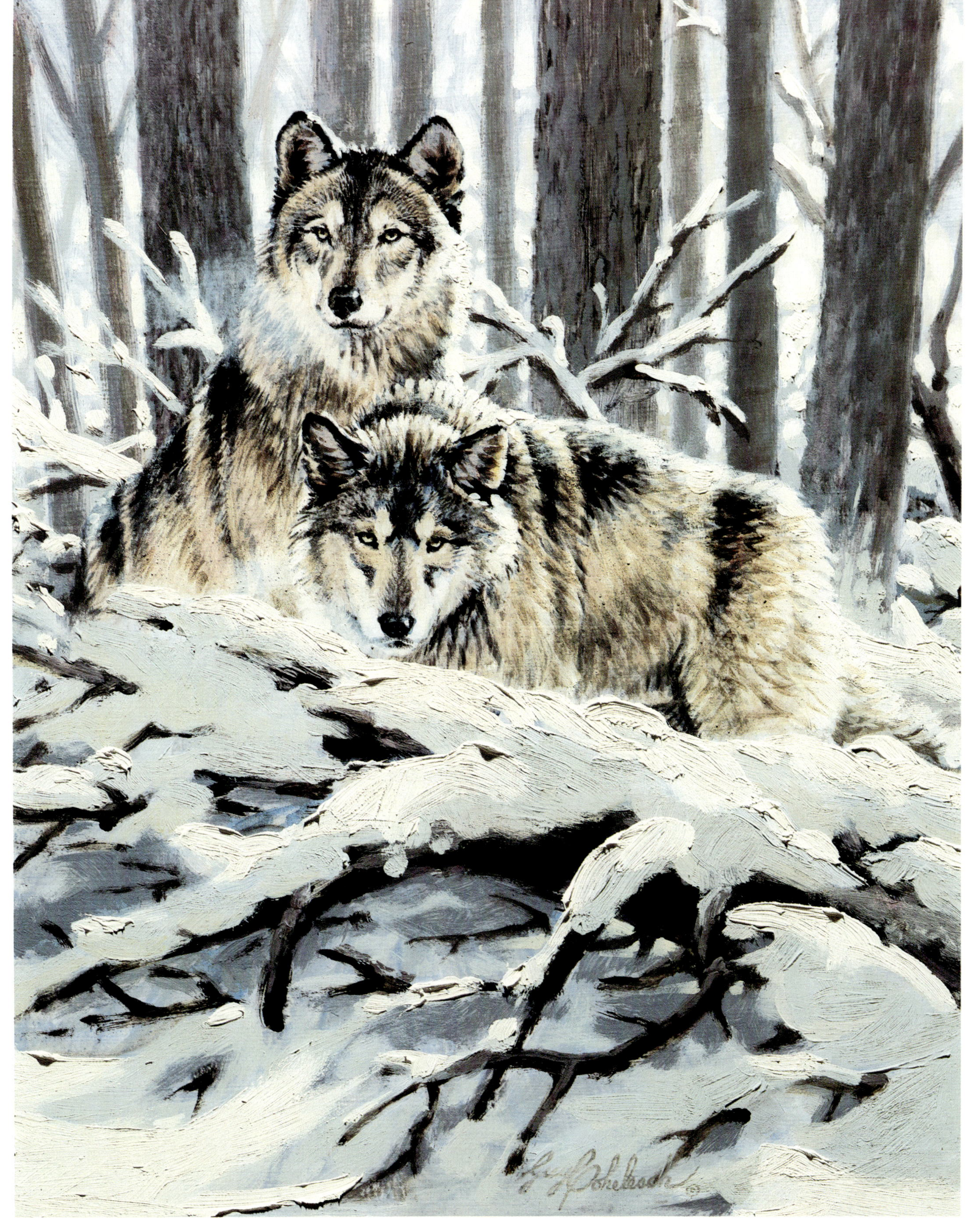

Colors in nature are deceptive to virtually all but the trained artistic eye. On the surface, it is unbelievable that a red-gold and black animal could become practically invisible among stalks of bright green grass. That it is not only possible but commonplace points up the fact that grasses are not entirely green, but a combination of shades and colors—not just cool greens and blues, but warm browns and reds as well.

There are a lot of very warm siennas and ochres in green grass; there is always grass that has died and turned brown, and other grass that has grown up through it. These individual stalks, while not obvious to a quick glance, provide an opportunity to put in some vibration—in this case, to reflect the color of the tiger's eyes.

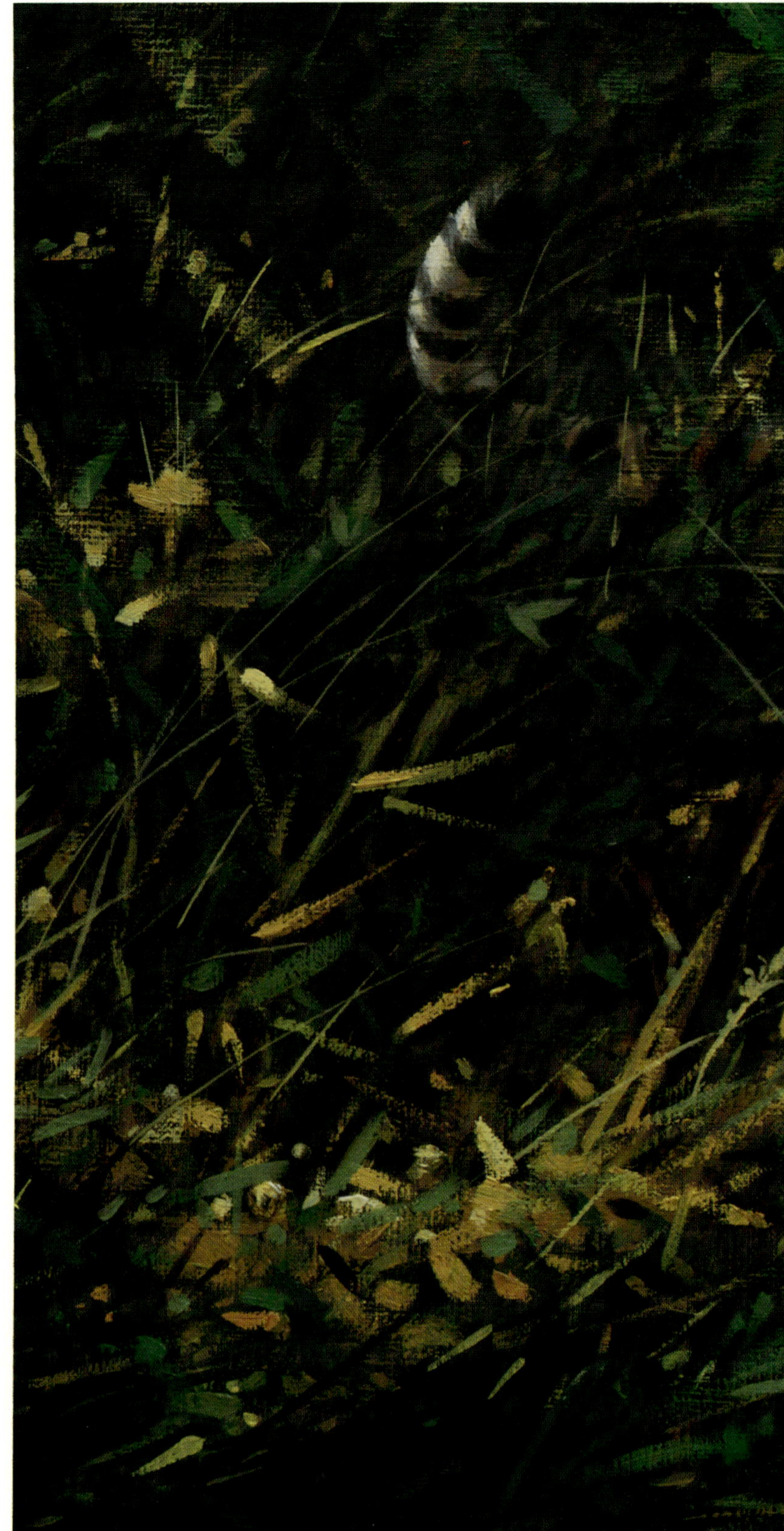

Stripes in the Grass, 30 X 15, Oil on Canvas

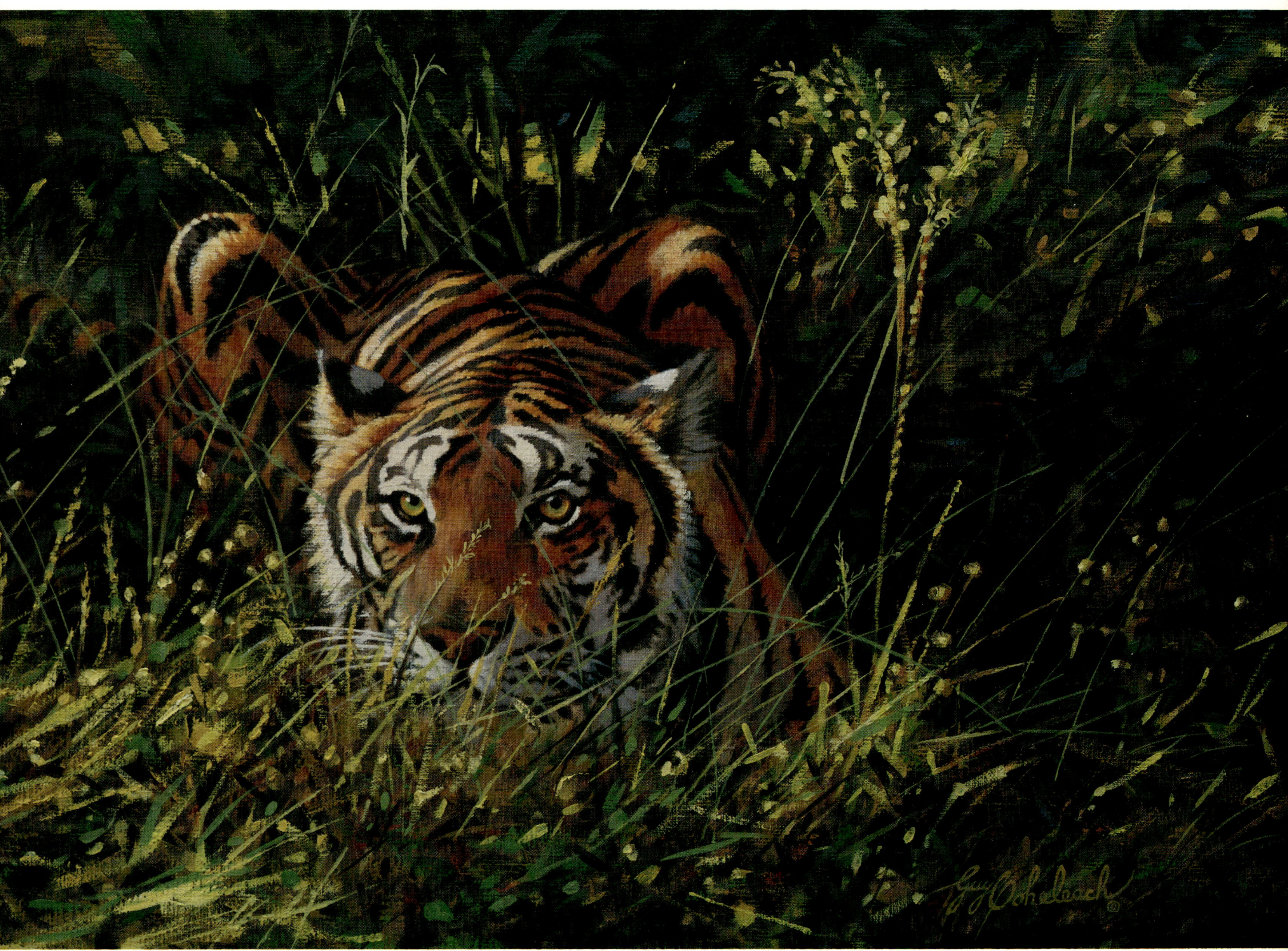
Guy Coheleach

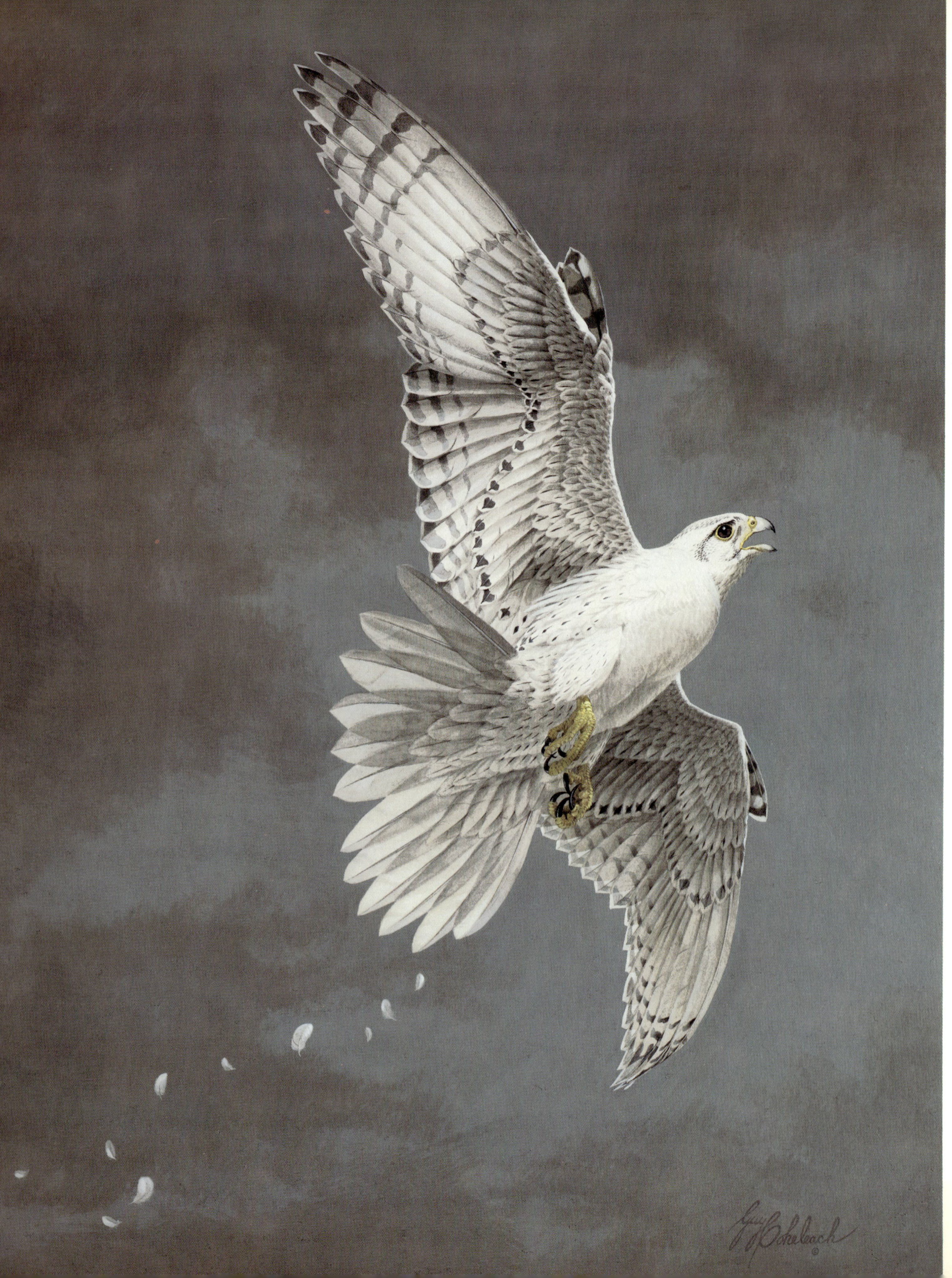

This may not be great art, perhaps, but I like to think it is great—or at least good—portraiture. It is a simple painting of a highly detailed gyrfalcon against a neutral, cloudy sky. Done this way, the sky serves a very real purpose: it gives the viewer's eye a place to rest, away from the detail, yet allows it to return to study the detail. I've found this to be important, although a viewer may not be able to articulate why he does or does not like a particular work.

Again, Coheleach has used his successful technique of victor and victim, but with the prey out of the picture; in this case, the feathers of a luckless ptarmigan drift from the gyrfalcon's talons as it rises and slows at the end of its swoop.

White Gyrfalcon, 30 X 40, Gouache and Acrylic on Illustration Board

This is the type of painting I would never dream of putting out as a print, and yet it is probably one of the finest pieces in the book.

It is a small painting, done in 1963, and almost exclusively with a palette knife. It is essentially a painting of design, of mood, of texture and technique. The fence in the foreground breaks up the big white block of snow on the bottom, and frames the mouse and owl. The end result of the chase is left to the viewer-whether the mouse escapes, or the owl eats.

Snowy Owl, 12 X 24, Oil on Illustration Board

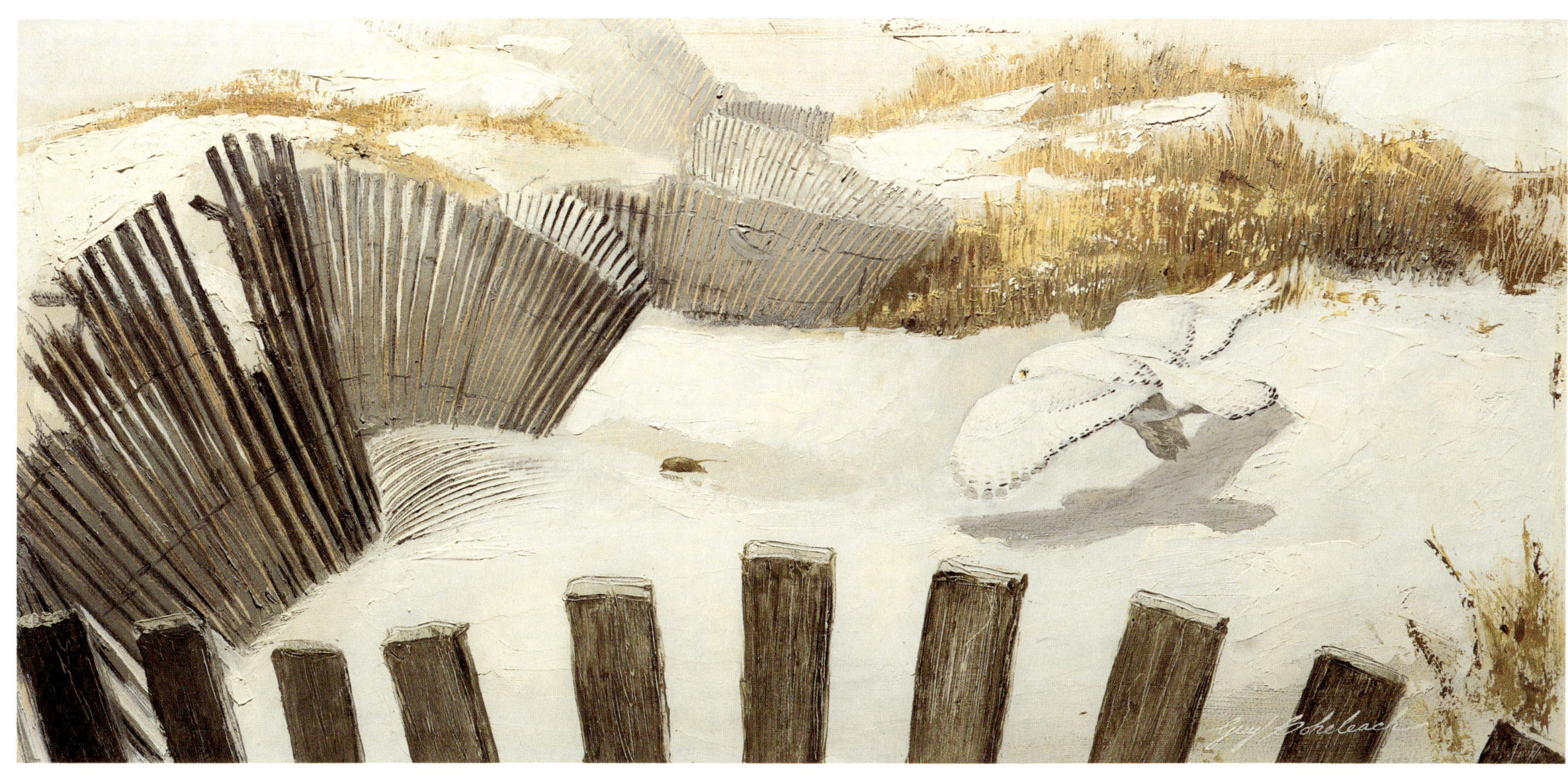

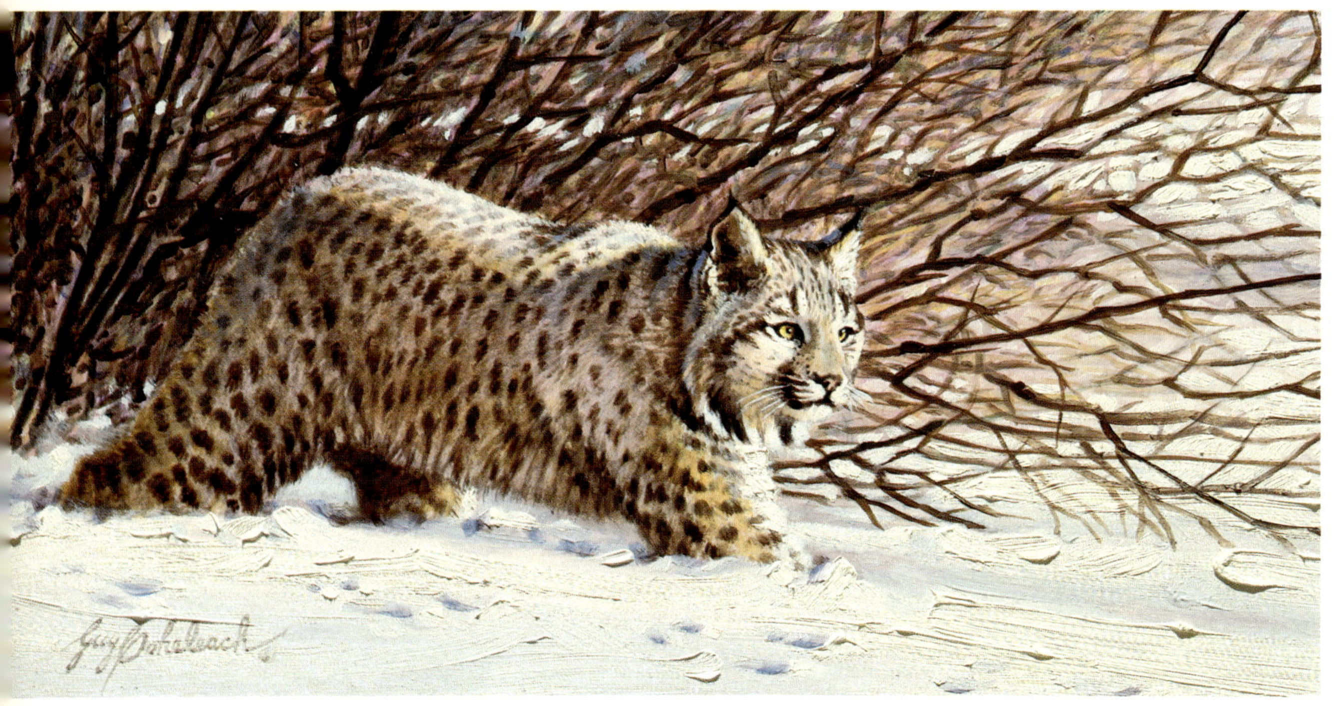

Bobcat is a very small painting, what gallery people call a "miniature." It was painted for one of the many miniature shows held around the country, and illustrates the difference between painting large, and painting small.

A miniature painting looks fine when you see the original, because people don't expect a great deal of detail. But in a book, when you reproduce a six- by twelve-inch painting and a three-by nine-foot painting to the same size, the small one starts to look clumsy compared with the other.

The main reason is scale. In a miniature, there is no room to delineate everything without getting the piece to look overworked. This painting looks more textured, primarily because of its small size. The ridges of thick paint are closer together than they would be on a large canvas.

Bobcat, 12 X 6, Oil on Masonite

Painted in 1983, this oil on canvas reflects Coheleach's fascination with snow.

The artist can do so many interesting things with snow. Most obvious are the strongly contrasting images — the brilliant, silvery-white patches of snow in the sunlight as opposed to the dark shadows of trees.

The warm-colored feathers on the bird's back are reflecting light onto the snow. This creates a nice dimension, a kind of third level in between the grouse and snow. I also like the play of light on the bird's head feathers, which appear almost transluscent.

Grouse and Snow, 20 x 30, Oil on Canvas

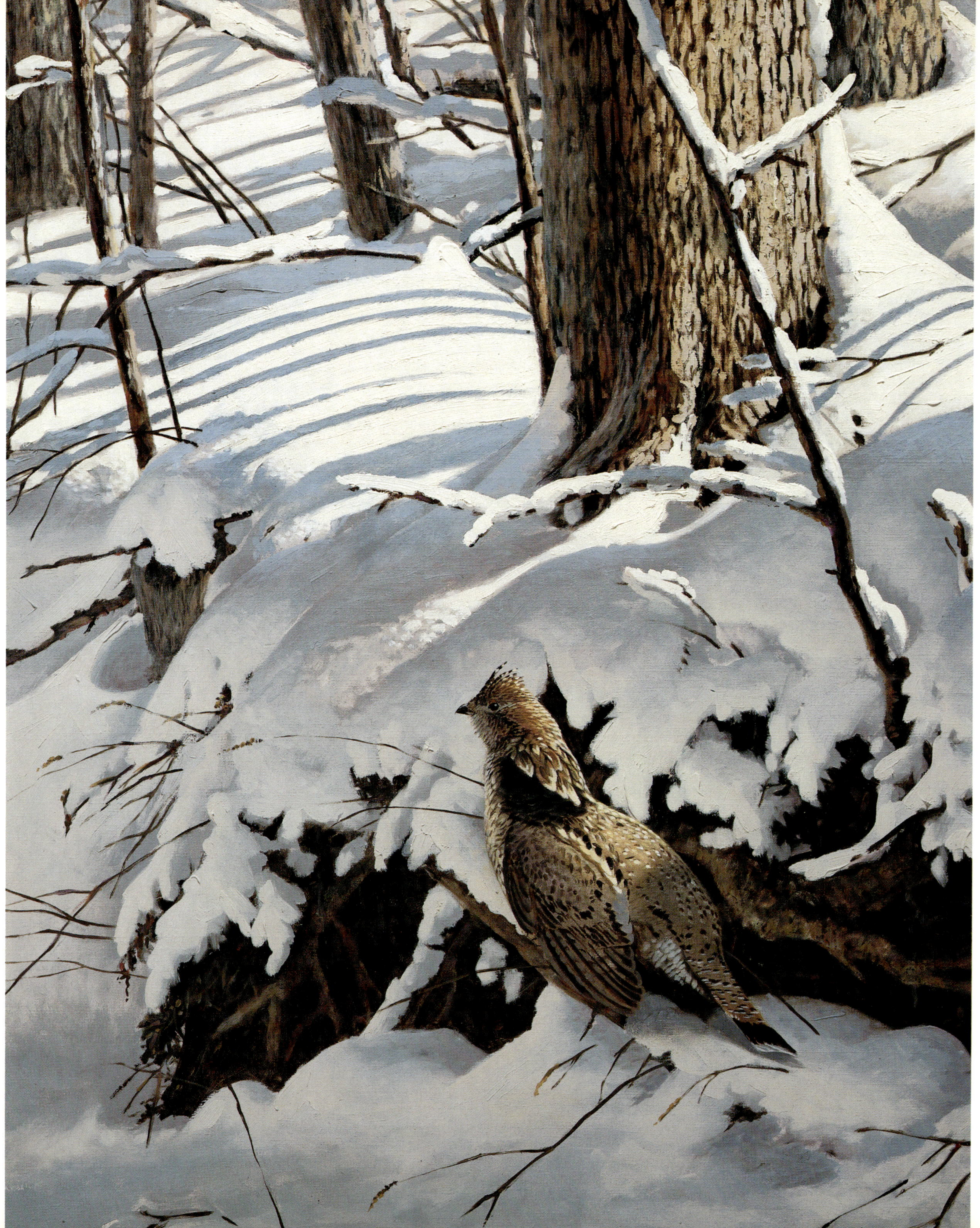

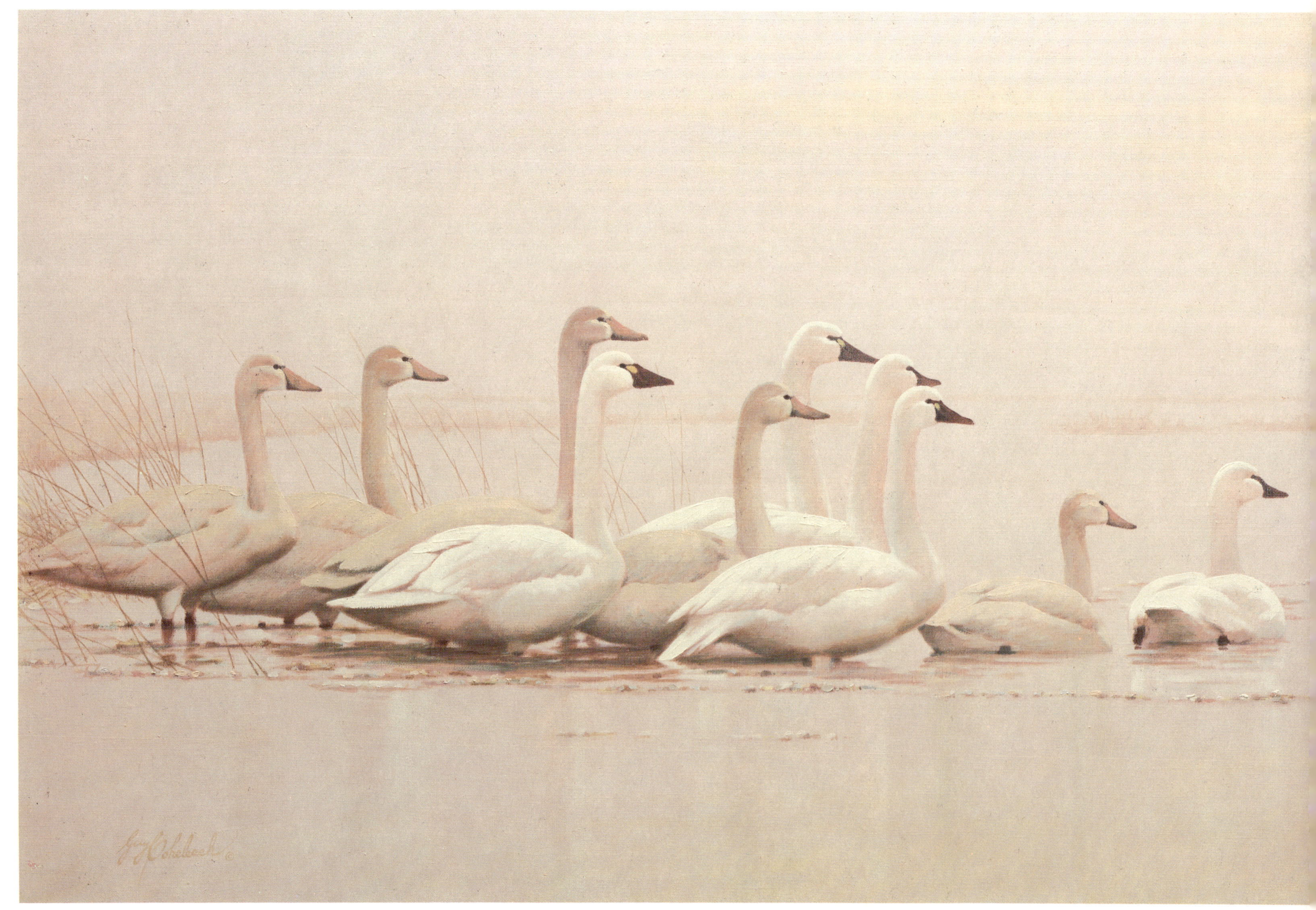

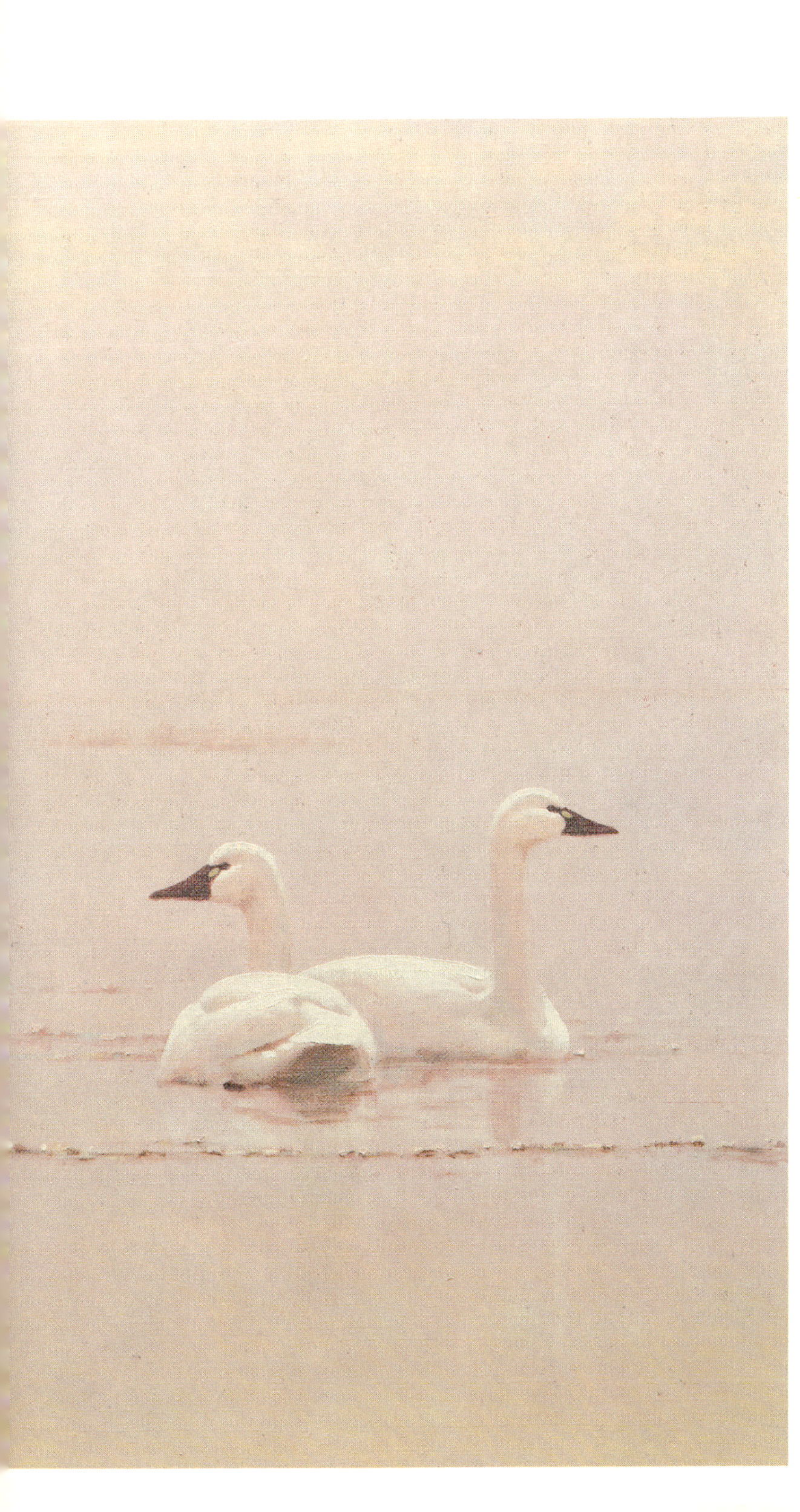

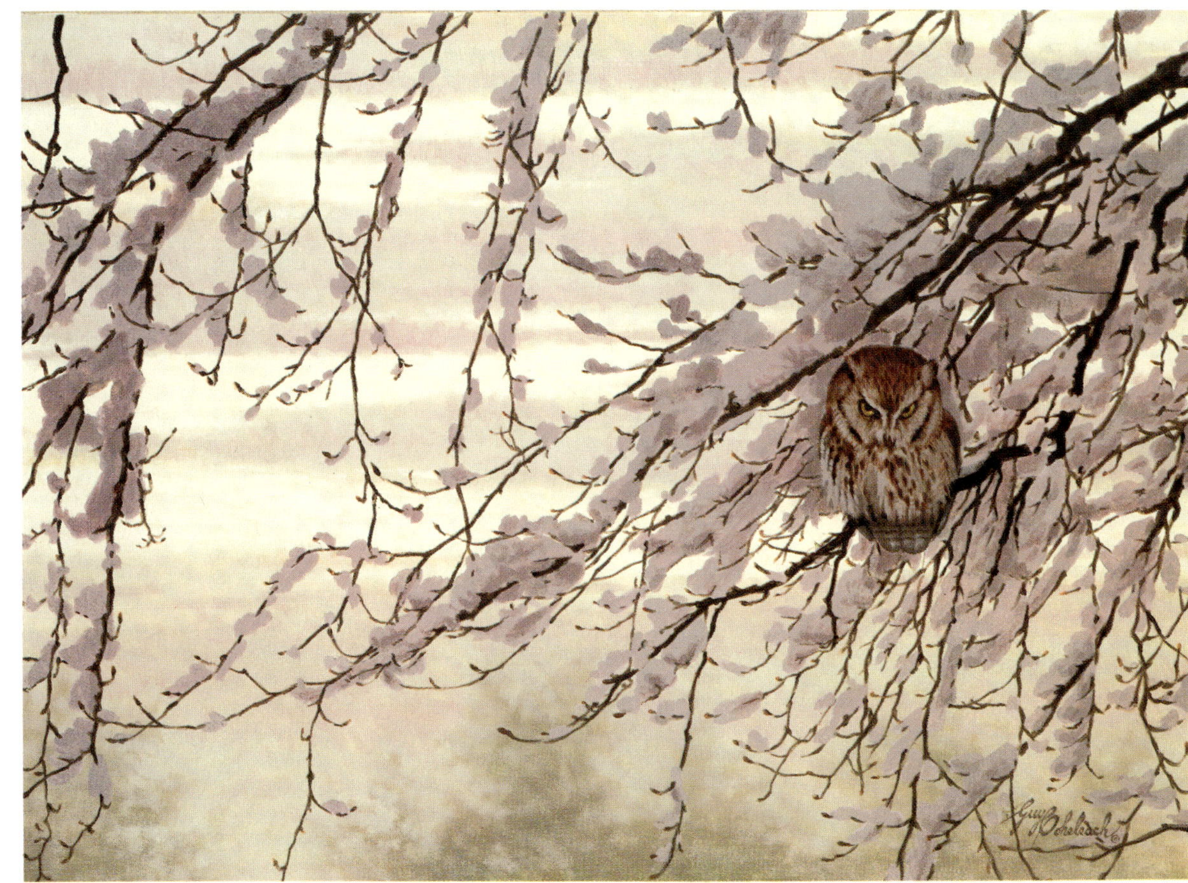

A painting in soft, muted light, where the atmosphere is thick and foggy, and the horizon gets lost behind it...

I achieved the effect by coming back in with a wash, to mute the colors. However, I usually don't like looking at things through a milky film, which is the danger you run when you take this approach.

Whistling Swans, 44 x 24, Oil on Canvas

The eye of the artist is the eye of the beholder; the difference is knowing what you are seeing.

Snow is pure white. Everyone knows that. If you took that magenta, put it on a white palette and said 'that is going to be snow,' people would think you're crazy, that can't be snow! Everything is relative; I suppose you could paint snow black if you paint it at night.

Tudor Point Screech Owl, 22 x 30, Oil on Canvas

Neck and Neck was conceived at a Kenya game park, where Coheleach watched two giraffes stroll up to a stone and concrete wall, then extend their long necks to feed on succulent green vegetation several feet beyond the barrier.

I had always wanted to paint giraffes, particularly in a long, horizontal format. Suddenly, here was the design I had been looking for. I sketched the animals, then did the finished painting back home.

In the mixed-media painting, Coheleach has contrasted the warm, reddish colors of the giraffes with the cool, purplish and gray background of the sky. The line of clouds keeps the eye moving to the right, since all the rendering is on the left.

Neck and Neck, 30 X 15, Acrylic and Gouache on Illustration Board

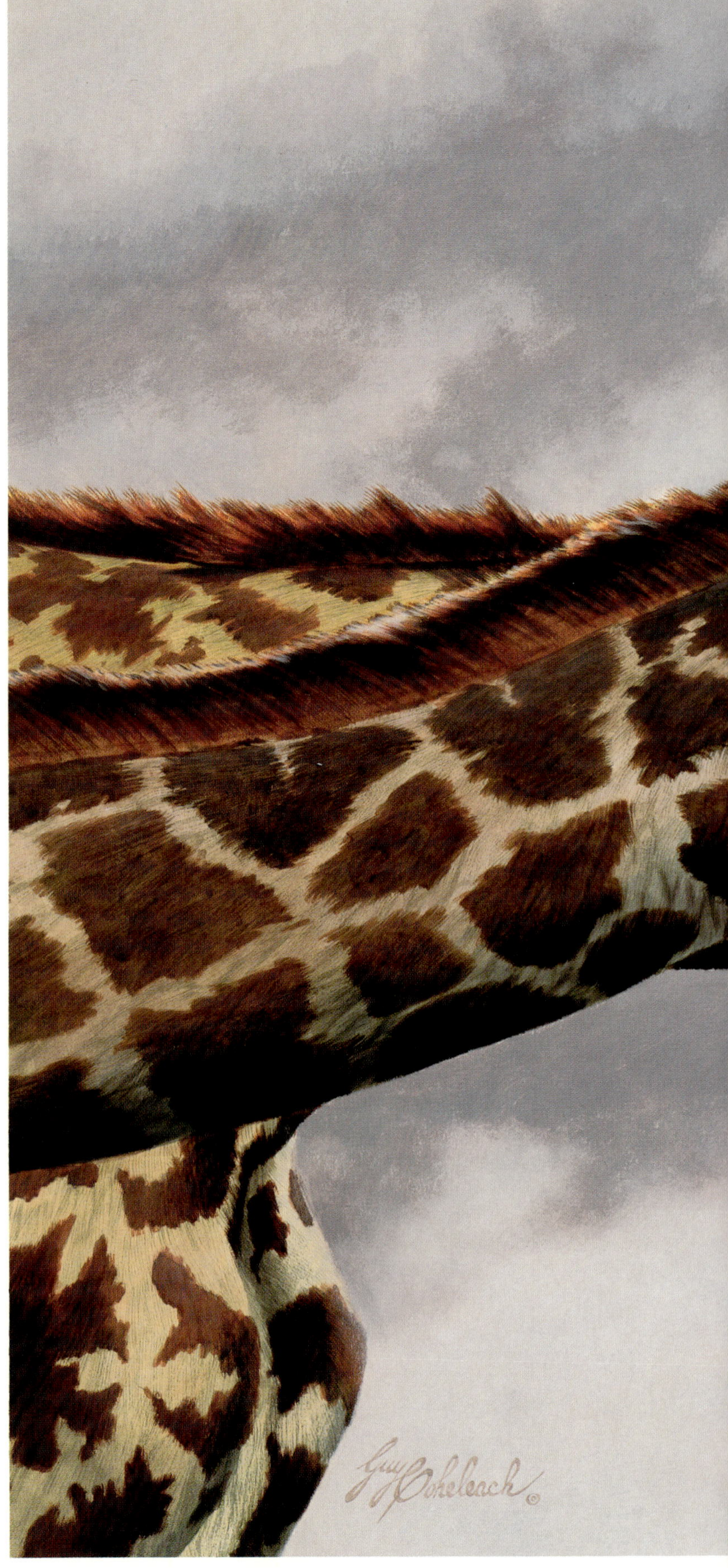

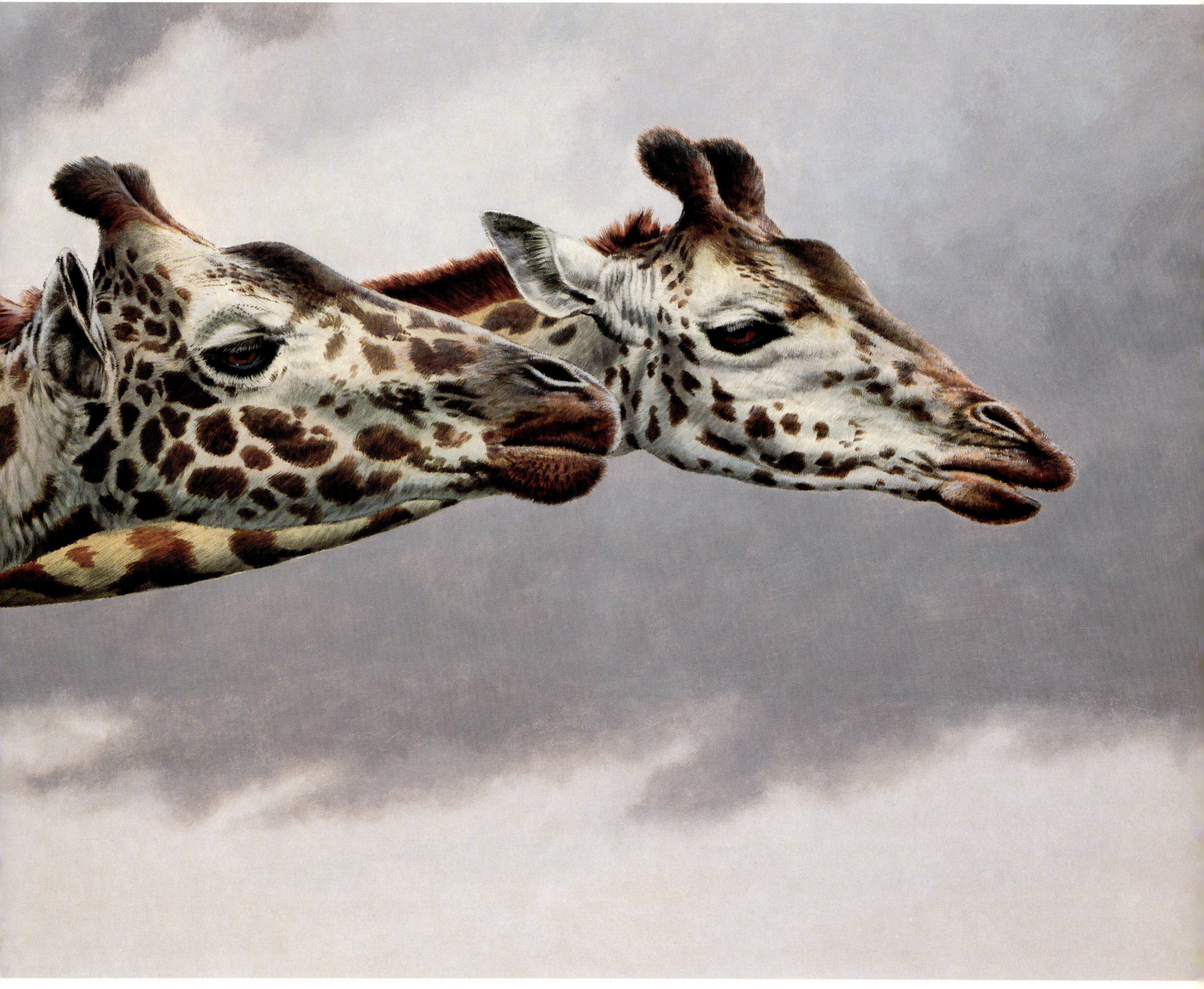

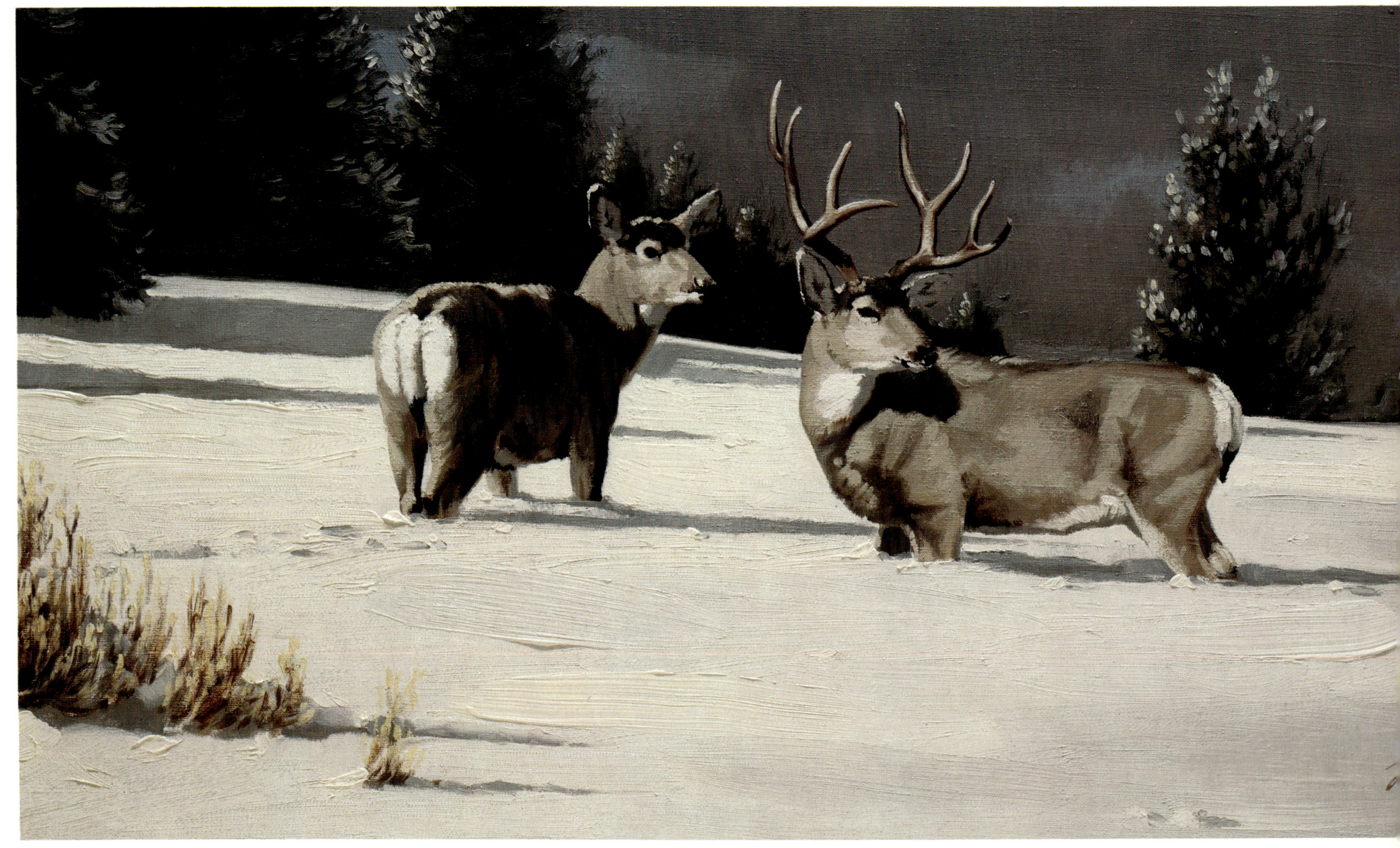

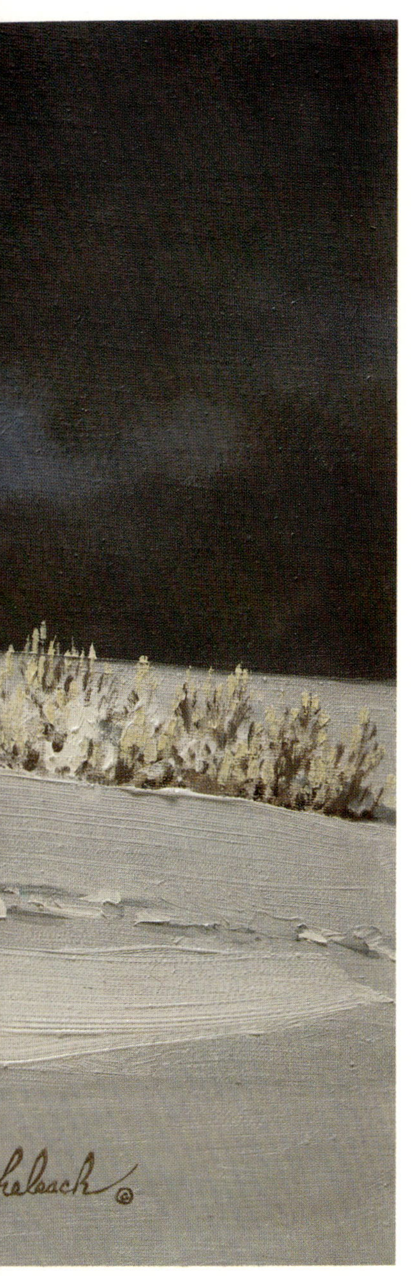

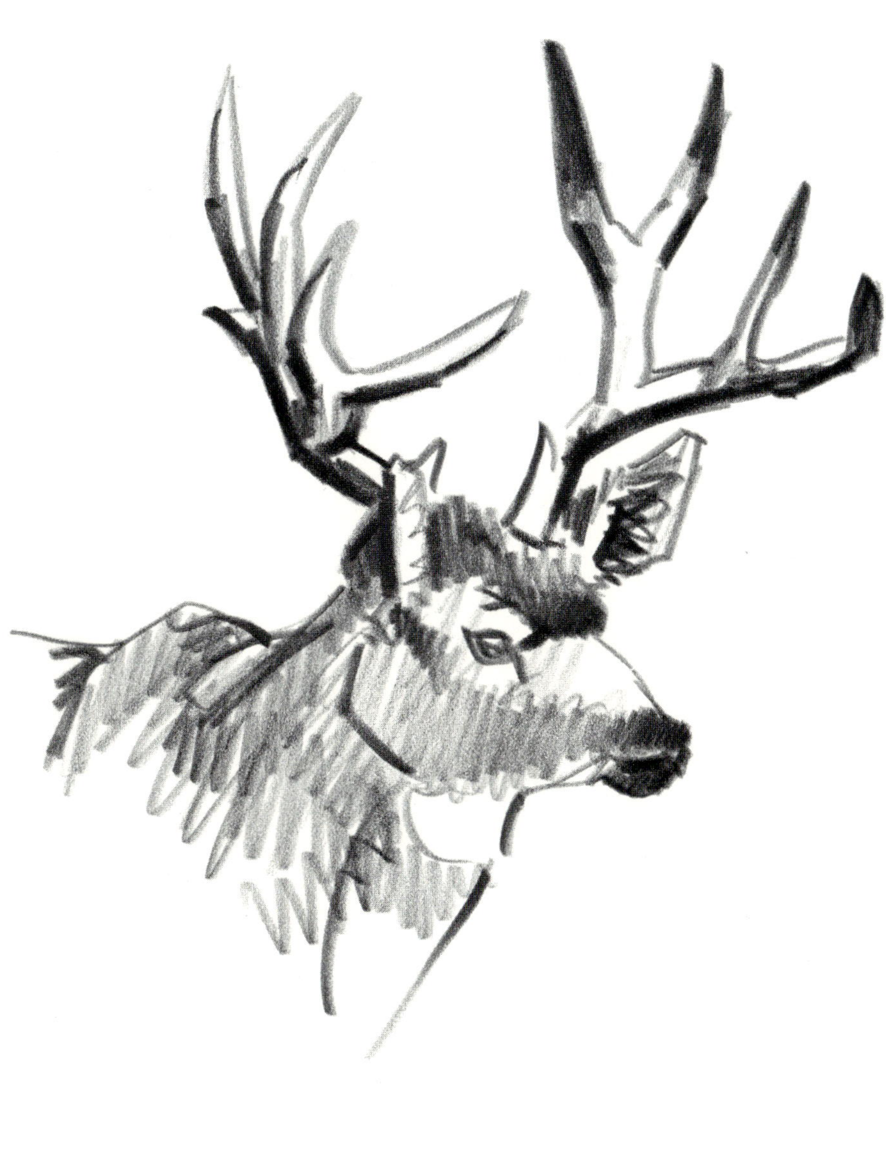

A painting is an assemblage of elements — in this case, a horizontal format, long shadows, textured snow, relatively little detail in the subjects, and the suspense of the unknown.

The threatening sky provides a good background for the buck's antlers as well as tension that enhances the foreboding imparted by the animals' intense curiosity about something—what?—off to the right, out of the painting.

Long Shadows—Mule Deer,
24 X 12, Oil on Canvas

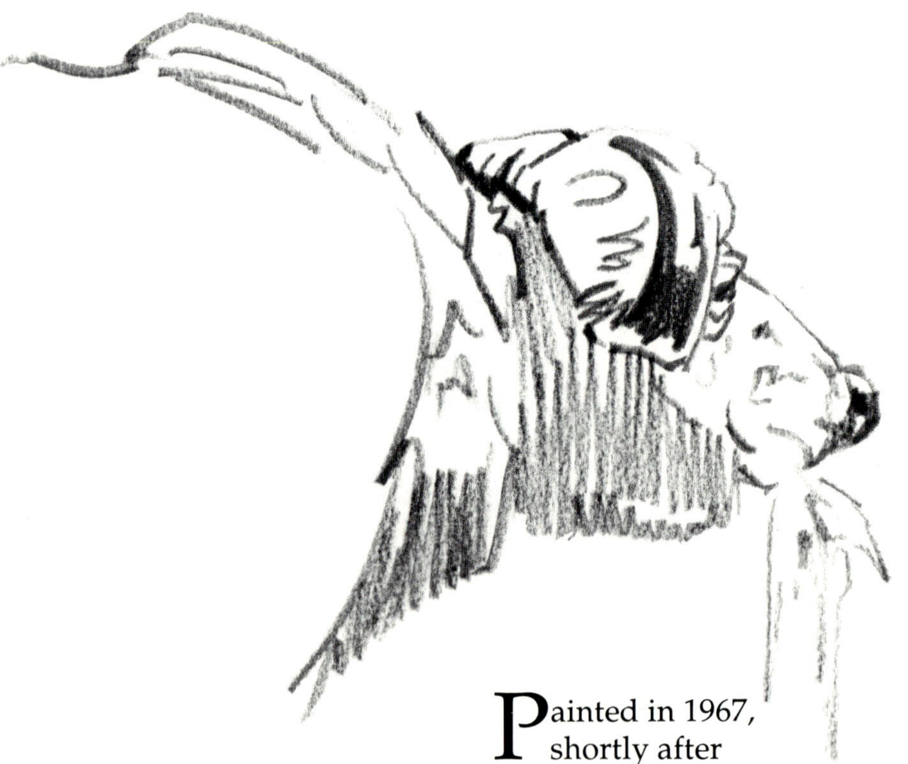

Painted in 1967, shortly after Coheleach's first visits to East Africa, *Rhino Under A Baobab Tree* is a "primitive" painting for him.

If I were doing it today, I would paint it a lot differently. I would do more with the reflected light under the branches, and use both cool and warm colors.

Still, it illustrates something of the type of painting I was doing then—a period that few people seem to know about. My work wasn't known, because I wasn't printing anything. Traditionally, this artistic, palette-knife approach has not sold well as prints, but I like doing it because it lets me get away from the shackles, if you will, imposed by the need to be absolutely, technically accurate in rendering an animal.

Rhino Under A Baobab Tree,
18 X 24, Oil on Canvas

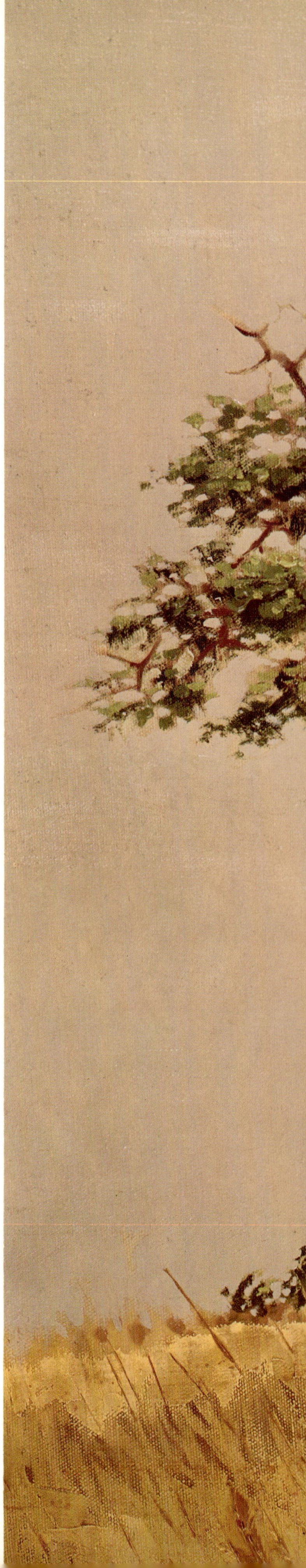

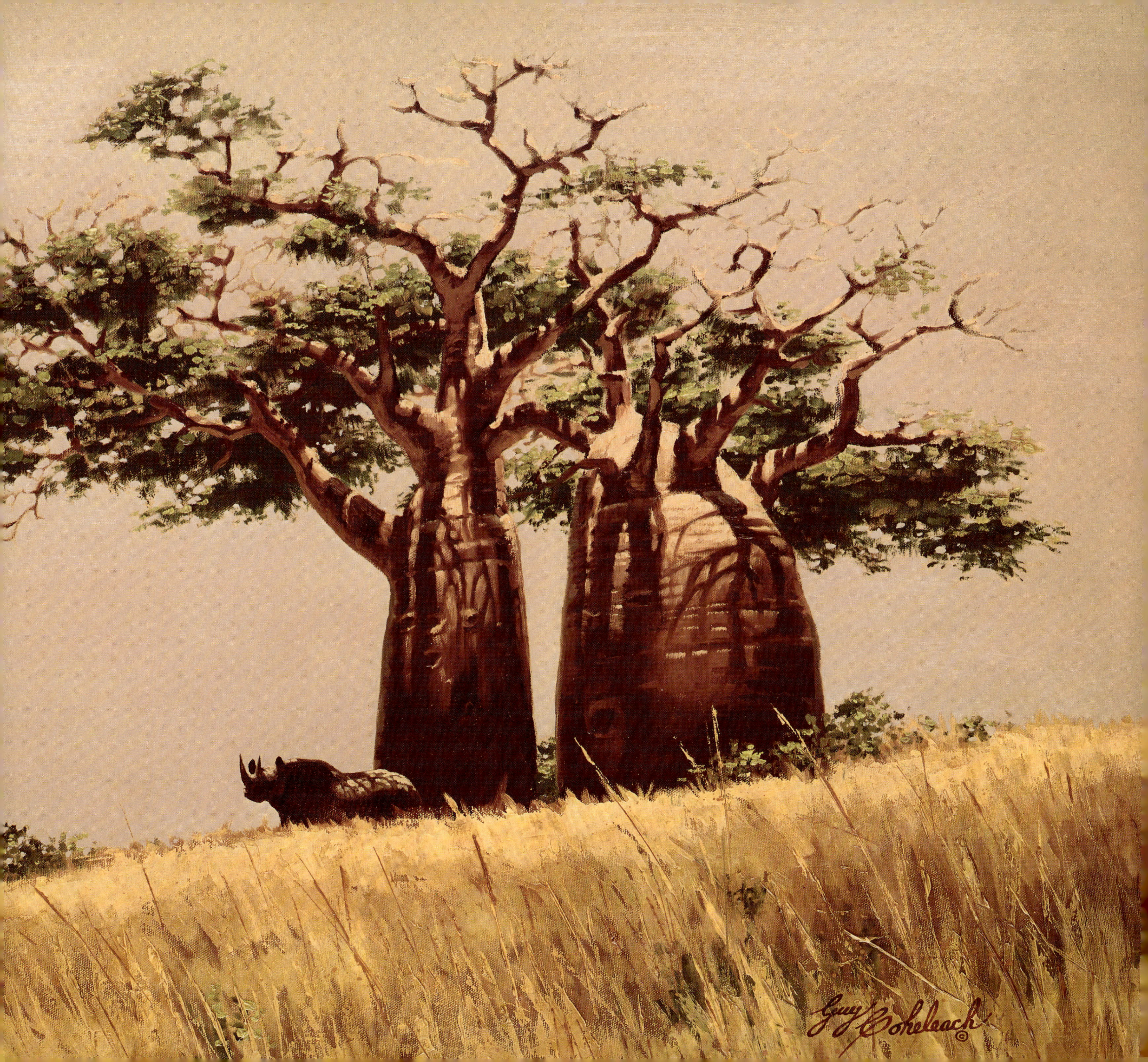
Guy Coheleach ©

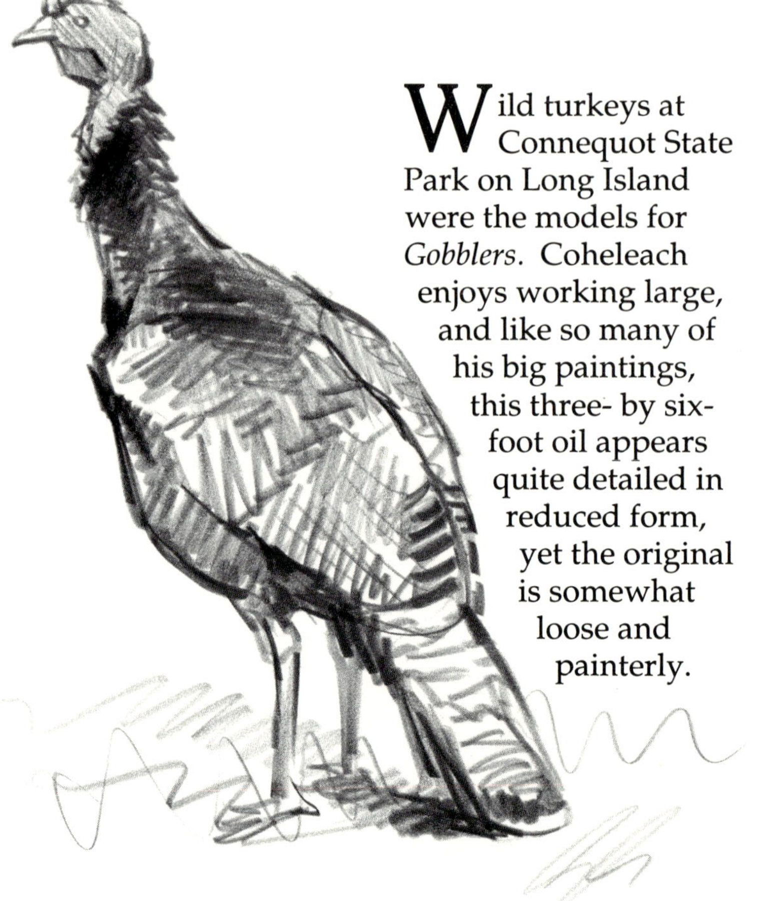

Wild turkeys at Connequot State Park on Long Island were the models for *Gobblers.* Coheleach enjoys working large, and like so many of his big paintings, this three- by six-foot oil appears quite detailed in reduced form, yet the original is somewhat loose and painterly.

Three horizontal lines—trees in the background, birds in the center, and autumn grass in the foreground—serve as basic design elements. For the composition to work, the turkeys had to be in a line, which is why you see the one on the left cut off, leading the procession across the painting.

I love painting turkeys. In fact, someday I would like to do one in real detail, Audubonesque, just the turkey against a white background with every shade on every little feather.

Gobblers, 72 X 36, Oil on Canvas

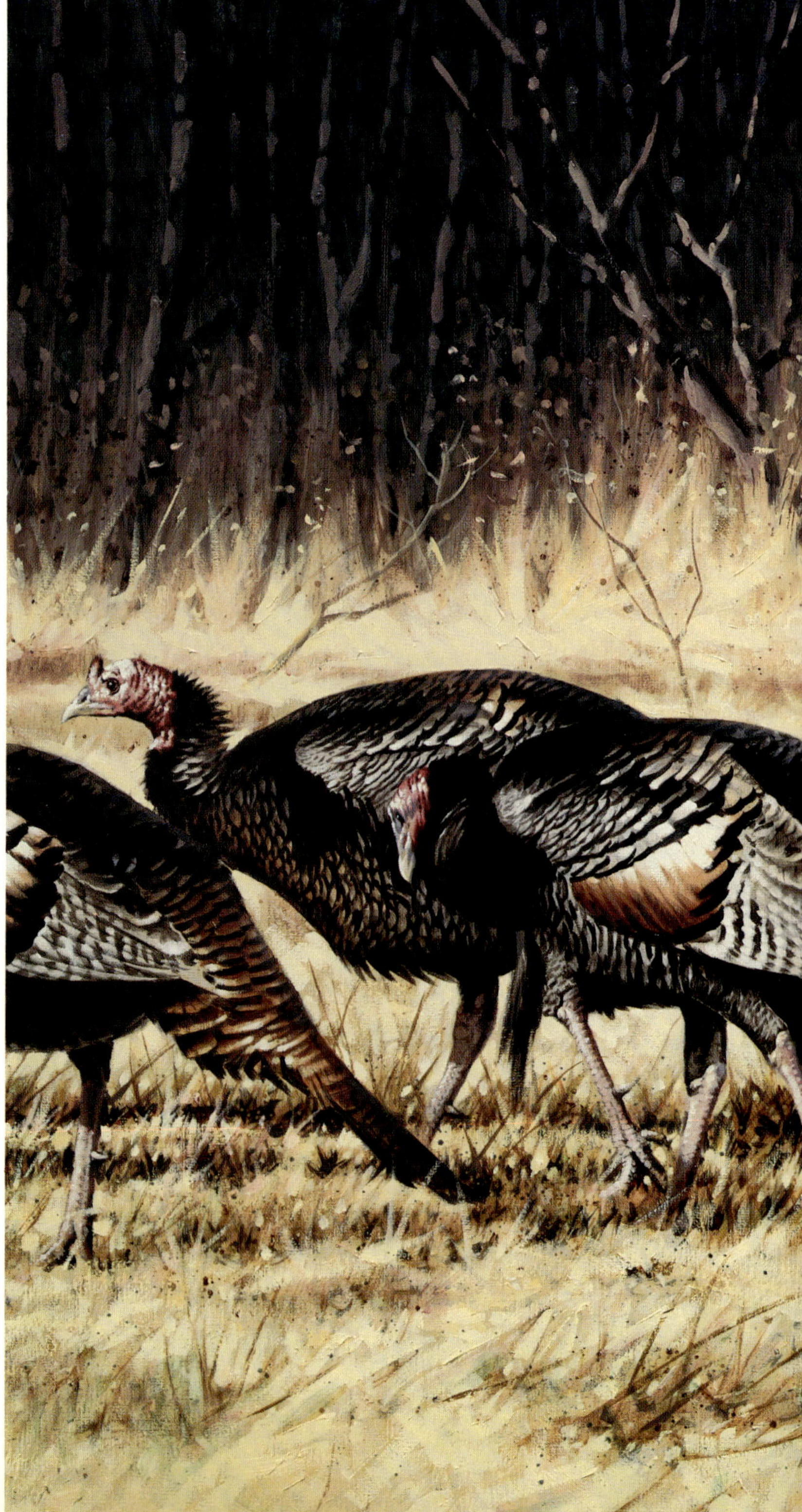

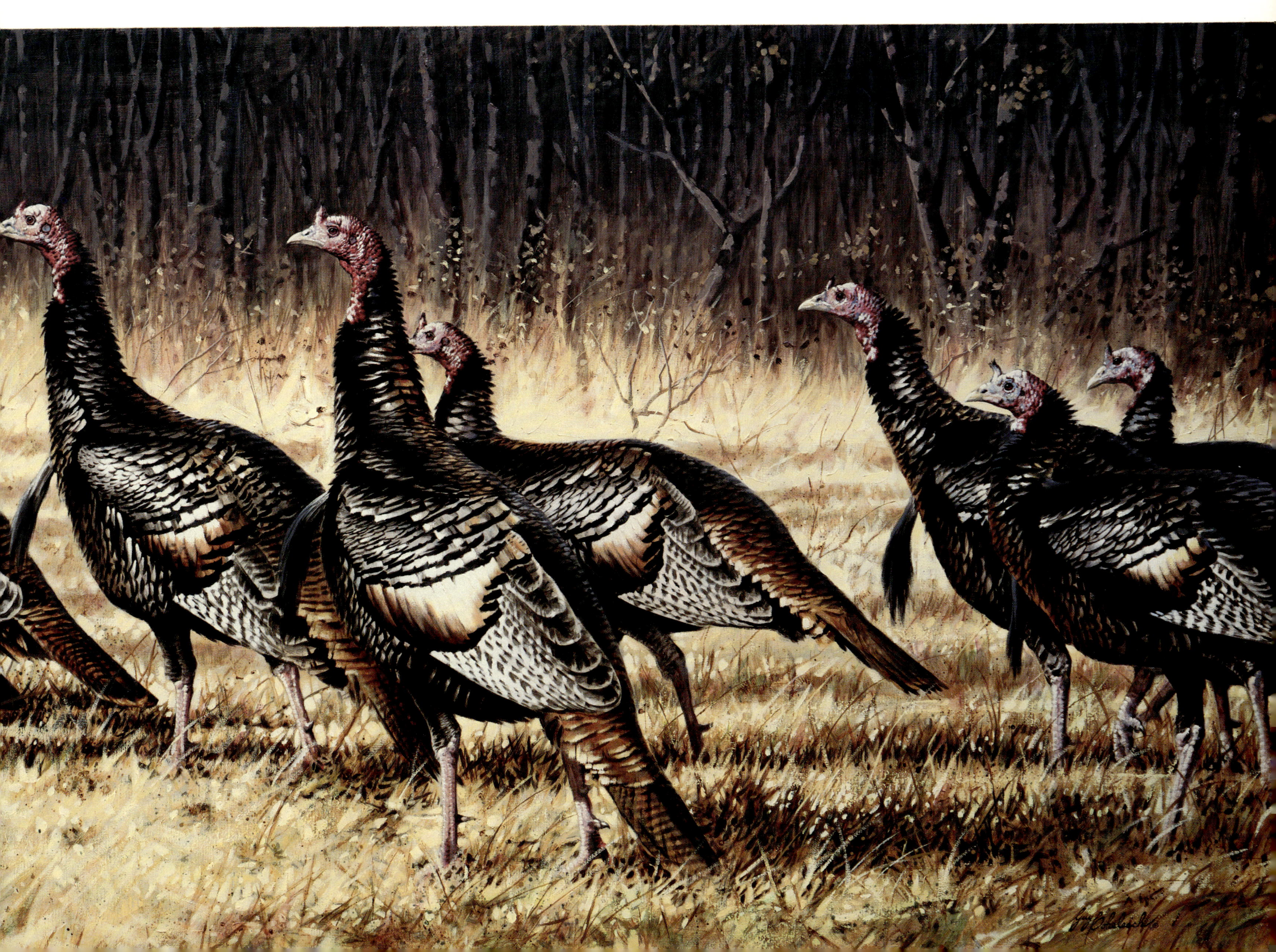

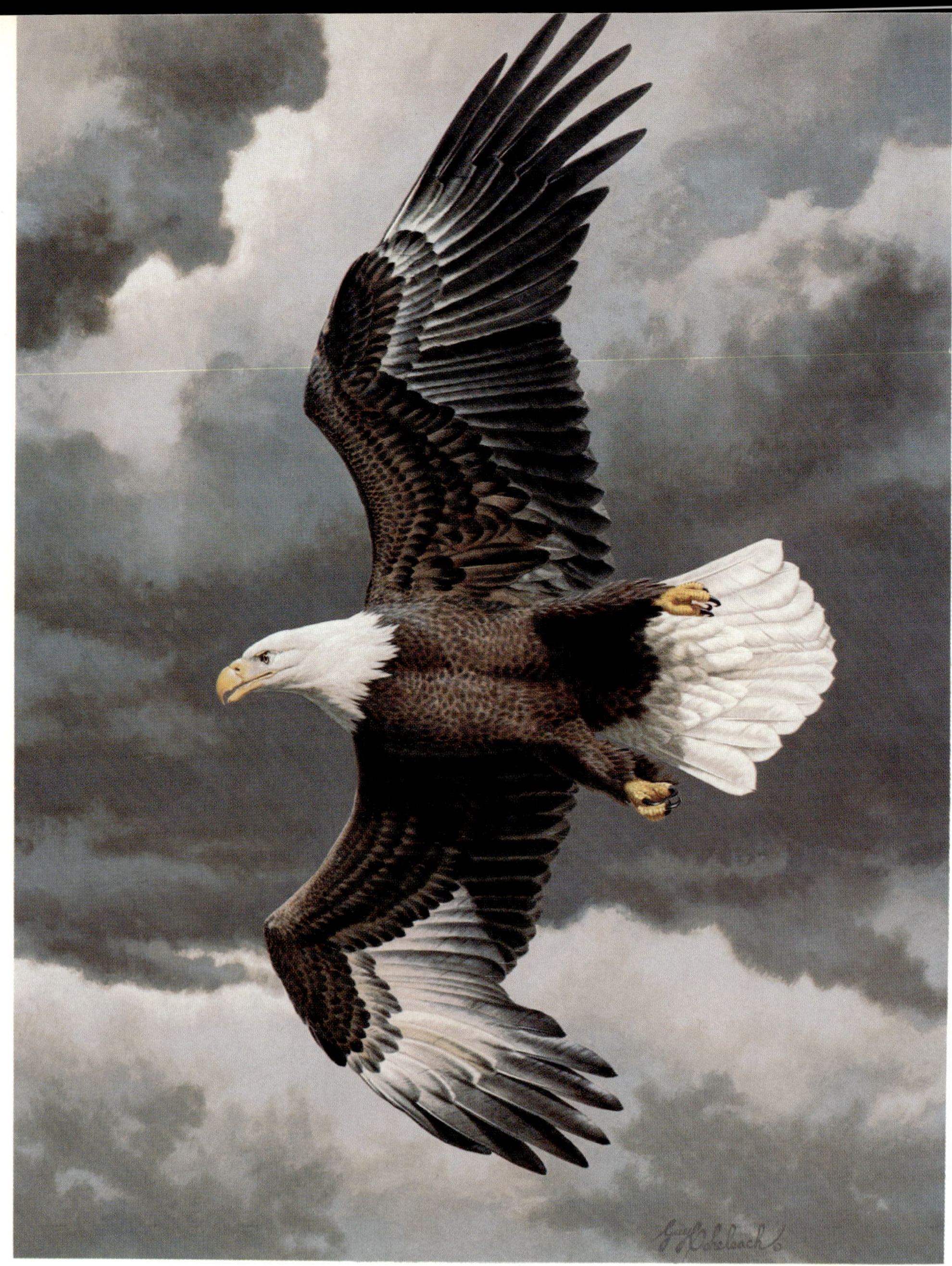

It is a magnificent bald eagle, swooping down through a turbulent sky toward its prey.

The bald eagle is a powerful bird and in this portrait I wanted to show a lot of force and motion. The clouds, if you study them closely, show an almost arrow-like direction to the left. This helps to convey the speed of the bird. Parting the clouds slightly also enhances the feeling of speed and direction.

When my publisher decided to make prints of this painting, he asked me to put mountains in the background. However, this is the way I like it, with just the clouds to impart a feeling of freedom and majesty.

Bald Eagle, 30 X 40,
Acrylic on Illustration Board

Here, I wanted to show the sneaky side of cats. Usually they slip through the shadows toward their prey or hunt at night. Seldom do you see them silhouetted in strong light, where other animals would spot them from miles away.

And here we see Coheleach's skill in painting a boulder-strewn landscape.

Sometimes it can be difficult to paint rocks and boulders that are believable. In this case it was fairly easy because I had good reference. My first step was to paint their forms, then the highlights and shaded areas, and finally the texture. In some areas I used a sponge to dab on paint; in others I spattered it on with a brush. But as I added texture, I was careful to maintain the same highlights and shade.

Shady Stalk—Cougar, 40 X 30,
Acrylic on Illustration Board

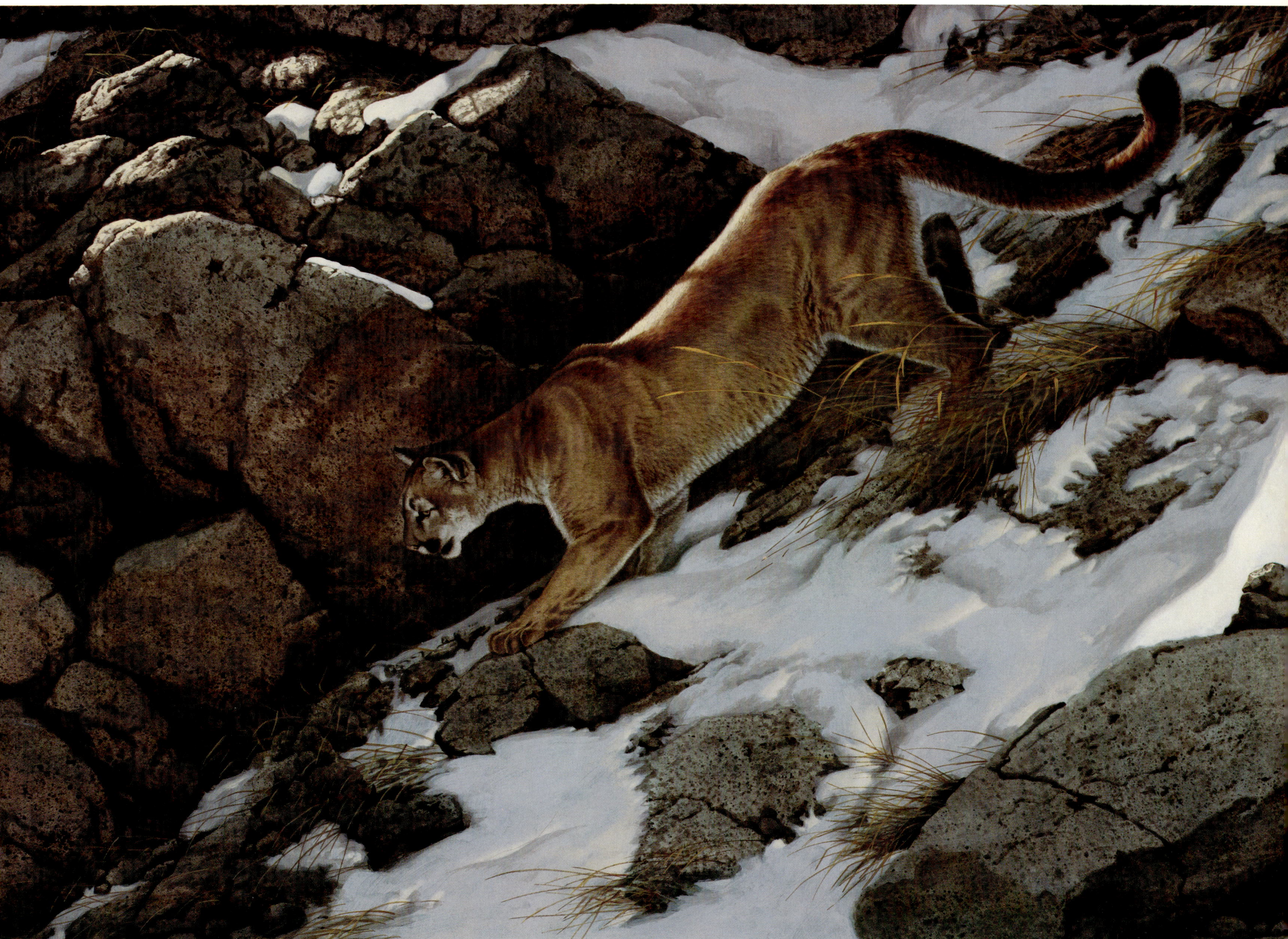

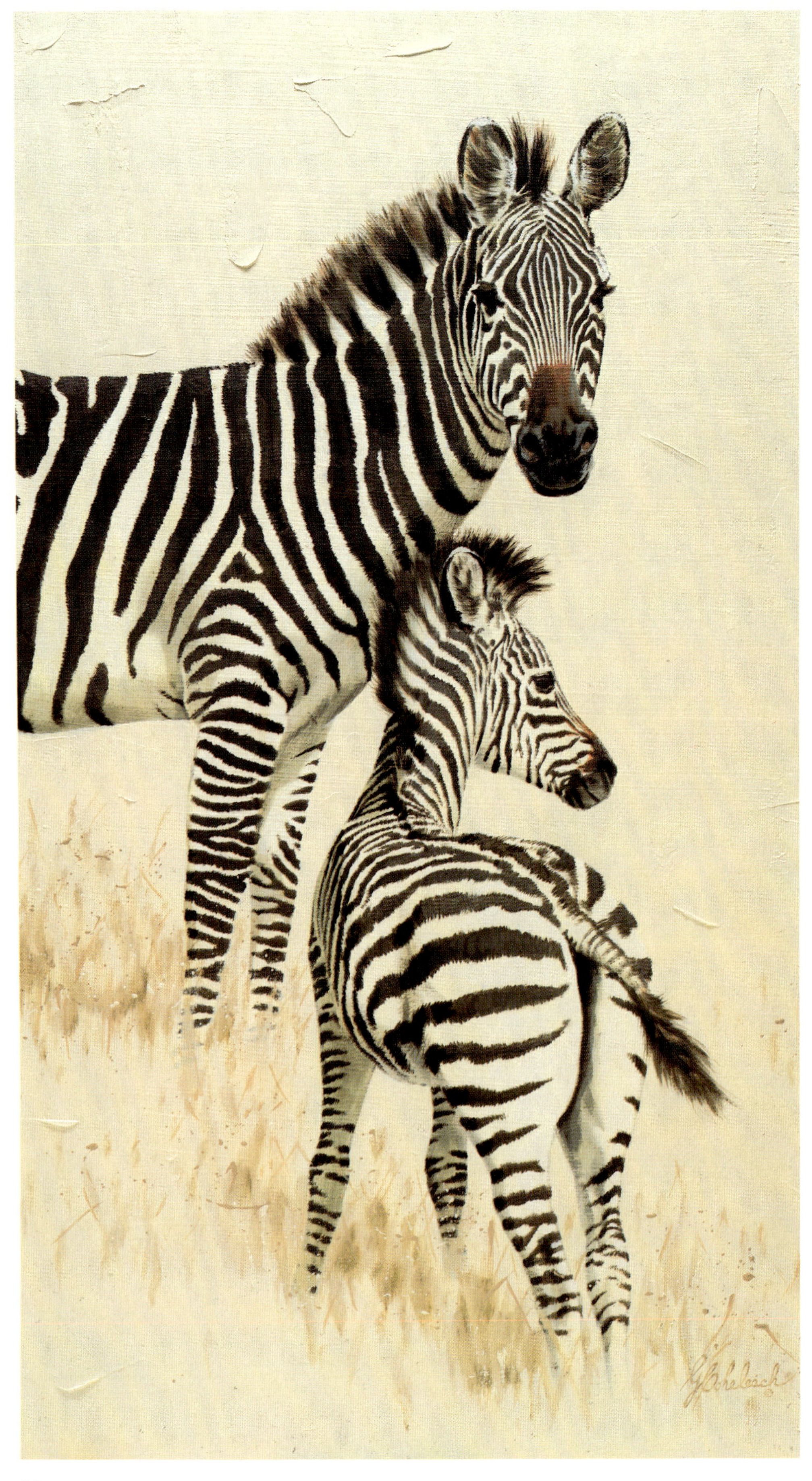

Zebras are a designer's dream with their wonderful pinstriping, which is every bit as different from animal to animal as fingerprints are among people.

As a commercial artist on Madison Avenue, Coheleach started out designing candy boxes and can openers for $55 a week, but within ten years became a highly-paid magazine illustrator. This particular painting was one of three Coheleach images featured on posters for the 1982 Knoxville World's Fair.

Zebras, 15 X 30, Acrylic on Masonite

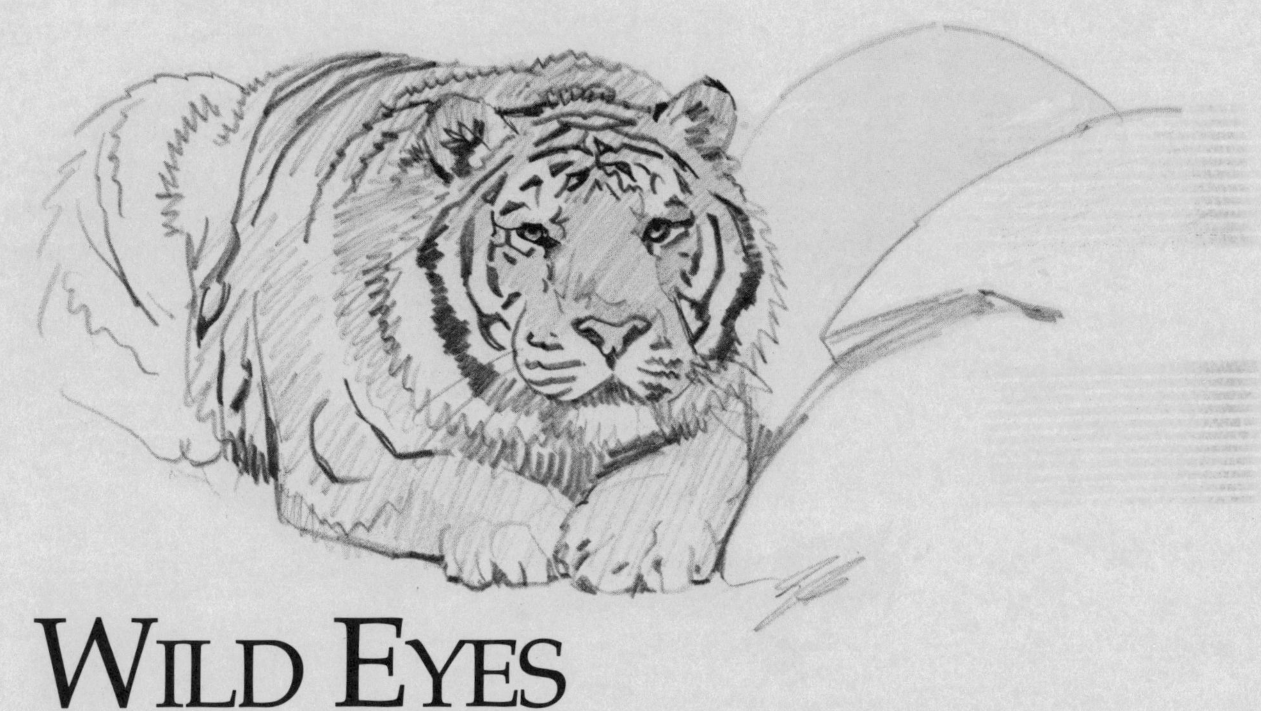

WILD EYES

At one point in our New Jersey odyssey, I asked Coheleach why he paints wildlife instead of, say, landscapes or portraits or still-lifes.

"I like painting landscapes; I put animals in them, although I don't have to. I used to paint still-lifes, and I don't enjoy it; you can do better with a photograph. I've tried portraits and I'm tired of making 90-year old dowagers look like 19-year old maidens; most portrait work, you have to stick so close to what is, you might as well use a camera.

"With animals, I can paint the soul and the character, and if you have the ability to paint, they are just wonderful subjects to work with. You paint a Siberian tiger and do a halfway decent job, he makes you look good because he is so beautiful.

"Leopards are the same; the elephant and the rhino are magnificent. One has power, one has grace, one has beauty, one is ominous. They are all different qualities you can put in, and if you do it well, they make you look good.

"Now, the warthog, of course, you might have a problem with..."

In Coheleach's life, interest in animals preceded interest in art. One of his earliest memories is his third birthday, receiving a toy handmade by his father, Gaetan, and finding an ant which had crawled inside. The insect frightened him, badly.

"I remember crying, I was so afraid," he says.

When it comes to animals, Coheleach is not reluctant to admit fear. In fact, when Coheleach the Storyteller discourses on the life and times of Coheleach the Hunter, very rarely is Coheleach the Hero. His heroes are elephant and Cape buffalo, steadfast, intelligent and valorous, in marked contrast to his own sweating terror,

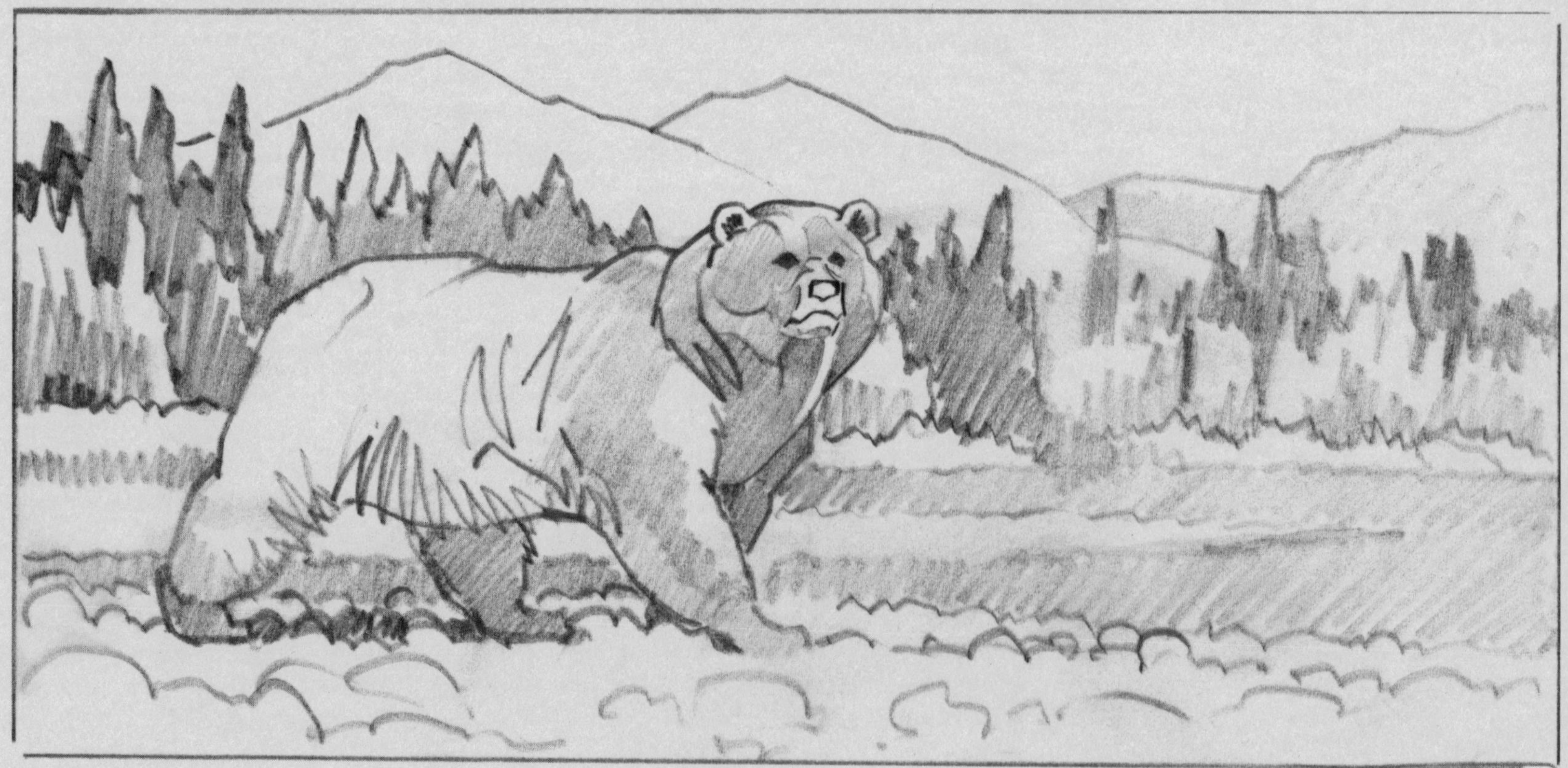

occasional bungling, and ultimate triumph through good luck and superior firepower. At least, that's the way he tells it.

Coheleach is uneasy about hunting. A man who has killed almost 100 Cape buffalo, almost certainly more than any modern hunter outside the African professionals, he speaks with enthusiasm, not of the killing, but of the animal and the hunt and the terror.

"Buffalo taste good, they're not endangered, they provide a lot of protein for the villagers, and nothing goes to waste except the grass in the stomach," Coheleach says, not once or twice, but half a dozen times — whenever the subject of hunting buffalo comes up.

Not a lifelong hunter, he does not seem to have the conviction of hunting's natural "rightness" felt by those who were raised to hunt by fathers who hunted, who grew up as hunters and return criticism with truculence. Or perhaps, living closer to animals and trying to get inside their skins in order to paint their real beings, Coheleach questions it all more carefully, doubtfully, regretfully.

"I didn't really hunt when I was a kid. Used to do some trapping, you know, blue jays in the back yard, and 'possums and muskrats and stuff. But then I found out there wasn't a helluva big reason to go kill the animals. I liked being out there, being in it, being part of it, but I never liked the killing."

As a kid on Long Island, Coheleach shot the odd squirrel and went hunting a couple of times in the Catskills, with his brothers, after whitetail deer. The experience left Coheleach with mixed feelings.

"These stories about people writing C-O-W on cows and having them shot is not funny; they are very true stories. Guys go up there that can hardly read if they can read at all, and for some reason or other this macho thing gets hold of them and they feel they're big men because they have a big game rifle and can kill something..."

While these hunts left him less than respectful of once-a-year hunters, they did imbue him with a sense of the real value of hunting.

"I found out very quickly, you know, the camaraderie of the hunt, eating together, having a few drinks and sitting around the campfire are every bit as important as the hunt itself. Maybe more so.

"When I look back at the African trips, I remember the terror and the anxiety and the hunt and everything else, but the most joyous times were when you come back and sit at the campfire and tell your stories with the next guy...

"This place I'm building here..." Coheleach motions around the half-built patio that flanks his New Jersey home, cut into the steep hillside and towered over by thick bush in the blackness, "One of the most important things I'm putting in — and I've never seen anybody put one in a patio — I'm putting in a firepit, a place for a campfire.

"I bet in the spring and fall, it will be the most popular spot around the house."

Coheleach may be ambivalent about hunting for sport or hunting for trophies. But he has no doubt whatsoever of the importance of hunting to art.

"A guy today could go into a library and never be outside the city, and see pictures of wild animals, and paint them, and paint them to the degree they'd be accepted. It could be done.

"He'd never really know the soul of the animal, not having witnessed it, not having hunted it, not having been chased by it, not having seen it fighting with others or feeding its young. Photographs just don't do it.

"As an artist, you can paint the predator/prey relationship one hell of a lot better if you hunt, and if you've had something chasing your ass."

So in the interests of artistic integrity, Coheleach has had his ass chased. He has also had it charged, chewed, swatted, ambushed, stomped, almost tusked, and generally subjected to attempted mayhem by a variety of large beasts in varying degrees of annoyance — with his proximity, with the company he kept, or with him personally.

The most notable instance was in 1972. A Coheleach elephant painting had been rejected by a woman buyer who had made a special trip to the Palm Beach World Wildlife Fund auction to buy it. Upon seeing the actual painting, however, she turned it down because, as a hunter of elephant, she recognized a game park animal when she saw one. And as a hunter, she wanted a portrait of an animal with fire in his eyes.

Thereupon Coheleach headed for Zambia determined to see exactly what she meant. In the Amwell Press anthology *Hunting the African Elephant*, Coheleach describes the encounter in a piece entitled "Fatal Encounter — Almost!"

"I had been informed by an acquaintance at the bar while in Lusaka that if you step into the charge of an angry elephant, it will stop or turn because 99 percent of the time they are bluffing," Coheleach wrote. "He and I went down to the river to a game park whose rules were not very important to the insurgents (returning to Zambia from incursions into Rhodesia, and given to shooting up the game parks for laughs)."

Frequent encounters with trigger-happy terrorists had turned these animals into anything but docile game park pets. With luck, Coheleach and friend would get to test the theory on animals with serious social problems. Along the river, they found two elephants browsing. Coheleach approached one from behind. Hearing him, the elephant wheeled, his ears went out, his trunk went up, and he "shook the whole damned riverbed with that blasting roar which everyone calls a trumpet."

"I must admit even now that the sense of exhilaration which surged through me was incredible," Coheleach wrote. "That invincible feeling that moves immature machos surged through me.

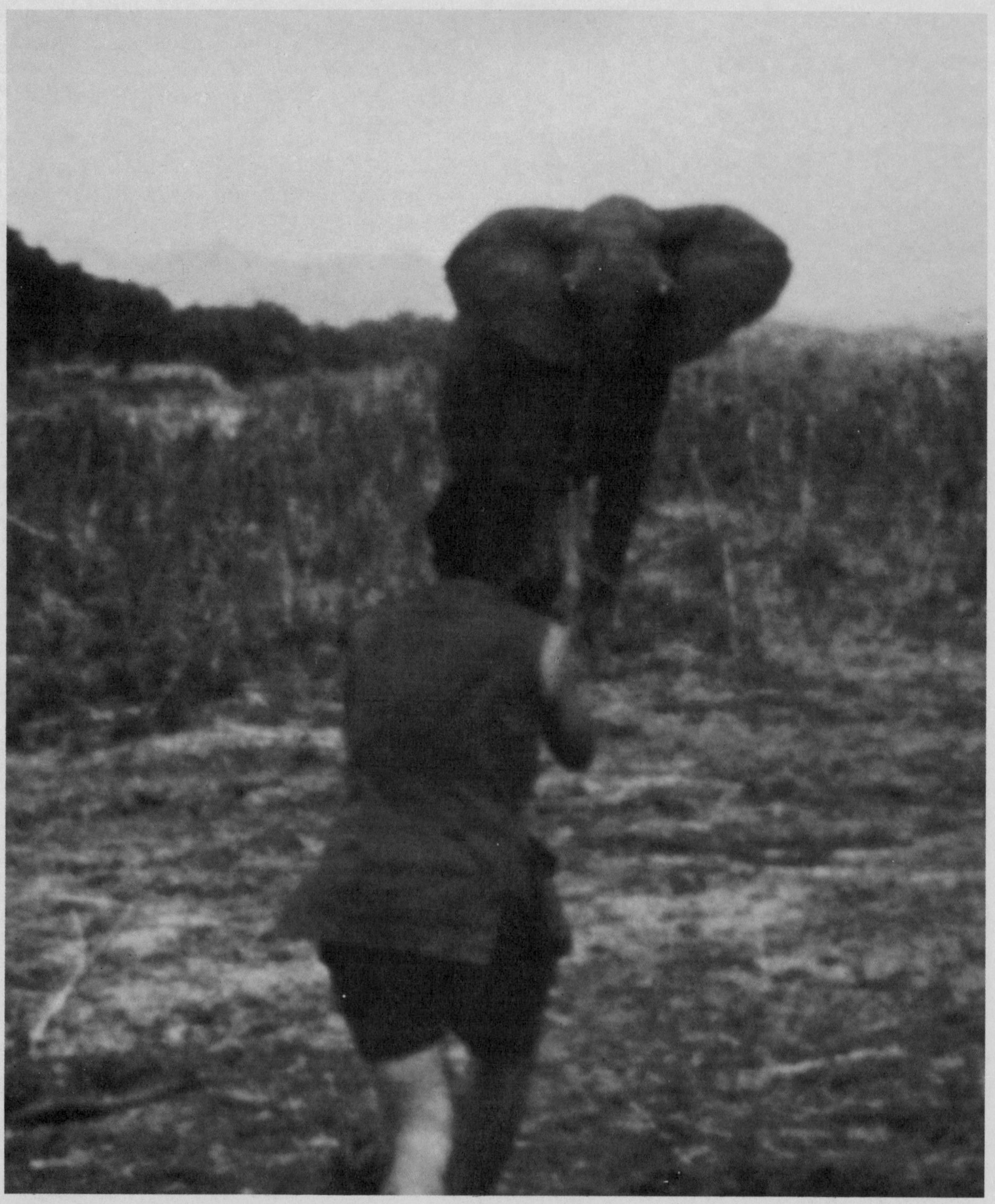

"I remember throwing my brand-new movie camera up in the air in sheer elation."

That elephant made one more bluffing charge, and departed downriver in search of more congenial company. Now a self-acknowledged expert on playful pachyderms, Coheleach turned to the second elephant, a monster whose sheer size made his three-foot tusks look like twigs, and who proceeded to put on "quite a performance." As his companion recorded the whole sequence on 16-mm film, Coheleach tried to provoke one last mock charge with the aid of a "good sized rock."

At which point, the elephant had had enough.

Coheleach: " 'Get the hell out of there!' my mentor screamed as I finally realized the elephant was having no more of my nonsense. His movie footage stopped at about this moment. Mine kept going until, with intermittent pans of the ground and sky, the last frame was filled by just elephant tusk.

"I threw my camera at his face and ran like hell. Heading towards the riverbank, I turned to see where the monster had stopped, only to find his outstretched trunk about three feet from my head. At this moment, I knew it was all over..."

It would have been, too, but for a couple of strange strokes of luck.

"My physical body remembers pain in my chest, legs and back. I remember lying on the ground with sand in my mouth and face, and a tsetse fly buzzing in my nose. I remember looking up and seeing the whole sky filled with elephant. I remember being hit twice on the head with what must have been his tusks. I remember hearing a shot and having those huge feet landing between my chest and knee; between my chin and shoulder and brushing my back. I remember hearing another shot and more feet brushing me, somehow never landing on me. The elephant finally stumbled off to feed a half hour later with the rest of the herd. I remember Eric yelling for me to get up, but I couldn't."

"Eric" was Eric Balsam, the head of the game park. Hearing trumpeting from the river, and already suspicious of the intentions of Coheleach and his friend, he had come down to investigate. What he found was a huge elephant in hot pursuit of a small human. The shots Coheleach heard were Balsam firing to drive the animal away.

The strokes of luck that saved Coheleach were, first, that the elephant was too tall to allow him to drive one of his relatively short tusks into Coheleach's prostrate form. So, he decided to dispatch his tormentor by kneeling on him; second, Balsam managed to put a bullet into the elephant's honeycomb skull above the brain, dissuading him from punishing Coheleach further, but without causing him to fall dead on the artist.

Coheleach's accounts of the incident, written and oral, are laced with words like idiot, nitwit, imbecile and fool. Few, involved or uninvolved, would disagree. The

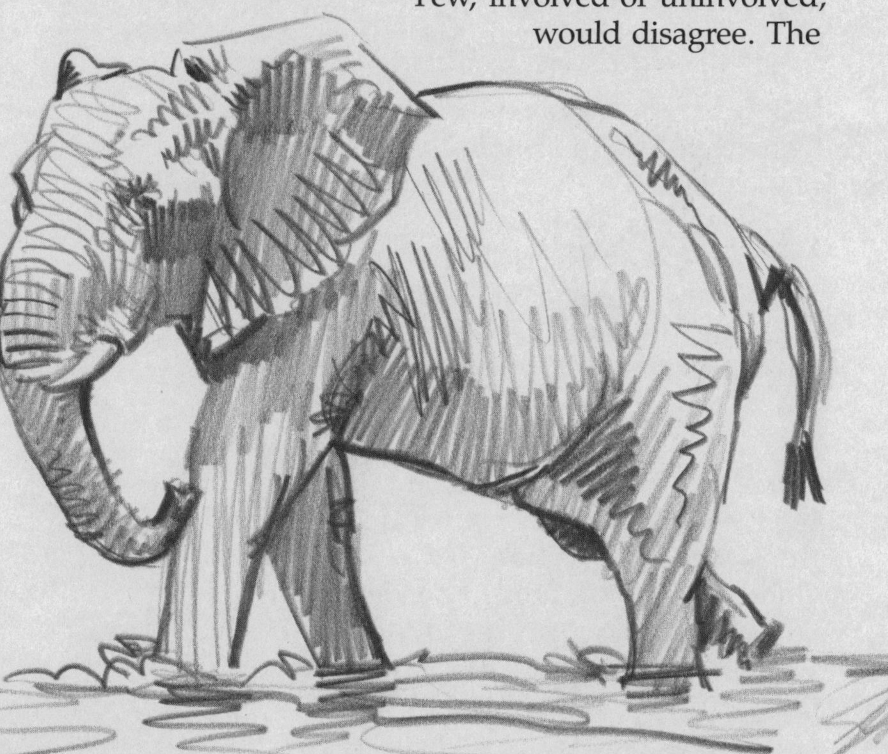

Enlarged from a tiny frame of 16mm movie film, Coheleach advances toward the huge bull elephant that almost took his life. Seconds after this picture was taken, the animal charged, knocked the artist down and tried to crush him beneath his massive forelegs.

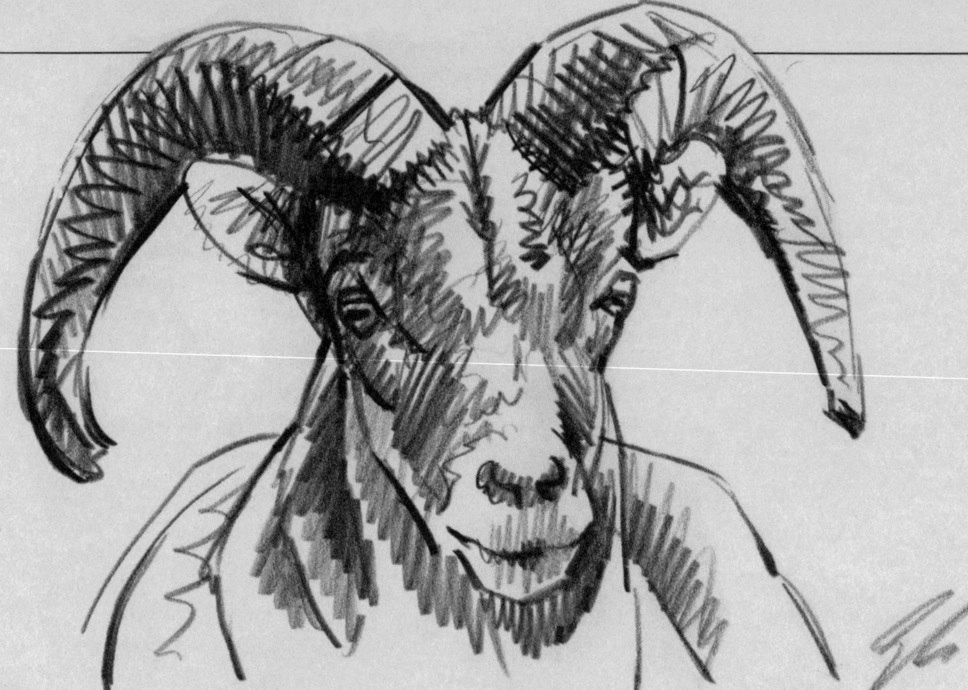

elephant, for instance, left no doubt about his views on the matter. On a painting of a greater kudu that Coheleach later painted for Eric Balsam as a gesture of thanks, he wrote, "To Eric Balsam, to whom this intrepid, but foolish wildlife artist owes his life."

Today, viewing the stark footage on a VCR in Coheleach's peaceful studio in darkest New Jersey, without sound, without narration, the black and white footage has the surreal violence of a nightmare. Watching it once, twice, the images on the screen never becoming quite defined, seeing now a tusk, now perhaps the outline of an ear, until blackness overwhelms the screen, it is easy to see why Coheleach does not like to watch it himself, and why for years afterwards even the word "elephant" induced trembling terror.

But, as he wryly points out, he had now seen an angry elephant, and his approach to life, to animals, and to art would never be quite the same.

The 1972 World Wildlife Fund auction in Palm Beach began several trains of events. For one thing, Coheleach's two paintings, one of a leopard, the other of the rejected game park elephant, sold for more than the rest of the offerings combined (two other buyers wanted that elephant, even if the huntress did not).

Over the years, Coheleach's donations in support of conservation projects have become so cumulatively large and almost routine that they are taken for granted. Estimates of their total value are in "the several millions;" it would be impossible to put a firm figure on them. At a minimum, they total several times what most of us earn in our entire lives. And lest you think they also add up to a fat tax deduction for Coheleach, you should know that artists are allowed to deduct only the cost of the paint and the canvas: what the painting sells for means nothing. Of course (and we should hardly be surprised) were he to die, the reverse would be true: his heirs would be taxed on the full market value of the art. This fact causes Coheleach, never a lover of tax collectors, no small degree of bitterness.

Yet his donations continue, and surface in the most unexpected places. Last week, I opened a bulky envelope from Safari Club International's Conservation Fund, and out tumbled five Christmas greeting cards, each a reproduction of a different Coheleach painting: a lion, a moose, musk oxen, a black jaguar, and his famous bighorn sheep and puma painting, *Rocky Mountain Chase*. Each was "Wildlife Art Courtesy of Guy Coheleach."

His conservation work earned him, in 1976, the title "Conservationist of the Year" from the African Safari Club of Washington, and the list of beneficiaries of Coheleach's dedication include the National Wildlife Federation, National Audubon Society, The Fund for Animals, Inc. (Coheleach is one of the few people in the world on speaking terms with both Cleveland Amory and the hunting elite), Holy Land Conservation Fund, National Foundation for Conservation and Environmental Officers, assorted zoos, universities, and Game Conservation International (GameCoin).

Another train of events begun by the conversation with the elephant hunter was the transformation of Coheleach's art. He became dedicated to realism, not so much in painting every hair and feather, as to ensuring that each animal had the right glint in his eye. A direct result of his near-fatal encounter with the Zambian elephant was *Charging Elephant*. Painted in 1974, the elephant is transplanted from the Zambian riverbank to the dry East African plain, and his tusks are a little larger. But the look in his eye is unmistakable. That is one upset elephant — an animal no hunter would mistake for an effete *boulevardier* of the game parks.

Coheleach's route to becoming perhaps the preeminent modern painter of African wildlife began, like so many things in his life, by accident and fortuitous coincidence.

In the mid-60s, he broke his leg. Hobbled, he took to driving home to Long Island by way of the beaches to look for hawks where he could observe them from the car, and one day he happened to drive past a trap-and-skeet range. Curious, he stopped and asked a few questions. Typically, the shooters handed him a gun, offered some suggestions, and Coheleach limped up to the firing point, where he proceeded to break 19 out of 25 clay birds.

Up to that point, his experience with guns was limited to shooting squirrels, deer hunting in the Catskills, target shooting with a .22 at Cooper Union, and rifle range experience in the Army, where he was quite successful at copping three-day passes by beating the rest of the division in basic training targetry. As it turned out, Coheleach was a natural, and in 1966 he won a trip to London for the Winchester National Trap and Skeet Championships.

Coheleach quickly parlayed the trip to London into a photographic safari to East Africa. Once there, he was hooked. Until 1974, however, this African experience was limited to pursuing animals with a camera, usually in game parks. After his 1972 experience in the role of prey, however, he determined to find out what it was like to be the predator. And Coheleach being Coheleach, he did not start at the bottom.

"Quite frankly, I wasn't interested in hunting non-dangerous plains game. I didn't want to hunt the predators, the big cats. The rhino fascinated me, but they're practically gone. And in 1974, Kenya closed elephant hunting," he says.

So by process of elimination, Coheleach landed himself a bout with *m'bogo* — the Cape buffalo — in many ways the most frightening and dangerous of all African game. For Coheleach, the pursuit of buffalo was to become an obsession, but his first encounter was not a wild success.

"We were up on Mount Kenya (home, historically, of some of the meanest buffalo on the continent) when I shot my first buffalo. Screwed it up; something spooked him just as I pulled the trigger and a young one jumped in front. I ended up making a fairly good shot on the wrong buffalo, a young one with no horns to speak of, and the professional hunter had to finish him off."

Since then, more than 90 buffalo in all, every animal Coheleach has brought down with his Champlin-made custom .460 Weatherby has been a one-shot kill, or at least has gone down for good on the first shot.

"You see, my whole theory of hunting buffalo is, anchor that son-of-a-bitch. He may still be alive, but at least I know where he is. If he goes off with a heart shot or a lung shot into the thorn bush, I don't know where he is, and finding out is not a lot of fun. I firmly believe in putting them down quickly, immobilizing them — if possible, by breaking the spine. It's easy if you know where it is (the Cape buffalo's spine takes a curious zig-zag between the head and the shoulder, unlike other animals with straight necks, but it is not readily apparent because of the massive muscle structure in the neck) and when they're hit in the spine they go down like they've been hit with a steam shovel."

Coheleach quickly became a regular on the African safari circuit, known personally to many of the professional hunters. He also became known as an excellent shot and a cool head in a crisis. As such, and knowing of his intense interest in seeing animals close up for art's sake, he was often invited along on safaris, or on the professionals' private trips to fill their own licenses, or to take part in animal control work where he could see the gritty underside of life and death in modern Africa.

It was on excursions like these that he shot many of his Cape buffalo, and most of the 19 elephants he has also killed, overcoming his terror of them in his actions if not in his gut.

He has also — the supreme compliment — been invited to accompany the professionals in pursuit of wounded lion.

"Not my lion — I'd never shoot a lion," Coheleach told me. "They're wonderful animals, and I don't feel like killing predators."

The big cats are Coheleach's particular love. He does not hunt the leopard or the lion. He is more likely to pay them homage than do them to death.

Photographs abound of Coheleach with a young leopard draped around his shoulders like a shawl. His daughter, Coleen, tells of bringing a couple of friends home for a swim in the pool on Long Island, only to find a 650-pound Siberian tiger lazily enjoying the cool water, swimming in lonely splendor.

"Better wait until Ruffles has had enough swimming," Coheleach advised, and the girls needed no second hint.

His adoration of the big cats manifests itself in many ways. At one point in the 1970s when, he says, he had a lot of money and no place to put it, he commissioned the great Italian shotgun makers, Abbiatico and Salvinelli, to make him a set of side-by-side shotguns, his own works of art reproduced on the frames and lock-plates in their incomparable *bulino* engraving. Prominent among the works chosen (although inappropriate, perhaps, for bird guns) were the big cats. Then, in 1982, he produced his extraordinary book, *The Big Cats,* an interweaving of science and art that may well go down as the best book on the large feline predators ever done, anywhere. And finally, Coheleach's personal stationery bears a portrait of a Siberian tiger.

"Given the choice, I could paint predators the rest of my life," Coheleach says. "Tigers, eagles, leopards. Dangerous creatures. I love them."

You almost get the impression that, being a natural predator himself, Coheleach would consider shooting another predator to be a breach of professional courtesy.

Yet, there is the hunting, the hunting...

"When you can smell that musk! You walk into the tall grass and all of a sudden you get a whiff of that musk. And God they're out here somewhere! It's absolutely bloodcurdling. Exciting as hell. But terrifying.

"I don't enjoy killing (animals) but I love hunting them. I love tracking them down. I love trying to capture them in some way. If it's not on canvas, it's, well, chasing them down. When you've got a buffalo looking down his nose at you like you owe him money — isn't that what Ruark said? — when his adrenalin is up...

"Elephant and buffalo, you know, they scare the hell out of me, absolutely scare the living bejesus out of me. I don't know whether I'll do it again...

"I probably will..."

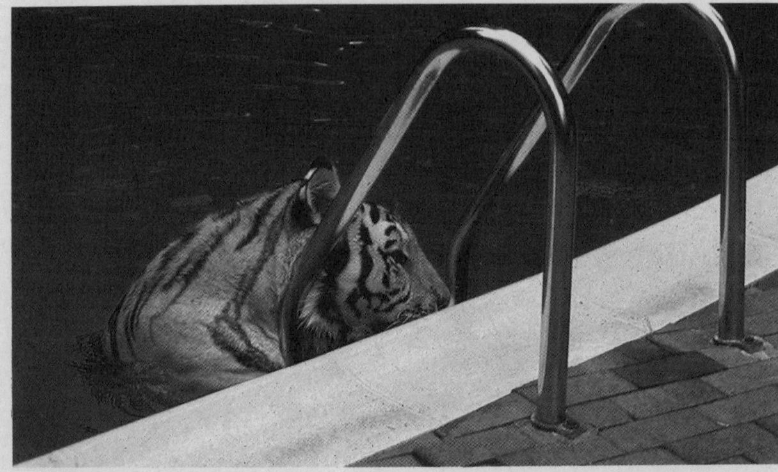

Coheleach took this picture of a tiger in the pool at his former home in Long Island.

The visit was prompted by a need for pictures to promote Coheleach's book, *The Big Cats.*

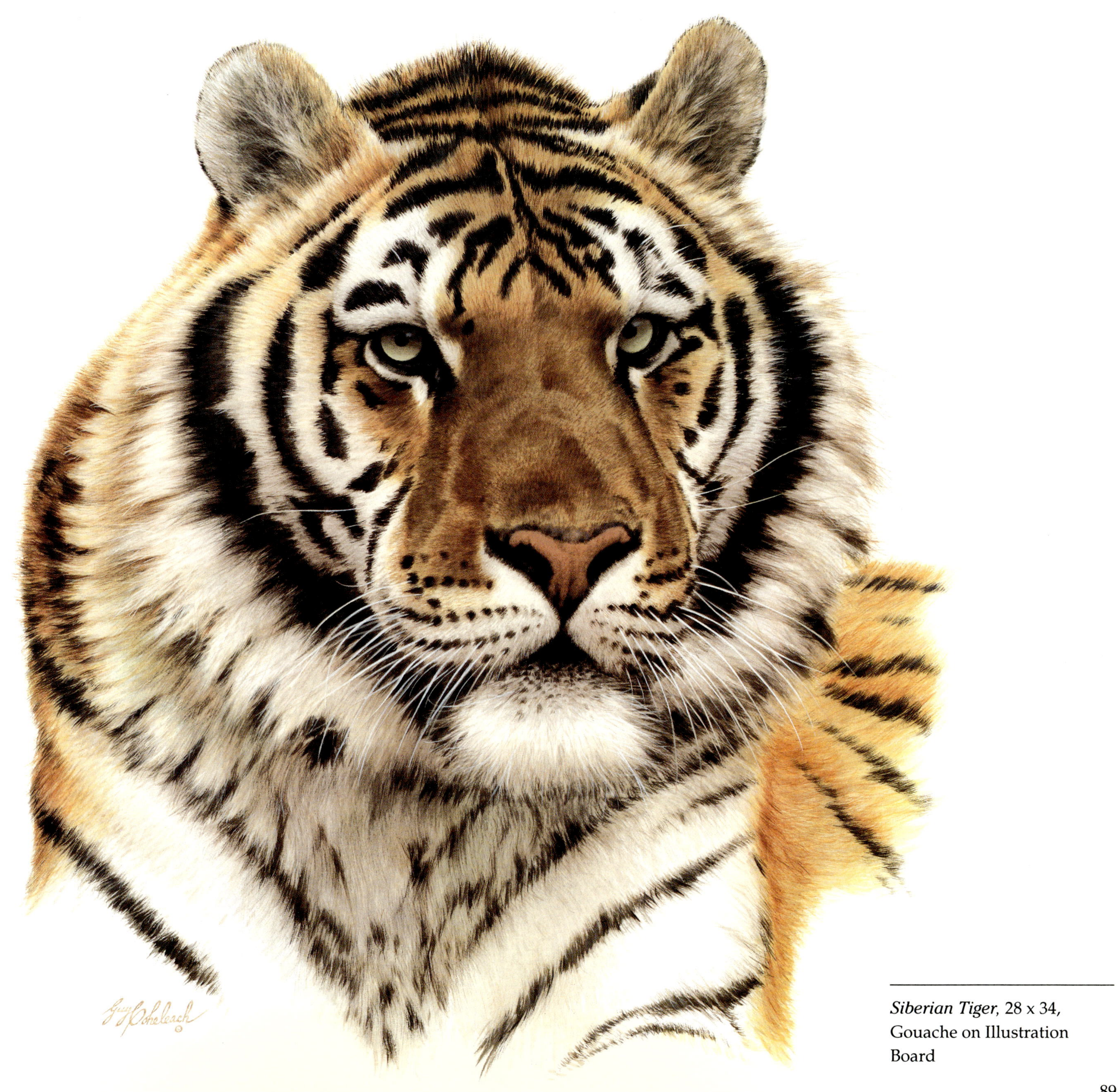

Siberian Tiger, 28 x 34, Gouache on Illustration Board

Painted in 1963, *The Chase* is one of Coheleach's most popular canvases. In subject matter, this depiction of hunter and hunted, with the outcome left to the viewer's discretion, is definitive Coheleach.

This was the first of many chase scenes to appear in his paintings — hence the simplicity of the title.

The detail reflects his knowledge of African animals:

The Thomson's gazelle is the most common prey of cheetahs, but usually it is too small and fast to interest the lion.

The Chase is also a superb example of composition and balance, displaying Coheleach's skill as both artist and draughtsman.

The Chase, 72 X 36, Oil on Canvas

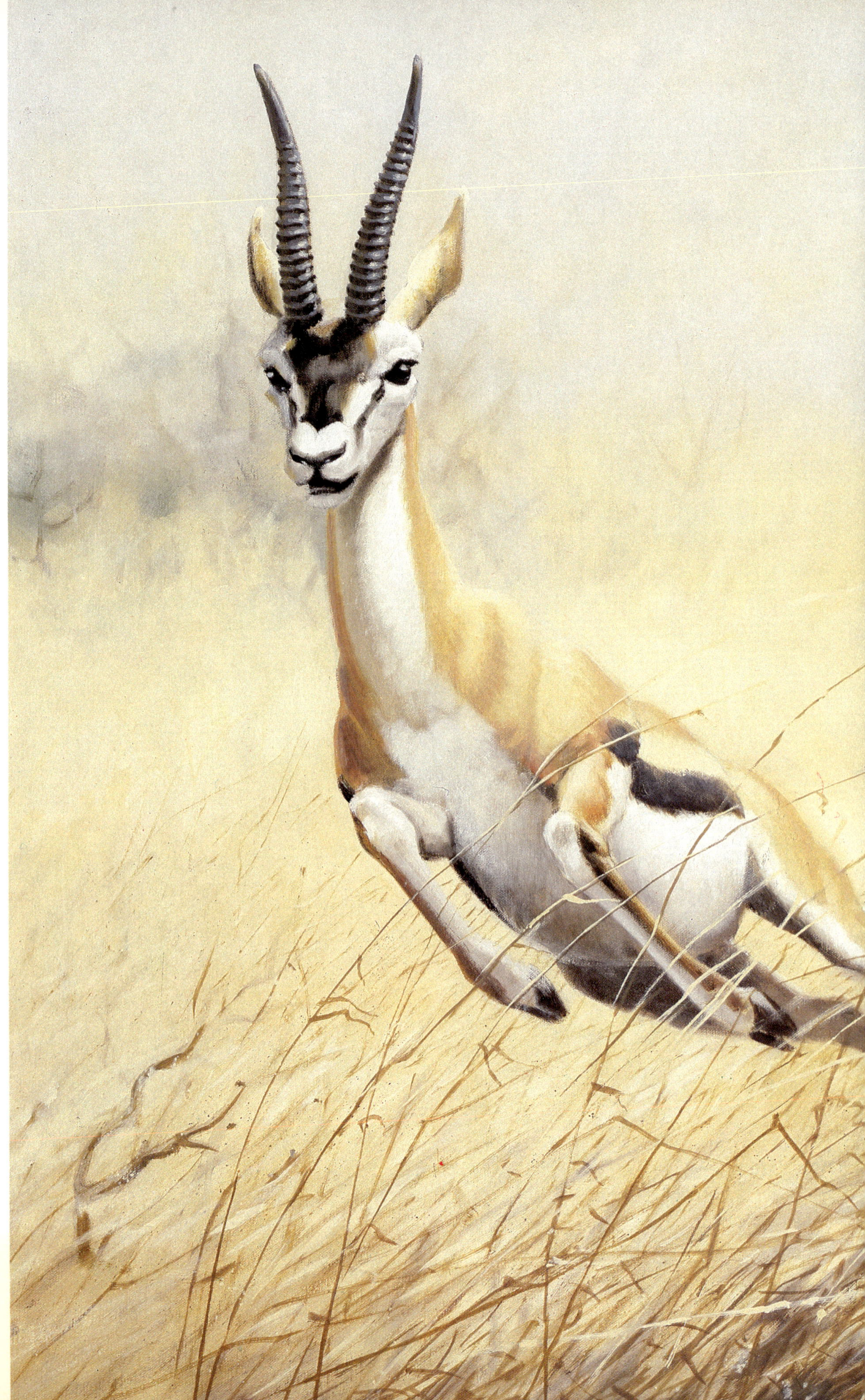

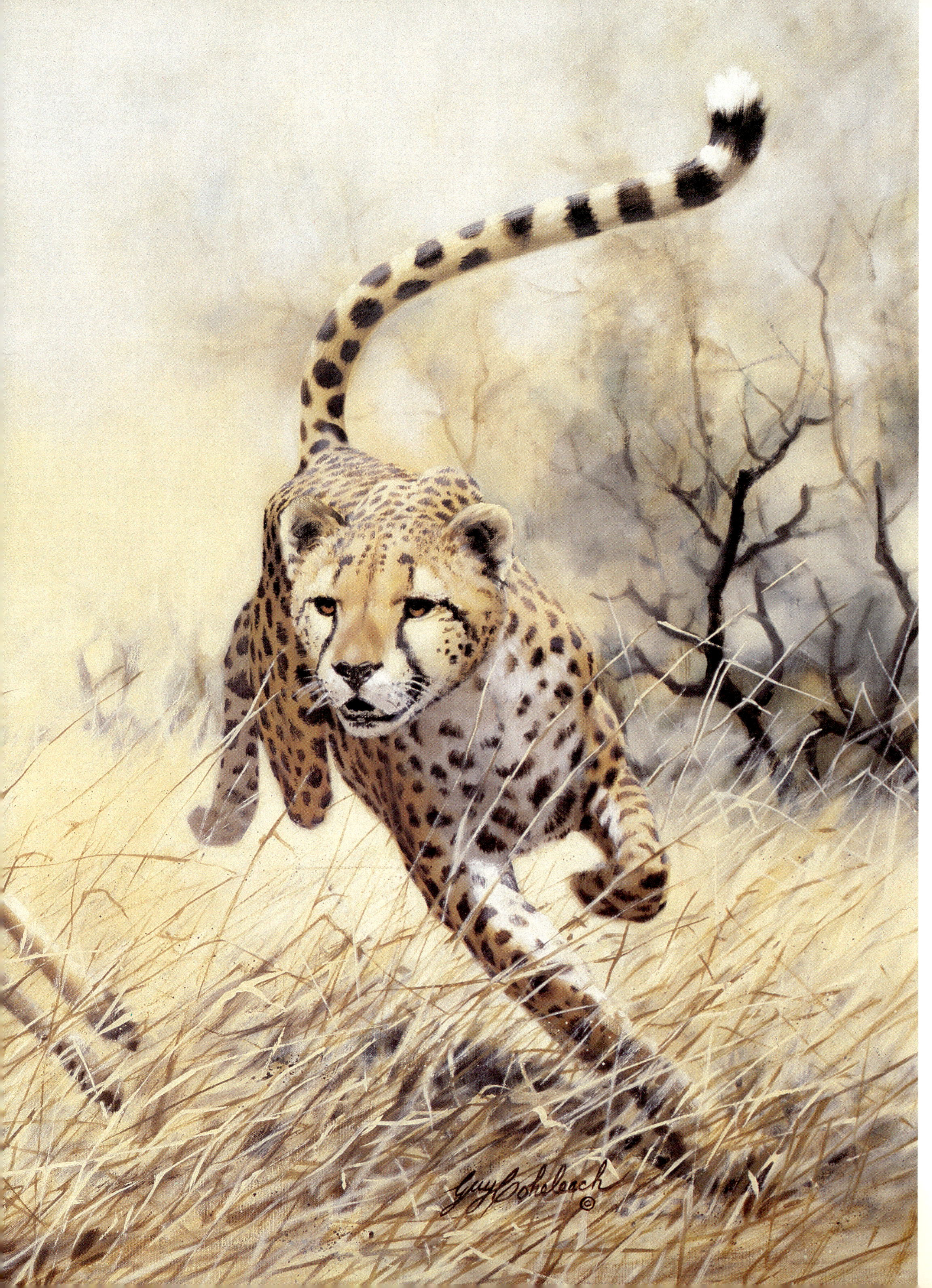
Guy Coheleach ©

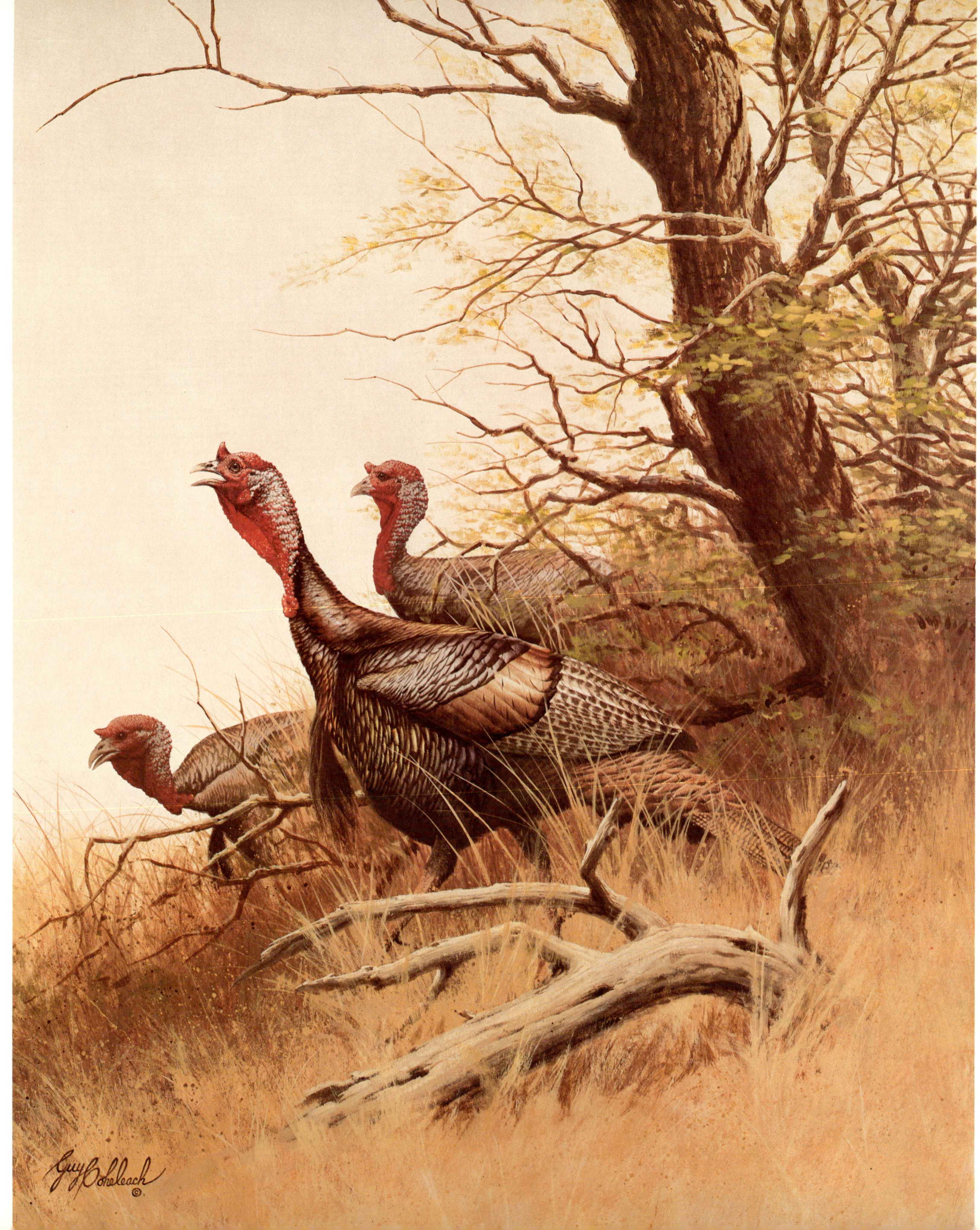
Guy Coheleach ©

Wild turkeys have feathers that appear to be made of sheet metal; they're very shiny and iridescent. So the challenge for the artist is to paint the bird's plumage so it looks soft and natural.

The scene of Rio Grande turkeys was painted for a private foundation that assists the widows of conservation officers killed in the line of duty.

Wild Turkey, 30 x 40, Gouache and Acrylic on Illustration Board

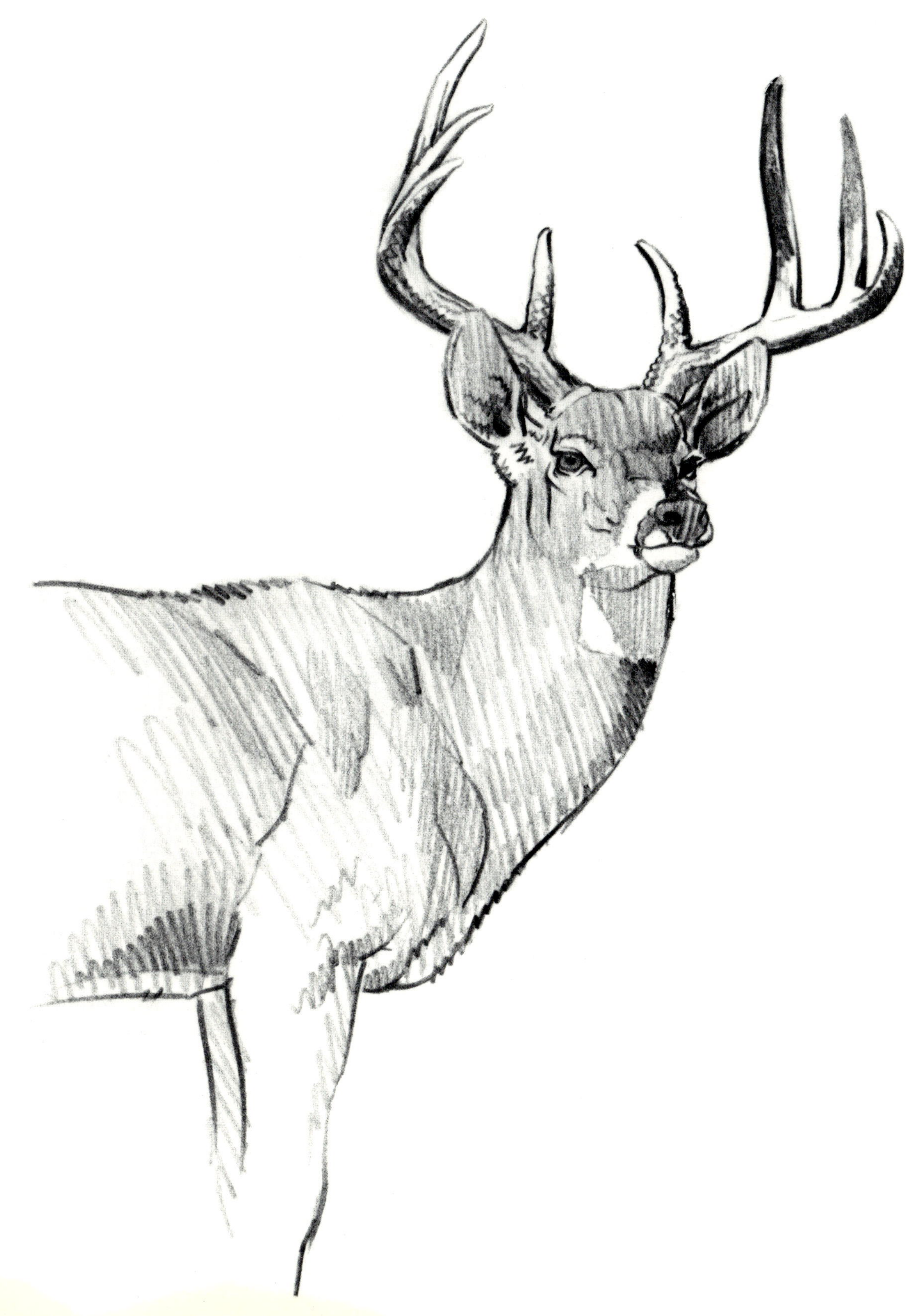

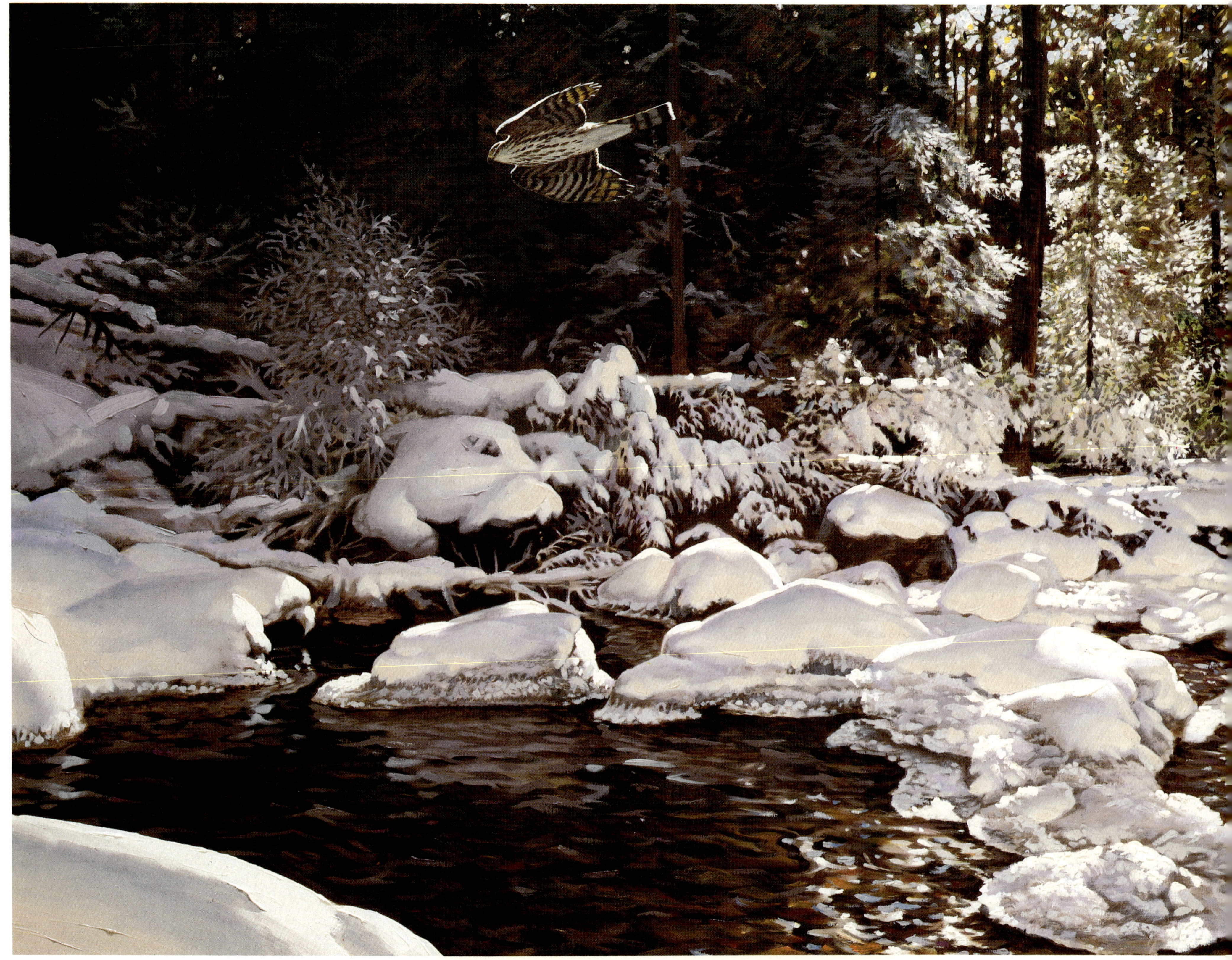

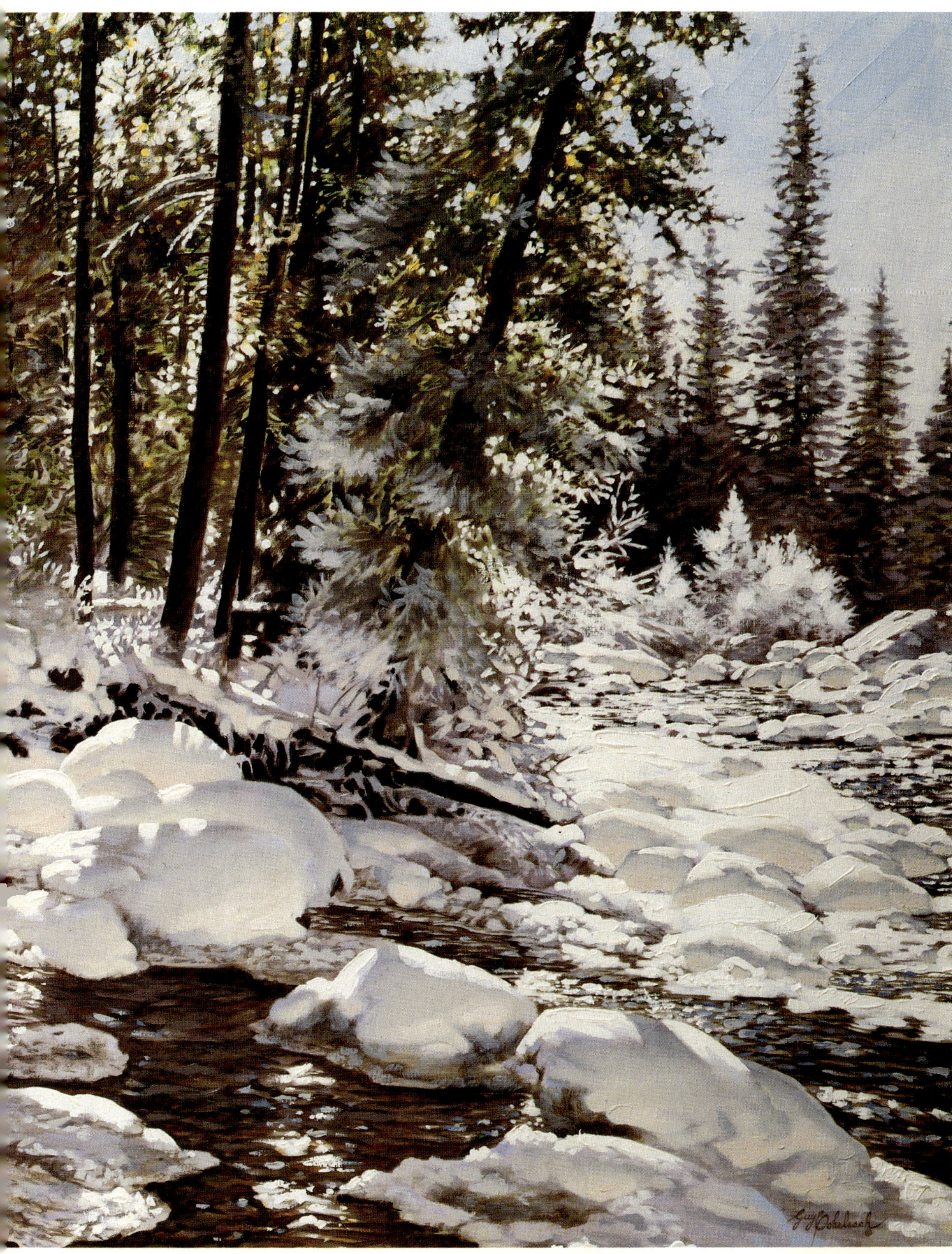

This is an example of the way I like to paint landscapes, quite large (three by six feet) and with a number of things to absorb the viewer.

First, there is the light filtering through the evergreens that provides a nice mix of contrasts on the water, snow, and trees.

The snow-covered rocks are in direct sunlight, and in real life they would be the kind of brilliant white that would hurt your eyes. But you can't paint snow that way; in fact, there isn't a piece of solid white on the entire canvas.

The trees behind the bird are darker than they would be in nature, because I wanted the backlit sharpshin to really jump out. The backlighting not only strengthens the hawk's outline, it gives an extra dimension to the painting.

Immature Sharp-shinned Hawk,
72 x 36, Oil on Canvas

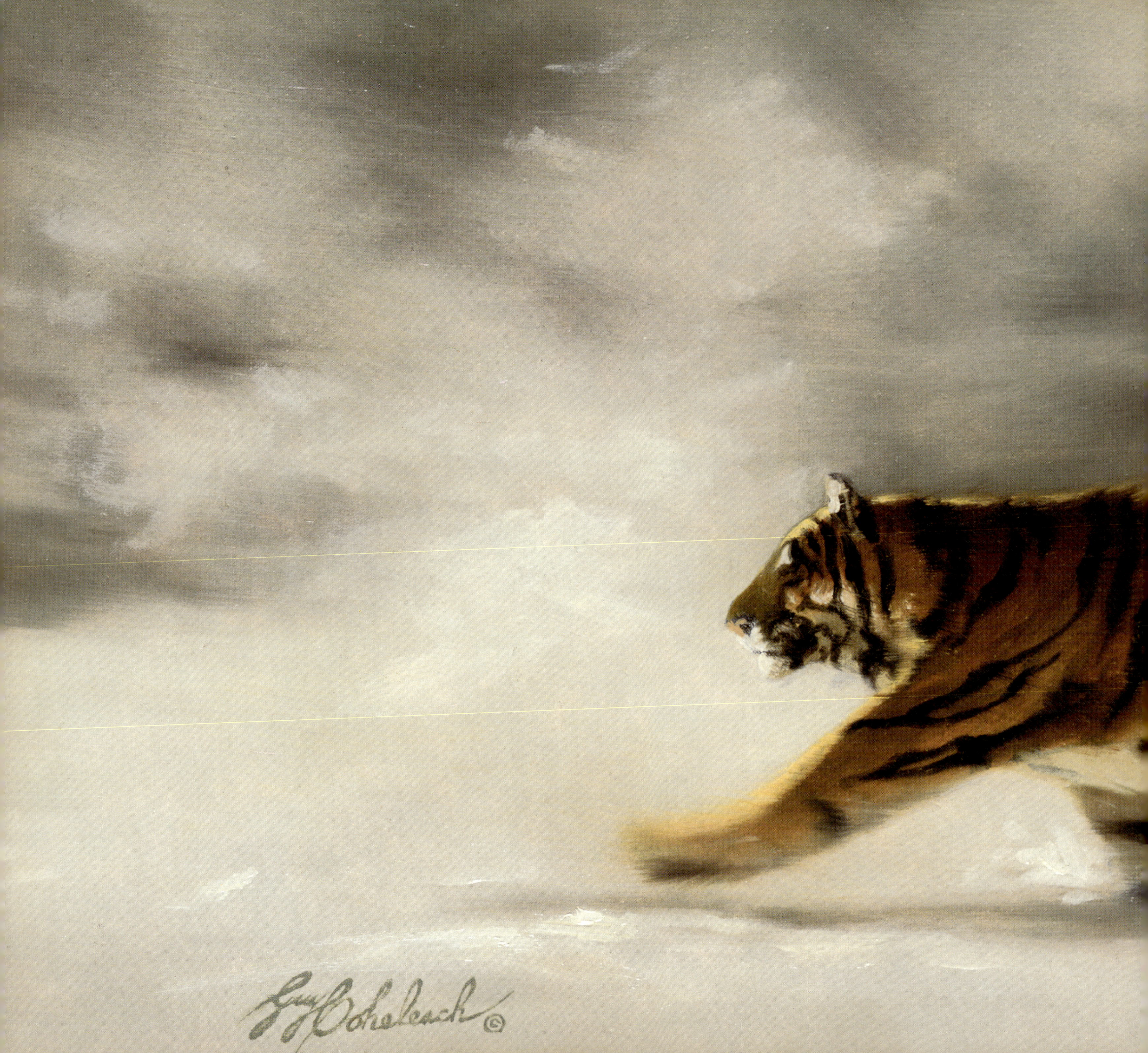
Guy Coheleach ©

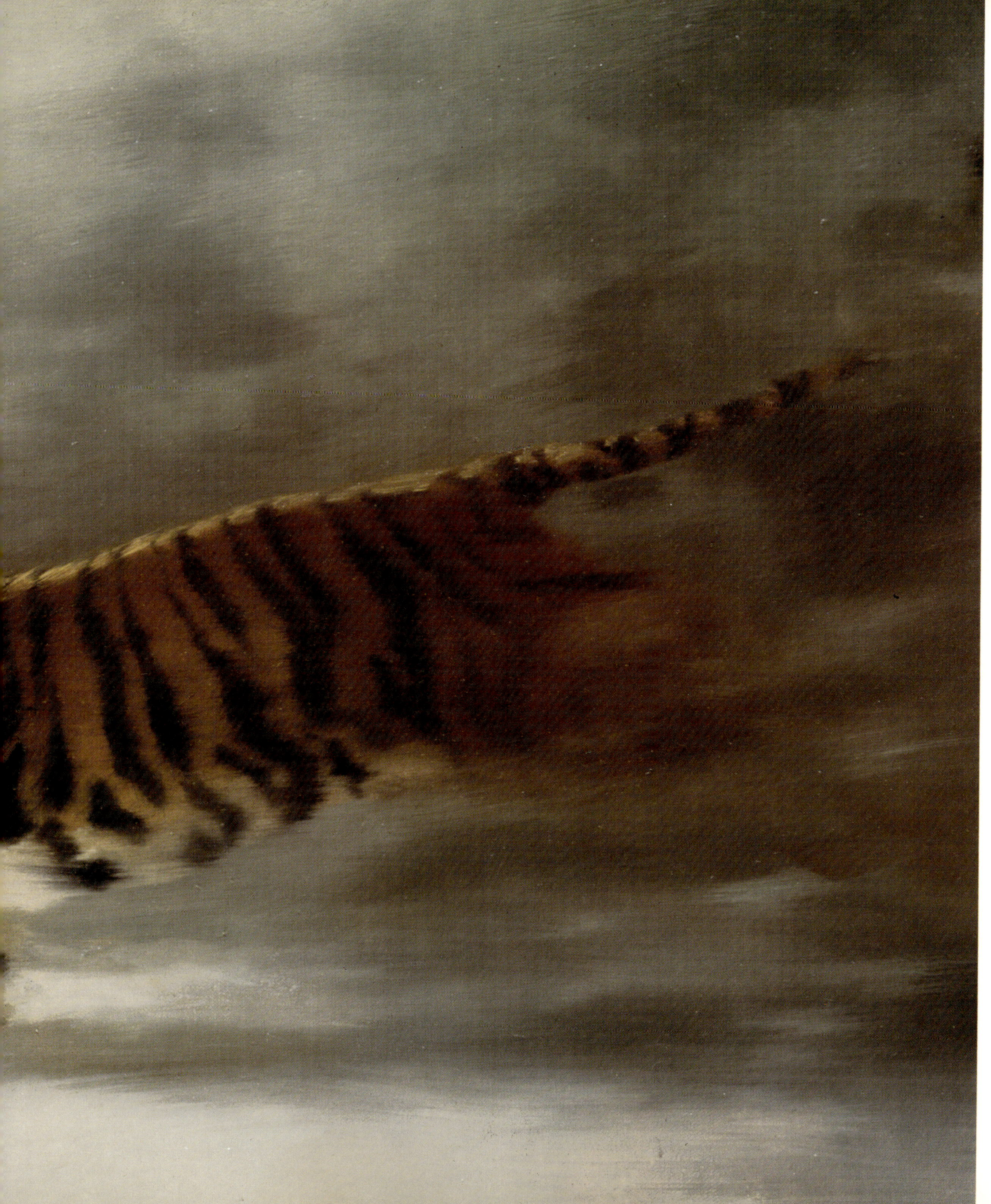

I have many favorite paintings. Some I like for their grandeur, others for their subtlety. There are those I prefer for their mood or detail; others for their painterliness.

Siberian Chase stands out because it became my favorite print. It proved to me that collectors of wildlife art will buy something other than pieces with fur and feathers rendered in meticulous detail.

I have always liked to work impressionistically, but I had never had the nerve to print such a painting. Siberian Chase was proof that at least some buyers were ready for more fine art in their limited edition prints.

I am sure there are better works of art among my paintings, but there is none I remember as fondly.

Siberian Chase, 20 X 10, Oil on Canvas

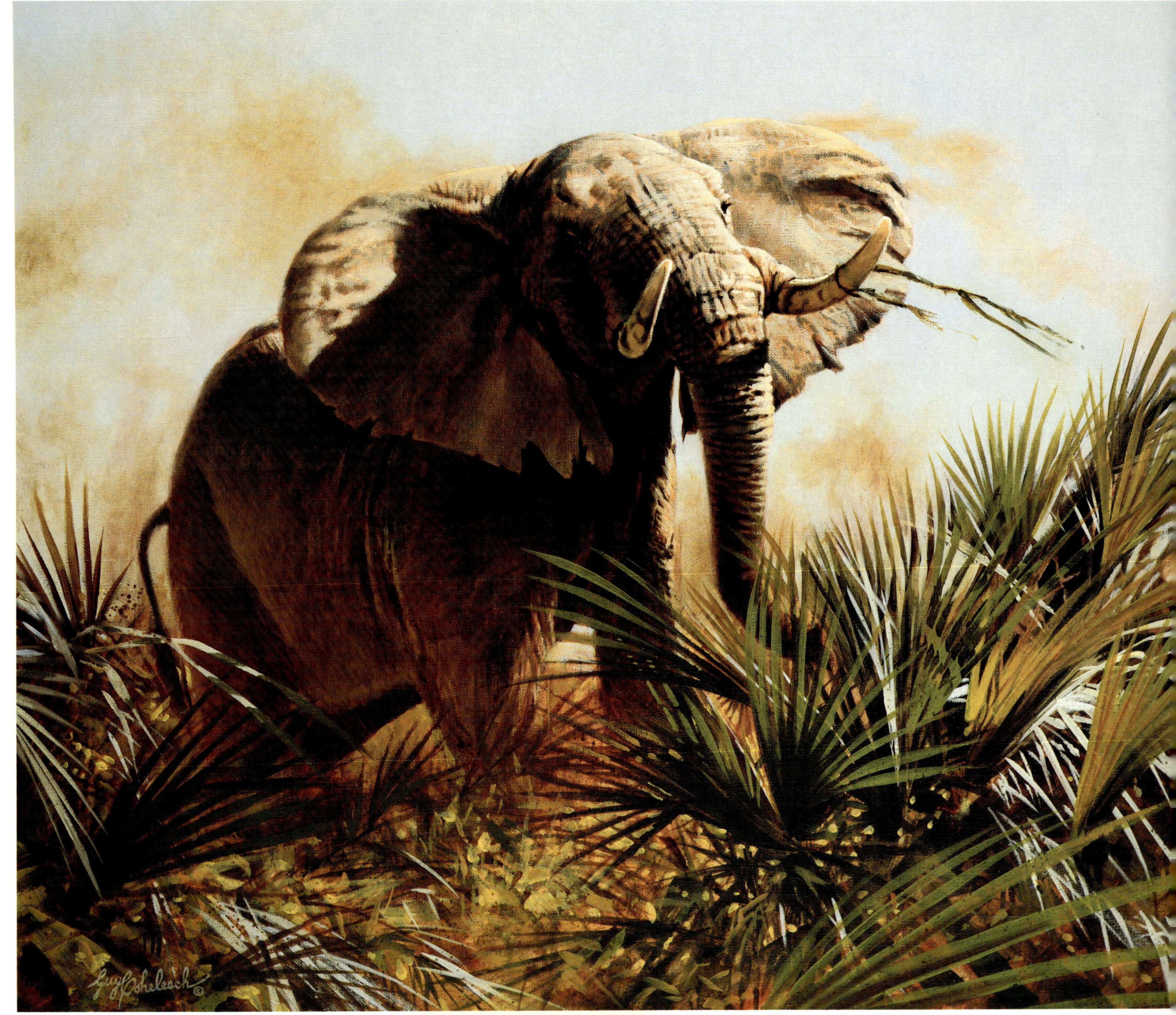
Guy Coheleach ©

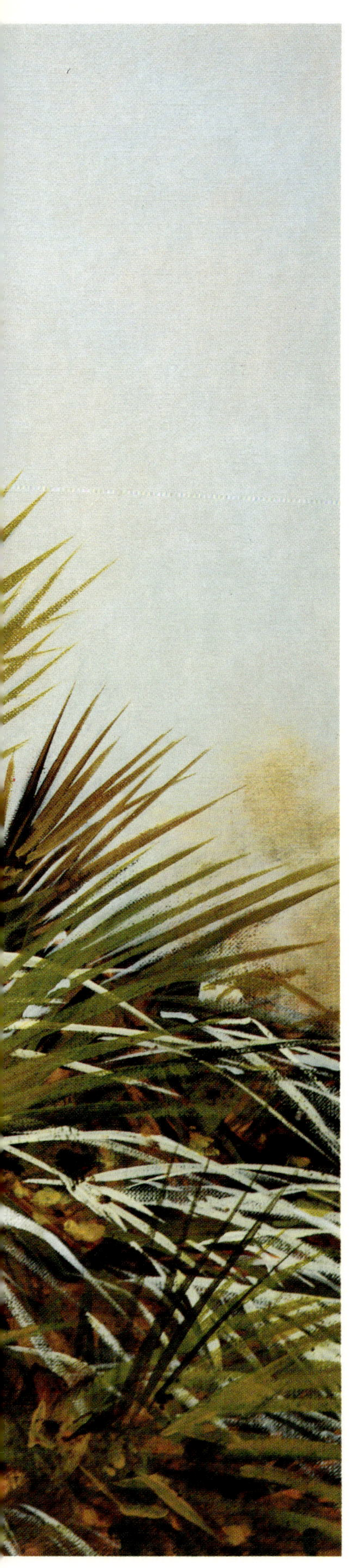

Since his brush with eternity at the end of an elephant's tusk in late 1972, Coheleach has become a connoisseur of pachyderm moods and mannerisms. Appearances, perhaps, to the contrary, this African bull elephant, under the sun in open country, is not charging.

He's just extremely irritated. He's tossing some dust around and saying 'All right, you guys, get outta here.' Which I would now do. Immediately. Charging, he'd be coming right at you.

The Last Ivory Hunt, 30 X 22, Oil on Canvas

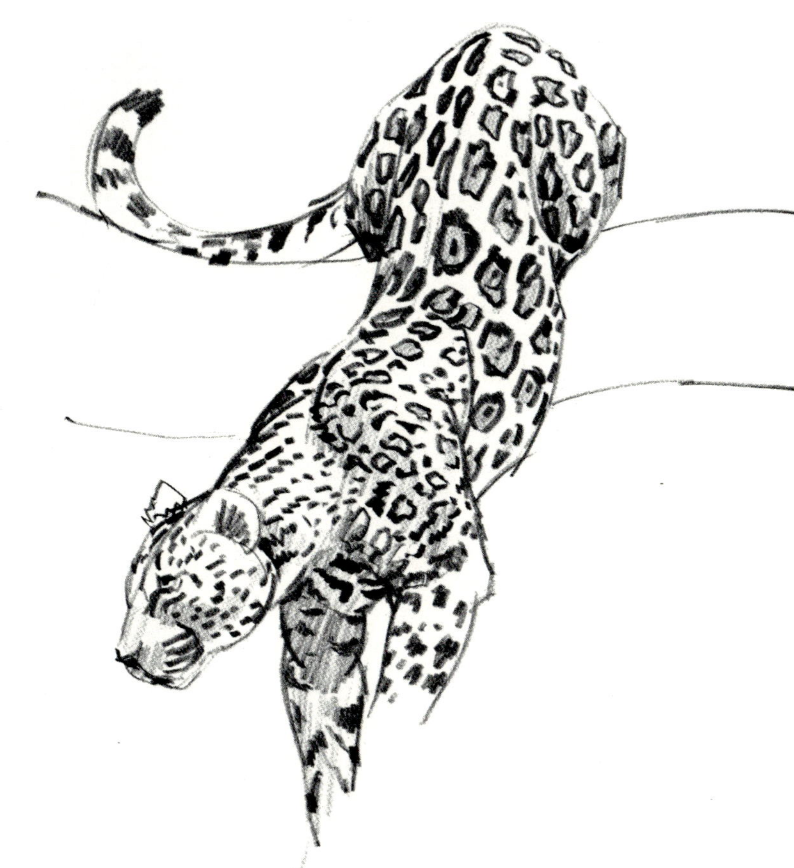

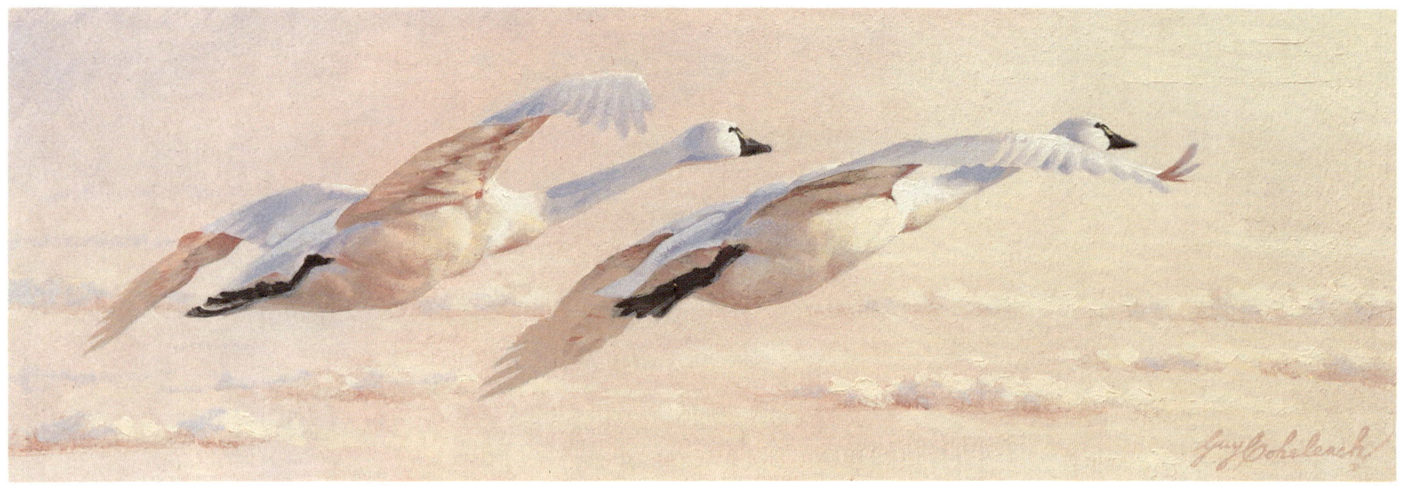

Occasionally Coheleach will re-explore certain themes that hold a special fascination for him. *Whistling Swans* (page 8), painted in 1981, captures the slow, lumbering flight of these graceful birds. *Tundra Swans,* above, was created for a miniature show in 1988. In each painting Coheleach faded the background into a misty obscurity, heightening the almost ghost-like flight of the birds.

The key to each painting is the play of various shades of gray. The blue-grays on the swans' bodies reflect the blue sky, while the warm grays reflect the light of the water underneath the wings, and all gradually fading into the distant water.

Tundra Swans, 15 x 5, Oil on Masonite

Although he had never seen a musk ox in the wild, Coheleach turned to his extensive photo library to create this painting for an *Audubon* magazine article. The adults have reverted to their classic "circle the wagons" defense, an armament of sharp horns facing their adversary which in the Arctic, probably means a wolf pack.

There is a charged air of excitement to the scene, yet one can almost feel the intense cold. The snowy foreground, the frosty breath of the animals, and the icy-blue sky leave no doubt about the frigid conditions.

Musk Ox, 18 x 14, Gouache and Acrylic on Illustration Board

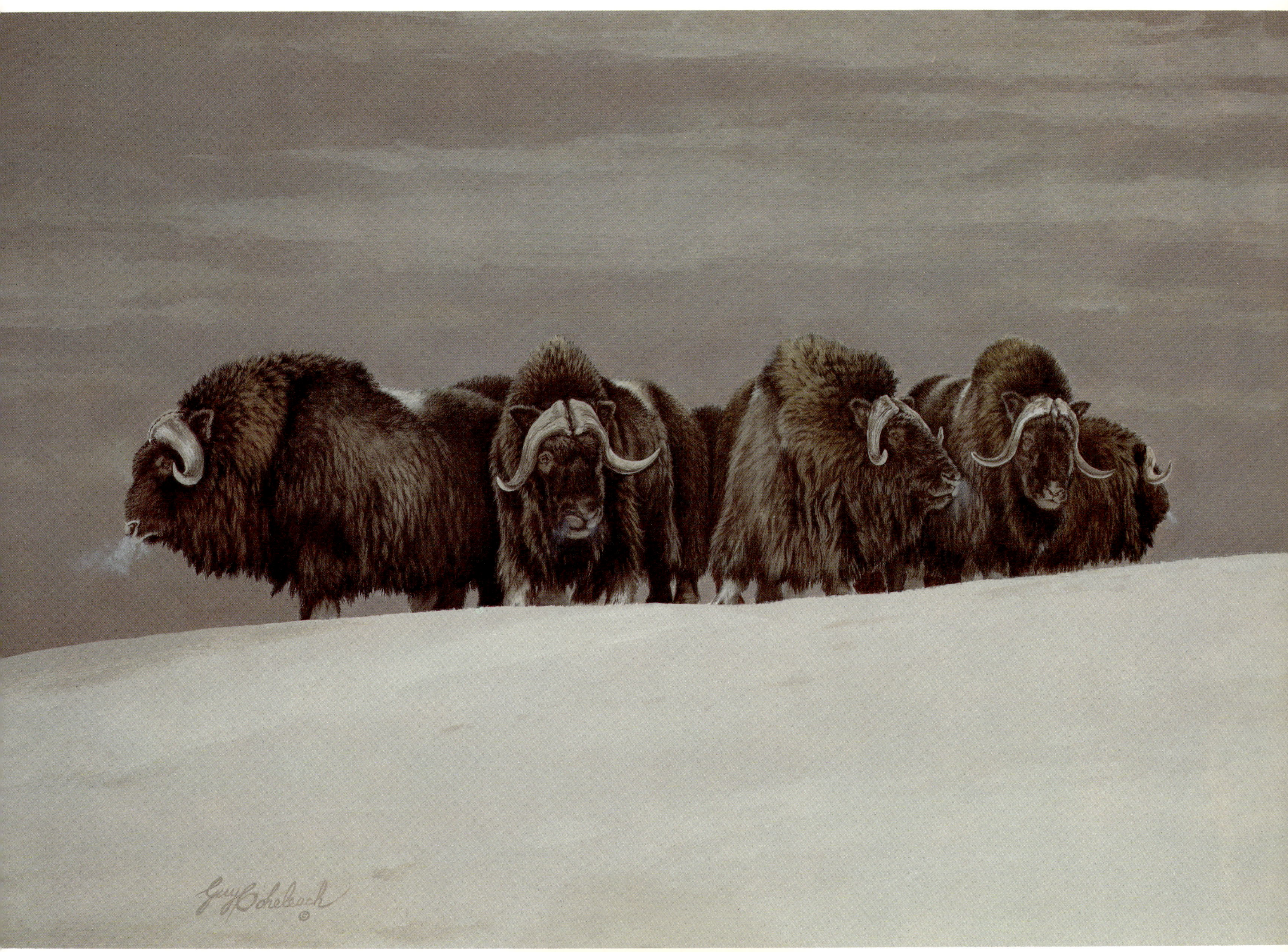
Guy Coheleach ©

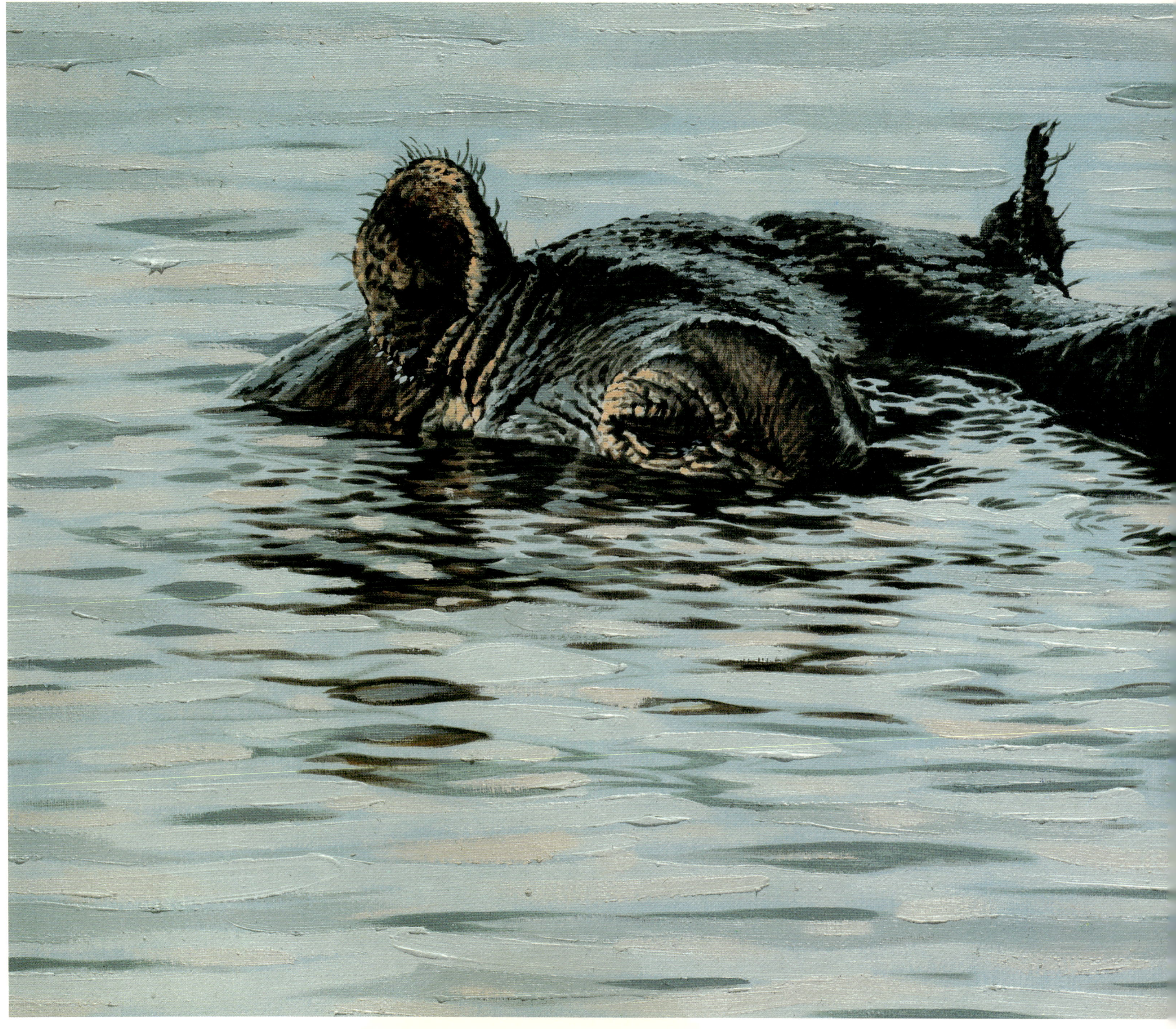

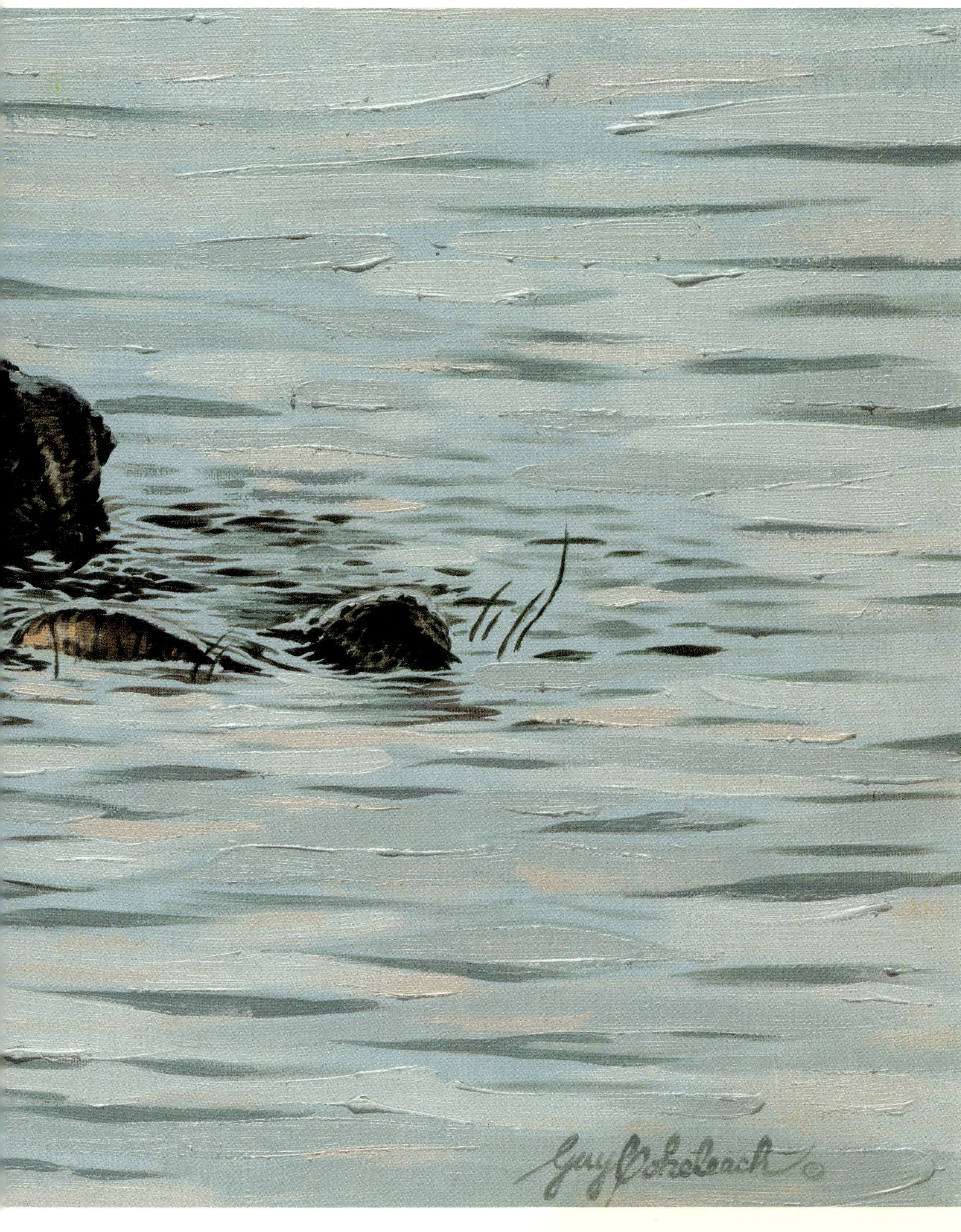

This is a fun painting, and I enjoyed painting it. Everyone seems to like hippos, but the truth is, they are one of the most dangerous animals in Africa. They account for more human deaths than anything else, with the possible exception of crocodiles.

The day after I left the Luangwa Valley, a man was killed on a walking safari. His group was walking in single file, the professional hunter out front and the man bringing up the rear. A hippo came down, and before the professional hunter could shoot, grabbed the man and carried him right into the river. That was the last they ever saw of him...

They are very, very cantankerous animals, and the guy just happened to be in the way...

River Horse, 24 X 12, Oil on Canvas

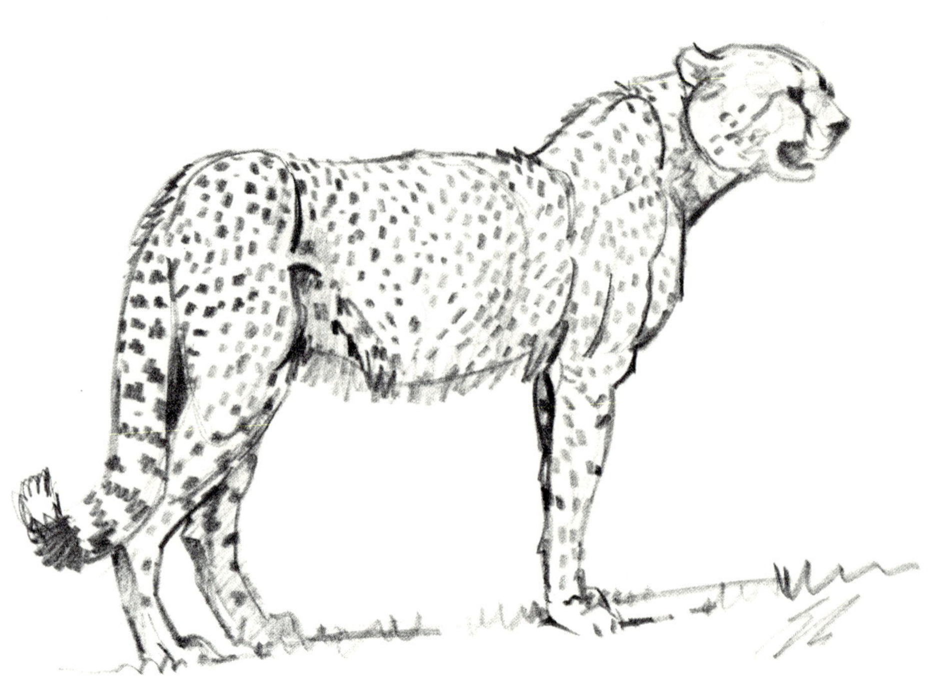

I did this painting the same time as The Chase, using the same palette. I was in a rush so while the oils on one painting were drying, I worked on the other.

I have seen a lot of cheetahs in the wild. Well fed, they appear loose and lazy, which I tried to convey here. But on the hunt they radiate intensity.

And their speed really is remarkable; it's one of those things in nature that you really can't comprehend until you see it firsthand.

Of the many interesting characters that Coheleach has met on safari, one of the most fascinating was a sheep rancher whose land was virtually overrun with cheetahs. The rancher did not want to kill the big cats, so he would trap the animals, then transplant them to other areas.

In addition to live-traps, he caught a number of cheetahs by running them with dogs and then roping them. Once the dogs had a cat at bay, he would move in and grab the cheetah's tail while his natives tried to get a noose over its head. The guy was an absolute madman!

Reclining Cheetah, 40 X 30, Oil on Canvas

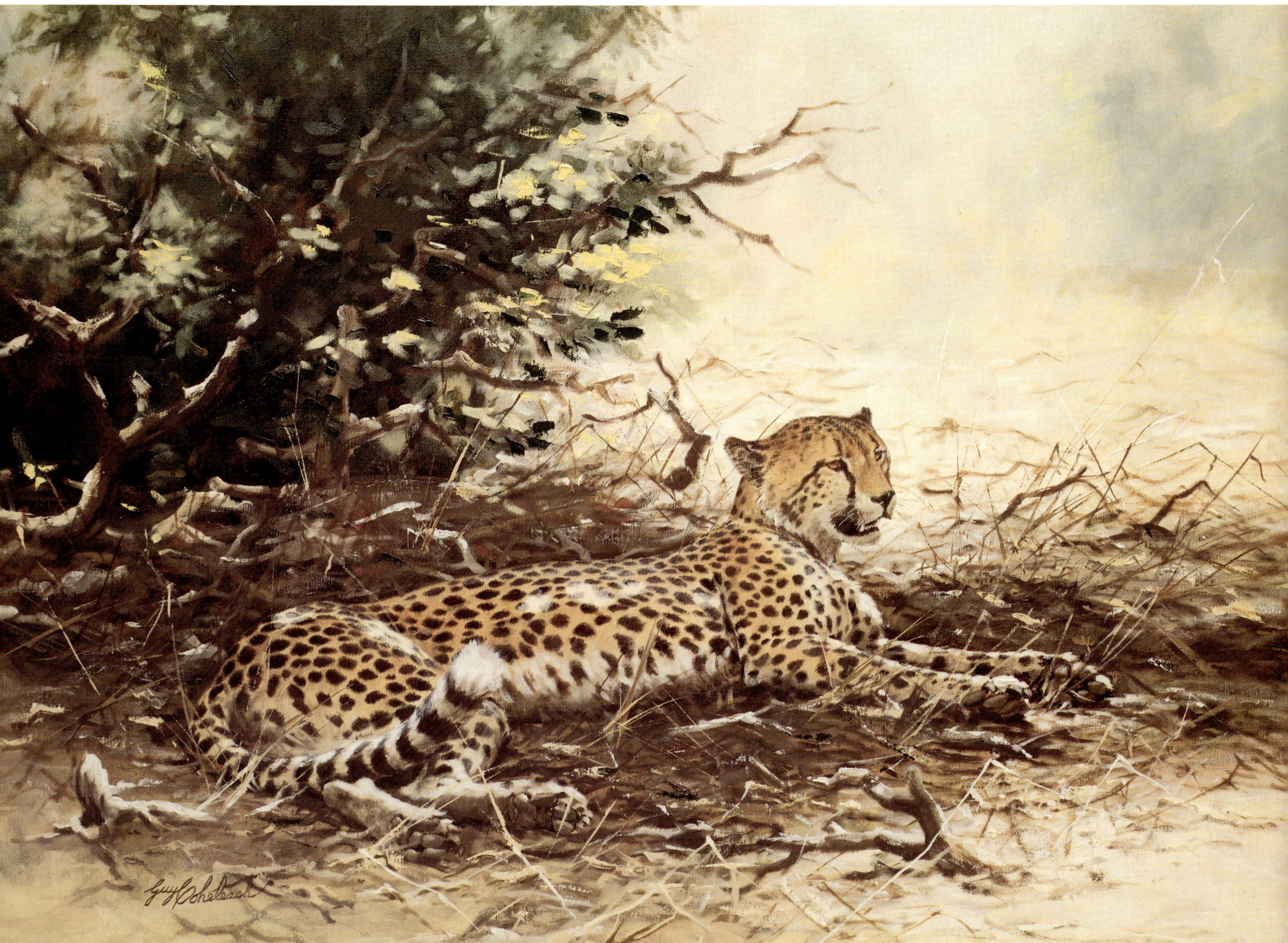

The Cape buffalo is one of Coheleach's favorite subjects, both to hunt and to paint. He was putting the finishing touches on this charging buffalo when African professional hunter Fred Bartlett walked up behind and said, "You just can't paint a Cape buffalo better than that."

Coming from a man who knows, it was the supreme compliment. This is a big buffalo, not really too old but in his prime. His horns are good — the classic Cape buffalo shape. The background is Botswana, where the bush is very light and as a result, the buffalo do not become badly rubbed. This buffalo has more hair than you would see on a buffalo from East Africa.

As he did in his painting of the elephant on page 162, Coheleach uses the position of the animal's body to denote speed. His mass is so far over to the side that only inertia of travel is keeping him on his feet.

It is one of those things that you paint instinctively, and as a result, people see a lot more action in it than they otherwise might.

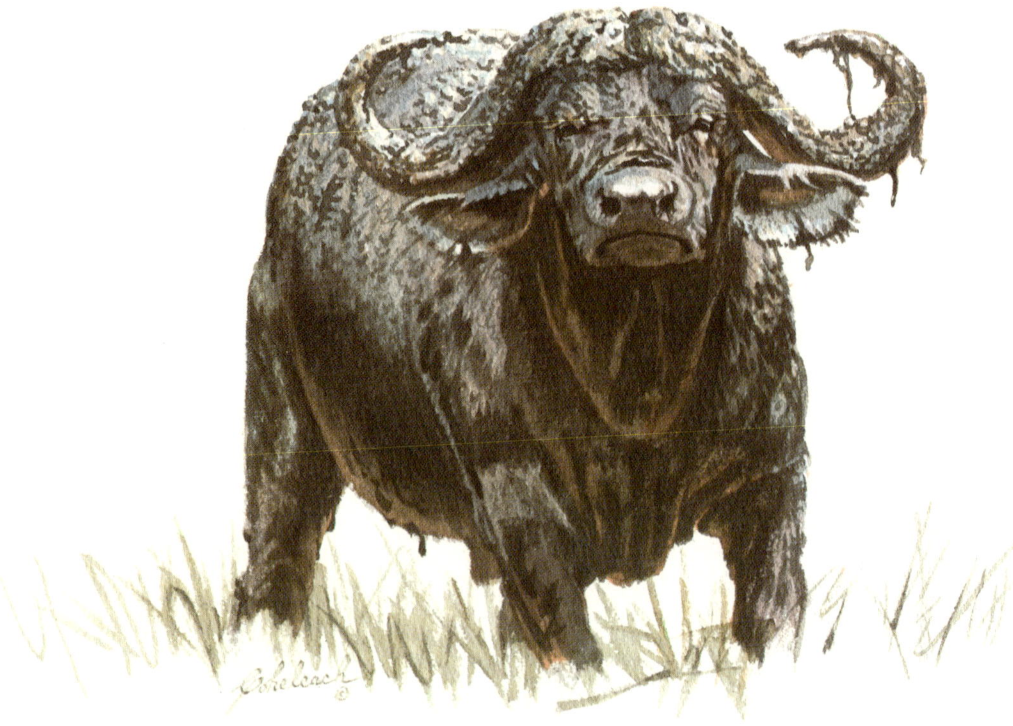

Cape Buffalo Bull, 10 x 8, Watercolor on Illustration Board

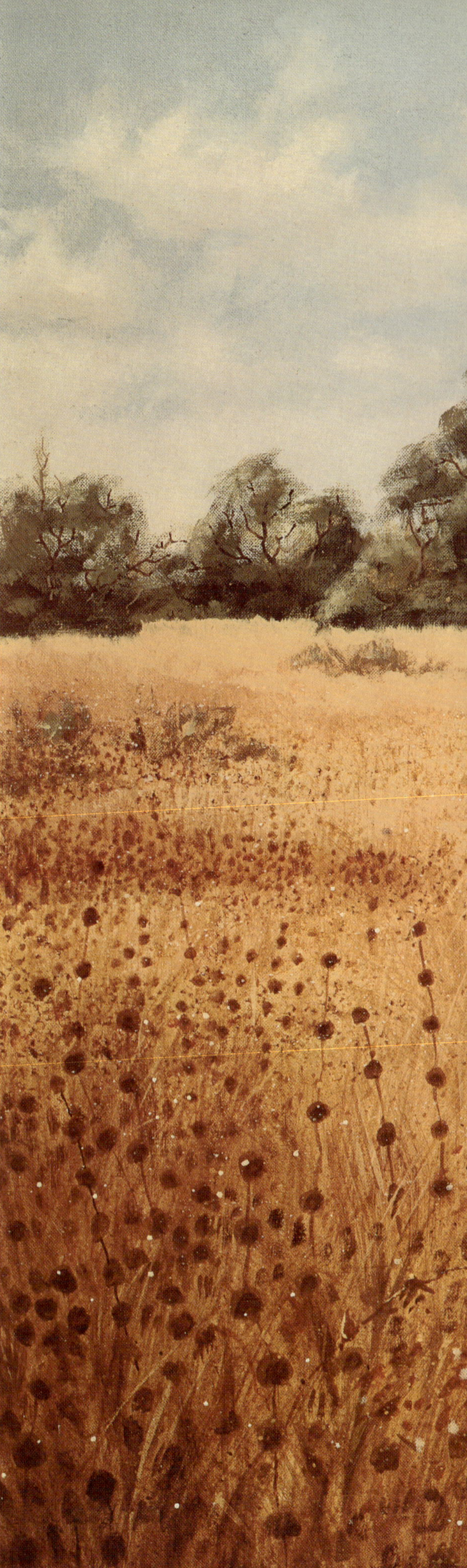

Cape Buffalo, 40 x 30, Oil on Canvas

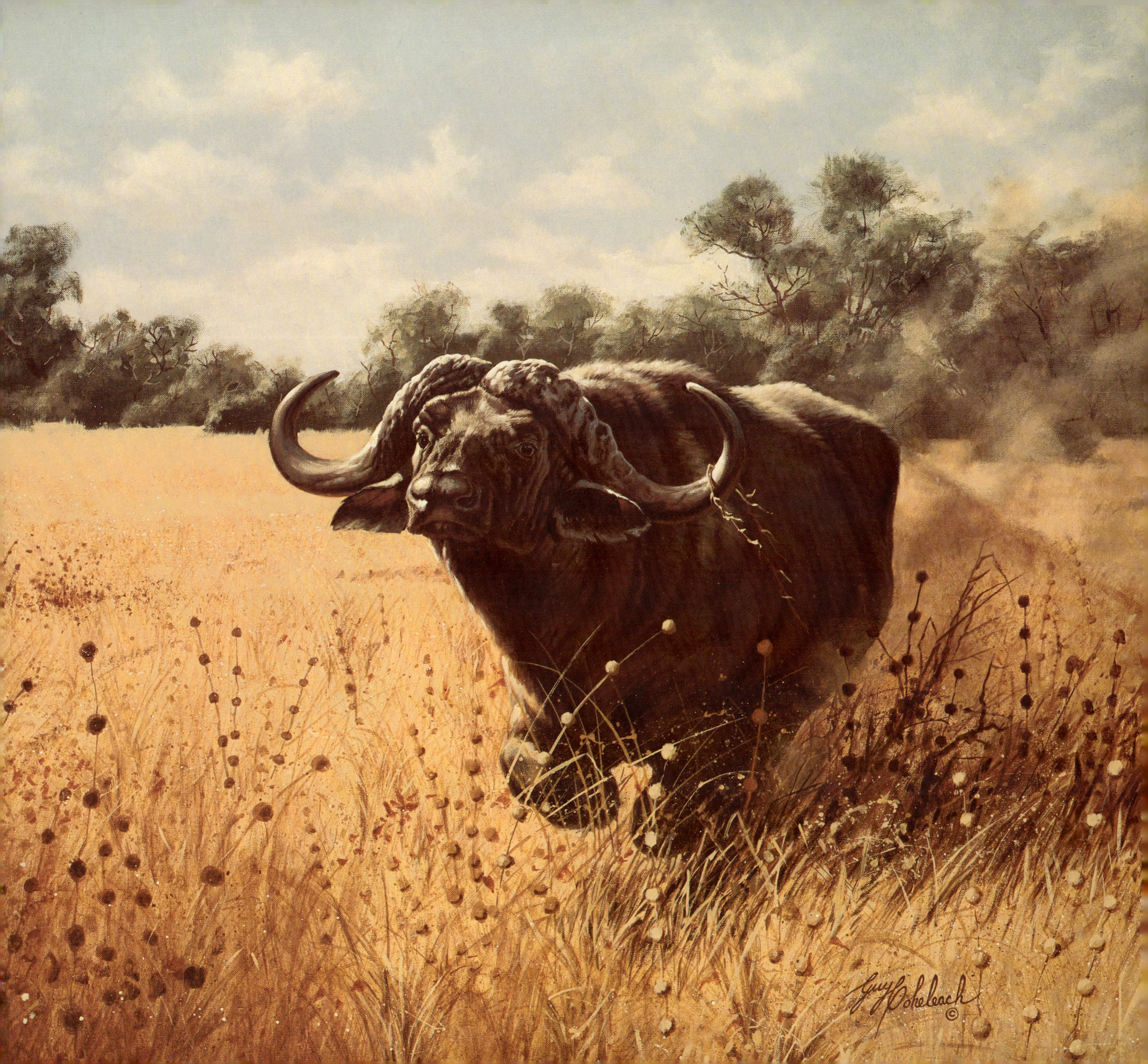
Guy Coheleach
©

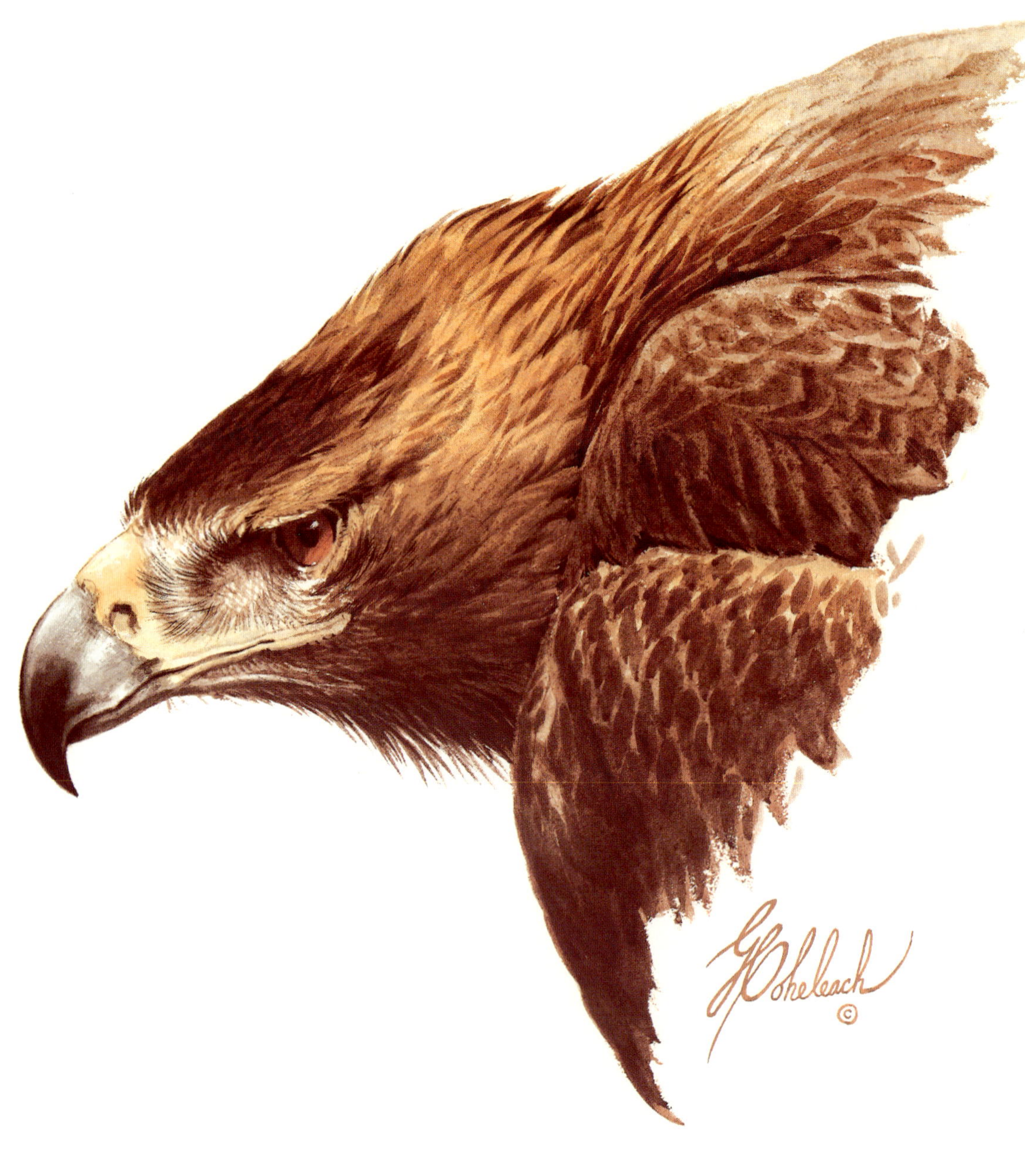

Just like the old saying, the eyes mirror the soul of an animal. If you want to paint something so it looks alive, you have to make the eyes right. You can make all kinds of mistakes on the creature's anatomy and colors, but if you screw up the eyes, it will appear lifeless.

I've always been conscious of eyes, on people and animals. You may not believe this, but I can look at the eyes and facial expression of a screech owl and tell you how many hours since he's eaten. I have spent hours and hours watching the little owls. When they are hungry, they look absolutely ferocious, with incredibly fierce eyes that go right through you.

The eyes of antelope and cows aren't as revealing as those of the predators. Still, if you paint them right, it's like looking into the heart of the animal.

Golden Eagle, 20 X 12, Watercolor on Illustration Board

Ambush, 30 X 40, Gouache and Acrylic on Illustration Board

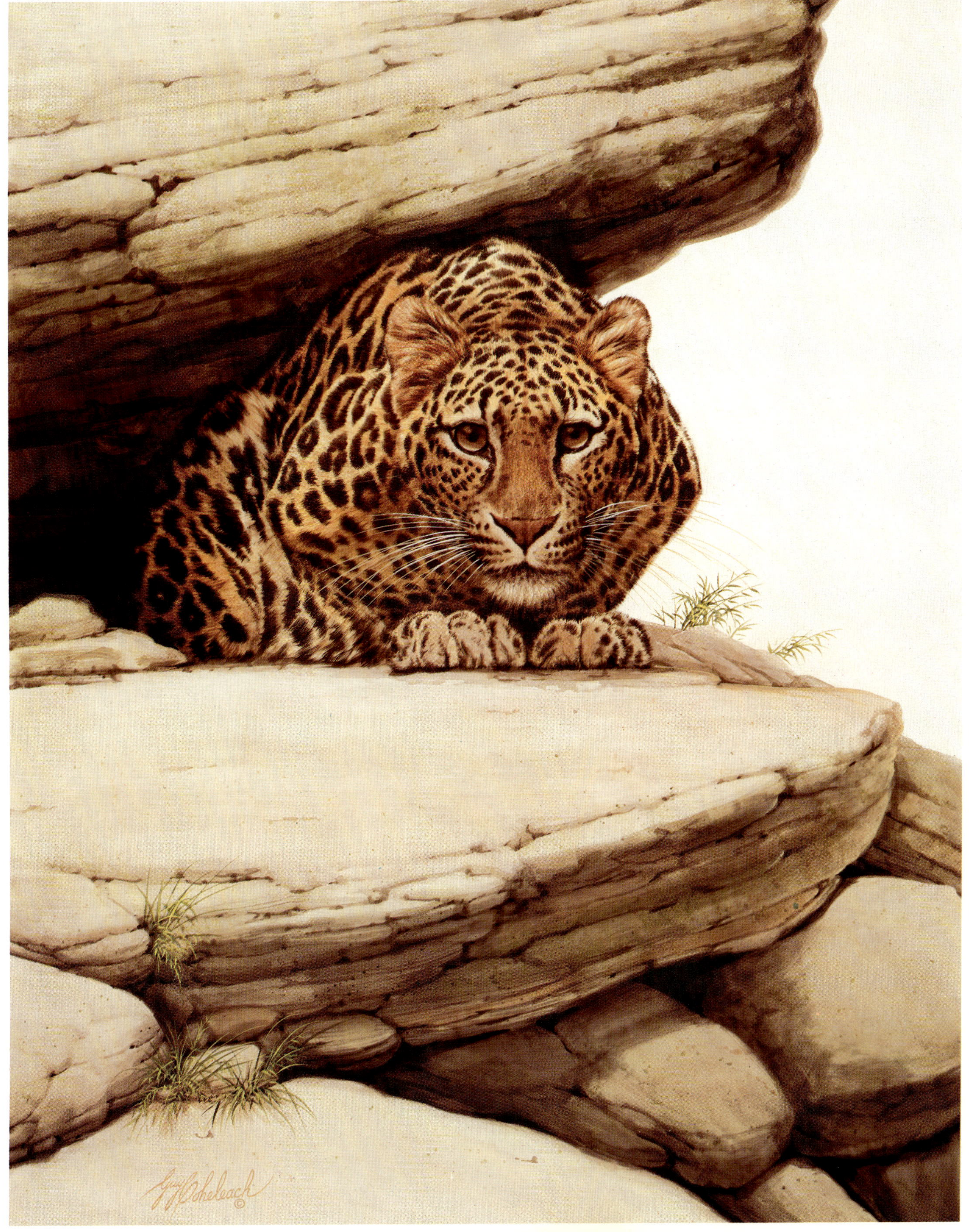

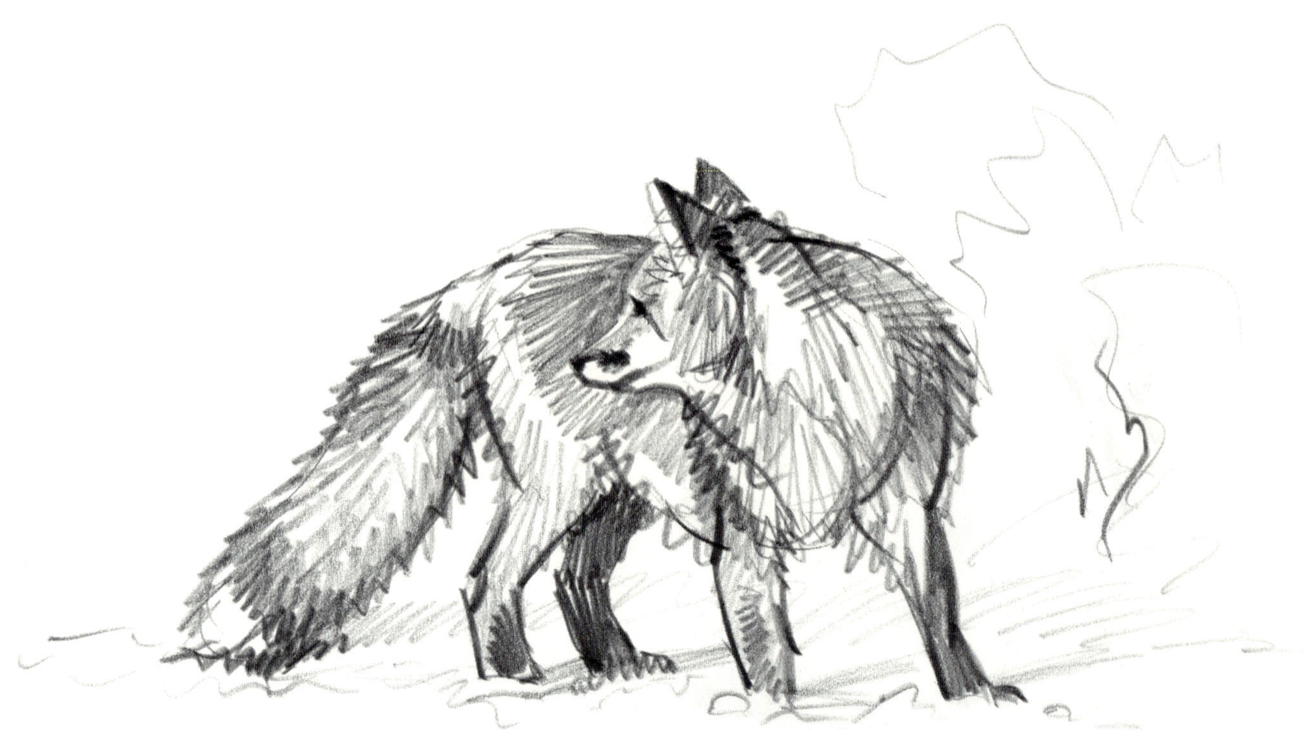

There is a lot of acrylic in this piece. I painted the birds first in gouache, then the background in acrylic. My last step was to touch up the geese with acrylic.

Acrylic dries quickly and is easy to use. You can boldly put something down and if it does not work, cover it over. With gouache, on the other hand, you have to think it out carefully. When working with acrylic, I often do my drawing right on the board.

Canada Geese, 40 X 30, Acrylic and Gouache on Illustration Board.

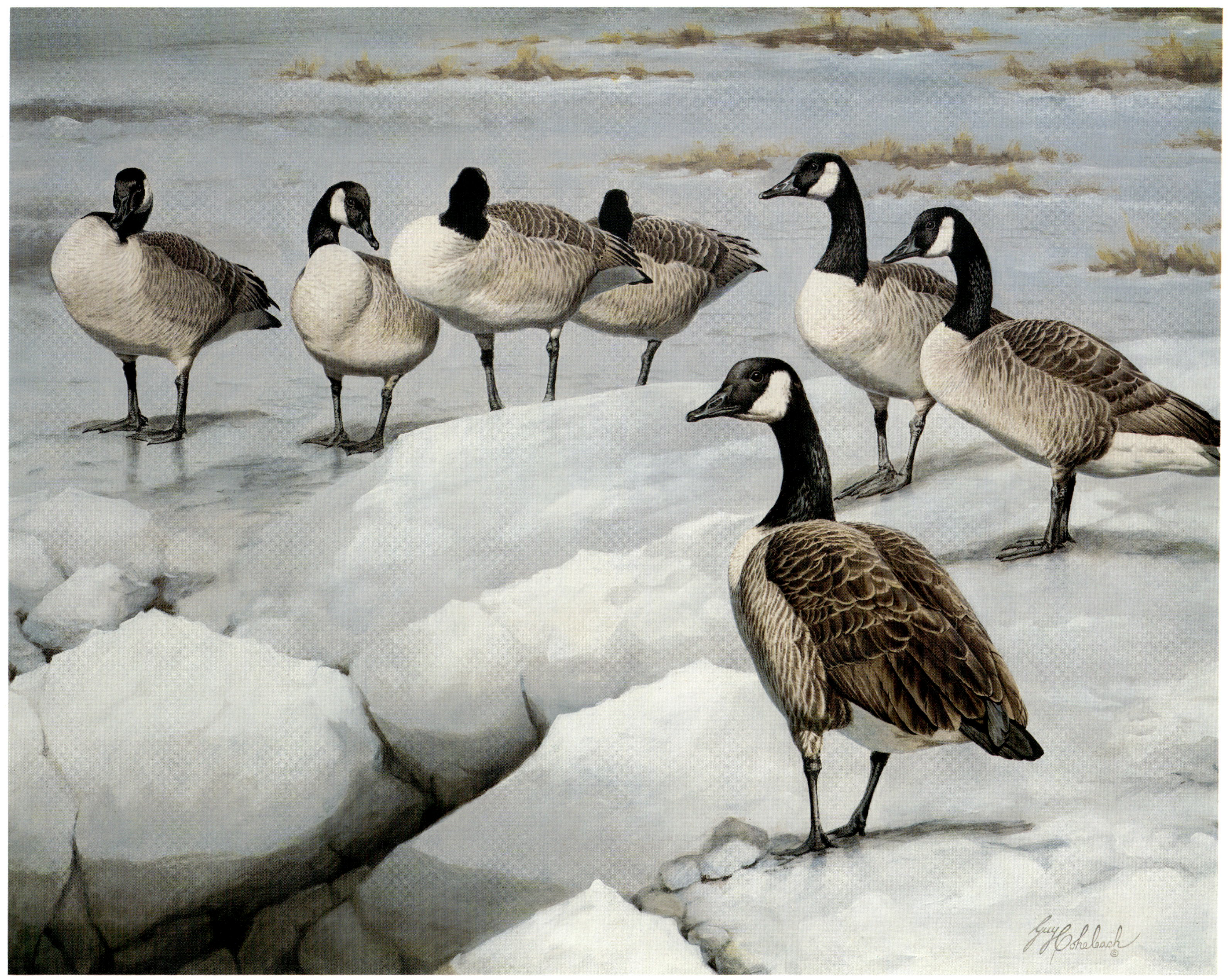

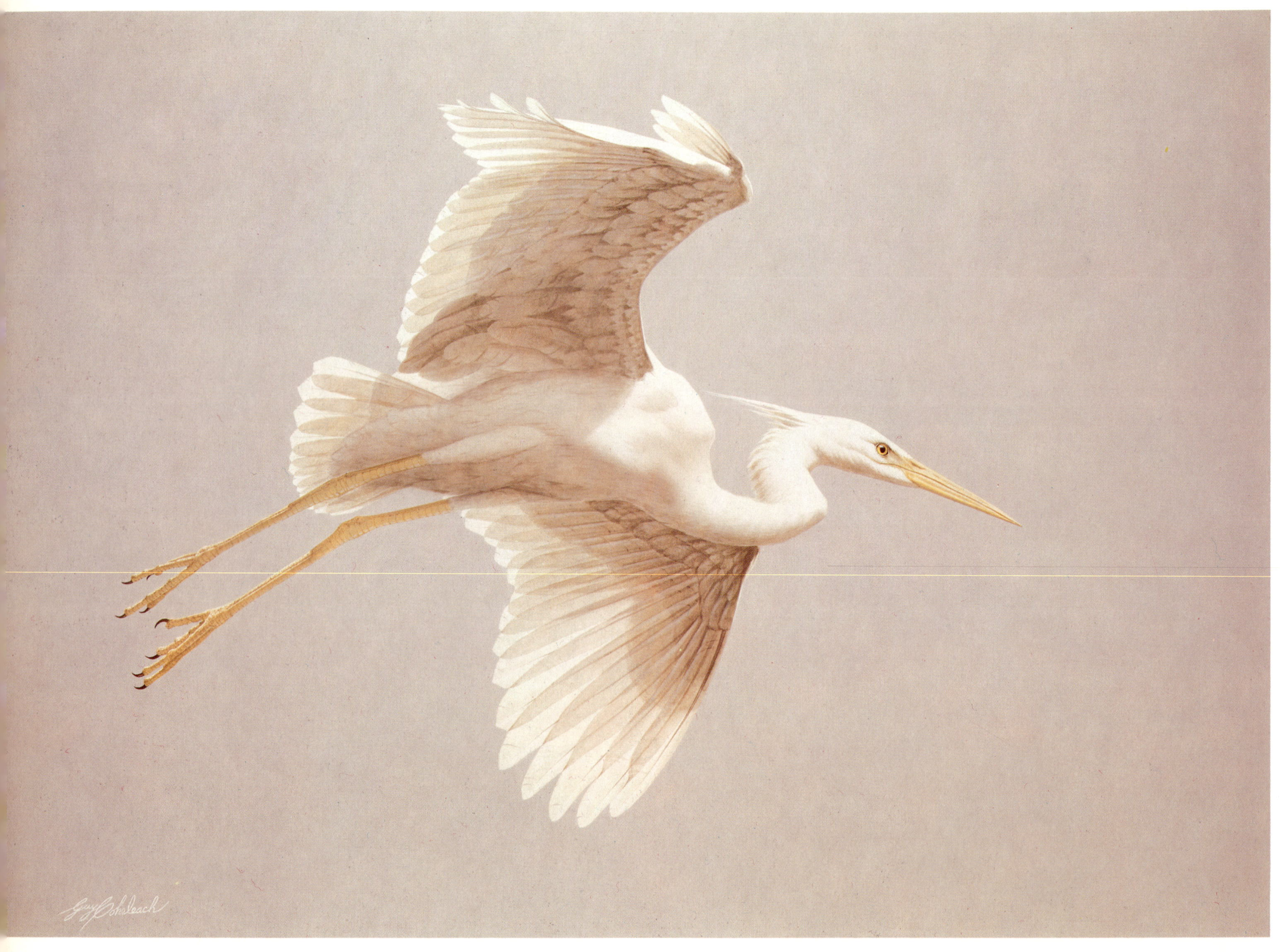

Now on the letterhead of the Audubon Society, this was painted in 1966 and was among a truckload of paintings hijacked in 1969; it was never recovered.

I particularly like painting herons and egrets in flight because it gives you a chance to play with their translucent feathers.

As always, Coheleach strives to portray the essence of the creature, in this case, the sinister look to a bird which, while stately and beautiful in flight, is one of the most ruthless killers in the animal kingdom.

Great White Heron, 40 X 30, Gouache on Illustration Board

Here is yet another painting earmarked for charity, in this case an auction for a local arts council in Florida. Coheleach set the mood with his choice of color for the watery background.

The pelican heads are a warm, yellowish white. The complementary color of yellow is purple, so to get the effect I wanted, I needed to make the water purple—and that is why there are all the pinks and lavenders. The somewhat jazzy mood is exactly the opposite of Snowy Egrets (page 175), where I was looking for a very subdued effect.

Brown Pelicans, 6 X 18, Oil on Illustration Board

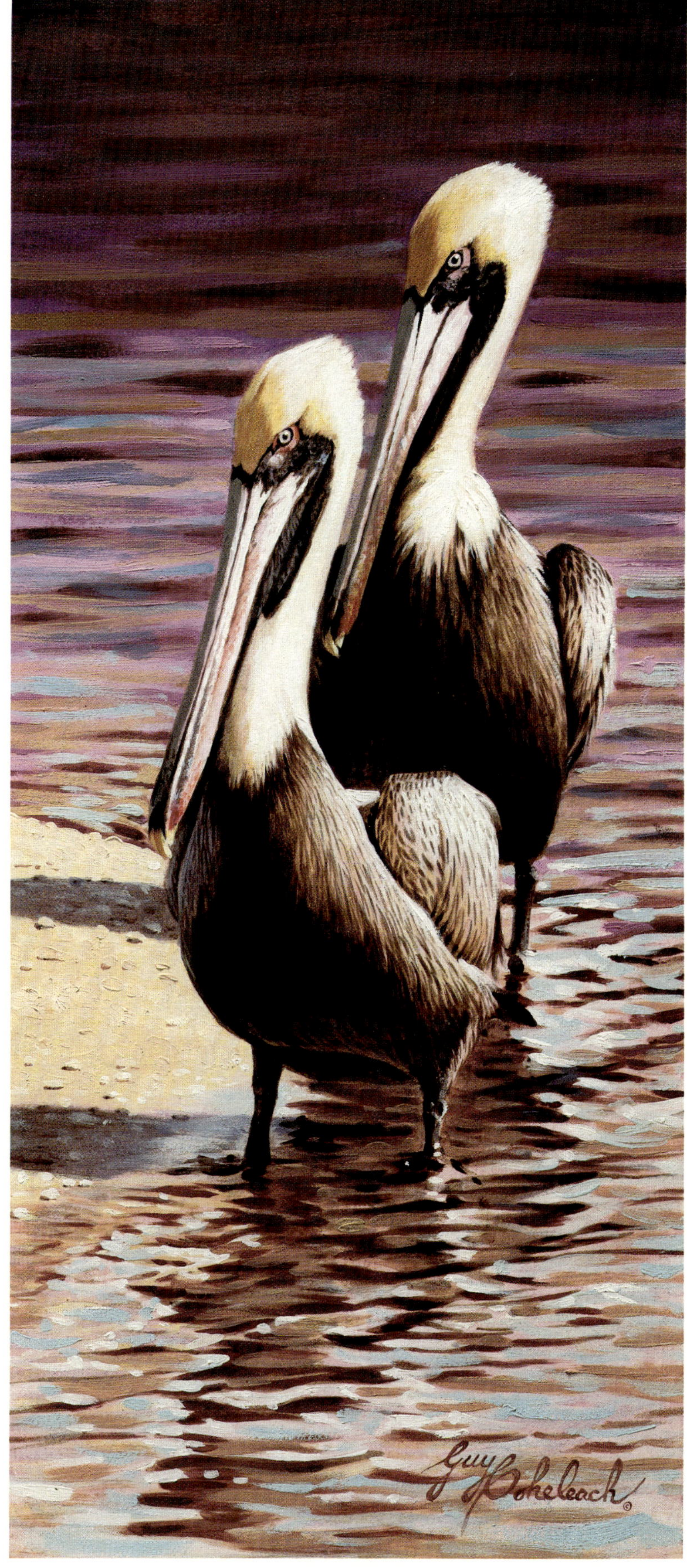

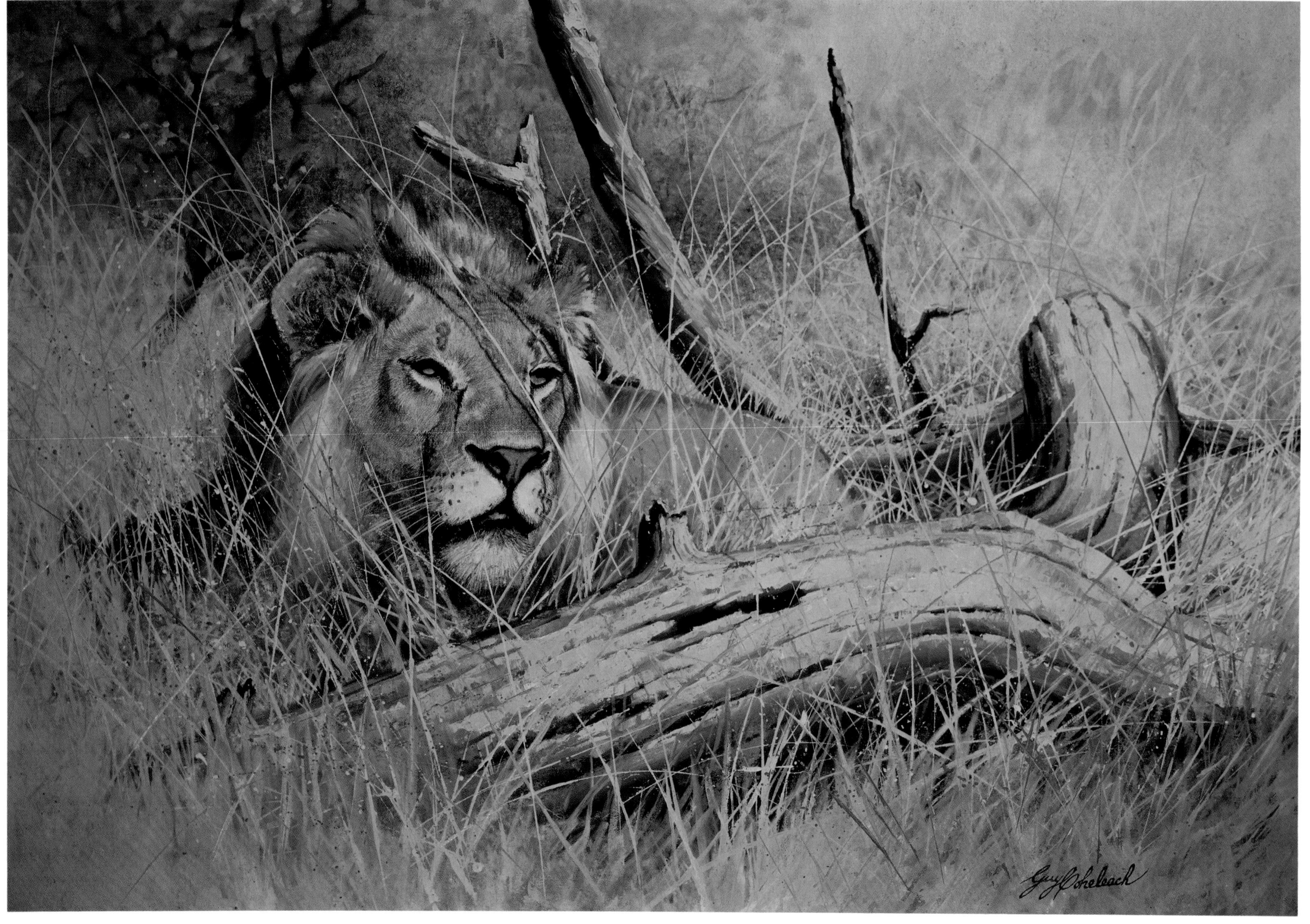
Guy Coheleach

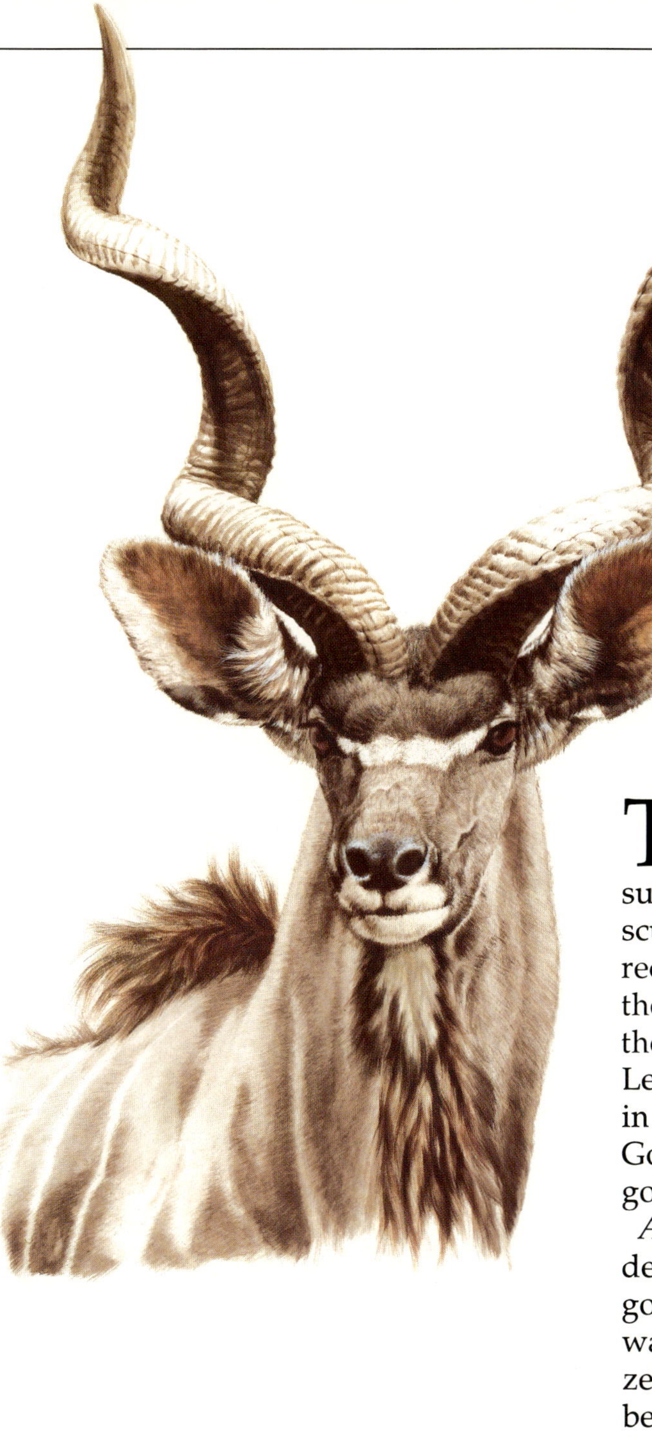

The lordly African lion has been the subject of painting and sculpture throughout recorded history from the Egyptian sphinx in the shape of lions to C.S. Lewis's children stories in which the Son of God is a lion with a golden mane.

Amboseli Ambush depicts a handsome, golden-maned male waiting to attack a zebra or wildebeest being pushed his way by other lions. Despite his king of beasts title, the male African lion spends most of his time eating, resting, and sleeping. He is somewhat slower and less agile than the female, which does nearly all the hunting for the pride. In fact, the big, conspicuous male may hinder a hunt simply because he is more easily noticed by prey animals.

Amboseli Ambush, 44 x 32, Oil on Canvas

Greater Kudu, 22 x 30, Gouache on Illustration Board

(overleaf)

A large painting in every way, with a great deal of texture and, most of all, a great deal of frantic action, *Attorneys and Bankers* was painted just after a period of legal turmoil in Coheleach's life.

Africa is a tough place. Even the king of beasts has to worry about the hyenas, and the hyenas worry about each other. The vultures want to get in on the action after the lions, but ahead of the hyenas and jackals because they can't fend them off. And, they have to compete with each other.

I grew up in a large family, and I got my hand slapped if I reached for something ahead of somebody else, before it was passed to me. I learned very quickly, since I sat next to my father's right hand. Vultures do not have that problem; if they are to survive, they have to get as much food as they can as fast as they can, between the time the lion leaves and the scavengers arrive.

The vulture's head and neck are very snakelike; devoid of hair and feathers, they are easy to clean after a typically rowdy and frenetic meal.

Attorneys and Bankers, 72 X 36, Oil on Canvas

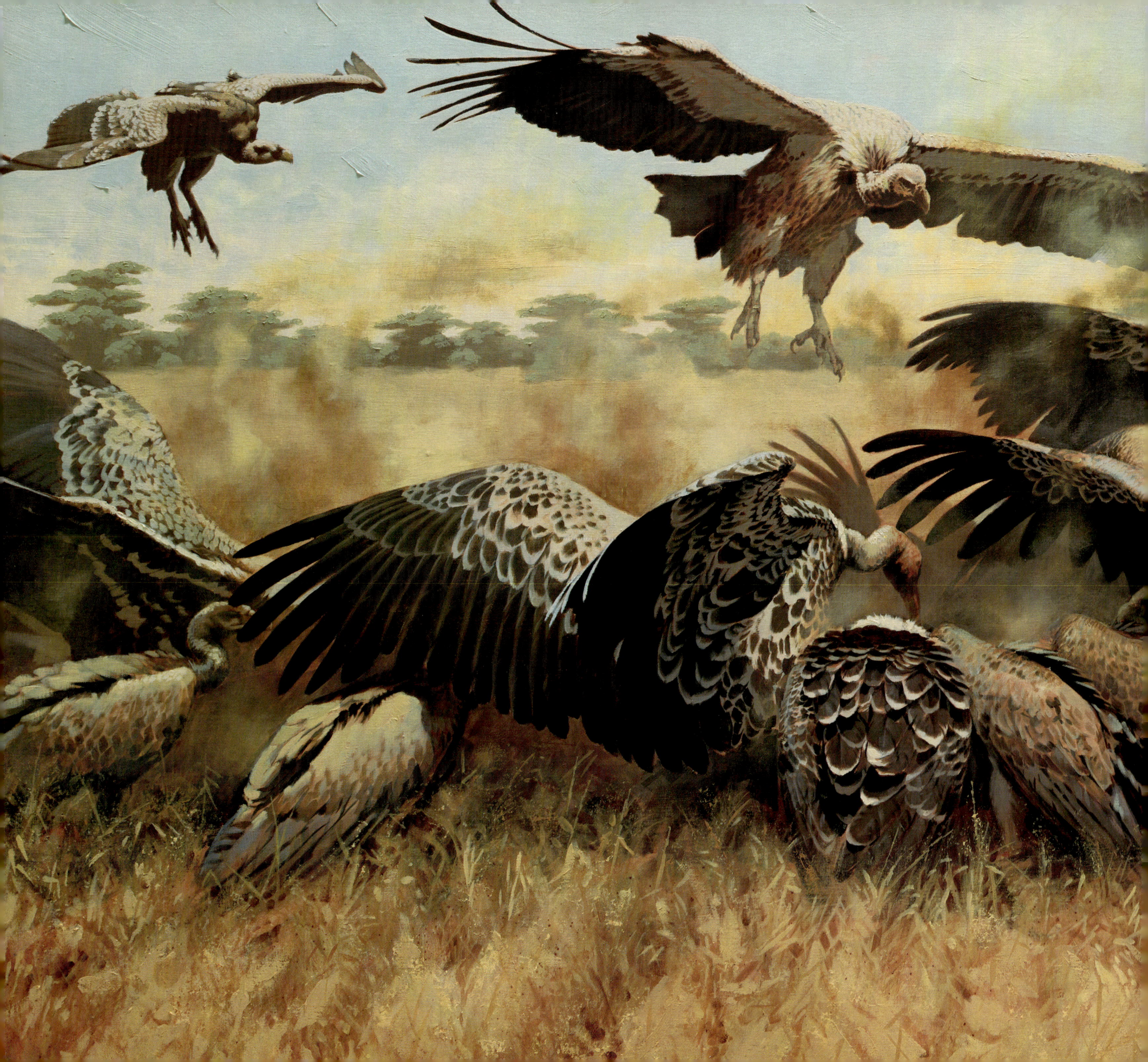

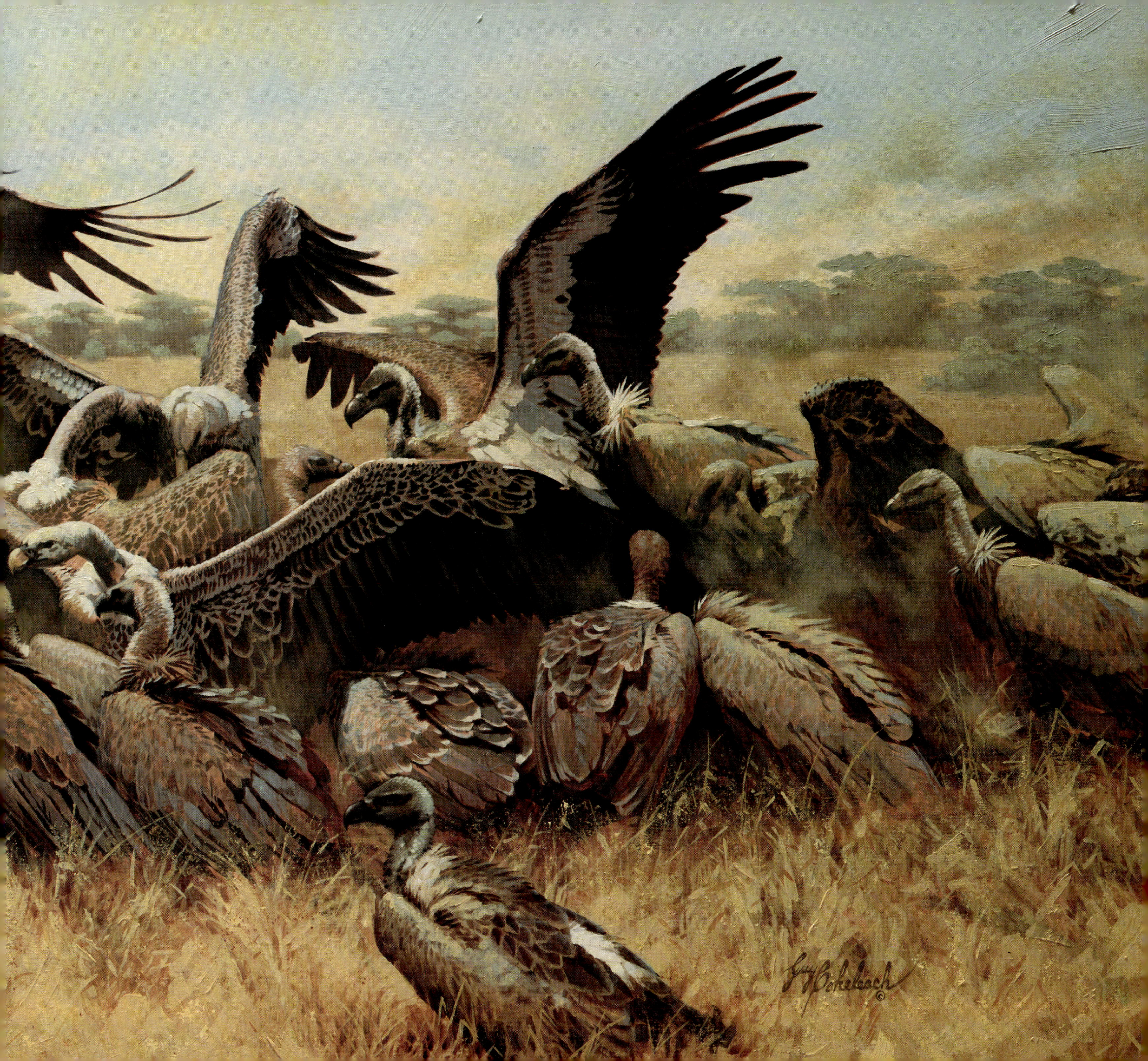

Paintings of wild animals can range from detailed portraits to broad impressions with bold, almost gloppy brushstrokes that create a particular mood or atmosphere.

In *Haree Moment*, Coheleach depicts a golden eagle swooping down on a snowshoe hare. The eagle's wingtips and the hare's bounding form are a blur of motion. To heighten the drama, he detailed the raptor's fierce expression and outstretched talons.

The painting works because of its breathless spontaneity—it's like the viewer has just rounded a woodland trail to see the life and death drama unfold.

Haree Moment, 72 X 36, Oil on Canvas

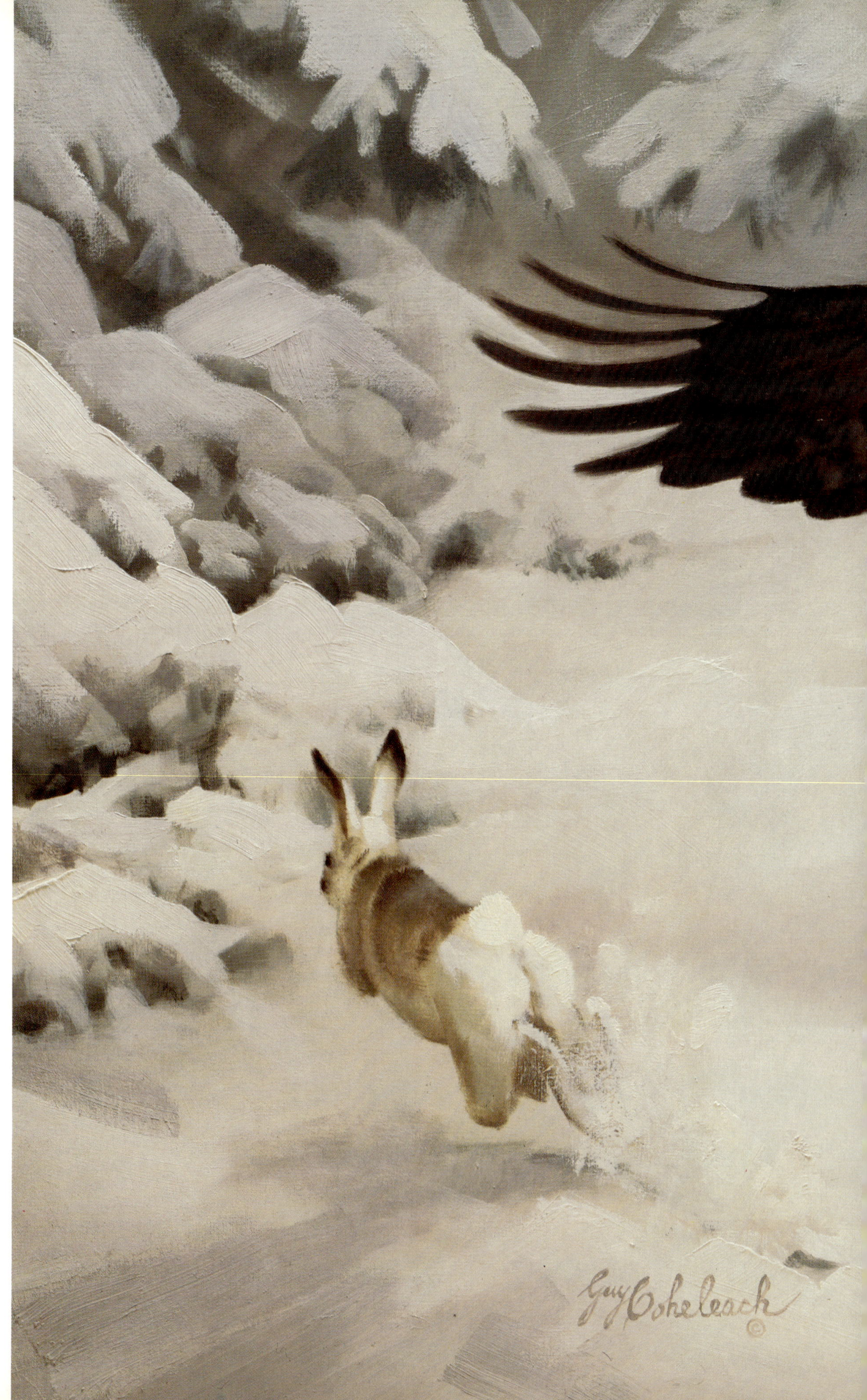

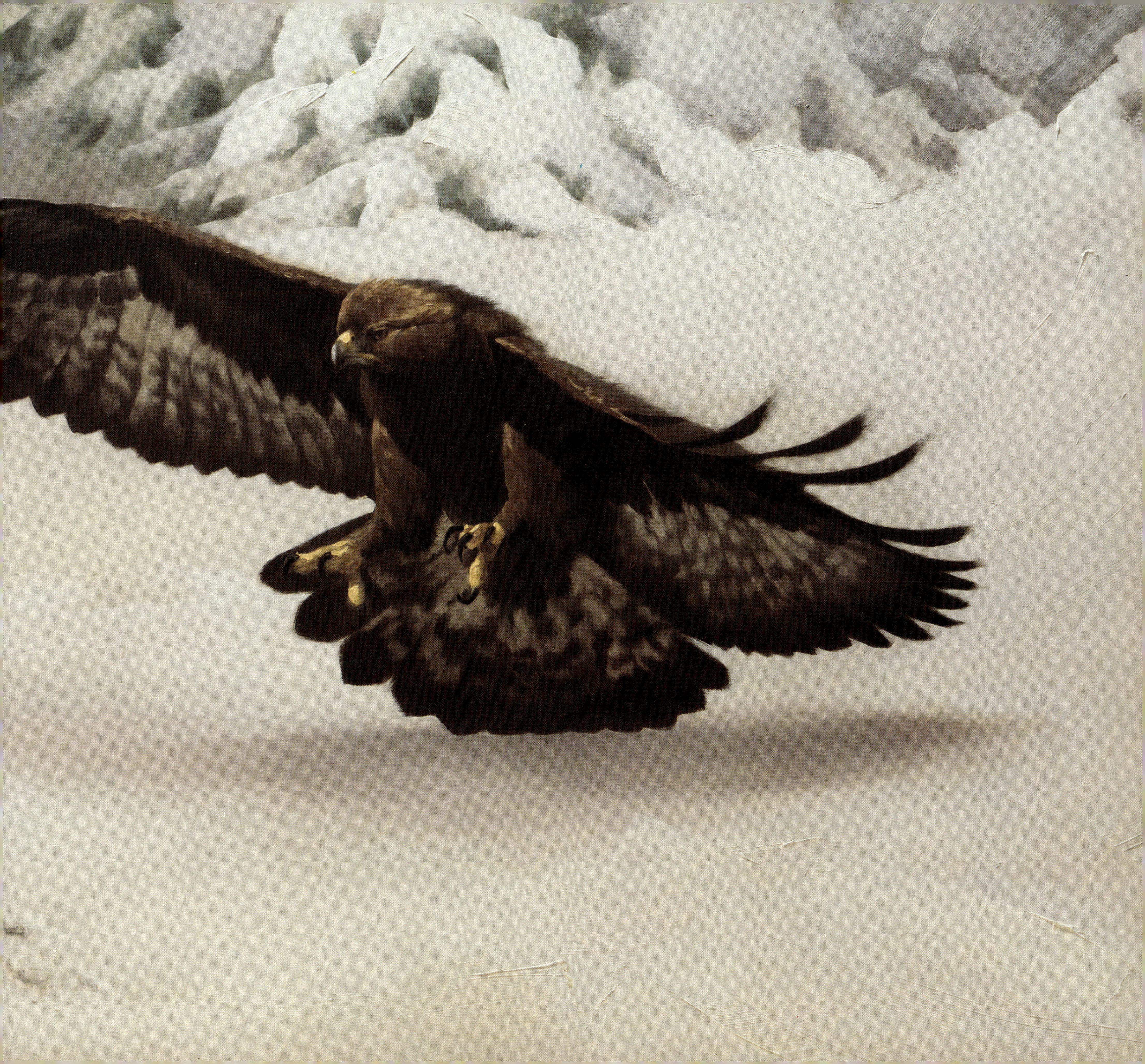

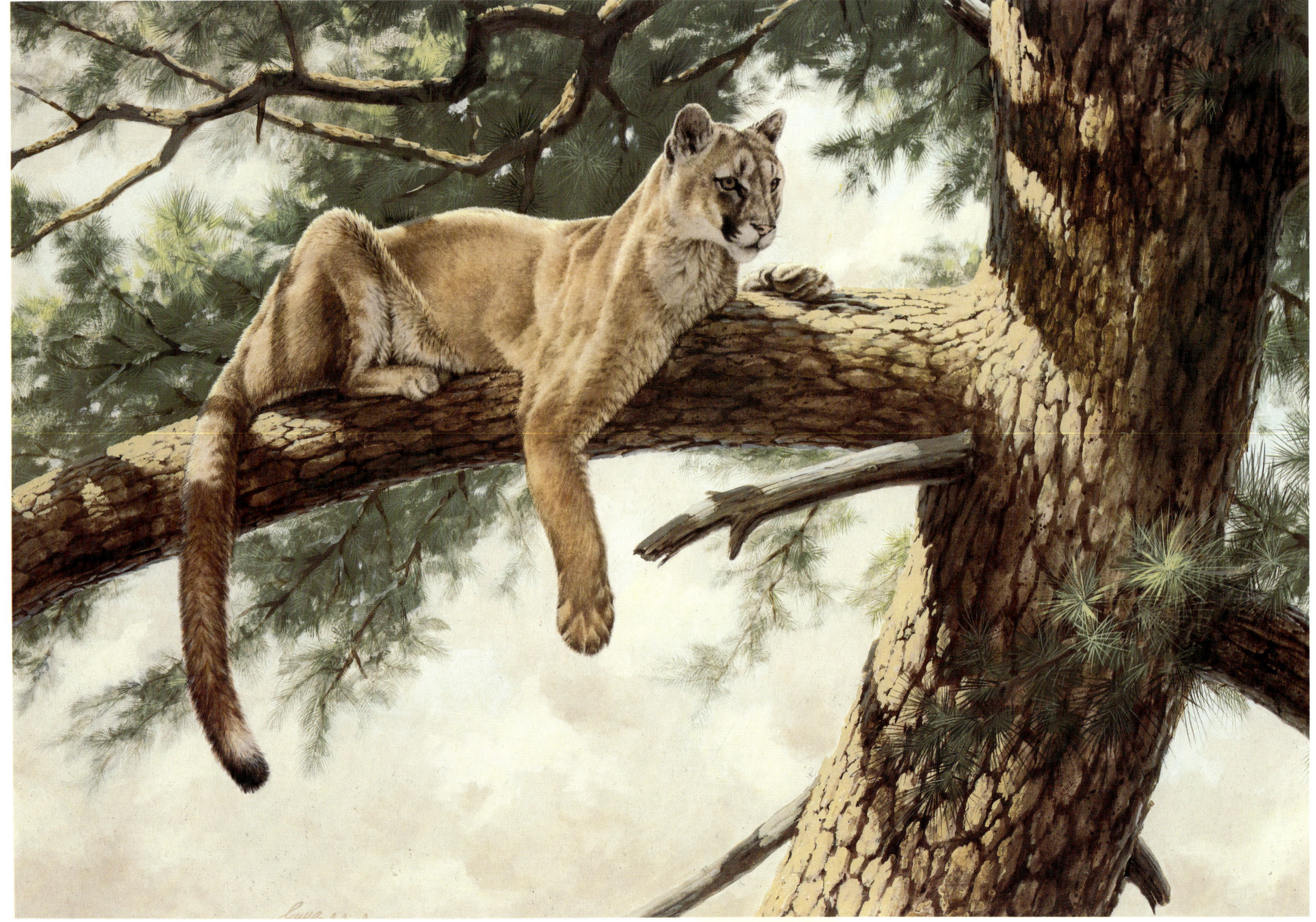

The owner of *Rocky Mountain Lion* is in the lumber business; after buying the painting, he told Coheleach "I just love that Ponderosa pine."

Coheleach accepted the compliment.

The comment points up the importance of correct foliage and background in detailed paintings. To ensure that the vegetation is accurate in every way—for the climate, the region, the season, and the animal—Coheleach takes dozens of photographs of the animal's habitat. He is especially thorough in areas where he has not spent much time.

When I was in Malaysia, for instance, I tried to photograph as much as I could and find out as much as I could about trees that leopards favor, and where they might be found. I have learned the hard way that if you make the slightest error, at least one bona fide expert will see the painting and notice the mistake immediately. It sure keeps you honest.

Rocky Mountain Lion, 40 X 30, Gouache on Illustration Board

This is a case where I experimented with underpainting; specifically, a base coat of orange wash. You can see part of it coming through in the shadow by the puma's chest, and in his face where I put white, yellow ochre and blue over the orange to bring it down.

When you paint, you will sometimes have bare canvas showing through. If it is just white canvas, it looks dull. If you have a color showing through, it can provide an exciting vibration.

Baby Puma, 18 X 14, Oil on Canvas

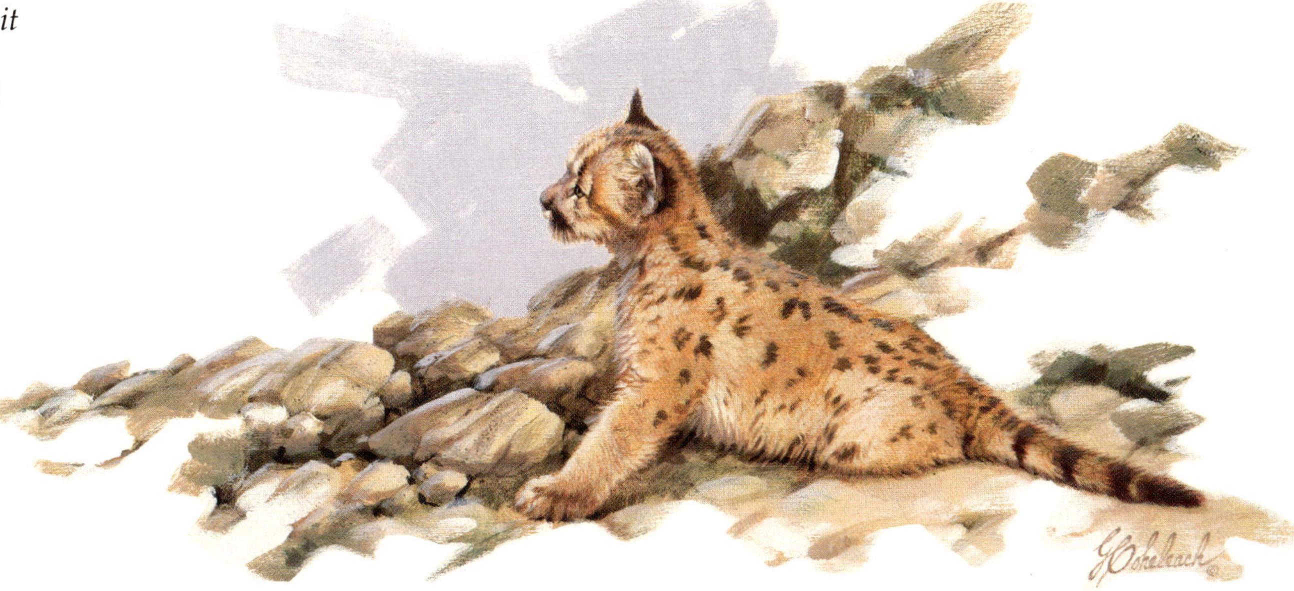

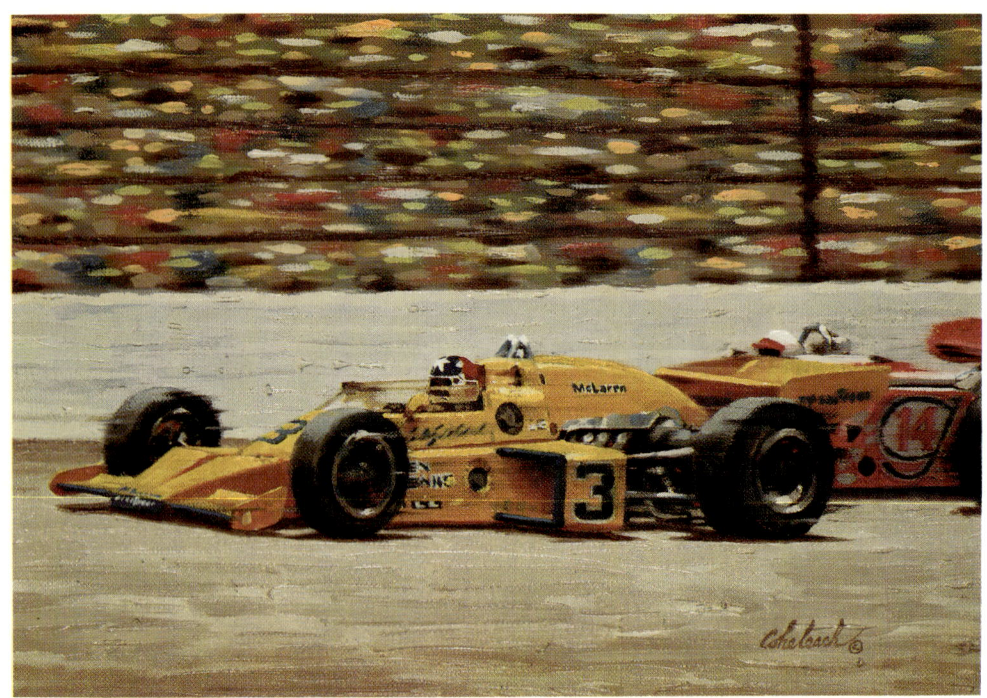

This painting of Johnny Rutherford passing A. J. Foyt in the Indianapolis 500 was done in the early 1980s. Coheleach once raced open-cockpit cars and remains an auto-racing enthusiast to this day. He painted the picture for a friend who owns Rutherford's car No. 3.

Race Car, 12 X 9, Oil on Illustration Board

Like the race car painting, this shows another dimension of the action work that I enjoy, other than wildlife subjects.

Most wildlife artists say they are uncomfortable painting people, and Coheleach is no exception. When he needs a break from wildlife, he usually turns to not-so-wild life, such as racehorses and racecars. The jockeys and drivers are merely adjuncts.

Horse Race, 24 X 12, Oil on Canvas

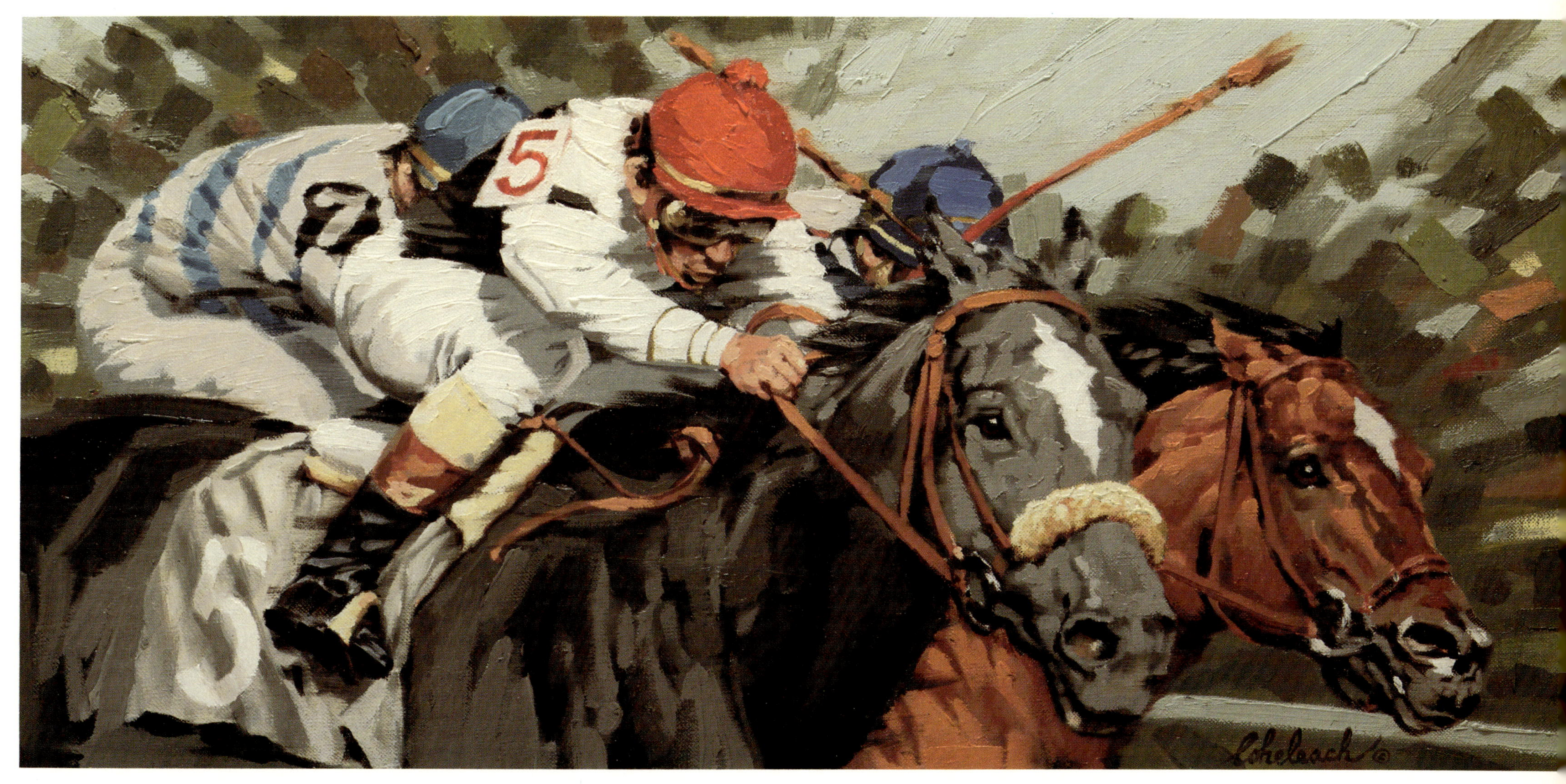

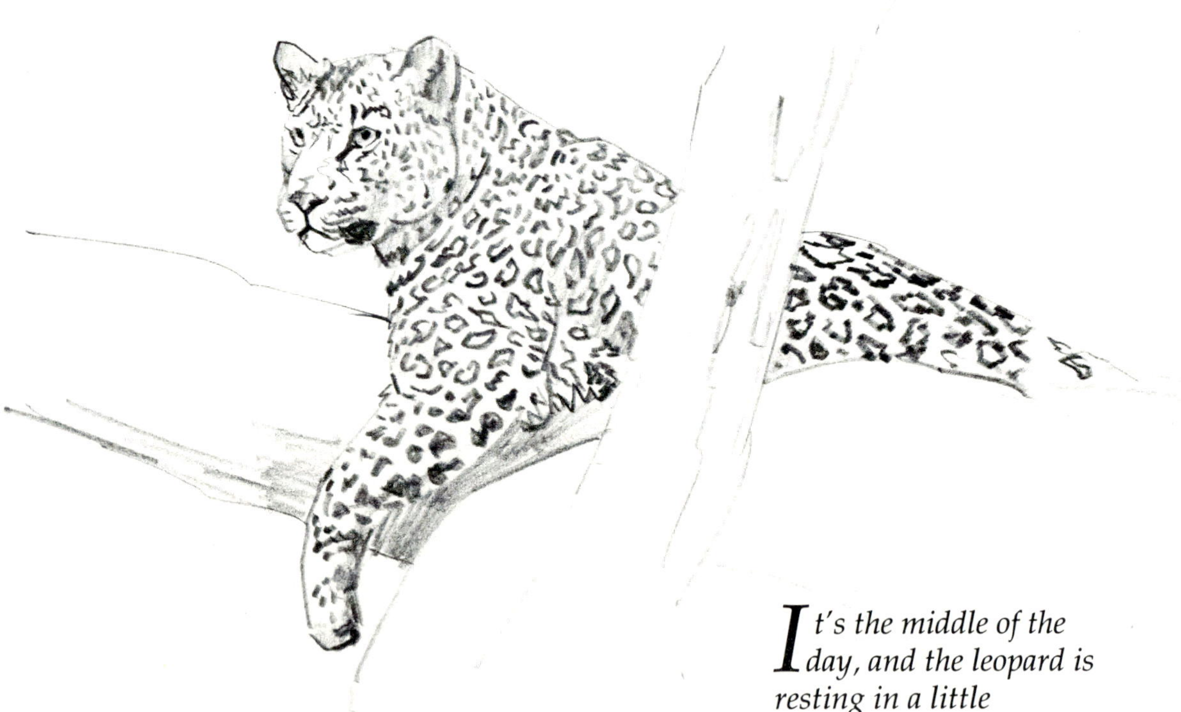

It's the middle of the day, and the leopard is resting in a little cubbyhole of rocks and brush. Something has gotten his attention and he's looking down the hill. Is that a baboon? Is that lunch? Is that a threat, or a meal, or an opportunity? Or should I just go back to sleep?

Coheleach has captured that indefinable quality that lives in every cat, from tabbies to tigers: a sleepy, bored curiosity that masks the alertness and the ability to spring from sleep to violent action in a whisker, and go back to sleep just as quickly.

Leopard's Lair, 44 X 24, Oil on Canvas

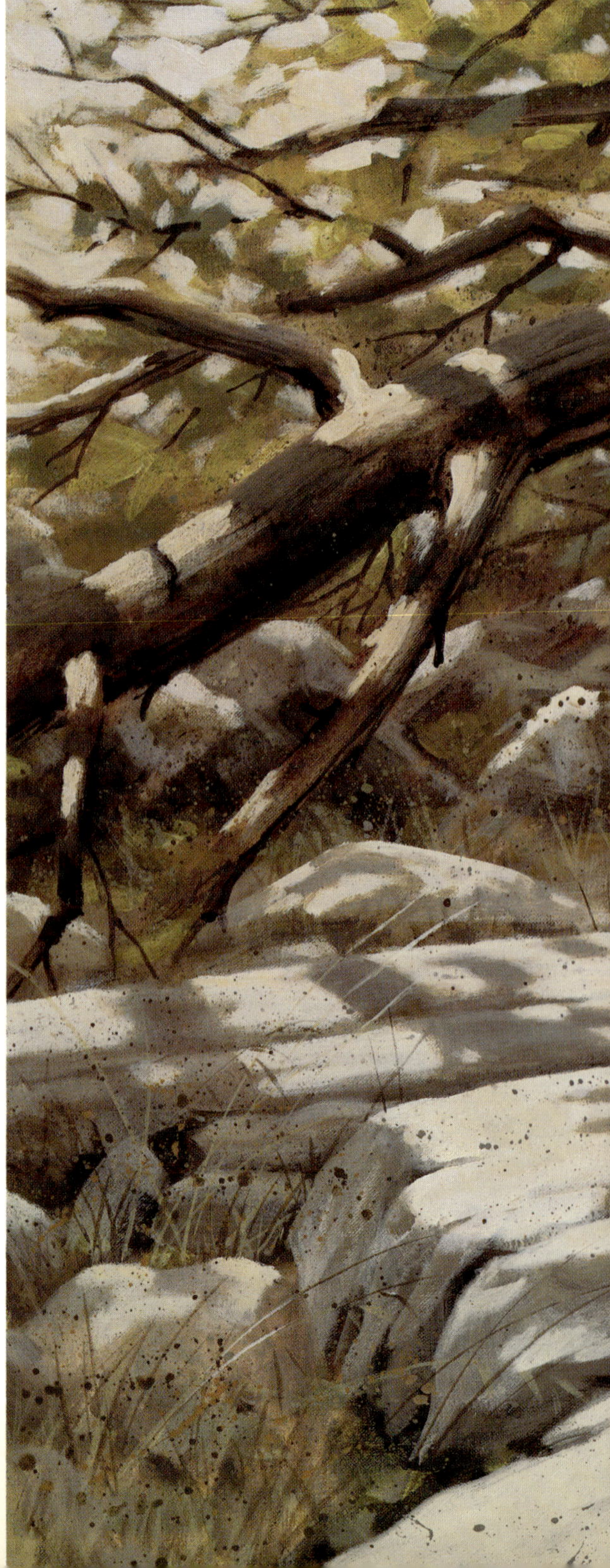

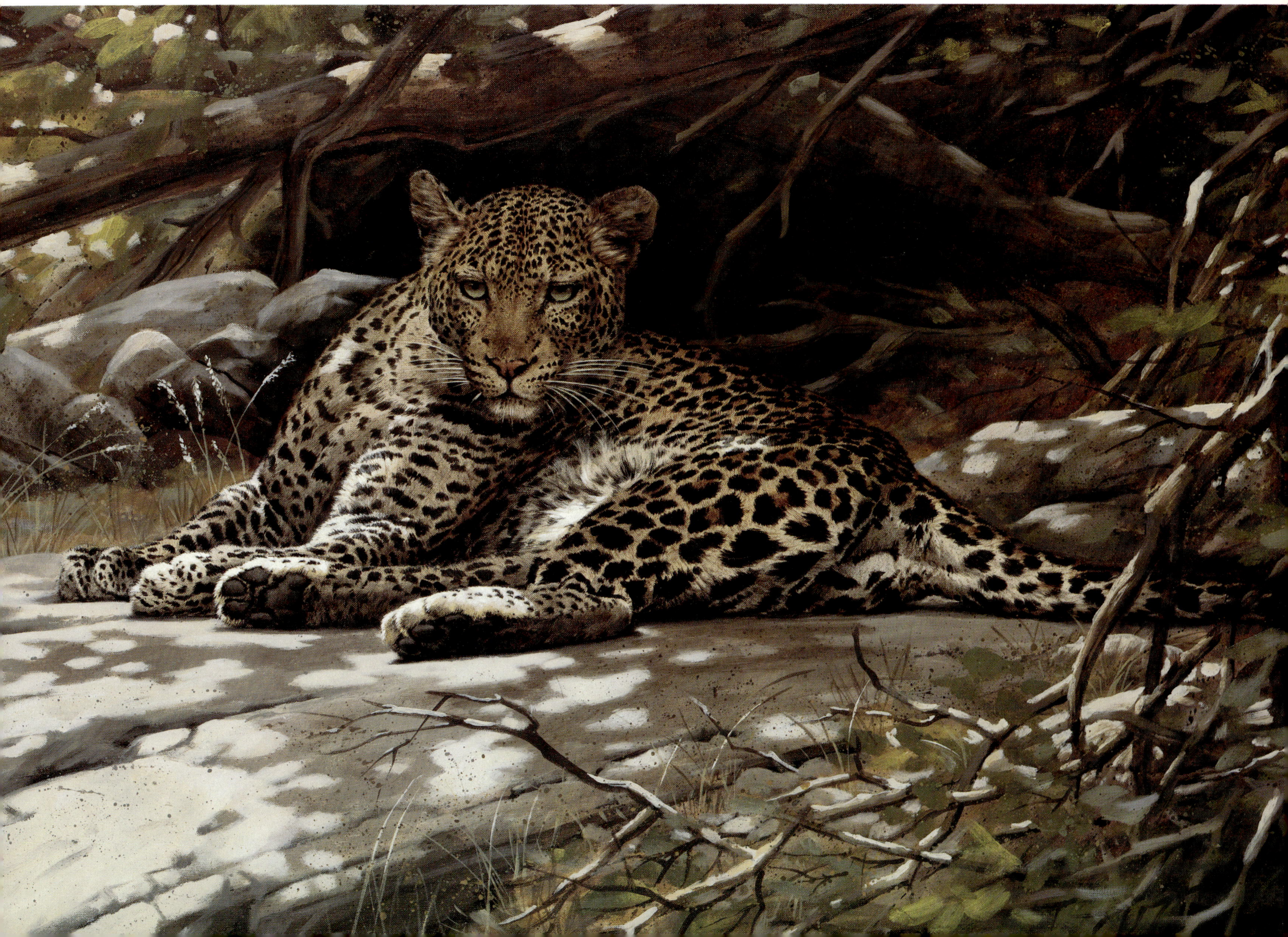

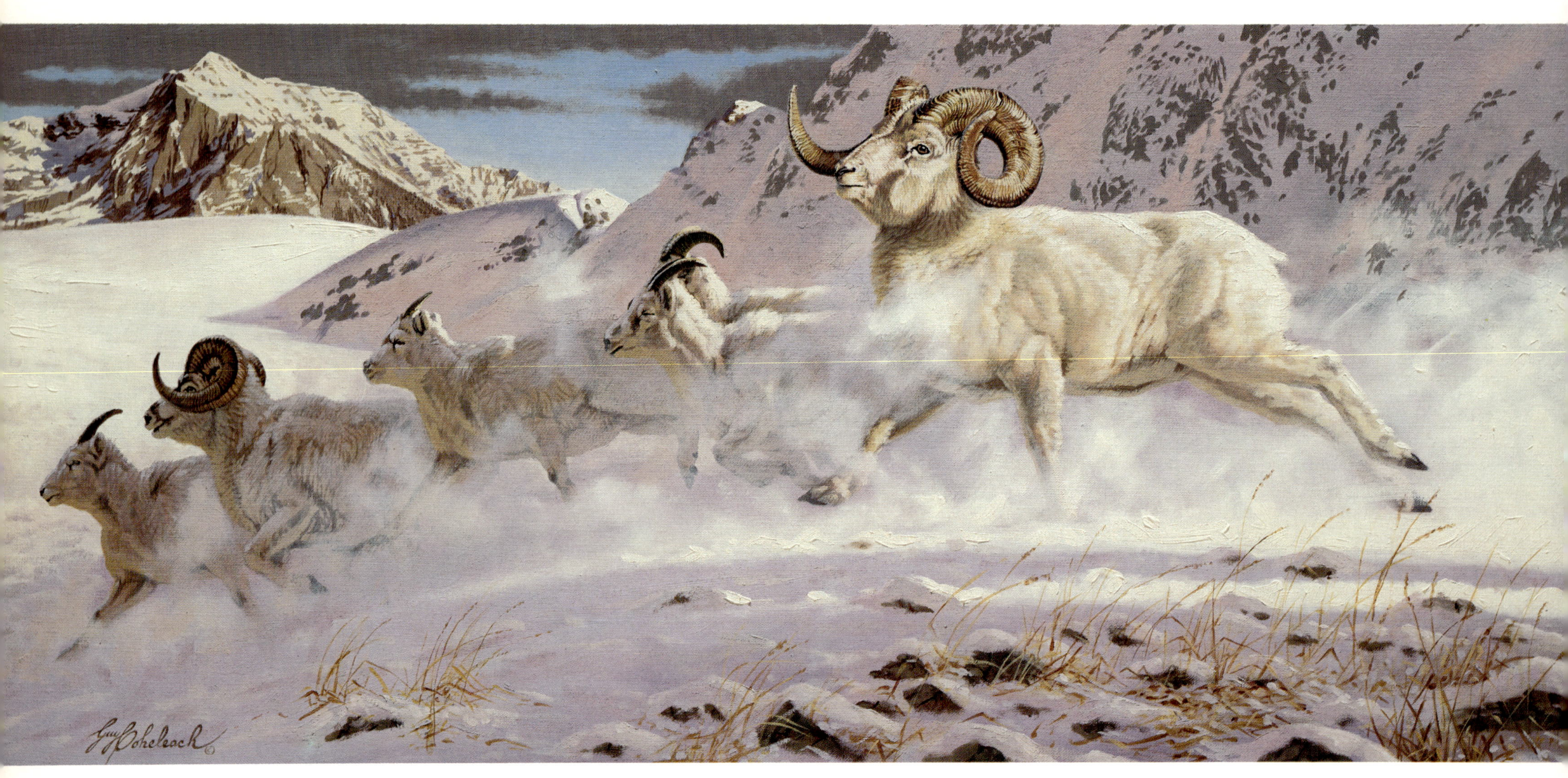

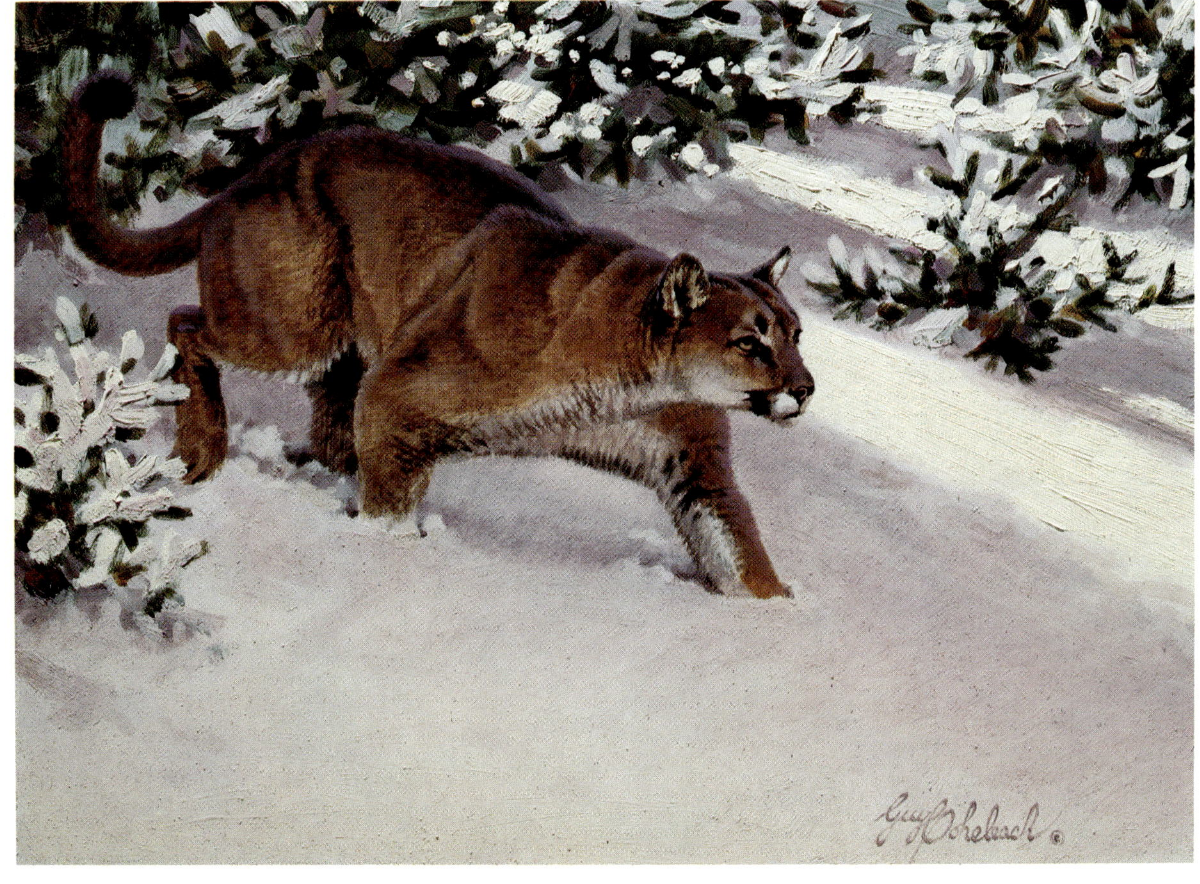

Long shadows at dawn and dusk enable the artist to create a stronger design. The key elements are more sharply defined and therefore, more dramatic. Conveying a feeling of motion can also make a painting more dramatic; in this case the snow kicked up by the racing sheep imparts a sense of motion and speed.

I have been to Denali National Park in Alaska, where if you move quietly, slowly, you can walk within several feet of wild Dall sheep. But sheep that are outside park boundaries are another creature altogether. I know hunters that have pursued them for weeks at a time without getting close enough for a shot.

Through The Pass—Dall Sheep, 36 X 18, Oil on Canvas

According to Coheleach, painting miniatures helps the artist on two fronts: simplicity and spontaneity.

You have to keep small paintings simple; if you make them too complicated, they become 'doodly.' But no matter what size you're working on, you should always strive to simplify.

Doing a miniature is like working on a big painting with a six-inch brush; it forces you to be more spontaneous, to paint the form and design first. This is another good thing about miniatures; you learn to interpret shapes.

Cougar, 10 x 8, Oil on Illustration Board

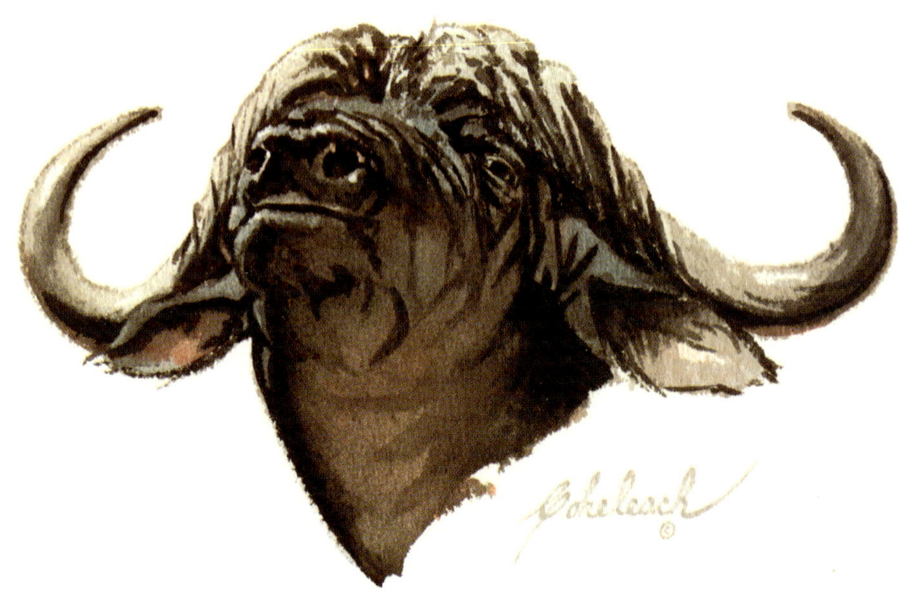

This is a very painterly painting—the grass is done simply, the elephant is very elephantine...

But like all good paintings, it tells a story—in this case, the story of the elephant's role in the overall African cycle of life. The pods of the sausage tree are a favorite food of elephants. They eat the pods, then pass the seeds in their feces, often many miles away. The result, in a few years, is another sausage tree, another elephant feeding station.

Elephant and Sausage Tree, 30 X 40, Acrylic on Canvas

Cape Buffalo Bull, 10 X 8, Watercolor on Paper

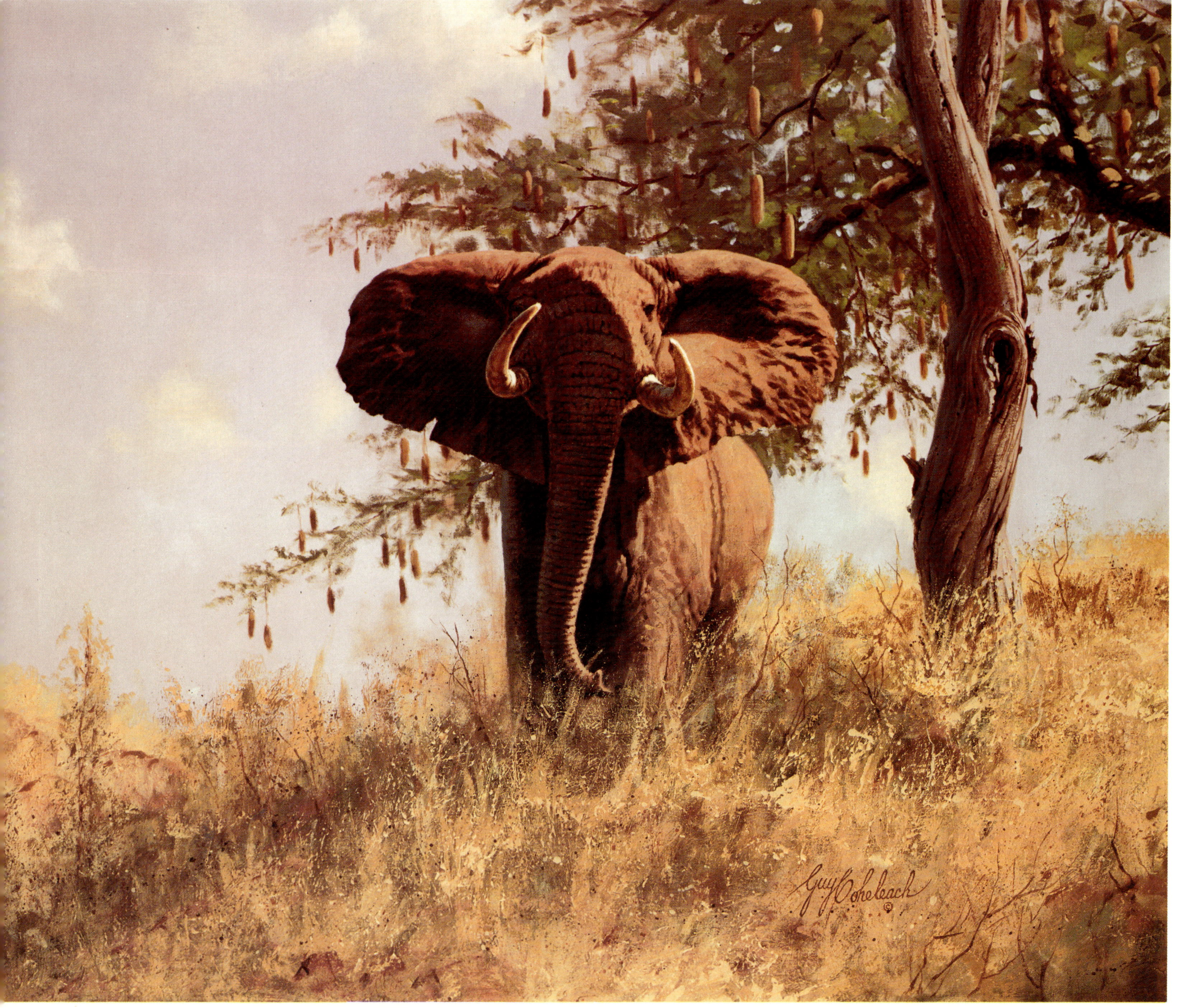
Guy Coheleach

Coheleach traces his career as a wildlife artist to an early and intense fascination with studying and drawing birds-of-prey. Consequently, *Peregrines' Return* was a source of particular satisfaction. It was painted in 1978 to commemorate the successful breeding of peregrines in captivity at Cornell University, an essential first step in the reintroduction of the endangered species.

There's a wonderful ending to this story. On my way out to Long Island recently, I saw two immature peregrines as I drove over the Throgg's Neck Bridge. I was told they were raised by young birds that were released years ago, so these were the grandchildren of the original peregrines raised in captivity.

Peregrines' Return, 30 X 40, Oil on Canvas

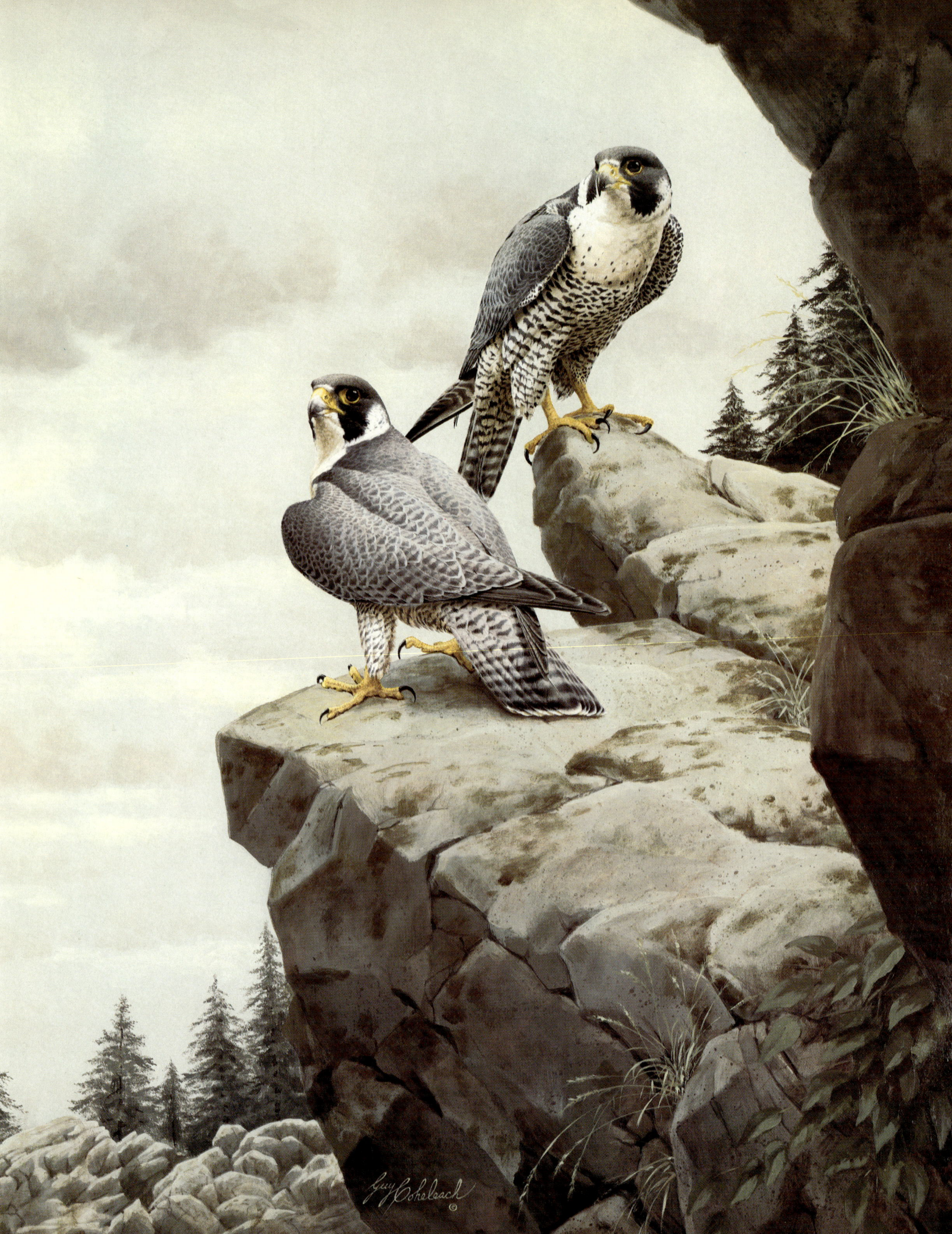

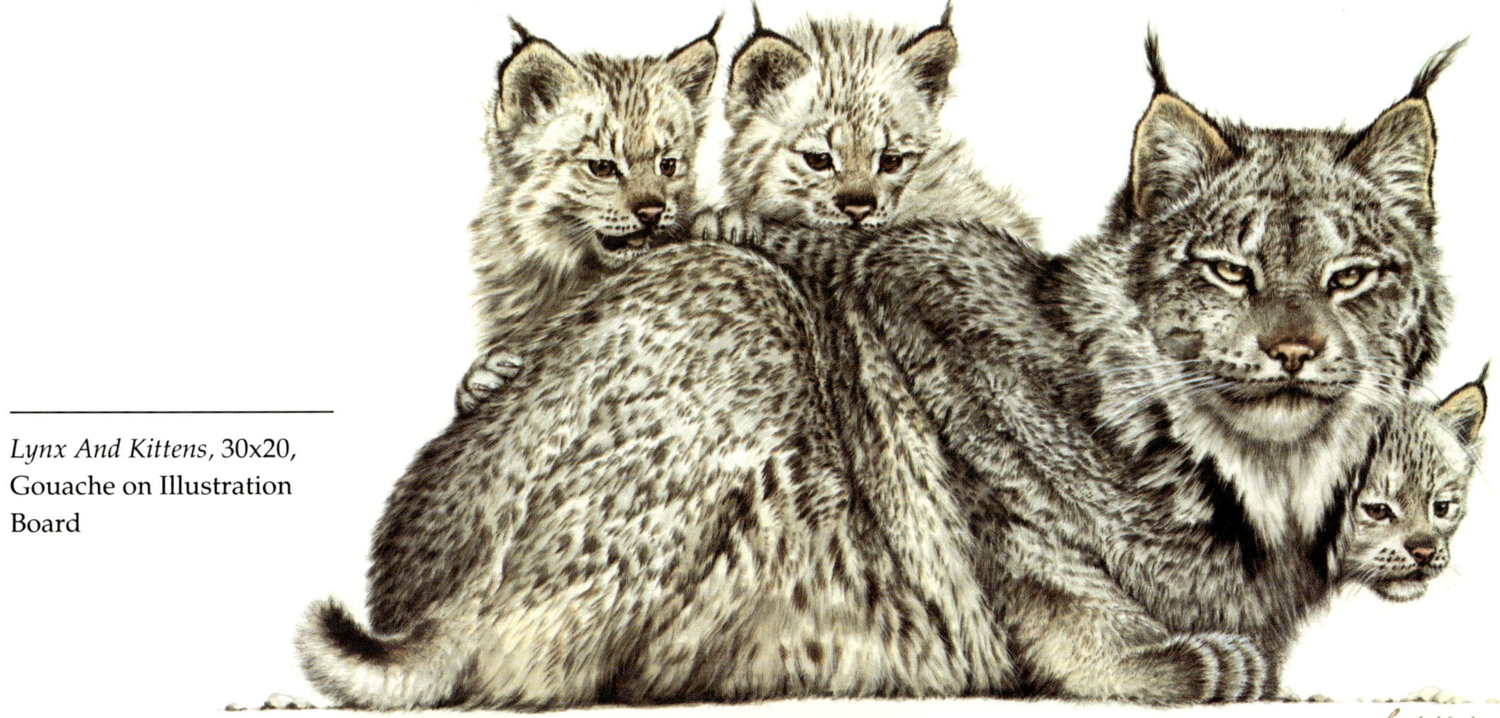

Lynx And Kittens, 30x20, Gouache on Illustration Board

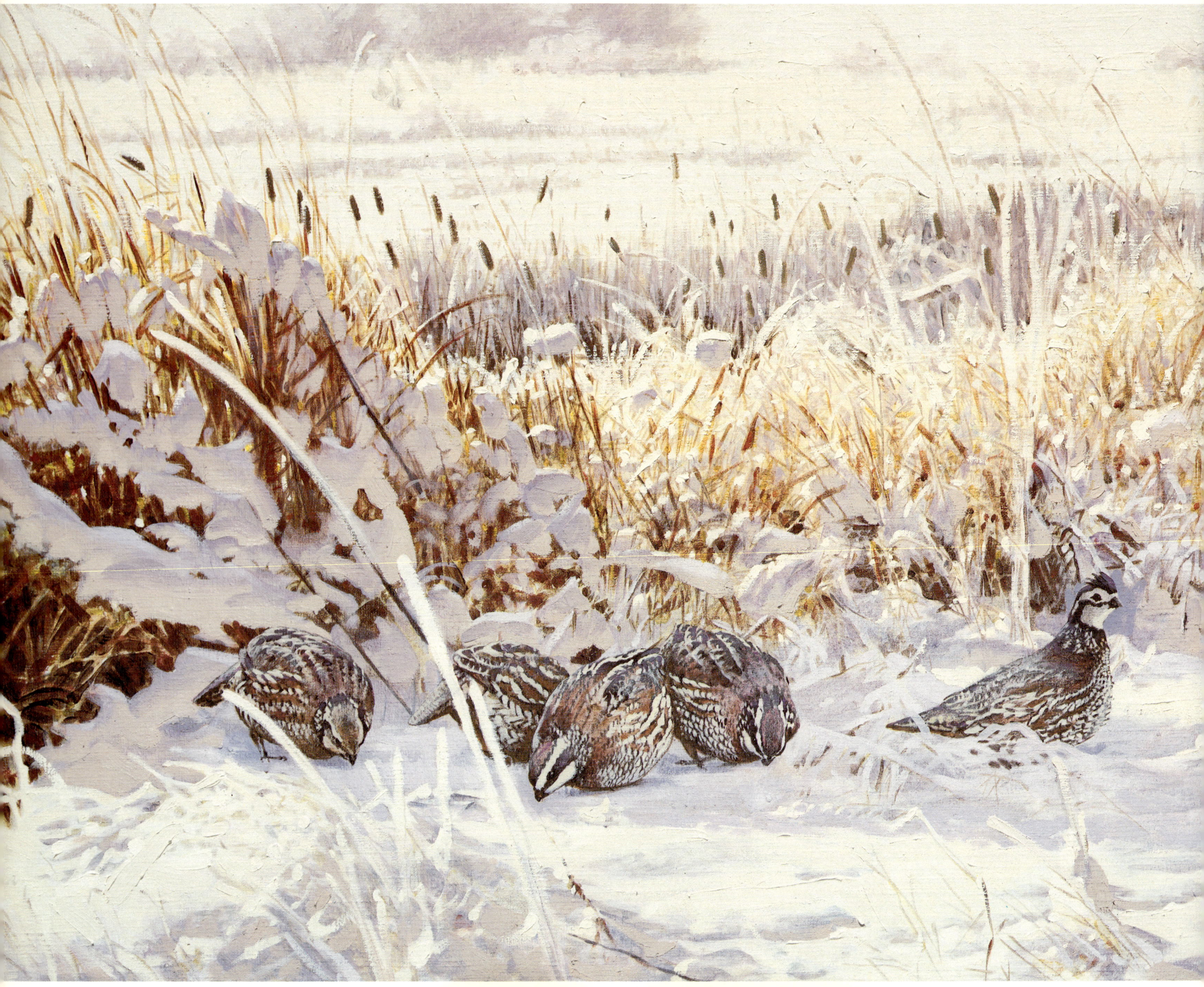

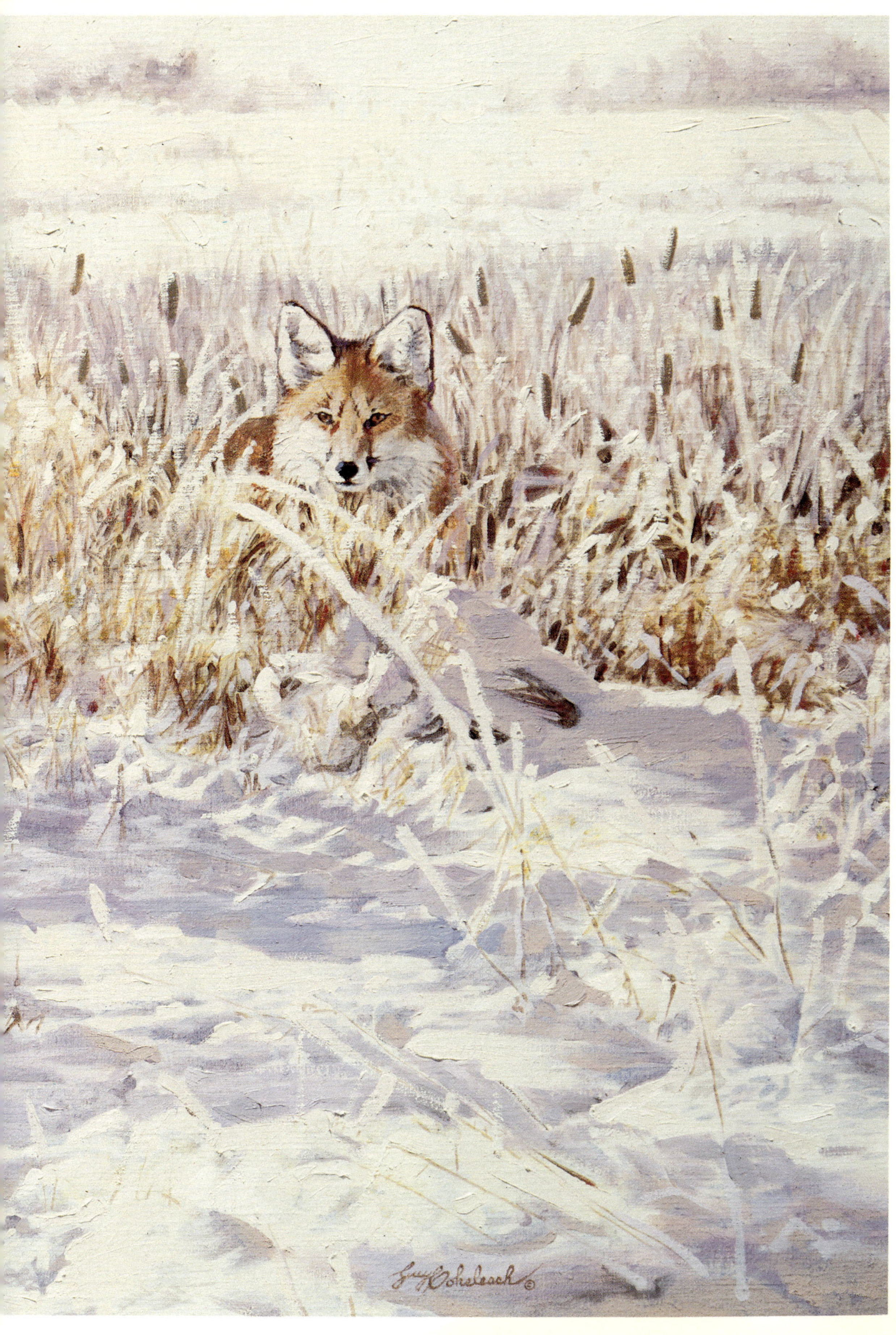

I was inspired to do this painting by tracks in the snow. I was on one of my jaunts near home when I came across some quail tracks. Before long, they were joined by the prints of a red fox and suddenly the quail tracks disappeared.

As in real life, I expect the fox in my painting won't get anywhere near these wary birds.

Red Encounter, 44 X 24, Oil on Canvas

*R*uffed Grouse in Winter* is a study in contrasting textures: hard bark, granular snow, soft plumage. The startling contrasts exist, not because the artist consciously included them to make the painting work; the painting works because the contrasts were already there, in nature.

I did not come up with the idea; I let the idea use me. These are intrinsic features of the scene itself, transferred through me onto the canvas.

This painting was done for the Michigan United Conservation Clubs to raise funds for the members' wildlife conservation efforts.

I have hunted grouse in Michigan—I shot at them, more than shot them. They give me a heart attack. I swear, if I'm going to die, it will be from the explosive flush of a ruffed grouse.

Ruffed Grouse in Winter,
30 x 15, Oil on Masonite

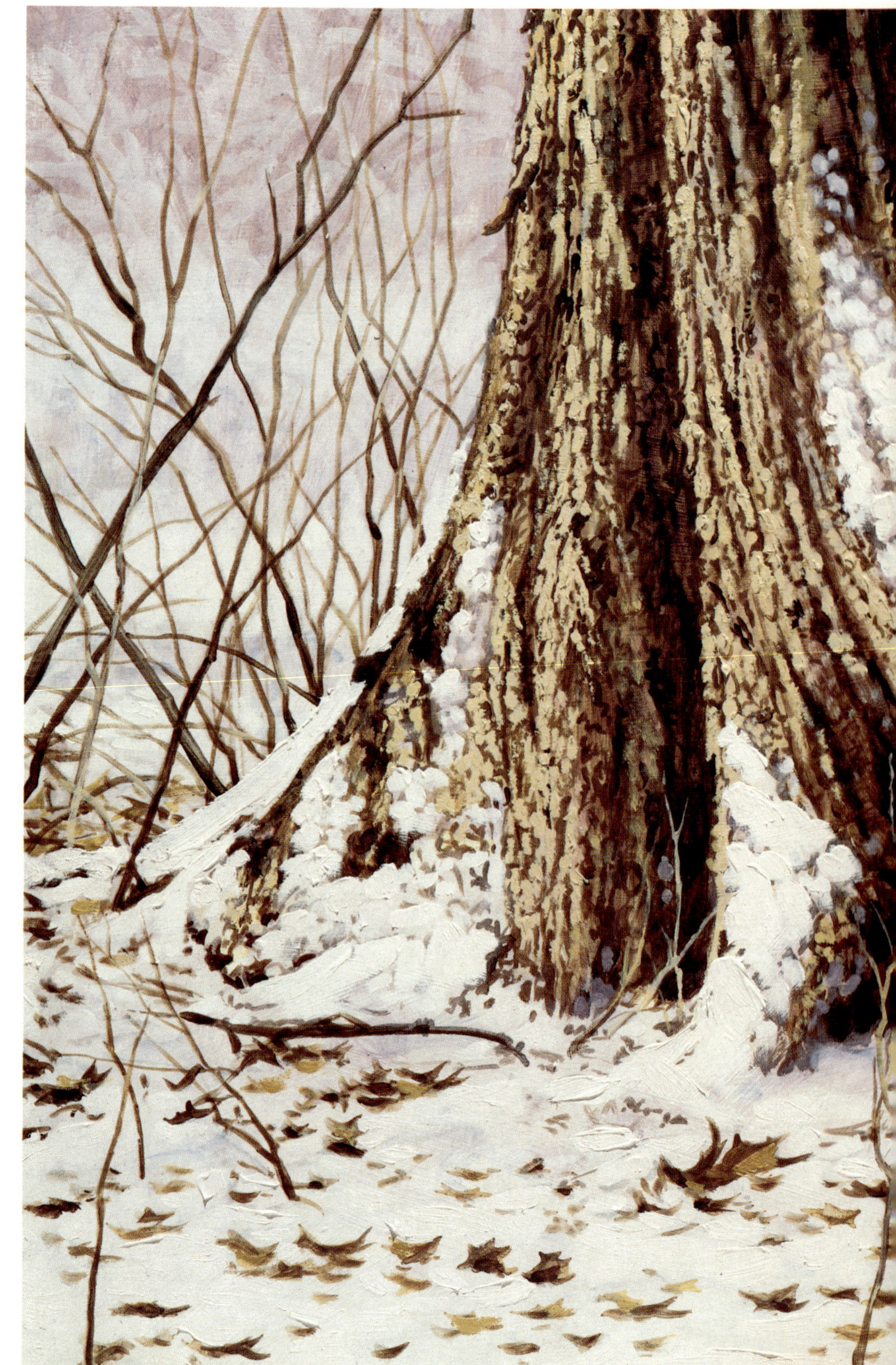

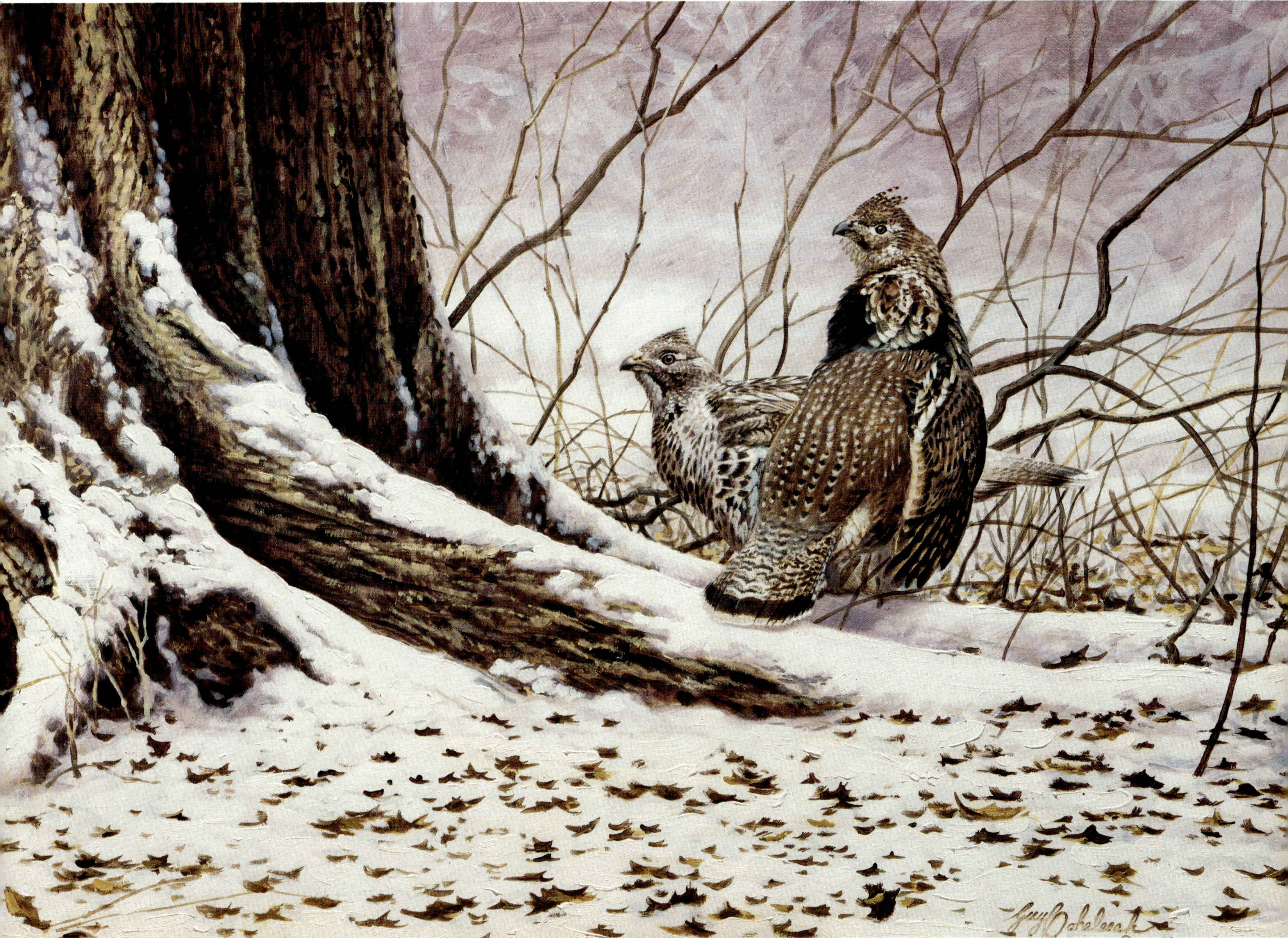

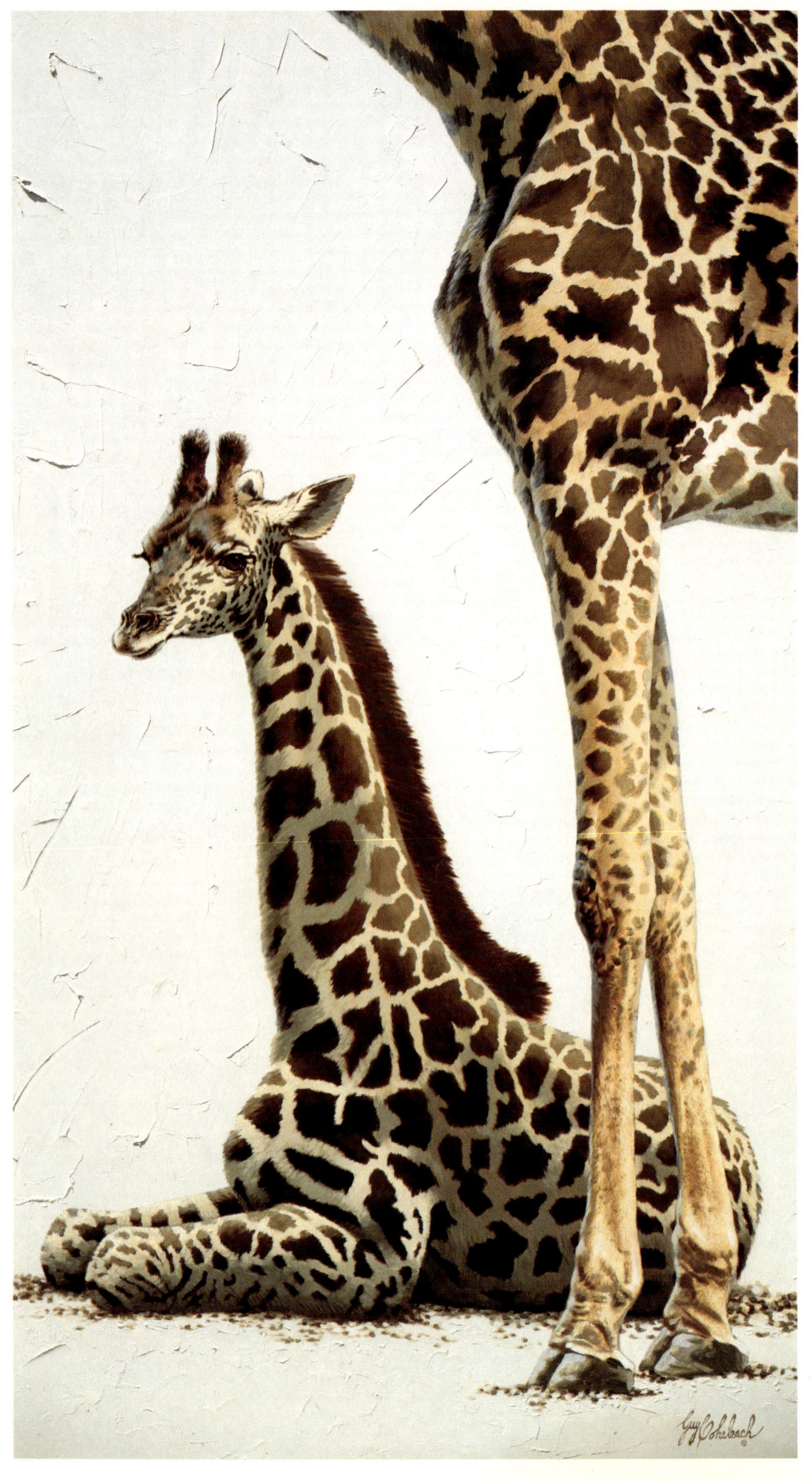

Working with a palette knife is a good way to show textures. It is the best way to show bright, clean colors. With a brush, you have hills and valleys; as a result, the highlights and shadows create a natural gray. Using a palette knife is a very arty method of painting, but it is difficult to create realism. It is like writing with your feet, with your shoe on; you don't have the necessary control over small areas.

This painting hangs in the stairway of the Giraffe Restaurant in New York City.

Giraffe, 36 X 72, Oil on Masonite

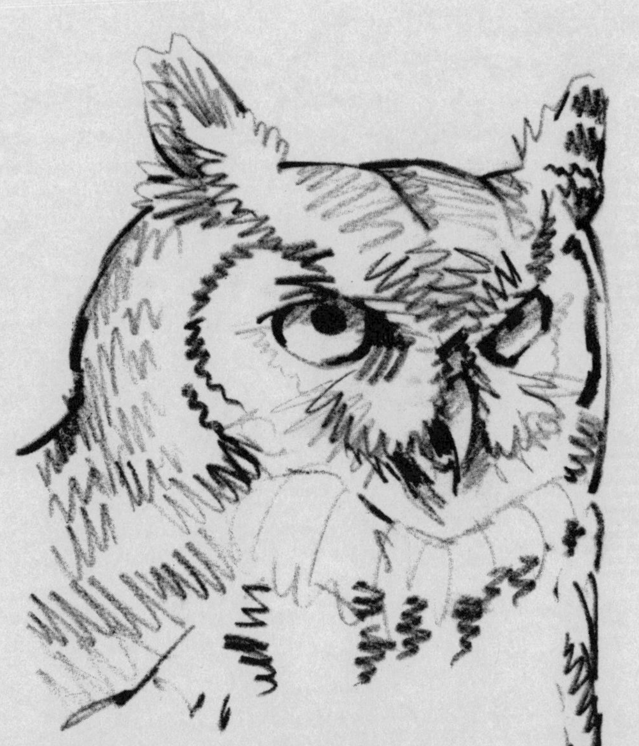

KNOWING THE DIFFERENCE

Guy Coheleach tells the story of painting a charging Cape buffalo. As he was adding the final touches, his house guest, Fred Bartlett, walked up behind him to watch. Bartlett is one of the best and most respected of the modern-day African professional hunters.

"He stood and watched as I finished touching up the eyes," Coheleach says, and he told me 'You just can't paint a Cape buffalo better than that.'

"When I get a compliment like that from him, and he's a man who knows, it doesn't matter that 99 percent of the people who don't know might prefer some other artist's Cape buffalo."

Coheleach estimates that fully one-third of his effort goes into making each painting "that extra one percent better." That's one-third of the painting time — it doesn't include his time spent in the bush seeing the animal firsthand so that he knows what that extra one percent is. A direct result of the Zambian elephant incident, this passion for ultimate detail, for the agonizing exact way it is, sets Coheleach apart from most other wildlife artists, and has made him an expert on the difference between animals in a zoo, and animals in the wild.

"Take a zoo elephant: you can see where they've rubbed, where they've gotten fat and paunchy, just like a zoo cat. Well, actually, it's a lot harder to tell the difference between a cat that's on a good diet and a wild cat, compared to a zoo elephant on a good diet and a wild elephant..."

(This is a degree of arcane discernment that is beyond most observers. In fact, it is beyond many wildlife artists. It is certainly beyond me.)

He continues: "It's like zoo deer, you know? They just lose their fear, they lose that tension in the eyes, they lose that life force; it's ... it's an electricity about them.

"You look into the eyes of a leopard in a zoo, and sure, you can get a lot out of them. But goddamn! You look into the eyes of a lion 30 feet away from you, and you're standing right in front of him, and you forgot your damned rifle .... lemme tell ya, they look a lot different. They do. Even with your rifle, whether you want to shoot or not, they look one hell of a lot different."

Knowing there is a difference, knowing exactly what that difference is, and knowing how to paint that difference: three tough steps, and Coheleach believes he has not completed them yet.

"My art is still very raw. I still don't know who the hell I am, style-wise. That's one reason I paint in so many different styles.

"When you look at all my stuff, you know, race cars, bottles of whiskey, roast beef, golf courses, horse races, birds, snakes, lizards, whatever! Portraits! They run the gamut from as tight as a drum to looser than anybody around; some are almost unidentifiable. But as far as finding myself as an artist, I haven't done it yet. Don't know if I ever will..."

Guy Coheleach's artistic talent first surfaced about age ten, scratched, illicitly, onto the covers of school notebooks. He got into all

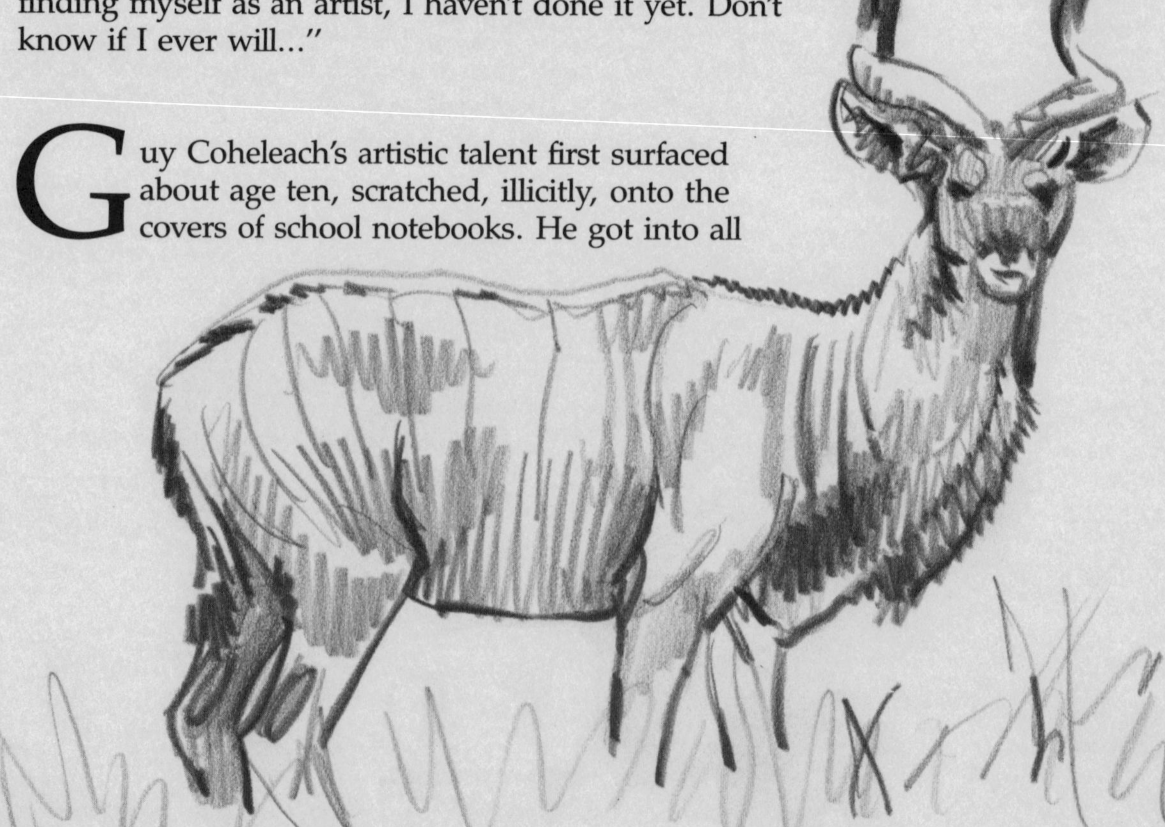

sorts of trouble for it, he says; the nuns did not approve of him defacing books — his or the school's. On the other hand, they recognized something beyond idle doodling and graffiti, and sent notes home with him "not so much to punish me, but just to let my parents know the talent was there.

"Apparently, they were pretty good," he says.

At Christmas time, Guy would get a drawing table, or an oil paint set.

"My parents never pushed it," he says, "But once they knew the talent was there and it was developing, they always encouraged it. And you know, one of nine kids and coming out the Depression, there wasn't a hell of a lot of money to throw around on stuff like that."

At Cooper Union, of course, he was confronted with the art styles of the early 1950s: New York avant garde, abstract — about as far away from wildlife realism as it is possible to get. Still, Coheleach tried it, and while it didn't take, it left him with one tangible: an eye and a feel for design, and an understanding of how important design is in a painting regardless of subject or style.

"I still do a bit of that, abstract ... not much since I left school, but some. I imagine I've tried just about every type of painting; representational, non-representational; you name it, I've done it."

And, usually, done it well.

In her book *Wildlife Painting Techniques of the Modern Masters*, Susan Rayfield uses Coheleach as an example of both how to render feather tracts of birds-of-prey with "meticulous realism," and how to use a "loose, impressionistic style" to suggest motion in a painting of a bird-of-prey attacking a rabbit.

Later in the same book, Rayfield calls upon Coheleach's expertise in "expressing motion with design." Finally, she uses a 1979 Coheleach vignette of three mallards on a white background, a painting of "extraordinary detail," as an illustration of how to capture the iridescence of feathers.

"Meticulous realism" and "loose impressionism;" conveying motion one moment through impressionism, the next through design; and being acknowledged as the master of all.

Coheleach tells a story of having ten of his paintings hanging in a gallery. Roger Tory Peterson, upon seeing the paintings and their widely differing styles, assumed they were painted by ten different artists.

"Roger was astonished to learn they'd all been painted by the same person."

Is this evidence of supreme versatility, a mastery of painting so great that it allows him to perform as a virtuoso in any style he chooses? Or is it evidence of a weakness — an inability to pick one style and make it his own, or to break away and do things that have never been done before?

To Coheleach, being new and different is not synonymous with being good, regardless of what the critics might think.

"Granted, they like innovation, or doing something new. If you do something that's been done, no matter how well you do it, they sniff and say, 'That's been done.'

"I could take a bag of garbage, put a canvas behind it, shoot through it, and have everything plastered all over the canvas, put a frame on it and say 'this is my explosive technique,' and some critic would be sure to say it's good.

"We go to gourmet restaurants because we want something done really well, done better than we can get anywhere else. We don't go there to eat gravel on a platter, and call it good because nobody's done it before. But that's basically what a lot of art critics try to shove down your throat."

As of right now, moving from detailed realism to loose impressionism and back again, Coheleach has not, as he puts it, "found my niche."

"Take Bob Kuhn and Robert Bateman: they are two super artists whose works are easily identifiable by their unique styles. An early Kuhn or an early Bateman is just as identifiable as their most recent work. It's a lot easier to recognize their styles than it is mine. Which is not to say that one is better than the other; just that we've developed differently."

Coheleach admires Picasso because he was a "great salesman who could paint ... an excellent example of somebody who came in and did something innovative, and was a great artist because he changed things."

The root of Coheleach's dissatisfaction with so much that is new — the grotesqueries of Van Gogh, Picasso, and occasionally El Greco, among the great artists of the past — is the deep belief that art should be aesthetically pleasing.

"You can have a poster that is not aesthetically pleasing, but has a message and has good design, and works. That's good functional art.

"Good fine art, to me, should be aesthetically pleasing."

Where does that leave *Guernica,* Picasso's acknowledged masterpiece?

"As a painting, I just don't care for it."

Coheleach reserves his greatest love for the impressionists: Monet, Manet, Renoir. And his favorite artist of all is the man who might best be described as the impressionist of wildlife art, Bruno Liljefors.

"Liljefors had more economy, and said more in his work ... and he just happened to choose Scandinavian wildlife, but oh God! When he did an eagle coming over, it was an eagle! You could tell those wings were made with a curve, and the air was sucking up the top of them and pushing up underneath them, and that was a great big heavy bird just floating down, coasting from the previous speed down, so he could pick off that rabbit...

"Or a peregrine! When he did a peregrine going through the marshes with the wind blowing and the leaves upside down so you see that silver part where the wind is blowing, you could feel the chill, the cold damp air!

"He was just marvelous.

"And you couldn't take one stroke of paint out of his

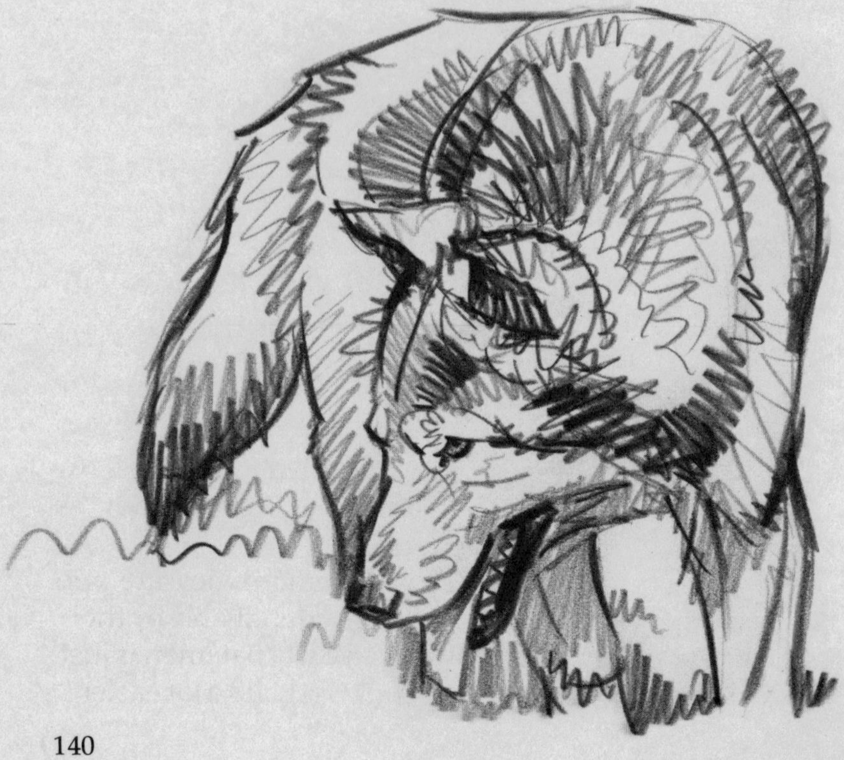

paintings without hurting the painting. And you couldn't make them a bit better by adding anything.

"To me, that's the way to go."

Coheleach also admires Carl Rungius and Wilhelm Kuhnert. Kuhnert particularly he accords the title of "all-time greatest painter of African lions," and a Kuhnert original hangs above the Coheleach fireplace.

There are those who would award that title to Coheleach, and their justification lies not just with his individual paintings of lions, leopards, tigers, and the other big cats, but with a major project which is unique in the history of wildlife art.

In 1982, Coheleach produced, in collaboration with Nancy A. Neff, a book called *The Big Cats: The Paintings of Guy Coheleach*.

More than just another coffee table compendium of pretty paintings, *The Big Cats* is a serious textbook on the large feline predators: lion, leopard, cheetah, tiger, snow leopard, clouded leopard, jaguar, and puma.

"I wanted to produce a serious academic work," Coheleach says. "I wanted it to be a textbook for scientists and students, as well as lovers of big cats and admirers of wildlife art. I wanted it to be a lasting tribute to the big cats."

As he tells it, he called up a friend at a major museum in New York and asked who was the resident expert on the big cats.

"He told me he had a gal working out in the back who knew more about the big cats than anybody."

The "gal" was Nancy A. Neff. She agreed to collaborate, on condition Coheleach did not refer to her as a "little gal" because it was not professional.

The book is a large format, 240-page volume with chapters covering every aspect of the natural history of big cats, from their evolution and place in the development of the order carnivora, to the biology of modern cats, to the genetics of cat coloration,

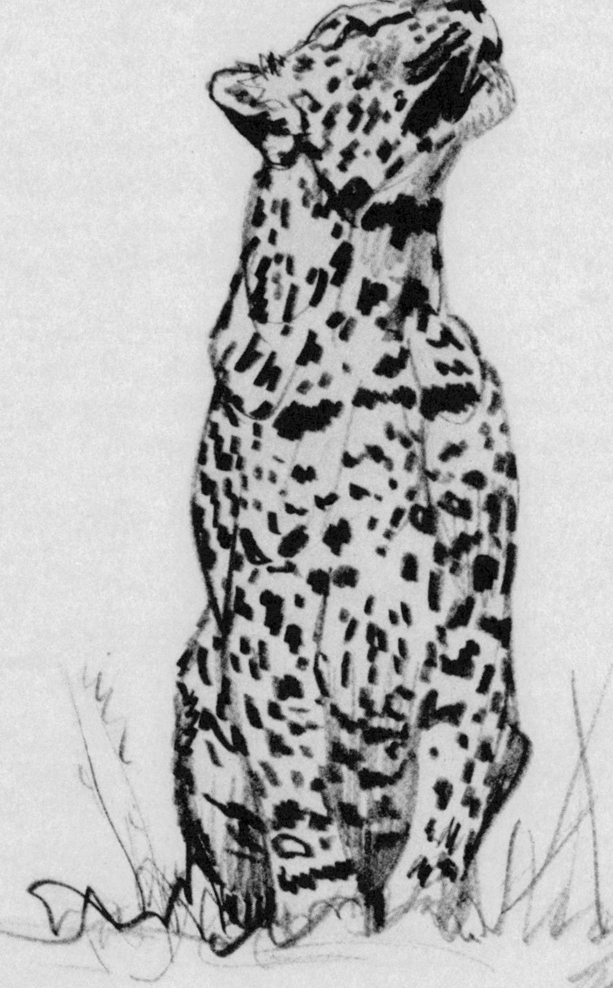

comparisons of cat's eyes with those of other meat-eaters, the mechanism of their retractable claws, and an explanation of why some purr and others roar.

The work is exhaustive. It was also exhausting. Everyone involved, Coheleach says — the author, the book designer, the specialists who prepared the intricate and detailed technical figure illustrations — put forth a superhuman effort.

It shows. The final product, when she saw it, brought tears to the eyes of Nancy A. Neff; it brought joy to the hearts of the publishers, Harry N. Abrams, Inc., and acclaim to everyone involved when it was made a Book-of-the-Month Club selection in 1982.

Coheleach's illustrations — 154 in all, including sketches, pencil drawings and 59 color plates — represent possibly the finest assembly of work on the big cats ever done.

Interestingly, it was about that time that Amwell Press decided to produce a five-volume series of anthologies on the African Big Five, and approached Guy Coheleach to illustrate the first two, *Hunting the African Buffalo* and *Hunting the African Elephant*.

Each contains five color plates and dozens of sketches and pencil drawings; as well, Coheleach contributed a chapter to each, drawing on his considerable expertise on Cape buffalo and elephant, both chasing and being chased by same.

He does not have the same enthusiasm for the work contained therein as he does for *The Big Cats*, but taken together they represent a unique side of Guy Coheleach: a willingness to use his art to try to accomplish something new, something bigger, something more meaningful. In one, great art complements a fine scientific text; in the others, he helped blend great wildlife painting with literary achievement. Like Hemingway's publishing of *Death in the Afternoon* and *Green Hills of Africa*, sometimes the attempting of something that has never been achieved carries with it a cachet, win or lose, that cannot be achieved by anyone,

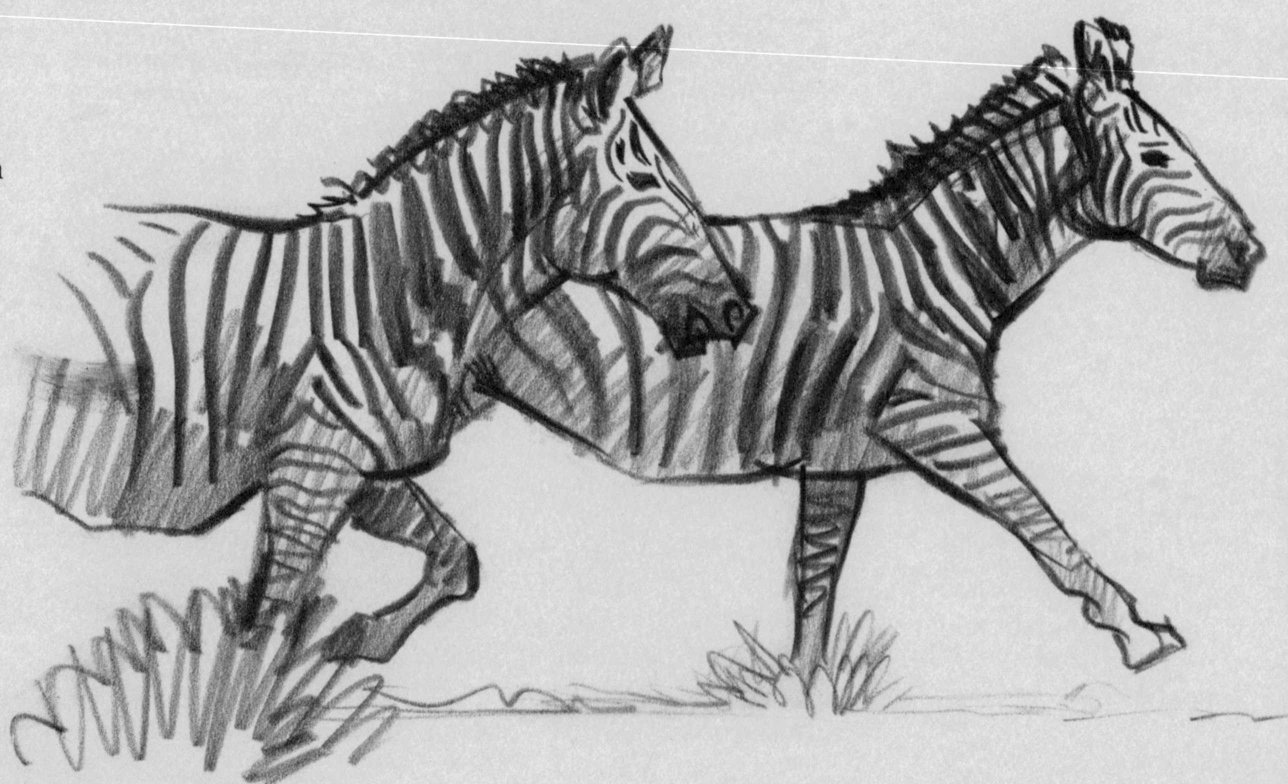

no matter how successful, who never puts it on the line.

The fact that, in the opinion of others, all three projects were first-rate, is simply icing on the cake.

Over the years, Coheleach's art has earned him a seemingly endless list of honors.

His work has been exhibited at the Corcoran Gallery of Art, the National Collection of Fine Arts in Washington, D.C., the American Museum of Natural History, the National Audubon Society, the White House collection, and the Royal Ontario Museum.

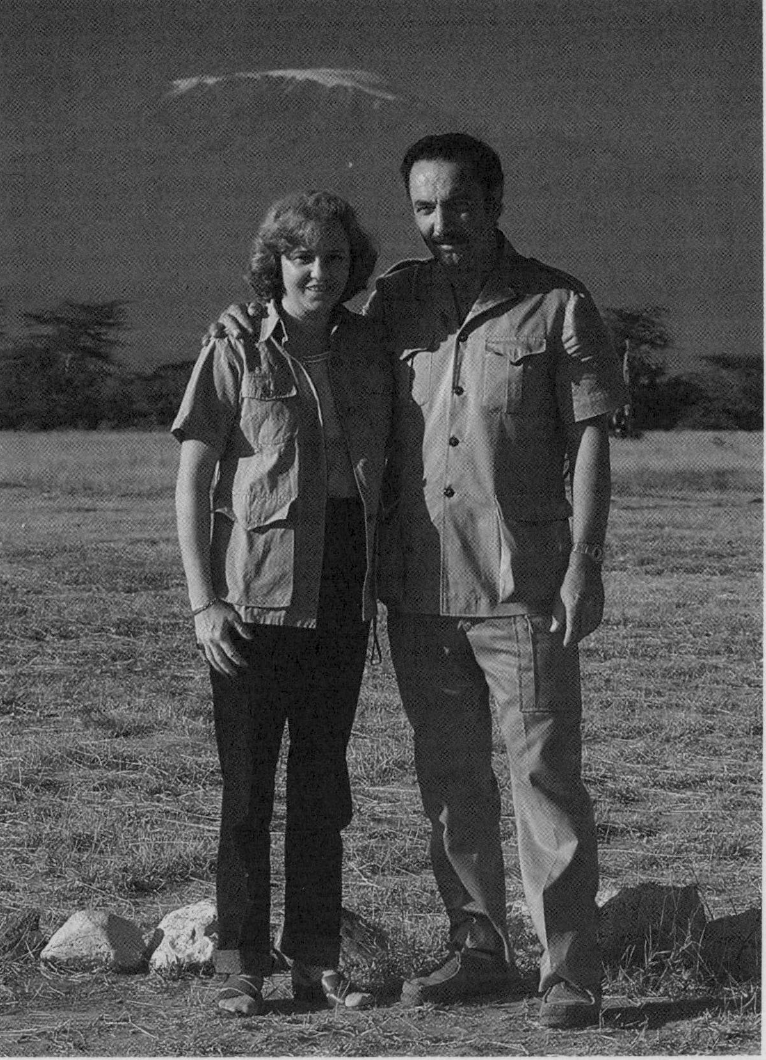

Guy and Pam on a 1977 safari in Kenya. Mount Kilimanjaro looms in the distance.

Prints of a Coheleach bald eagle have been presented to visiting dignitaries as a gift from the United States, and he was one of the first western artists to exhibit in Peking after the second world war.

Coheleach was awarded an honorary doctorate of arts from the College of William and Mary (1975), named Master Artist at the "Birds in Art" exhibition by the Leigh Yawkey Woodson Museum of Wisconsin (1983), and named Wildlife Artist of the Year by the National Wildlife & Western Art Collectors Society (1985). Between 1979 and 1986, he was awarded the Society of Animal Artists Merit of Honor six times, with the judging (since 1982) done by curators and professors of fine art from the host city's museums and universities.

All of this suggests an artist who has arrived — a painter who has established himself and, one assumes, knows where he fits in. But in Coheleach's case, no.

When Coheleach jokes that his favorite way to paint a cardinal is in the talons of a goshawk, he is only half joking. Death is a dominant theme in his work: death, the imminence of death, and the inevitability of death. It is one of the elemental facts about nature, which he has learned in his determined pursuit of firsthand knowledge about what life in nature is like. This he has translated into works of art which portray life for both predator and prey not as he wants it to be, nor as he imagines it might be, but as he knows it to be.

He has been, he estimates, on at least 40 full-blown African safaris, either as hunter, guest, observer or hanger-on. He has killed, and he has watched others kill. He has watched predators kill their prey, and watched men kill predators, and sometimes he has helped to finish the job.

From this vantage point he is astounded at wildlife artists who go into the field so rarely, who might make one or two trips to Africa to photograph game in the parks, almost as one might establish credentials before retiring to paint from photographs or observations made in the aspic of the modern zoo, where nature's ration animals lead unthreatened lives, and nature's hunters have their dinner delivered on a plate.

"Only a handful that I know of have been to Africa more than once or twice," Coheleach says, not in judgment so much as wonder that an artist could sustain the pretense of knowledge based on so little and hope to get away with it. And of course, many do, because the knowledge of the art-buying public is rarely more sophisticated than that of the painters themselves.

Not every painter is privileged to receive a negative critique by an experienced elephant hunter. Or, having received it, to acknowledge the shortcoming and do something about it.

For a period in the 1960s and 1970s, Coheleach painted primarily for the print market. He painted what he knew would sell, and much of it was work he now dismisses as mediocre.

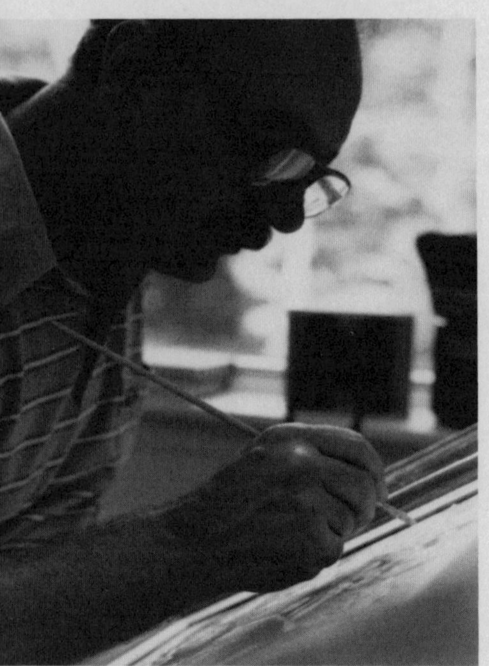

Coheleach at the easel in 1987. One of America's most versatile artists, he works comfortably in gouache, watercolor, acrylic, and oil. His subjects range from race cars to rhinos, his paintings from tiny miniatures to three- by six-foot canvases.

"Up until fairly recently, I just wanted to make money. Then I wanted to do good work as well as make money. And now I just want to do good work.

"I really don't think I've found my niche yet. I'm getting there, if I could ever get to the point where I don't have to worry about paying bills, now my kids are out of school...

"But hell, you still worry about your kids. I thought eventually you got over that, but it just seems to get worse..."

God," Picasso once remarked, "Is simply an artist like all the others. He invented the giraffe, the elephant, and the cat. But he hasn't got a style — he continues experimenting."

Guy Coheleach paints in oils and in watercolors, in gouache and acrylic. He begins each painting with a pencil drawing, and sometimes the pencil drawings are left to stand on their own, obeying Cezanne's dictum to treat everything in nature in terms of the sphere, the cylinder and the cone. Coheleach's spheres, cylinders and cones, black on white, move and mesh together like elements of a splendid machine, challenging the world with his draughtsmanship.

In the studio beside the house in Bernardsville, there are two complete drawing tables, one for watercolors and one for oils, set one behind the other like pupils' desks in a primary school, each with its own clutter of brushes, paints, and paraphernalia.

Today, it is oil — a red fox in the snow, the second of a set, almost finished. All that is left is to make the shadows on the snow exactly right. The fox sits, waiting, a debutante being made ready for the ball, sitting patiently as he is fussed over, being made *exactly right*.

Coheleach leans back and studies the fox, awash in the light that flows onto the drawing board through the big north window. The fox stares back unblinking, and makes not a sound.

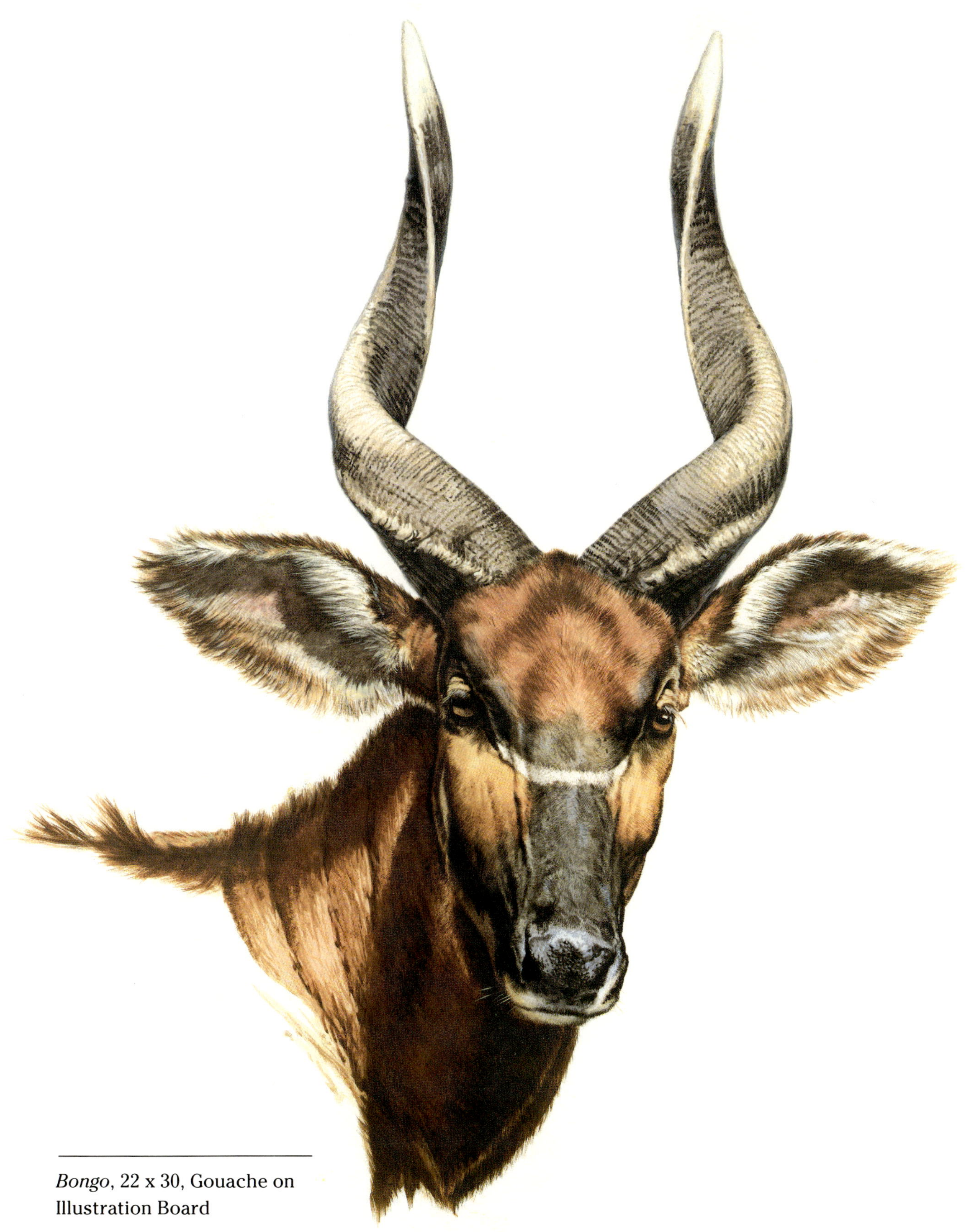

Bongo, 22 x 30, Gouache on Illustration Board

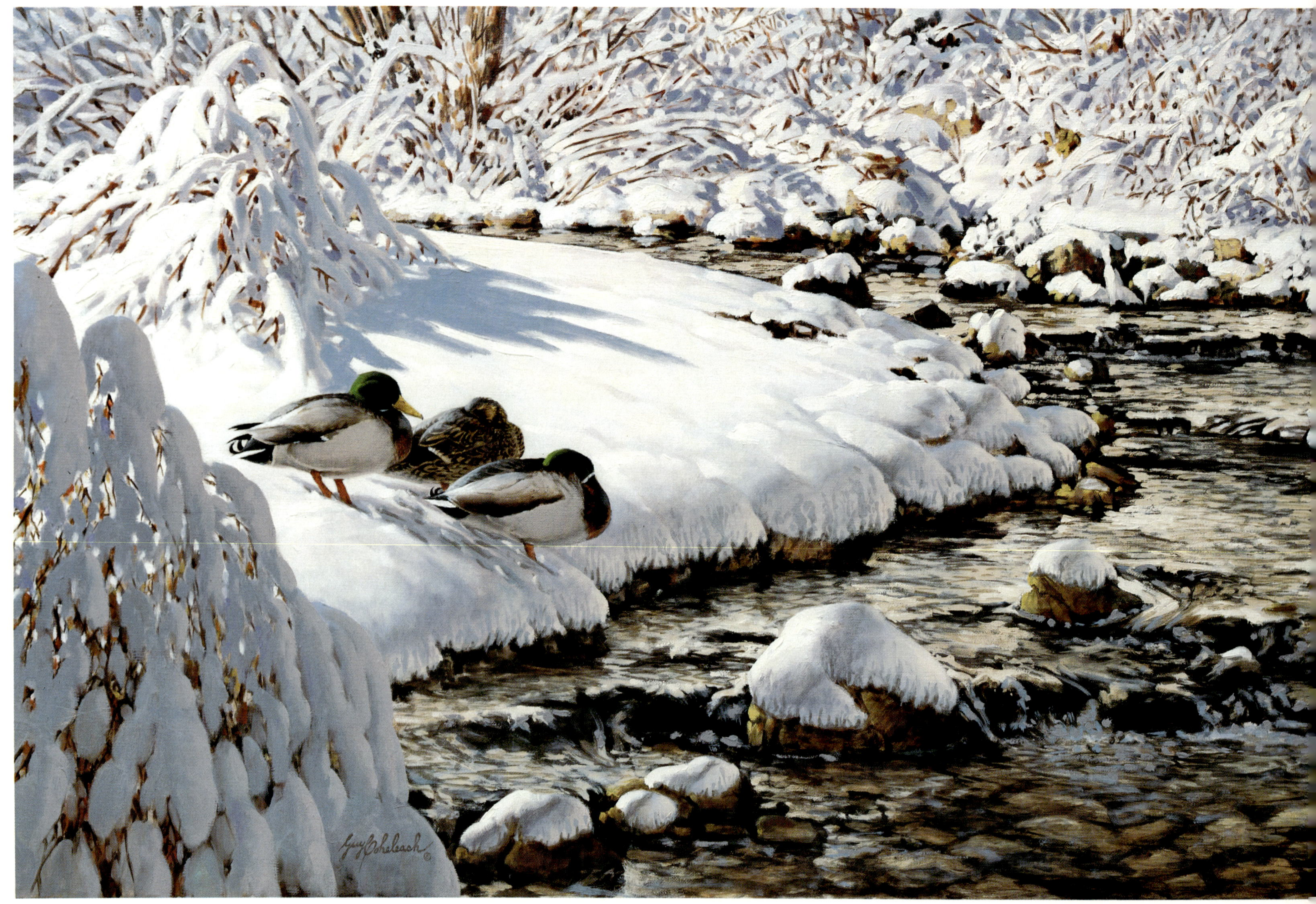

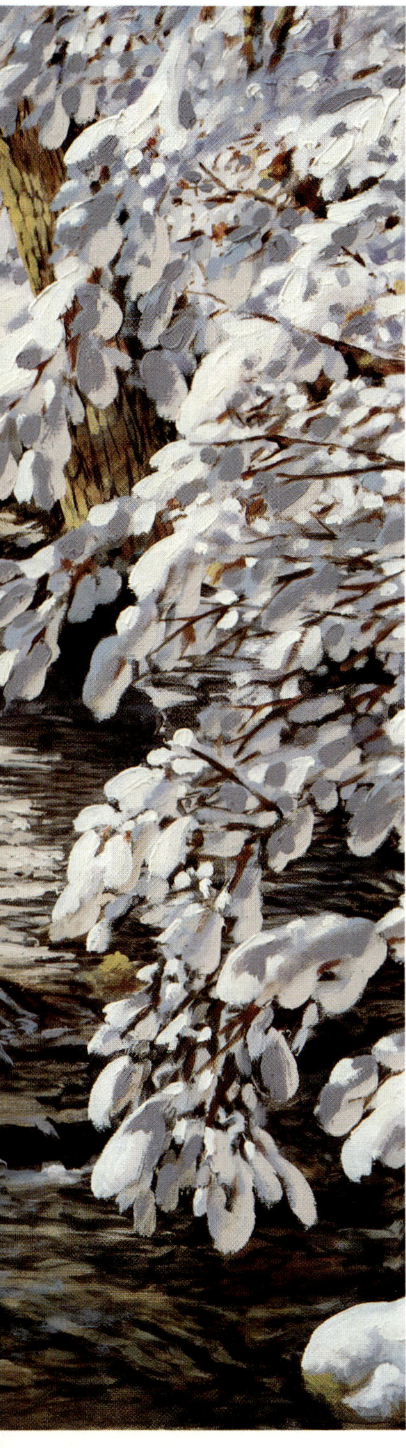

Throughout the northern tier of states, warm-water discharges from countless factories and power plants keep streams and ponds open year-round. As a result, more and more migratory birds stay all winter, enduring sub-zero temperatures and heavy snow as long as they have water and food. The mallard and Canada goose have become familiar sights in metropolitan areas like Minneapolis, Milwaukee, and Chicago, where dining on handouts from people who enjoy their presence has replaced feeding in cornfields.

I was asked to do a painting similar to Brightwaters Creek (see pages 46/47), and I chose mallards as the subject. The birds are very loosely painted, which helps to draw attention to the stream, which is really the focal point of the painting.

Mallards, 44 X 22, Oil on Canvas

Supposedly there are 18 distinct colors on the bill of a drake wood duck, and the bright scarlet of its eye may be the most intense red in all of nature. An exercise in pure color, very small, tightly rendered (as most gouaches are), Coheleach created this painting simply to show the spectacular beauty of the drake's courtship plumage.

The secret to iridescence is contrast and purity of color. I find the glaze approach works best. You can make a color much brighter if you apply it over white, rather than mixing the two.

For example, you could paint the green on the wood duck's head by laying down an opaque mixture of green and white. Another technique would be to paint it black or dark purple, then add transparent green over that.

Drake Wood Duck, 9 X 7, Gouache on Illustration Board

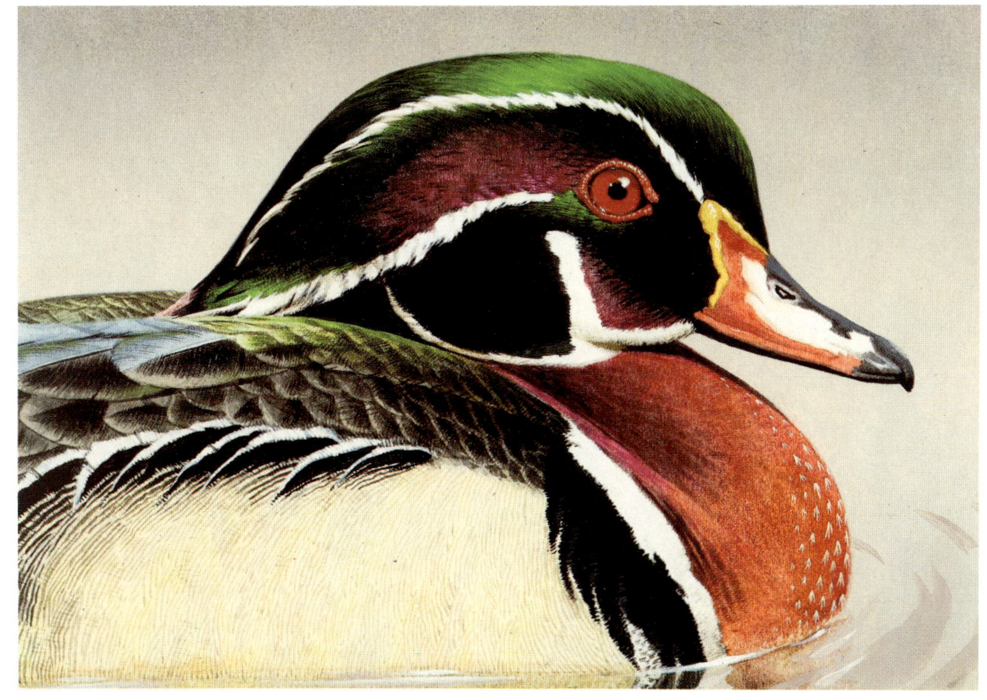

This is the way I like to paint. The sun is directly overhead, so it is hot, and you know it's hot. The bongo is standing in the stream. The strong shadows denote heat, but also provide, along with the vegetation, a nice contrast that accents the animal's colors.

More than just placing the animal in its habitat, Coheleach reveals its character. The secretive, reclusive, shadowy mood of this painting reflects the bongo's legendary elusiveness.

This particular bongo, however, has been seen by thousands since it was published by the Dallas Safari Club in 1986.

Bongo, 22 X 30, Oil on Canvas

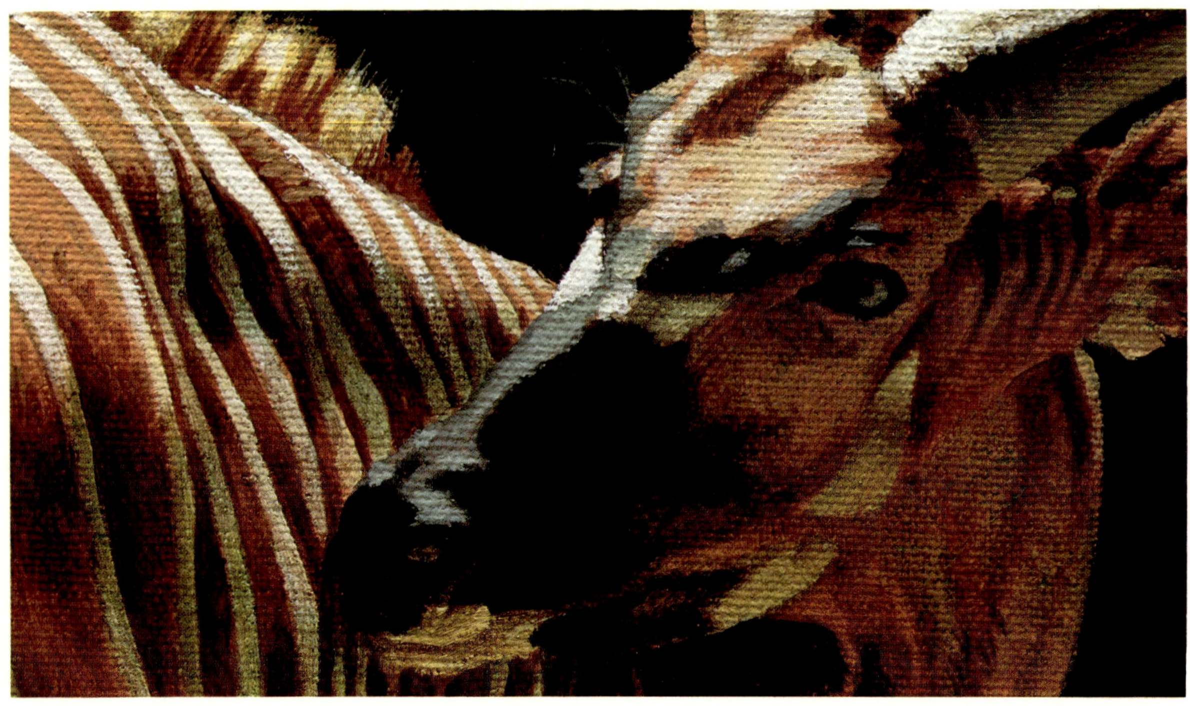

Detail of *Bongo*

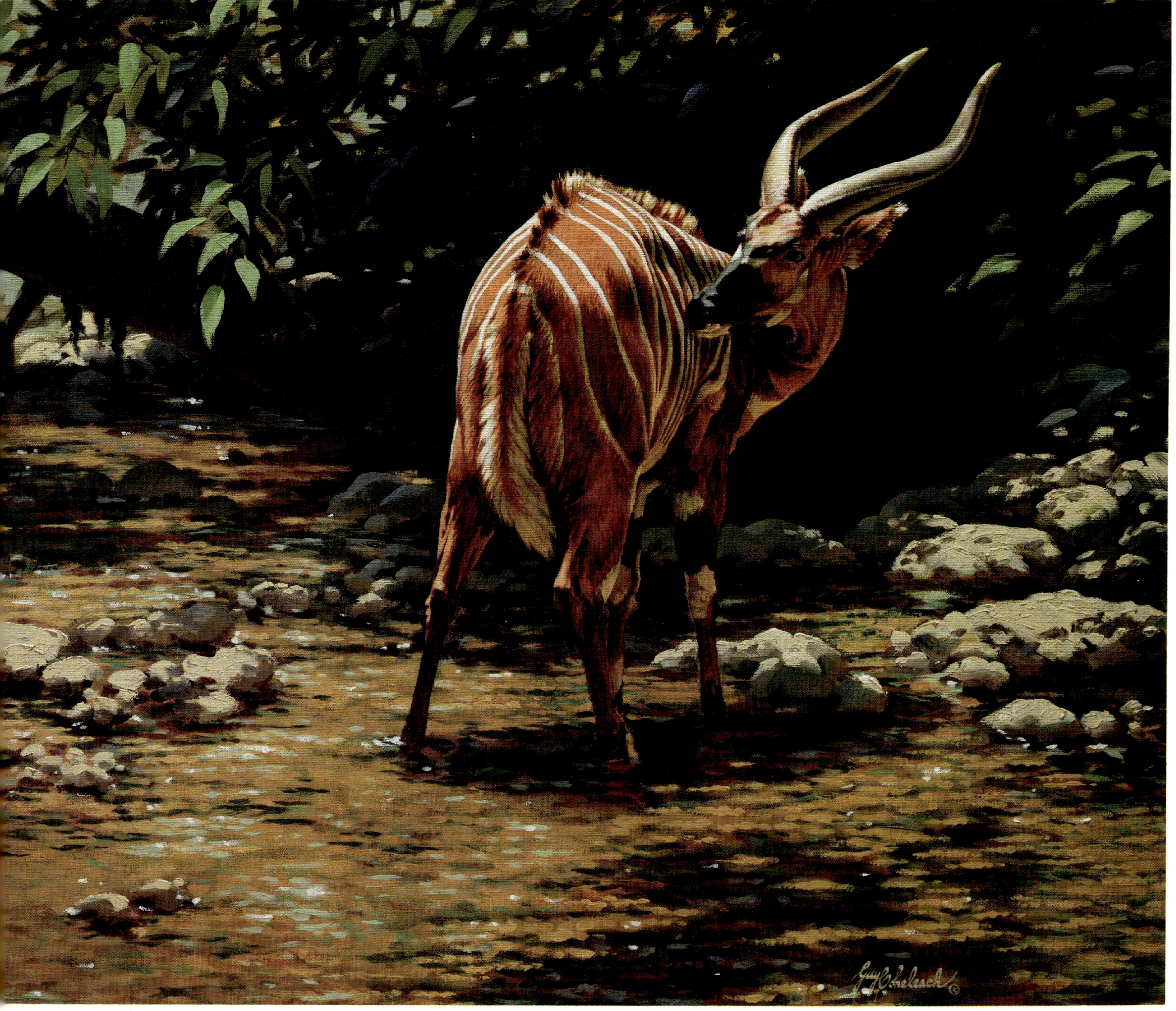
Guy Coheleach ©

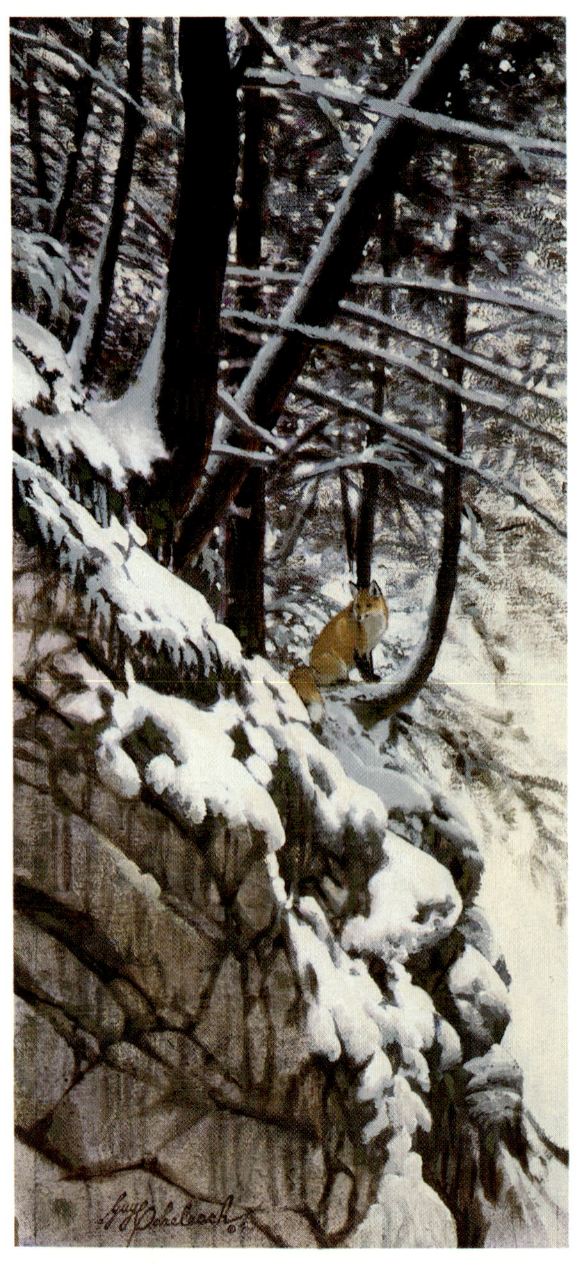

This is a rough oil sketch of the magnificent Clinton Gorge in New Jersey. I find it easiest to work on a 1:2 format; extreme verticals and horizontals are more challenging because you have to exercise more care when composing the various elements.

Clinton Gorge, 6 1/2 x 17, Oil on Illustration Board

The smallest brush-stroke on this six by three-foot canvas was made with a half-inch bristle brush. How long would it take to do such a painting?

It takes about 30 years to learn how; then it takes about a month to do the pencil drawing, and another three or four weeks filling in the colors.

Rariton Feeder — Red Fox, 72 x 36, Oil on Canvas

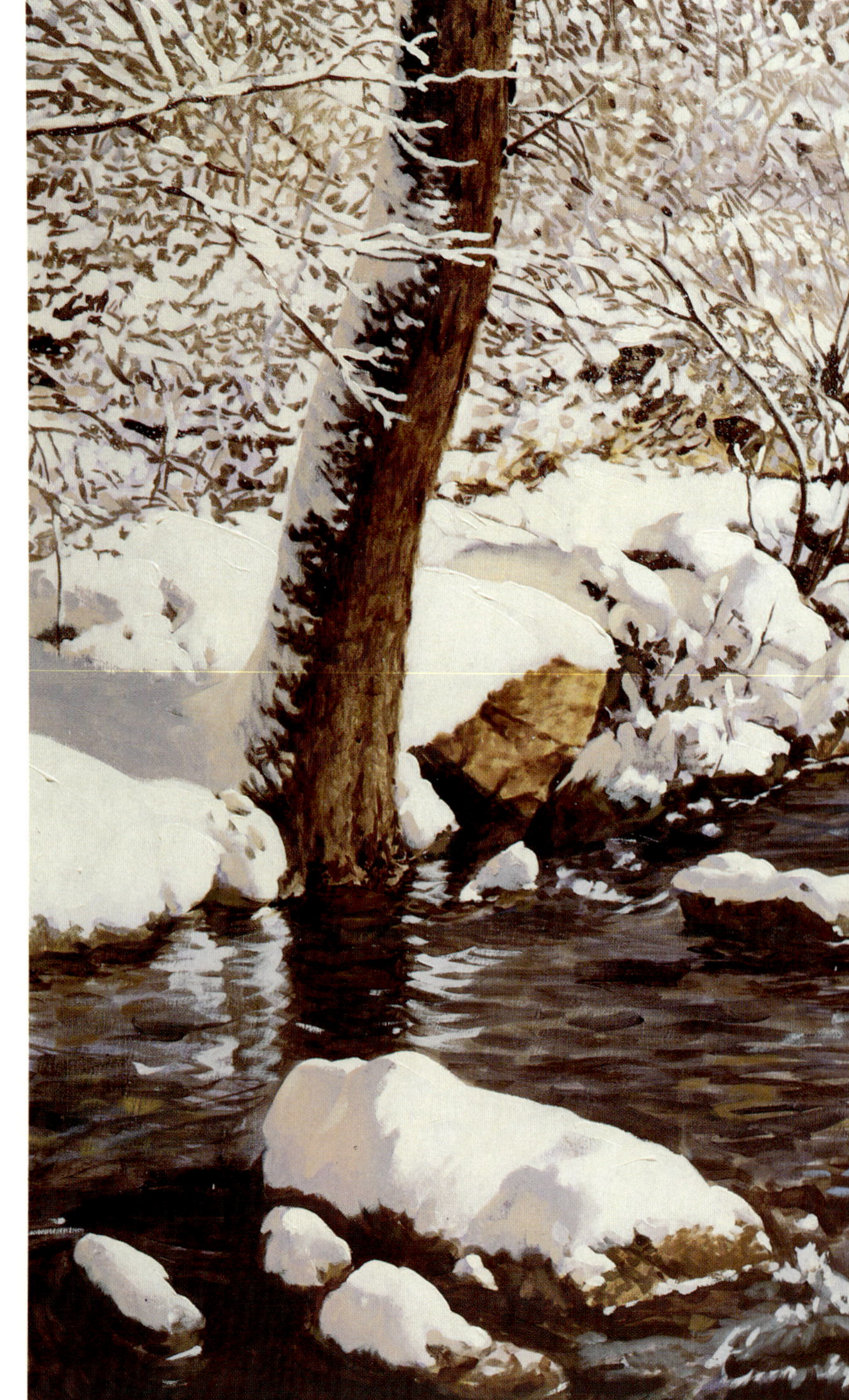

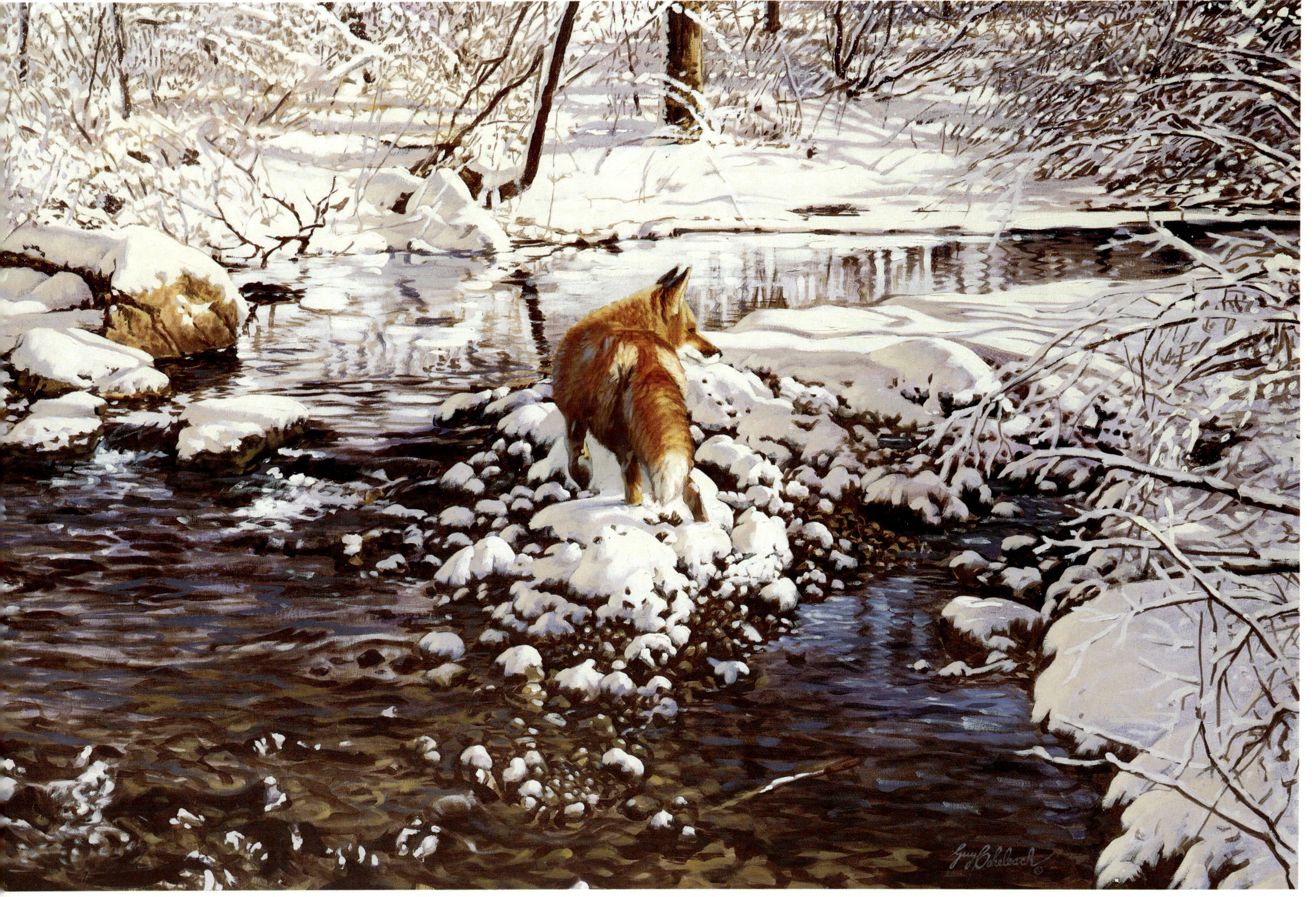

Guy Coheleach is the preeminent painter of the big cats and without question, the greatest leopard painter ever. *Liquid Leopard* is Coheleach at his best, painting his favorite subject at its best.

One thing that I love about this painting, aside from the dappled light, is the liquid look to the animal. Cats have incredible kinetic energy, and yet if they are not tense, their muscles are like jelly, and their skin and connective tissue like rubber. They can literally drip off a branch, but when they start to move, they turn to spring steel.

Liquid Leopard, 72 X 36, Oil on Canvas

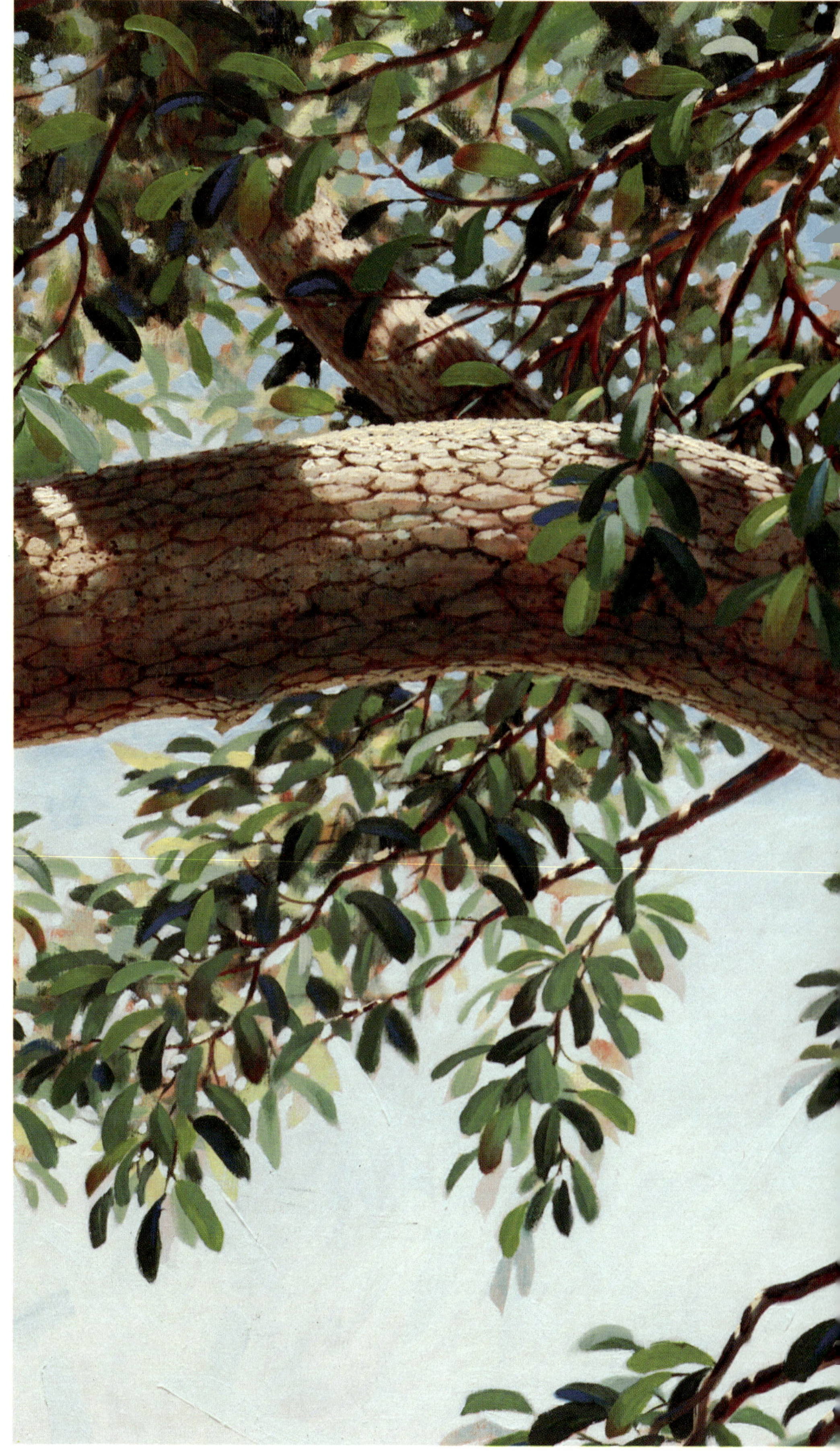

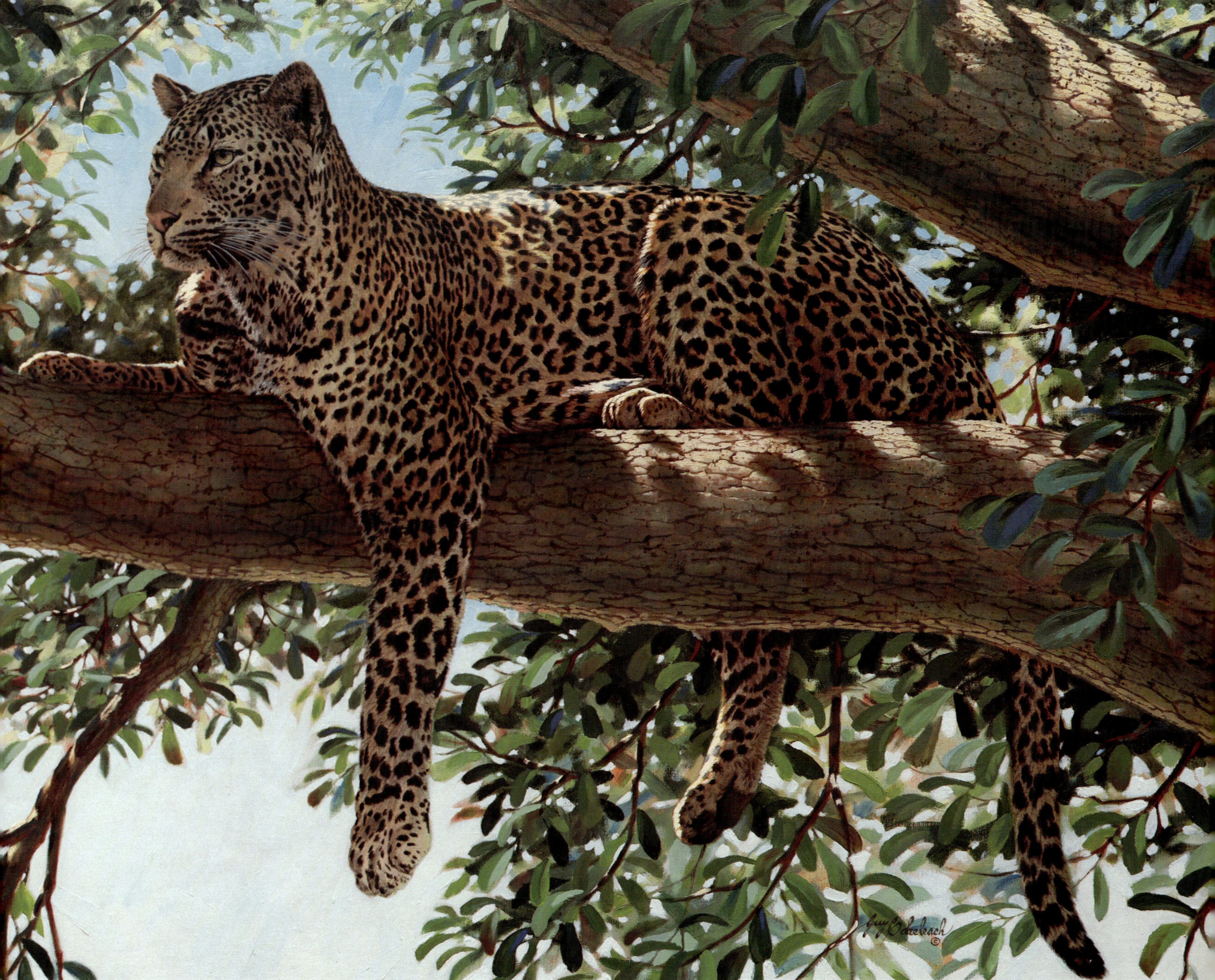

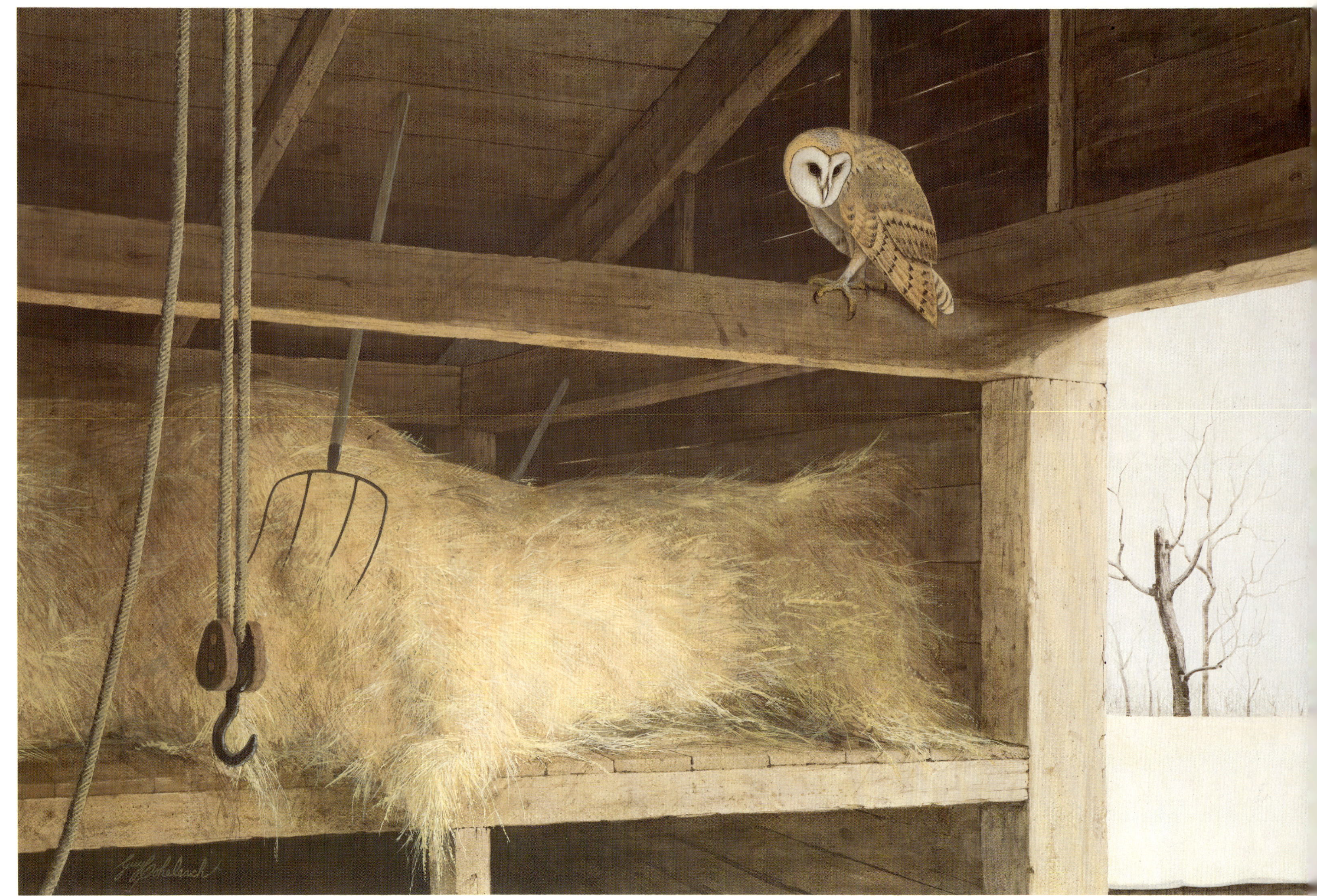

In the mid-1960s, Coheleach was approached to do a series for *National Wildlife* magazine; he would paint a specific animal and a writer would then do an article about the species.

It was just the opposite of normal illustration, in fact, and it was really one heckuva compliment. And when you think that this was done in the '60s, about 25 years ago...

I painted several works along this line, most of which sold before I started keeping photographs of my work. Today, I believe I could do a better painting, in oil, in about half the time. But I enjoyed working this way.

People have told me that it looks like a (Andrew) Wyeth. There's no doubt that I have been influenced by Wyeth, but not any more so than I have by other great artists such as Liljefors, Fuertes, Rungius, and Kuhnert.

Barn Owl, 48 X 30, Casein on Illustration Board

Coheleach has again used long shadows for good design, combined with a great deal of texture in the snow. Tension is provided by the confrontation which is only an instant away...

Sheep have so much character, so much bulk and massiveness. The big rams in their winter coats are built like fireplugs. Like elephants and freight trains, anything with that much mass is really fun to paint.

Bighorn Sheep, 24 X 12, Oil on Canvas

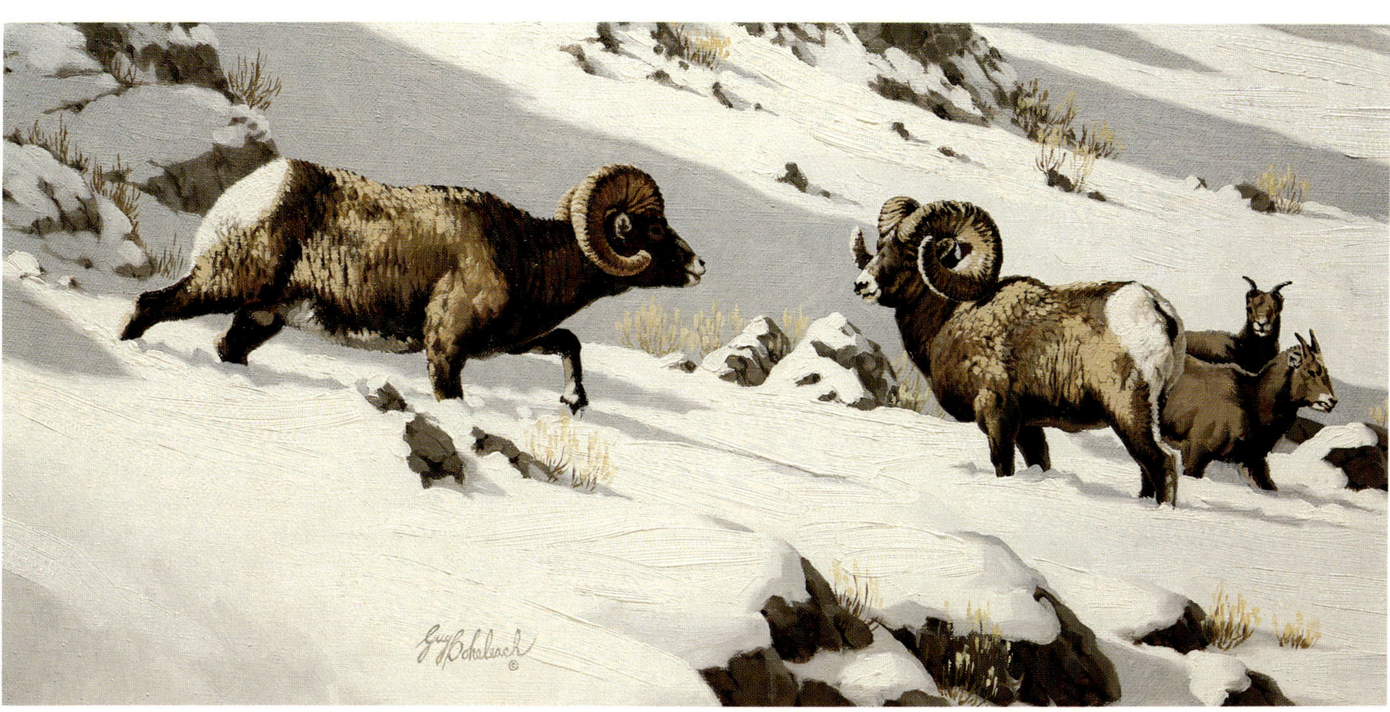

The paintings on these pages bring back vivid memories to Coheleach.

The year was 1962 and the young artist was determined to build up his portfolio of wildlife subjects — to reveal a diverse hand capable of rendering fish as well as elephants and eagles.

Coheleach lived on Long Island at the time. Using a rented rowboat and sandworms for bait, he would fish through the night, paint his catch in the morning, nap for a few hours in the afternoon, eat the fish for supper, then head out to catch another.

I kept up that crazy round-the-clock schedule for about four weeks. This particular painting is actually based on some 30 striped bass I caught over that period.

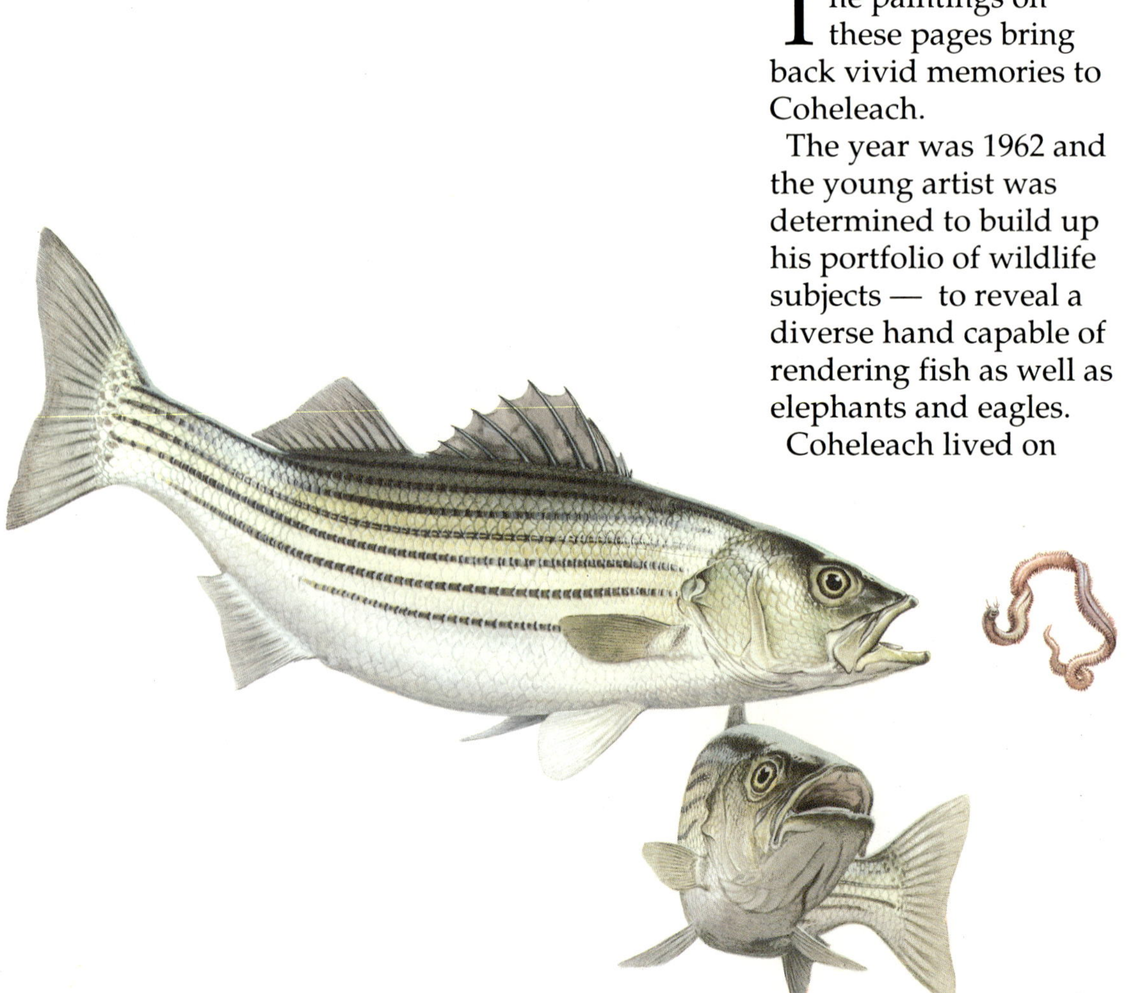

Striped Bass, 22 x 14, Gouache on Illustration Board

I love ospreys — everybody does. When I was a kid, before DDT found widespread use, ospreys were so common on Long Island that you could find their nests on the ground. I remember one giant oak tree on Orient Point that held three active nests. I used to watch the birds dive down out of the trees to snatch weakfish and bluefish — what marvelous hunters.

The osprey is one of the few birds that you can paint from underneath. The underside of an eagle is relatively dark and uninteresting, but the black-and-white pattern of the osprey's plumage provides a nice natural design.

Osprey, 30 x 40, Gouache and Acrylic on Illustration Board

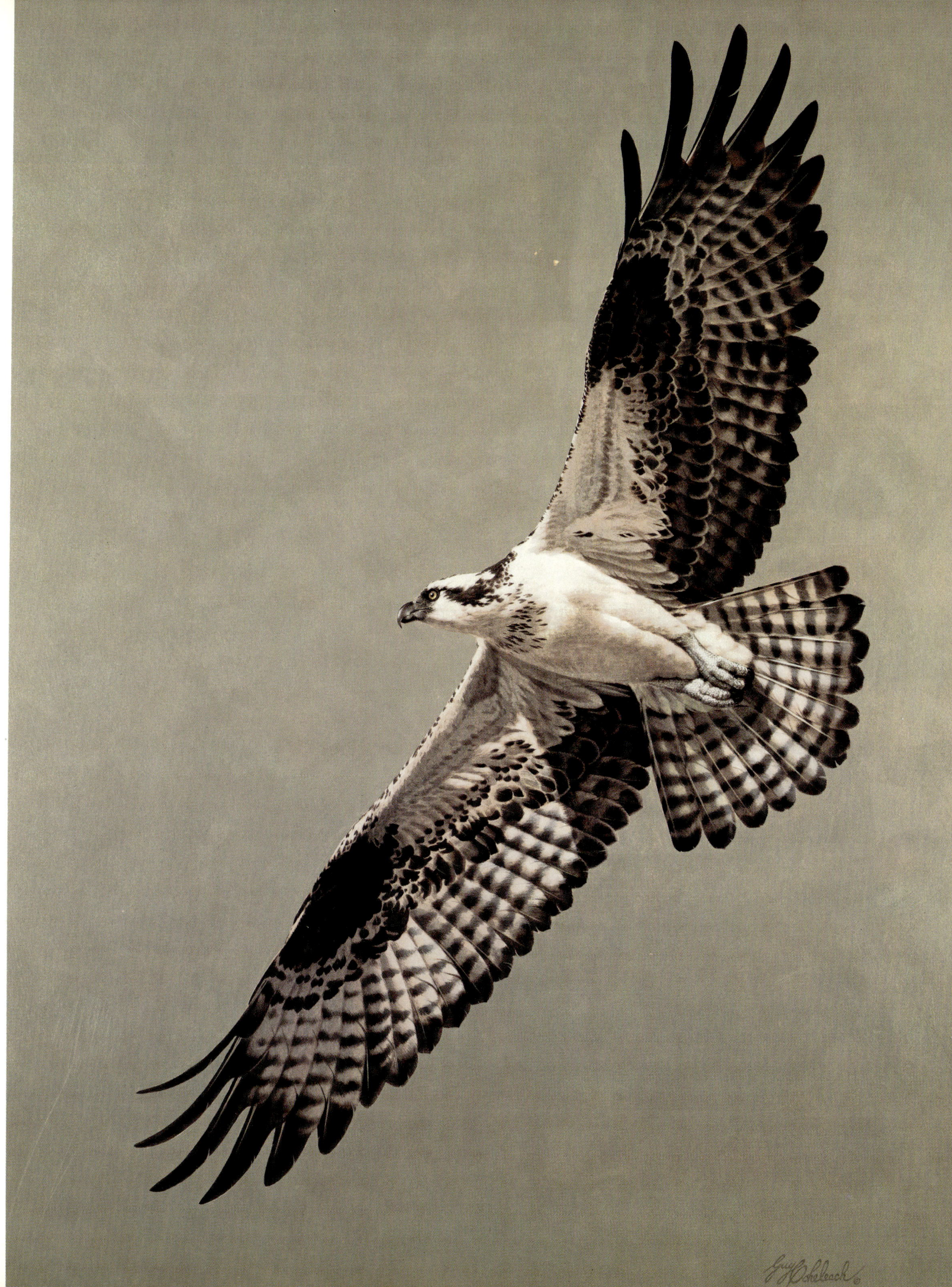

You're at the twelfth hole of Augusta National Golf Course in Augusta, Georgia, home of the Masters Tournament. Jack Nicklaus, winner of six Masters titles, is teeing off with Andy Bean.

I have done several golf paintings; this is certainly my favorite. In reality, the crowd around the hole would be closer to the action, but I kept it back to assist the overall design of what is essentially a landscape.

Five hundred prints were made of *Amen Corner,* most of which Coheleach keeps as gifts for people who are not wildlife enthusiasts. The original hangs in Jack Nicklaus's office.

Amen Corner, 44 X 24,
Oil on Canvas

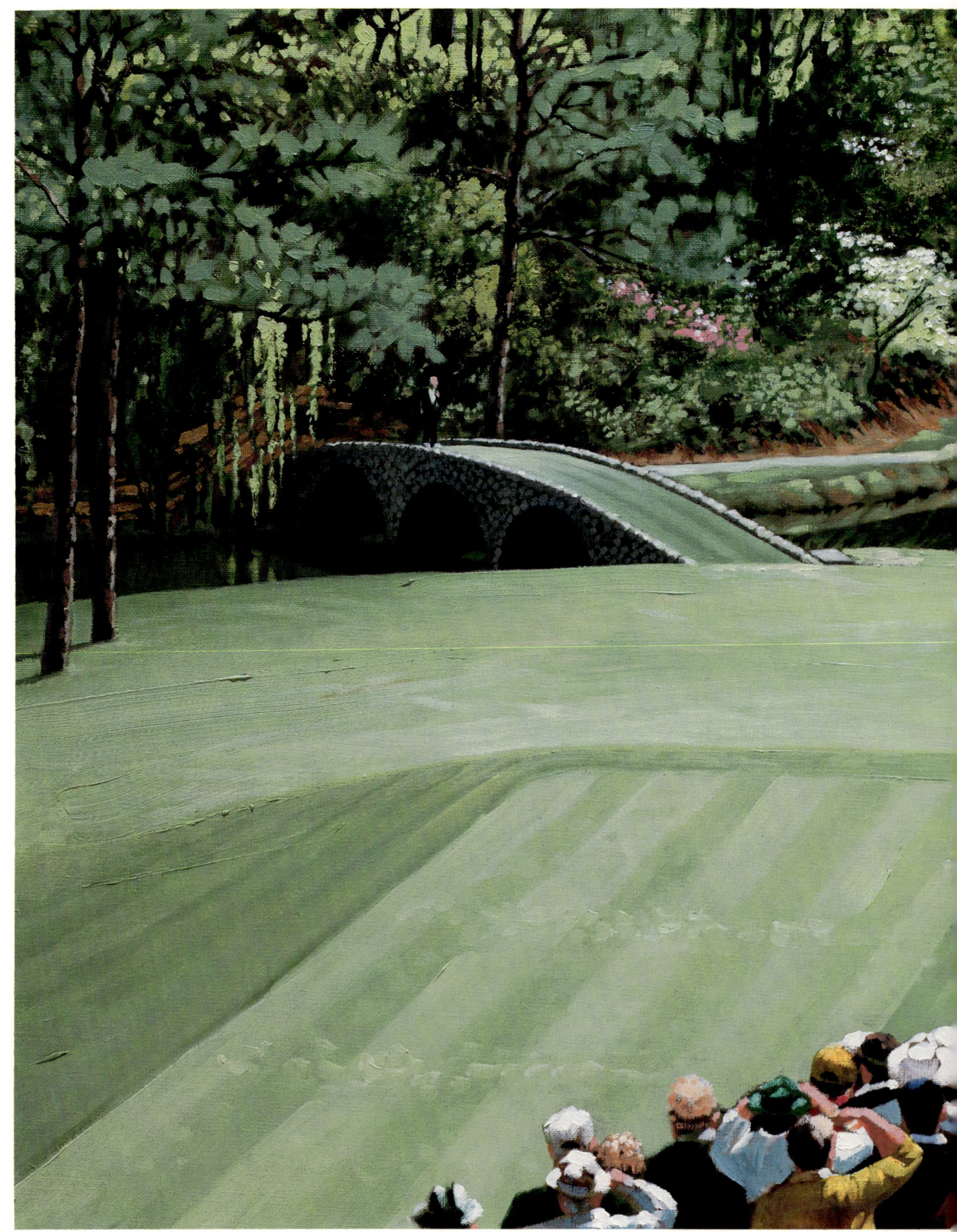

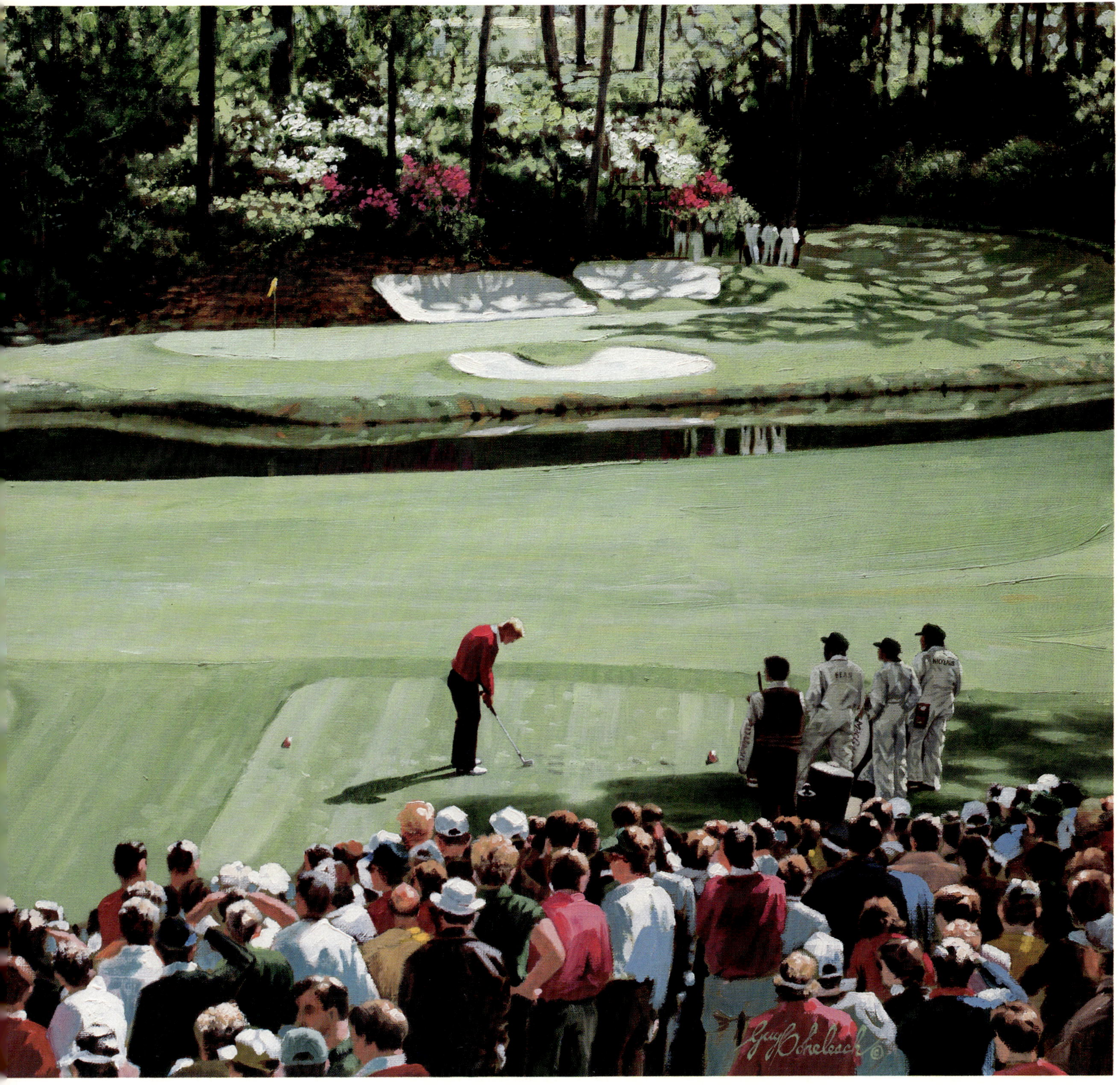

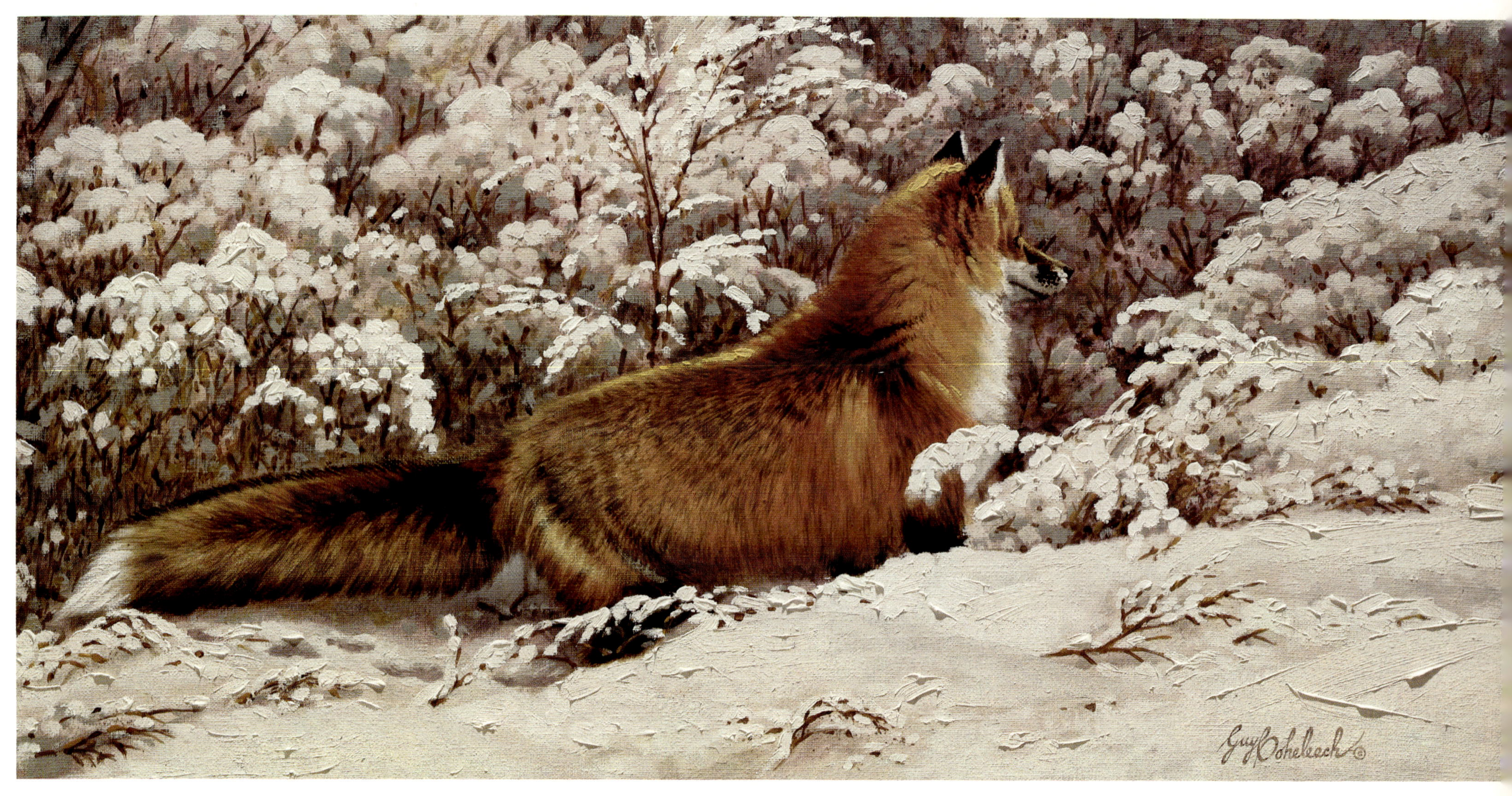

The canids, including foxes, wolves, and coyotes, appeal to the artist because of their character.

They give you an endless variety of expressions, both in their faces and bodies. This is Reynard in his winter coat, looking for mice or birds or anything else he can catch.

Foxes and coyotes are also interesting to me because unlike so many other wild species, they have either increased or held their own at the edges of civilization. Like crows and leopards, they will always be with us.

Reynard the Fox, 24 x 12,
Oil on Canvas

Anyone who has ever owned a bird feeder can relate to this scene. It is one of those subdued winter afternoons; you can sense the cold by the birds' fluffed-out feathers and the snow-covered branches. The blue jays have just eaten and now they are simply waiting to get hungry again.

I like this painting because of its design — the flow of its predominantly vertical lines — and because of its contrasting textures. I enjoy painting soft feathers against a cold, hard background.

Blue Grey — Blue Jay, 16 x 30,
Gouache on Illustration Board

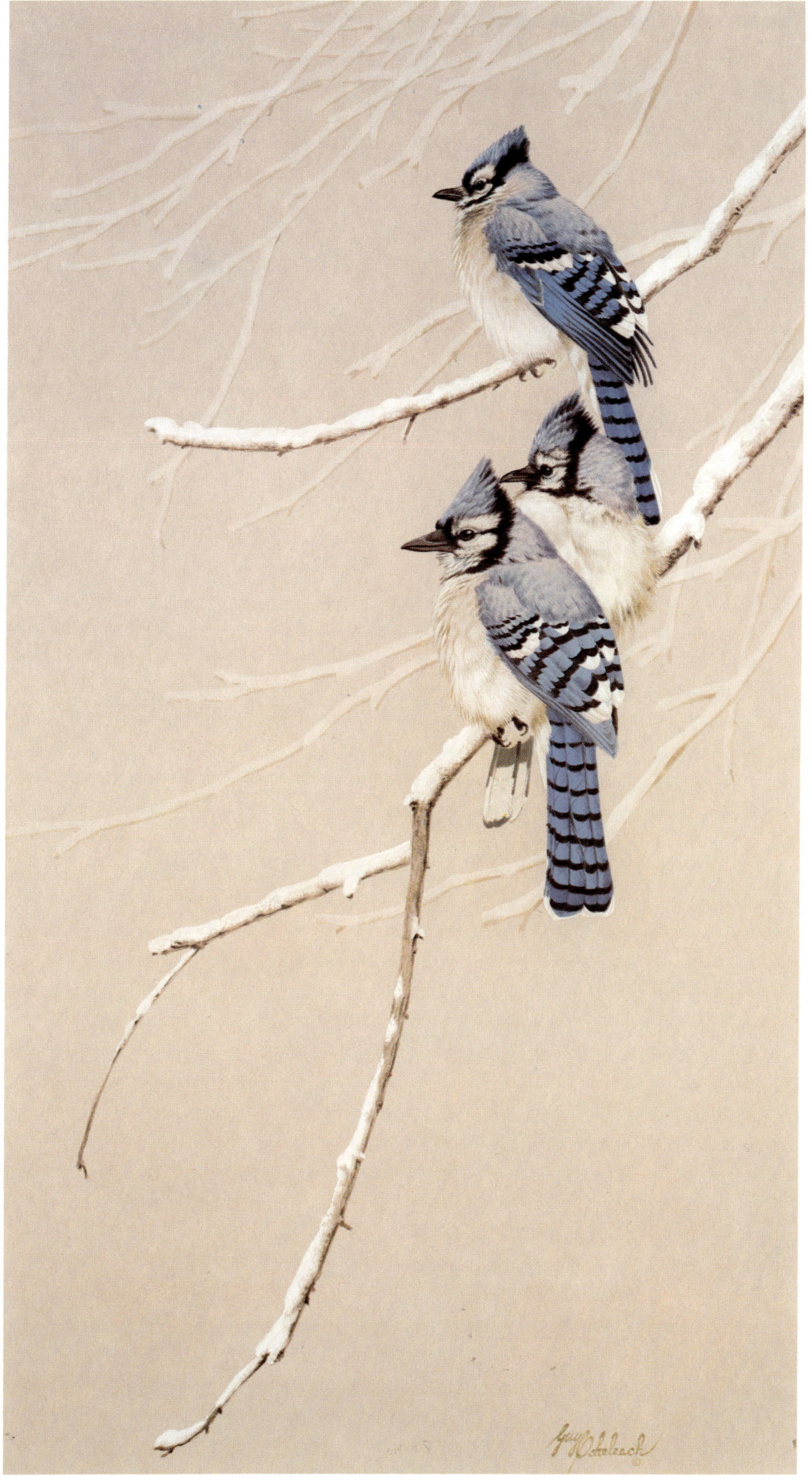

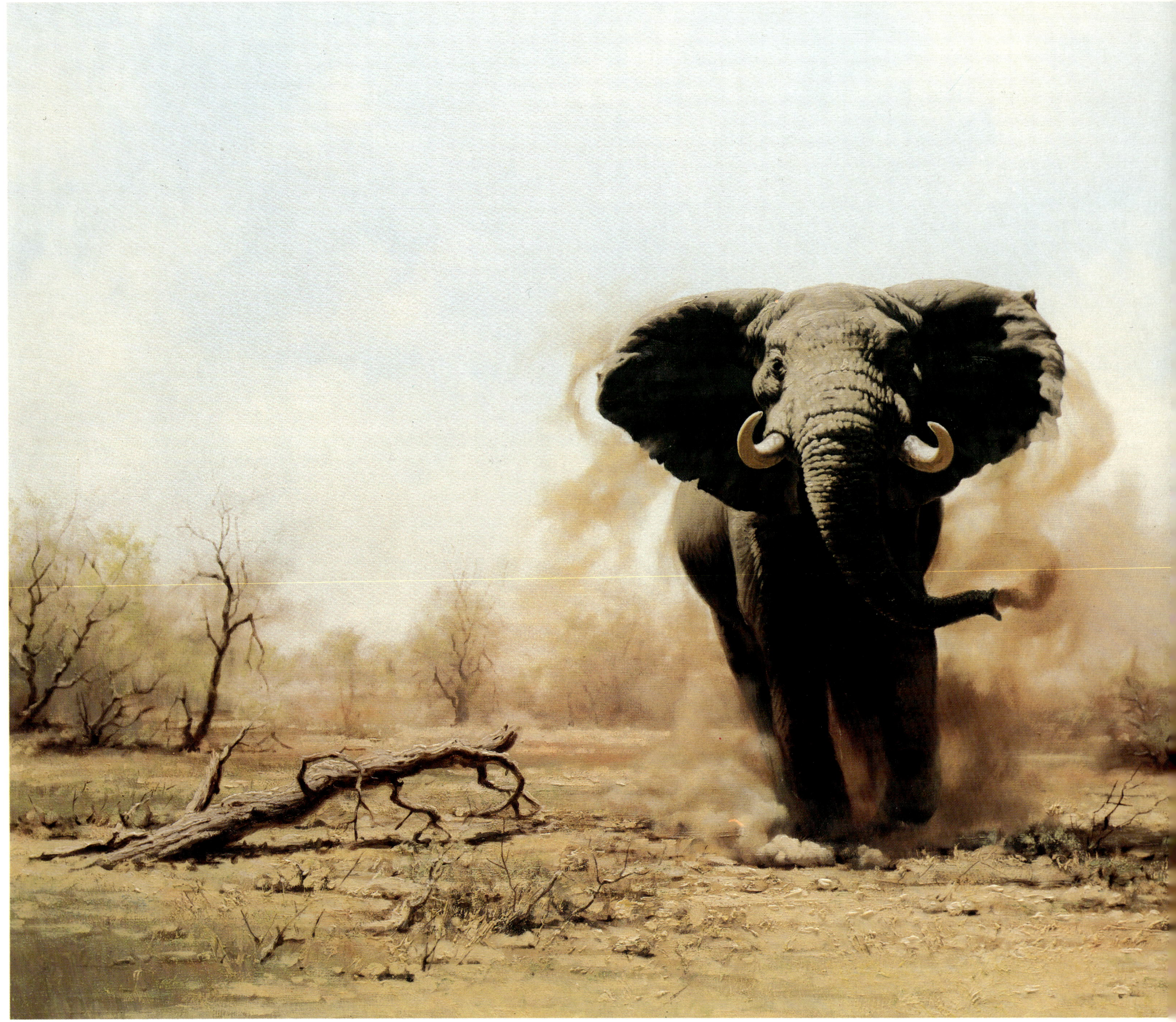

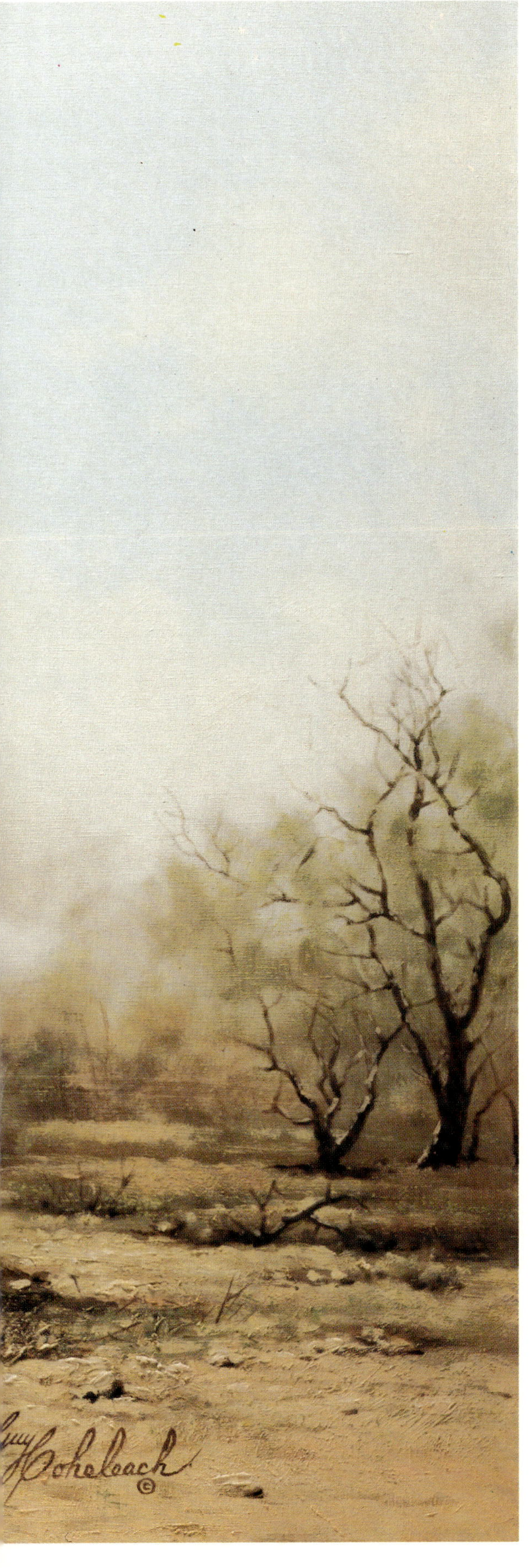

Coheleach's close encounter with an elephant has been told and retold. Here, he tells it again on canvas.

This is the painting I did after being run down by the elephant. I put much longer tusks on him, and placed him in a setting which is more East African than Zambian; otherwise, it's him. You know that he's moving because of the dust, and because he is tilted over to the side. He could not be in that position and NOT be moving.

That's him!

Charging Elephant, 40 x 30, Oil on Canvas

A pure watercolor with no whites or opaques, this portrait of a zebra, lazing away in the midday heat, was painted at Etosha Game Park in Namibia.

None of us remember sunlight directly overhead when it is cool or cold. Sunlight in the middle of winter, even at midday, is always on an angle. When it is directly overhead, it is summer or at the equator, it is nothing but hot.

Zebra, 8 x 10, Watercolor on Illustration Board

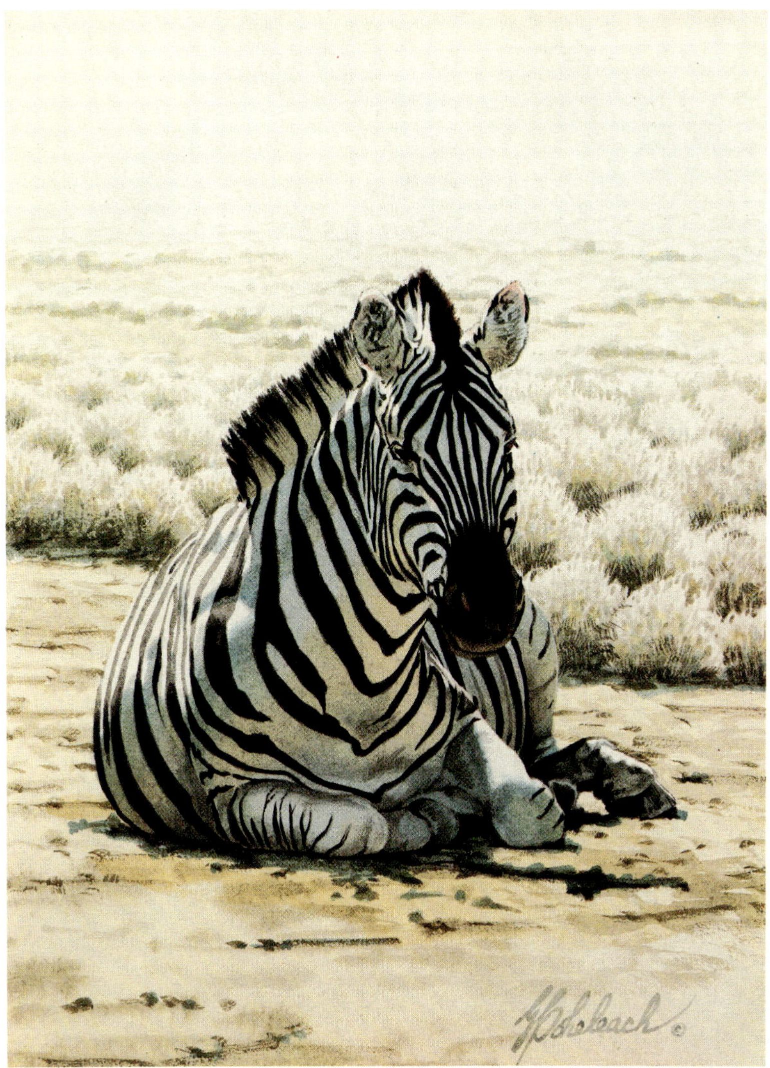

Rarest of all the big cats, the snow leopard lives on the treeless rocks and alpine meadows of the Himalayas and other mountainous areas of central Asia. In the Himalayas, its last major stronghold, only 200 to 600 individuals remain.

Coheleach painted the preening adult in 1979, in preparation for his book *The Big Cats*. The portrait of the snow leopard family was done eight years later, at the request of a friend.

There are many ways to paint fur. One is to paint every hair, which impresses people, but in a painting like this, it would be boring. You want to make it look like all the hair is there, but without detailing it. There are many little brushstrokes here. But you could paint this scene just as easily with a wet canvas — turpentine all over it — letting the spots bleed into the gray areas and showing no strokes at all.

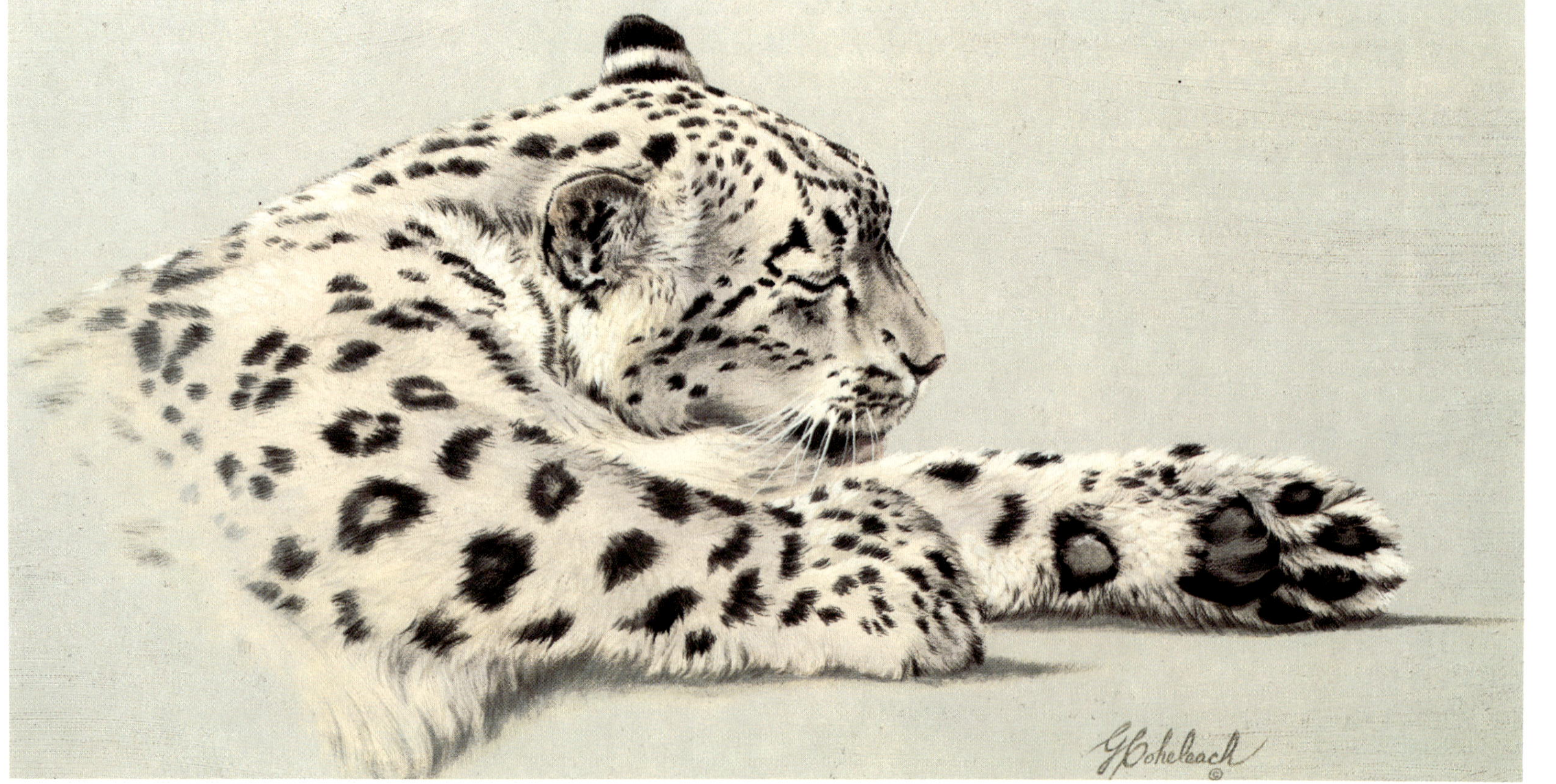

Preening Snow Leopard
24 x 12, Acrylic on
llustration Board

Den Mother — Snow Leopards,
44 x 24, Oil on Canvas

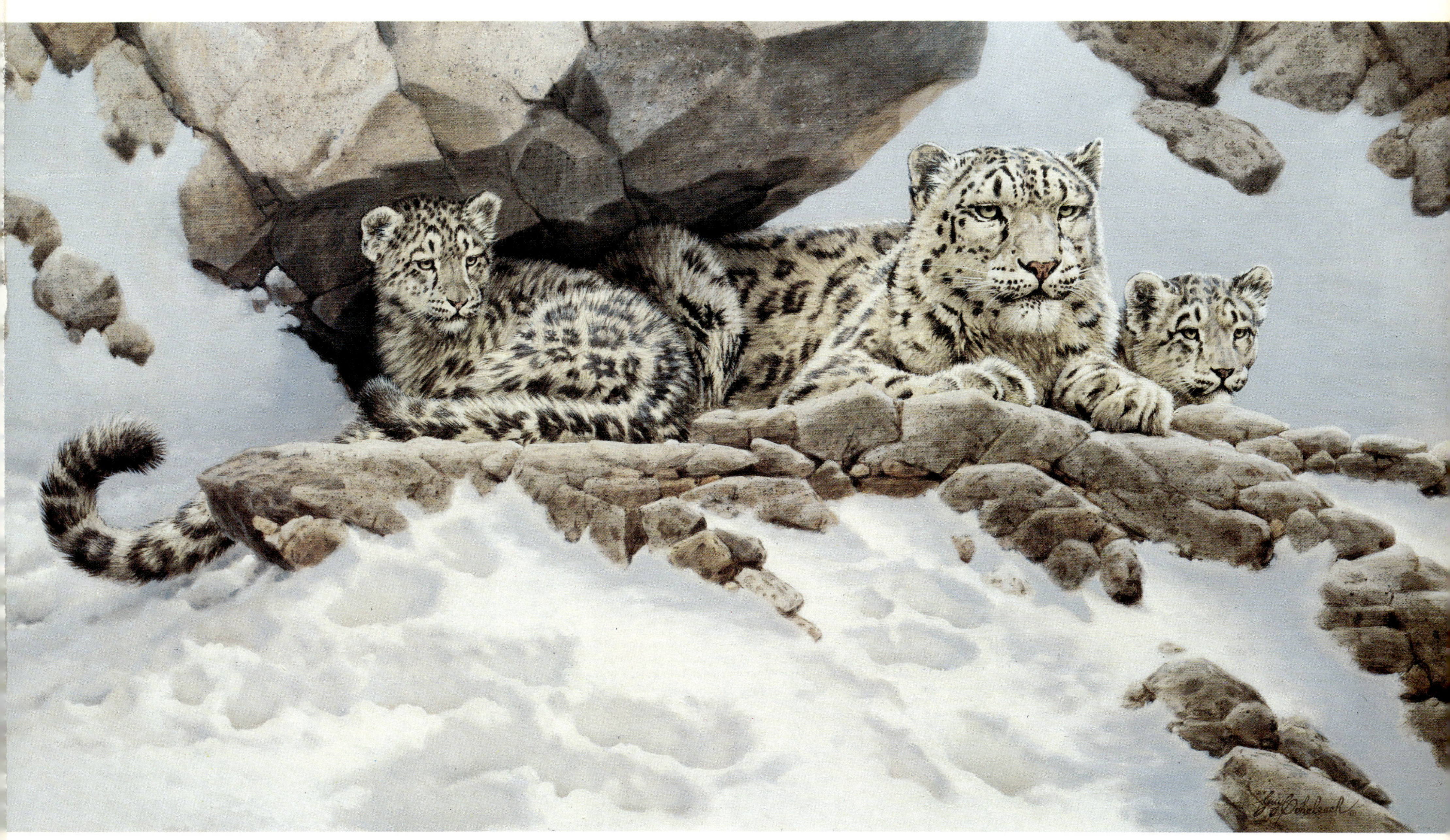

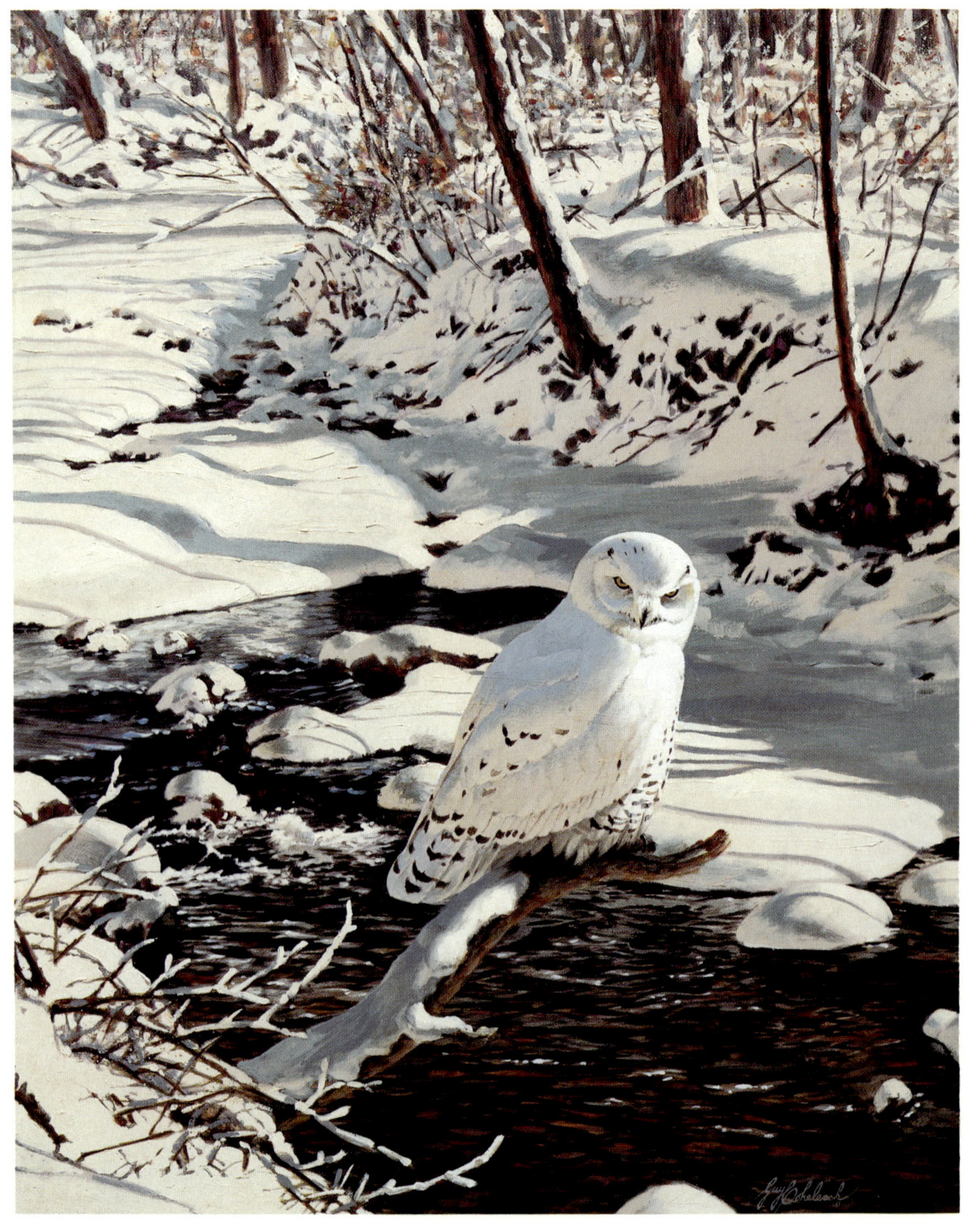

I can remember snowy owls from my boyhood days on Long Island. During winters when lemmings and voles were scarce in the Canadian provinces, these magnificent birds would drift southward into the States to search for food. I can still see their ghostly forms gliding across the dunes.

The snowy owl is a creature of open spaces. Here, I have used artistic license to portray it in a more interesting setting, an ice-choked stream and snowy woods that accentuate the bird's mottled plumage.

Snowy Owl, 22 x 30, Oil on Canvas

As the first of five projects in an American Heritage series, Coheleach was asked, in a painting, to capture the spirit of freedom. The result was this spectacular portrait of a bald eagle.

One of the thrills in nature is looking at a good sky. When I lived in Florida, I used to sit on the porch and look at the sky, miles out across the ocean. Pam and I once sat out all day and an evening, just watching thunder-storms. We watched five at a time. I could paint thunderheads forever.

Coheleach heightened the drama through skillful use of top-lighting on the clouds and by backlighting the eagle's dark wings.

Freedom, 30 x 40, Oil on Canvas

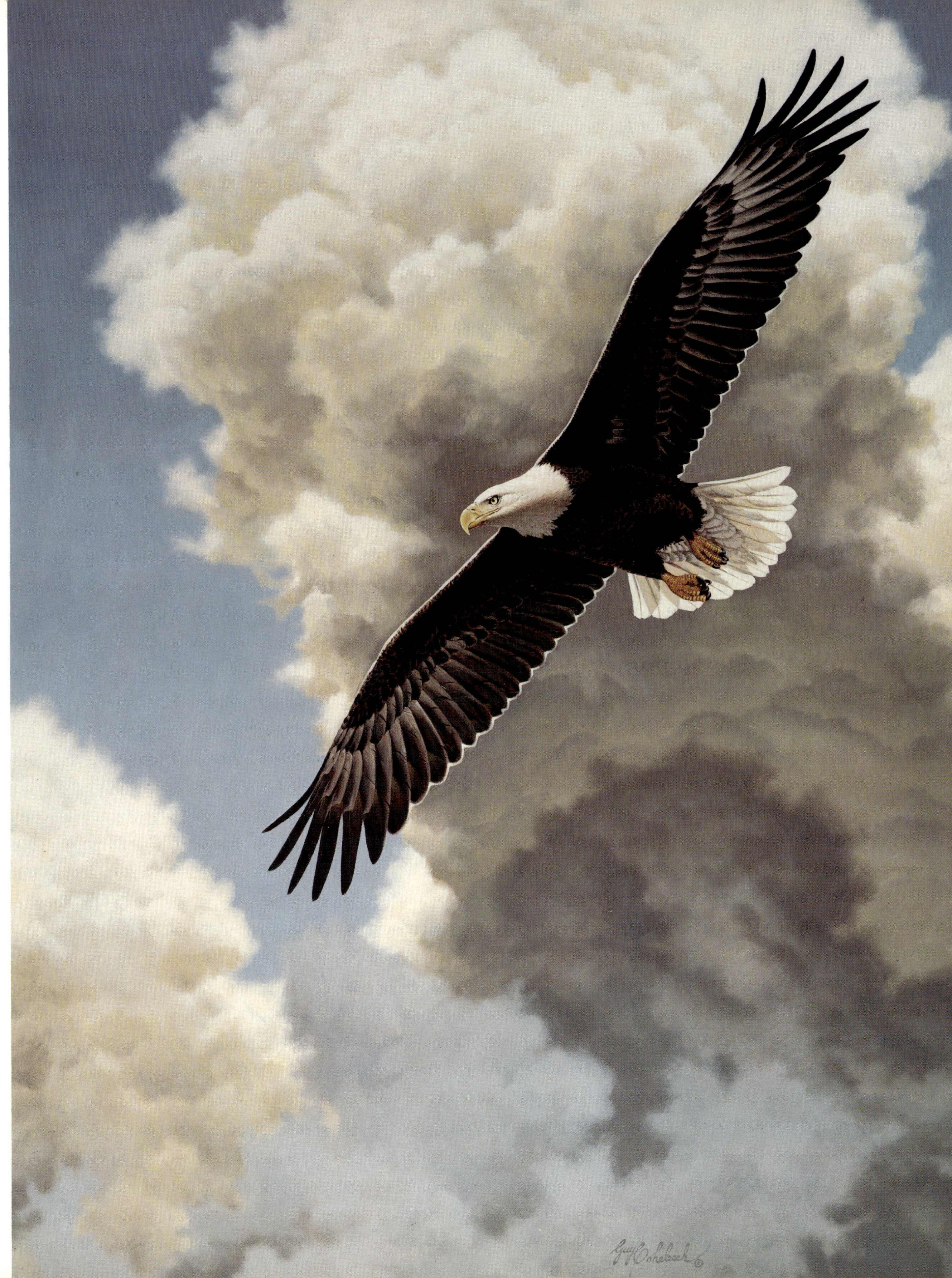

In this portrait of two Siberian tigers, the long shadows in the snowy foreground enhance design and movement. Coheleach painted two tigers rather than one to depict the fluid motion of the big cats.

It's like painting two or three birds in flight: you show one with the wing up and one with the wing down. The shape of one shows you what the other will be in an instant; as a result, you can almost see them moving across the canvas.

In other paintings where the predator is the subject and Coheleach has not wanted to detract from it by including the prey, he has suggested the fleeing creature by clouds of dust or snow, or by feathers floating down in the air. Here he uses a variation on that technique, indicating the prey by tracks in the snow.

Manchurian Chase, 44 X 24, Oil on Canvas

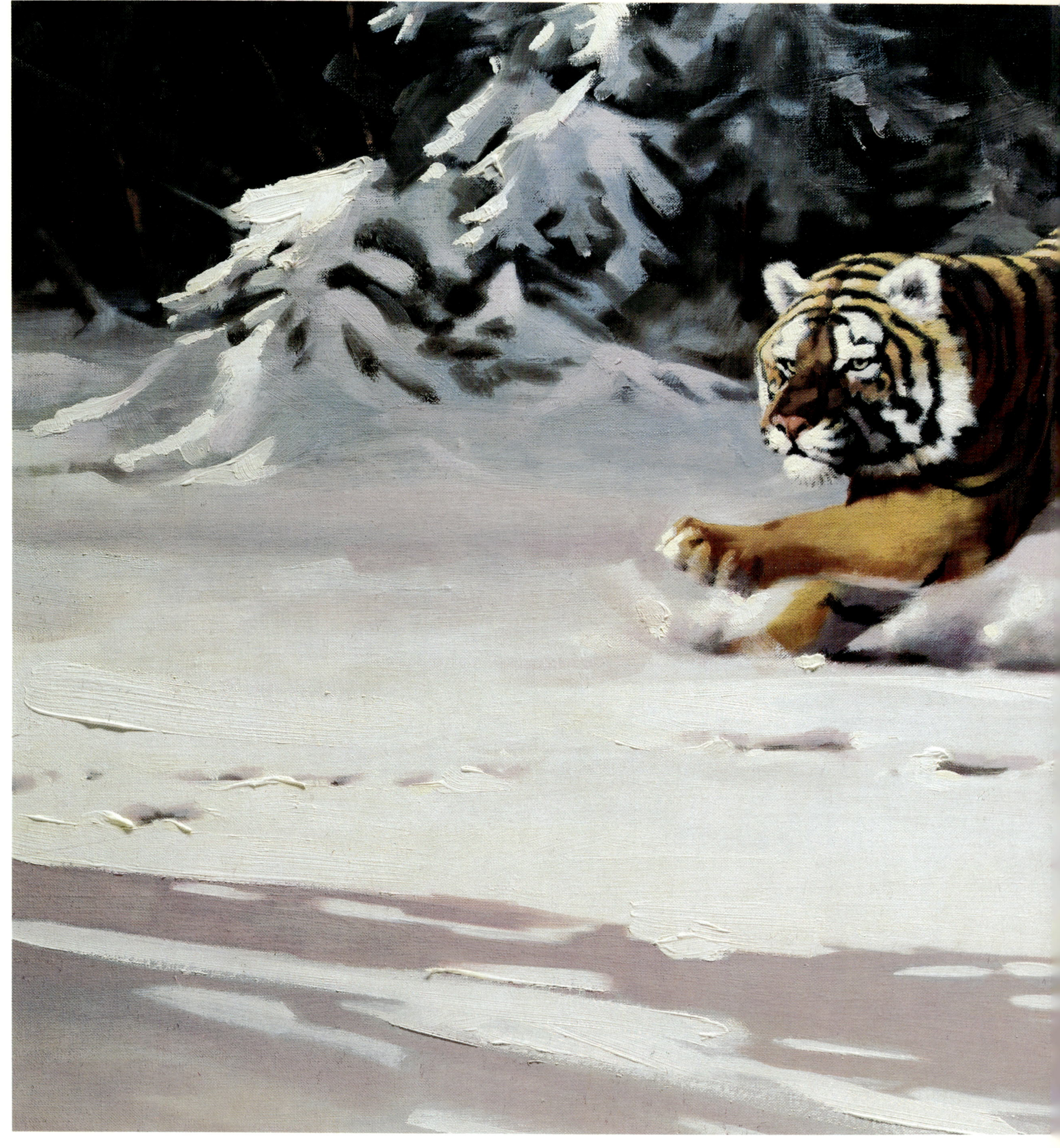

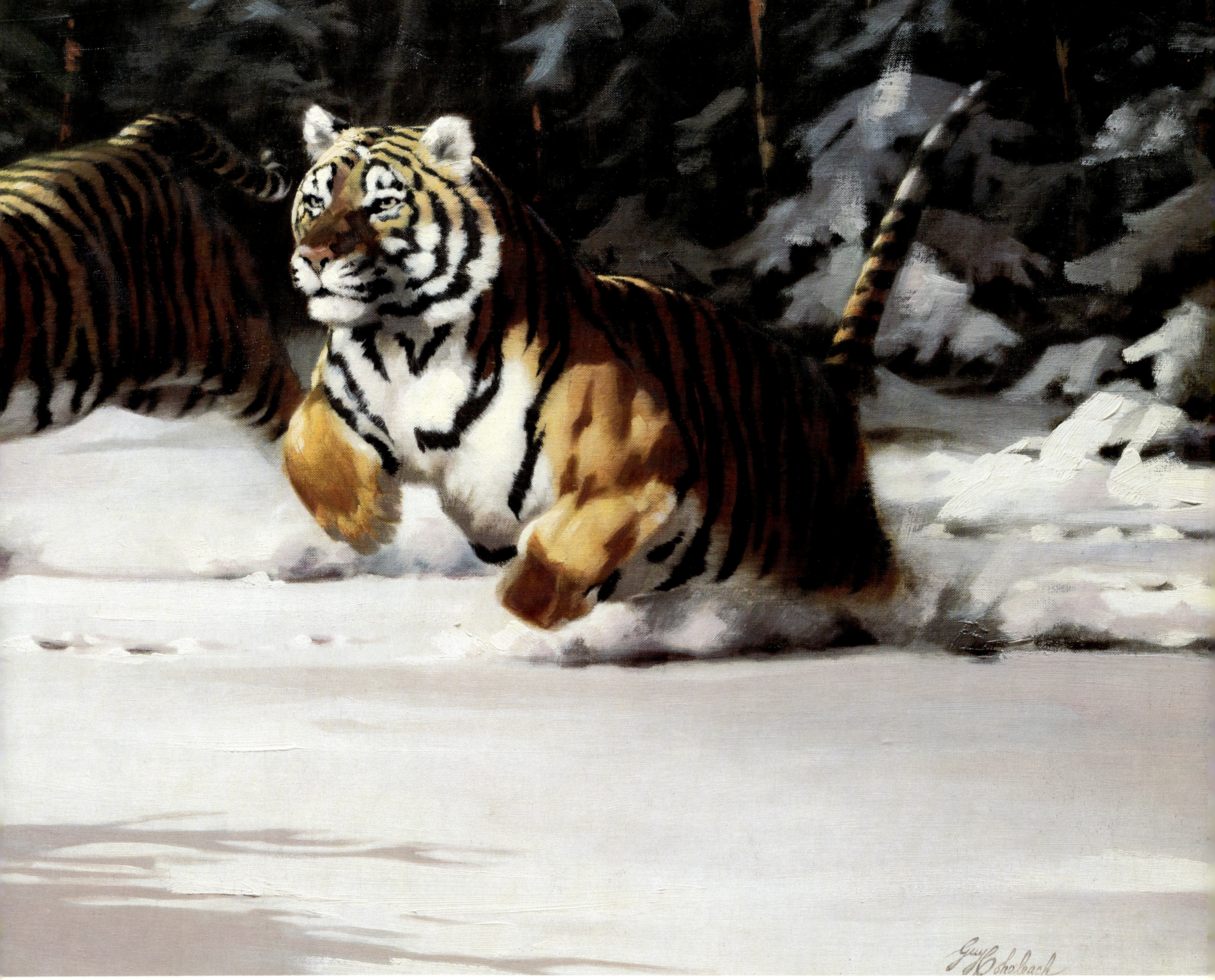
Guy Coheleach

Working on small paintings enables you to toy around with different styles, to experiment with colors, composition, and texture. As a result, you learn faster. Many of my small paintings incorporate happy accidents.

And miniature paintings can be a lot of fun. I would probably never depict a wart hog or ferret in a large painting, but these subjects are perfect for miniatures.

Interestingly, *Cougar* is one of the smallest paintings ever completed by the artist. This reproduction is actually larger than the original.

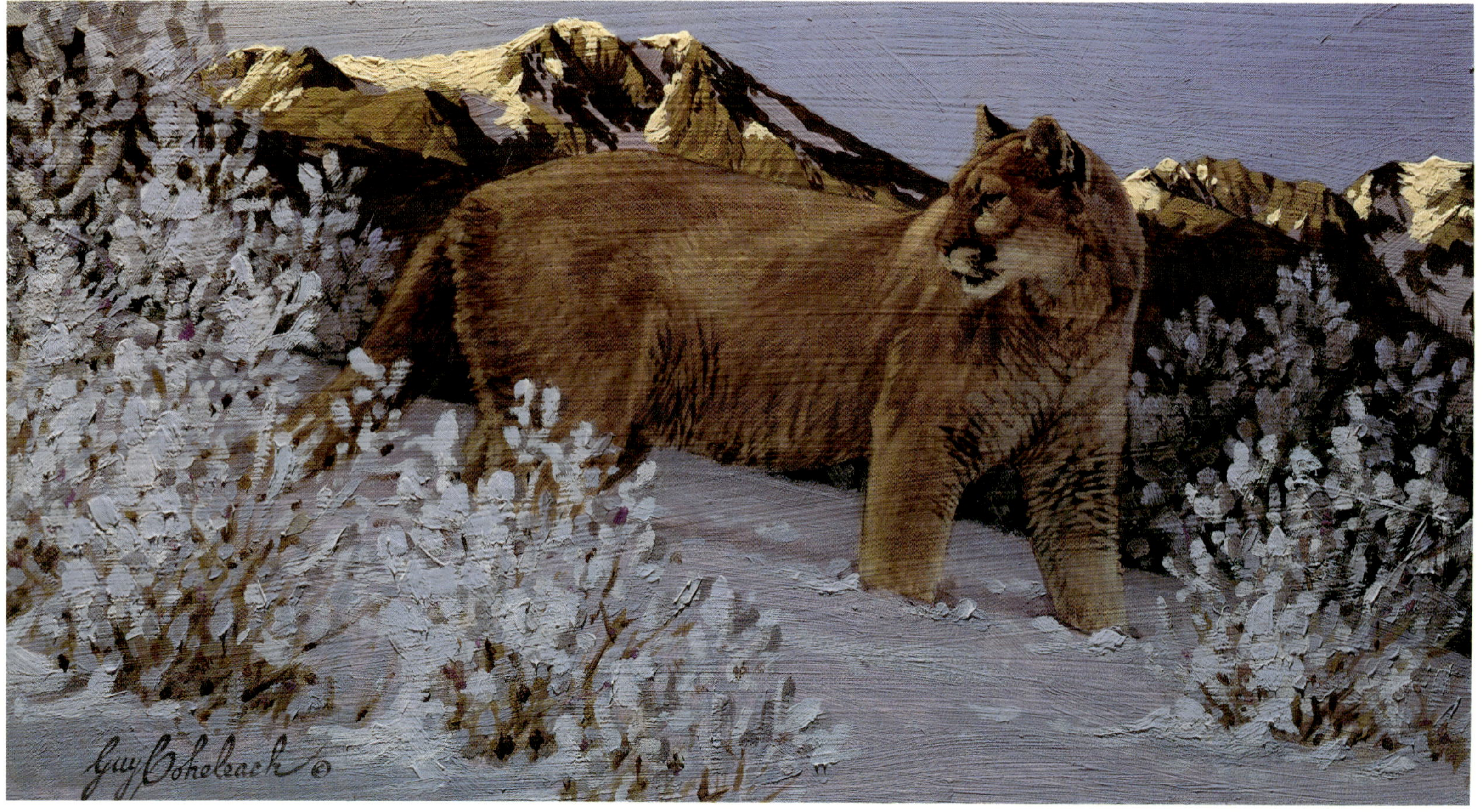

Cougar, 8 x 4, Oil on Masonite

This gouache painting depicts the strong bond between the female cougar and her cubs. She will nurse her young for about three months and remain with them for almost two years, protecting the cubs from other predators and teaching them to hunt.

Cougar and Cubs, 20 x 28, Gouache on Illustration Board

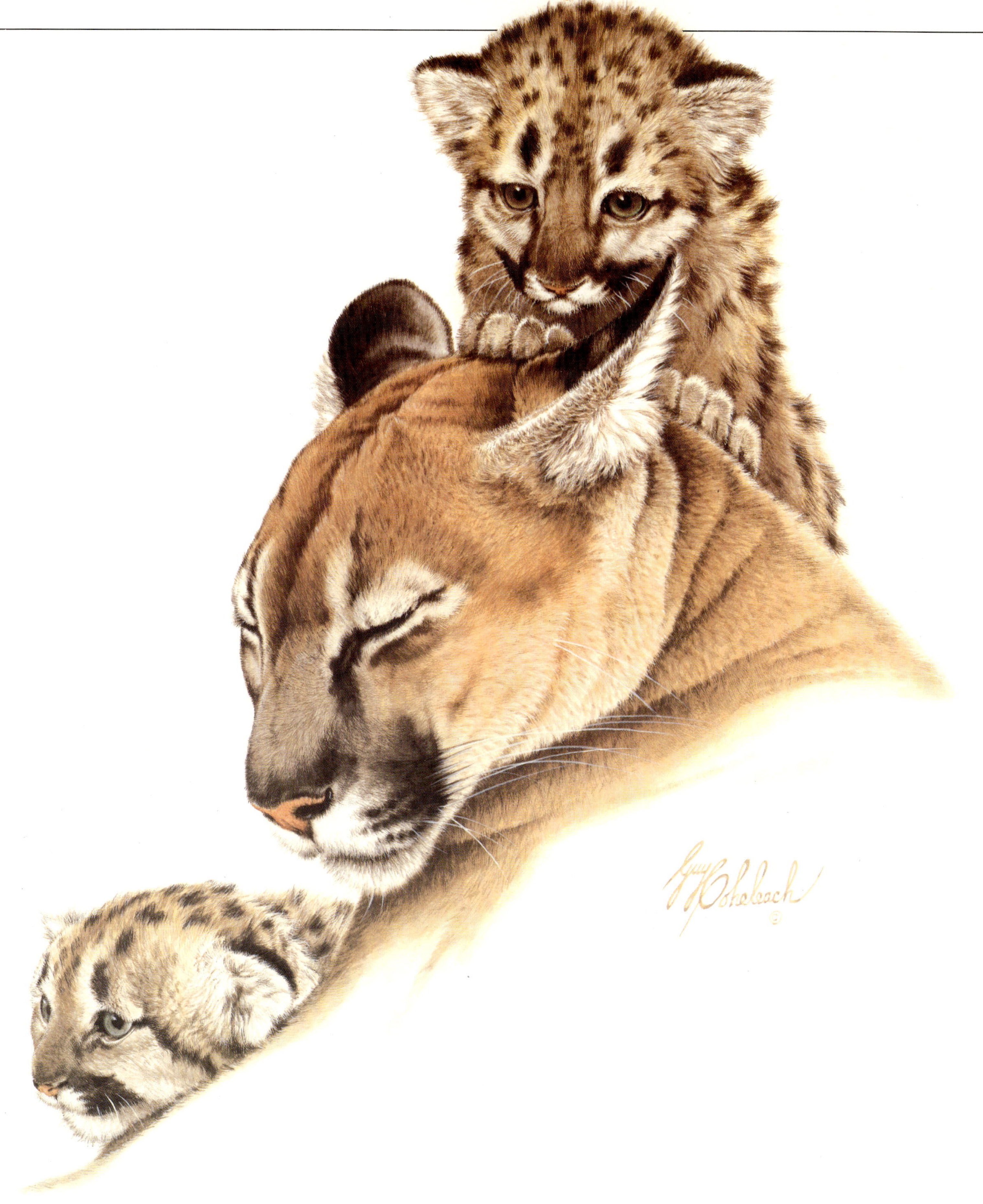

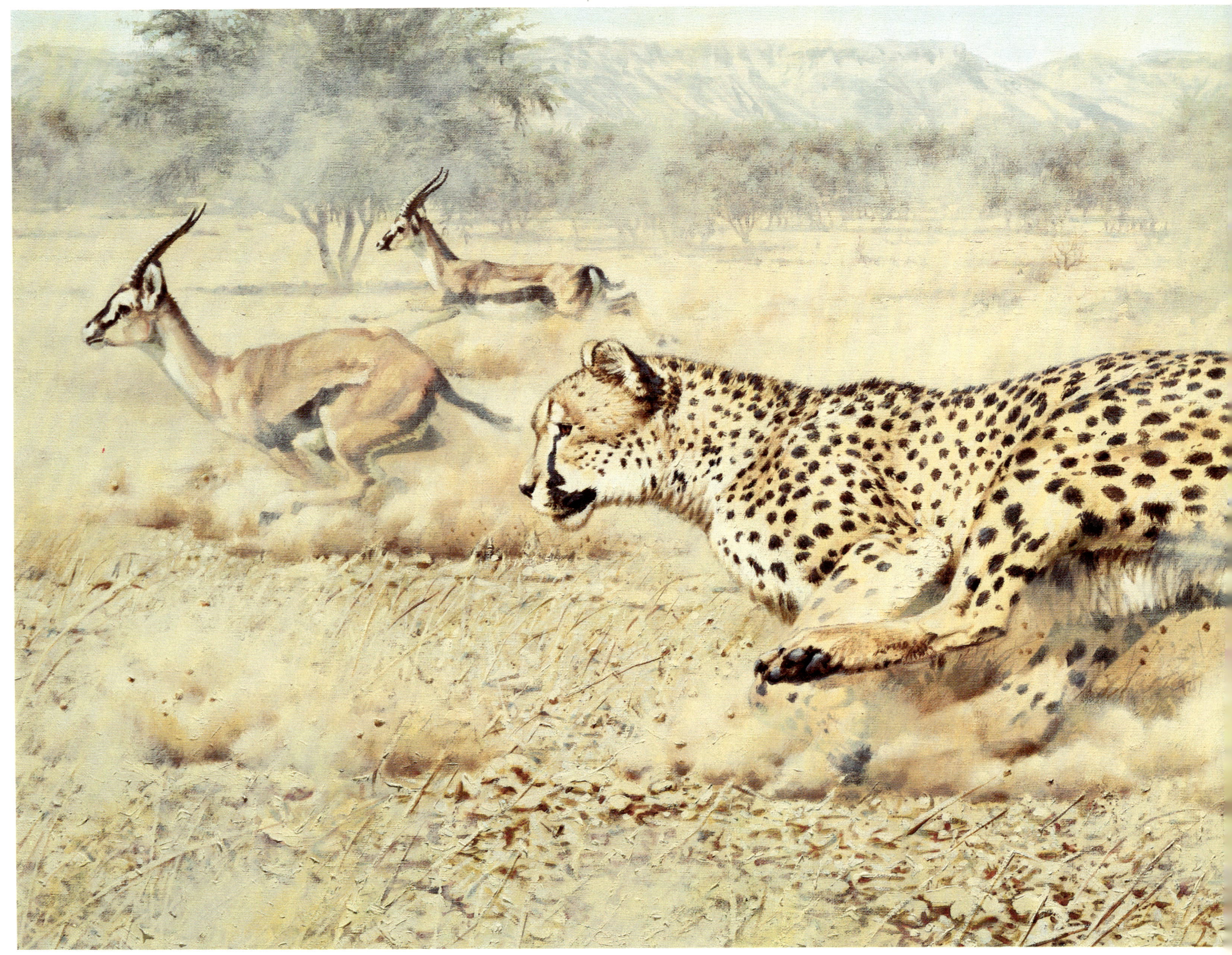

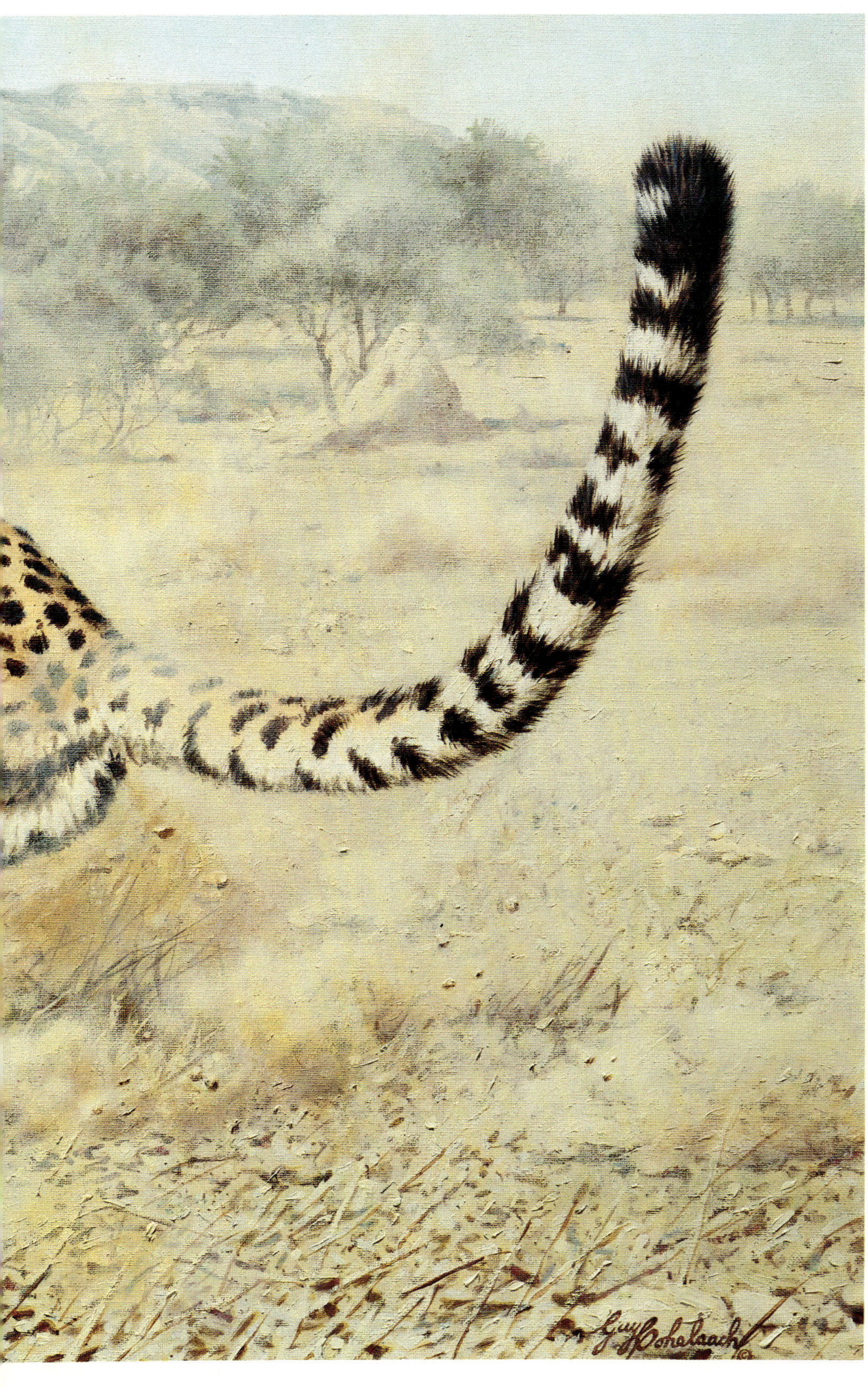

Angel, the star of *Angel's Chase*, is also a star attraction at the Cincinnati Zoo. In 1987 Coheleach was asked to paint a portrait of Angel, but in a wild setting. The result was *Angel's Chase*, which came about only after the artist worked out several technical and compositional problems.

First of all, the markings. To do a portrait of an individual animal, like a cheetah or zebra, each mark must be in exactly the right position. That's not a problem if you have a good photograph to work from and you paint the animal in the same pose. But to do that with the animal in a totally different position, allowing for perspective and muscle movement, can be an exercise in extreme frustration.

My second problem was even worse. I wanted to portray the cheetah in a chase scene, but she had to be large enough to be the focal point. If I put her behind the Thomson's gazelle, close enough that she was still important, she would have to be leaping to make the kill. But I didn't want to depict that actual half-a-second before a cheetah strikes. There are many people, even though they like the cheetah, who want to see the gazelle escape. I considered turning her head and having her chase one of the other Tommies, but then all you would see was the back of her ears. If the gazelle was coming at you, he'd be more important than the cat.

Coheleach solved the problem by having Angel pursuing a gazelle that is one step beyond the canvas; only a spurt of dust from its heels remains. Angel is the unquestioned hero of the painting, and the gazelle's fate is left to the proclivities of the viewer.

Angel's Chase, 44 X 24, Oil on Canvas

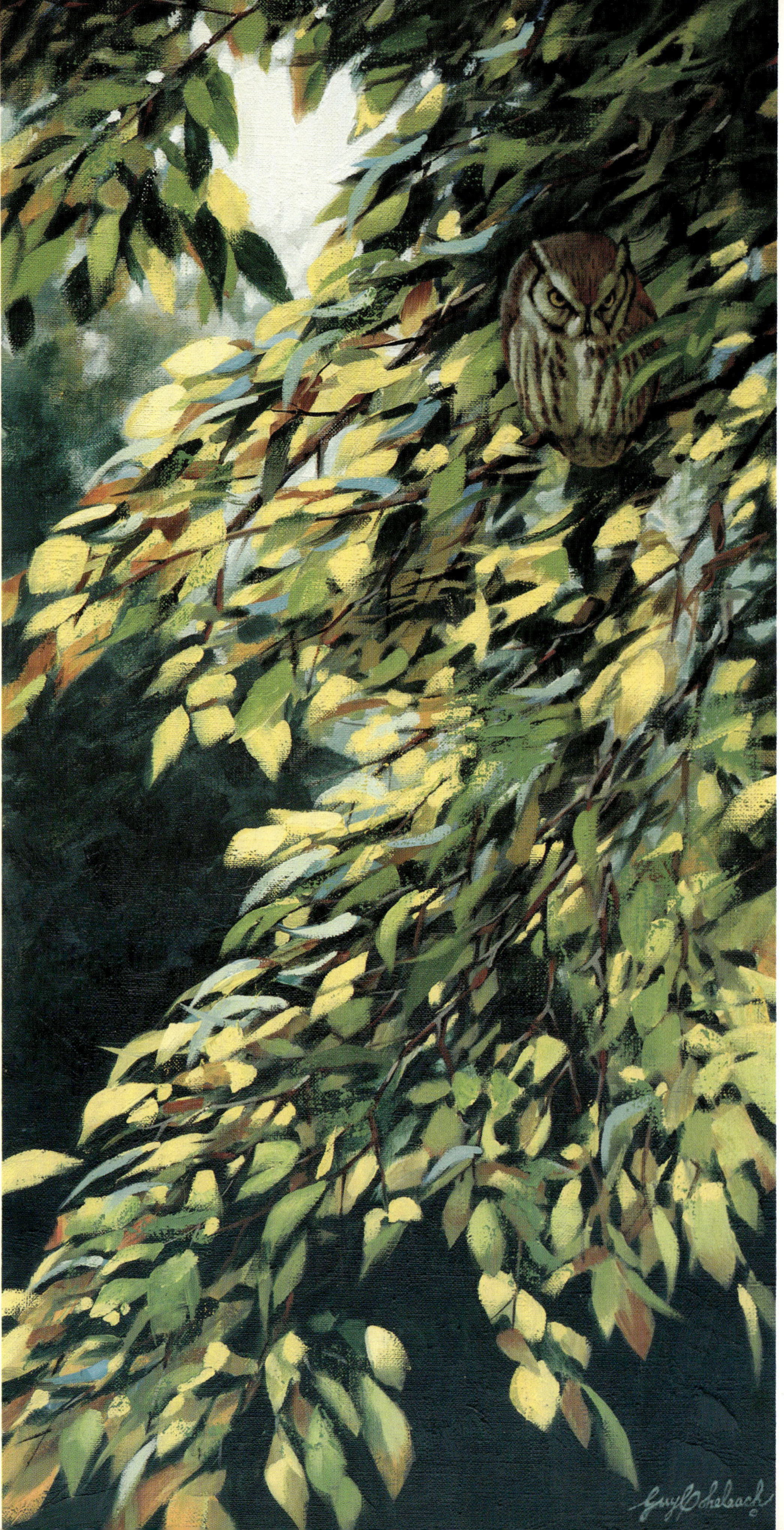

This is a small oil sketch of a screech owl in September, just as the leaves are starting to turn. The leaves form a tapestry of greens and yellows; the owl is brownish, but he is bathed in the bright colors of the leaves.

It is essentially an exercise in splashy color — a very loose oil in which each leaf is little more than a daub of paint. In approach, it is similar to Brightwaters Creek (page 46), although the technique is quite different. In Brightwaters, I set out to paint the water as the focal point. The ducks are loosely done, to draw attention to the water; they are not essential to the painting.

In this sketch, the opposite is true. There has to be a bird to give the painting a focal point; without one, it would look unfinished. And yet, my purpose was simply to paint autumn's brilliant colors.

Screech Owl, 12 x 24, Oil on Canvas

Snowy Egrets is an example of painting on commission and having it really work. *The customer came to me and said 'I'm a Florida resident, and I want a painting of snowy egrets—it's my favorite bird. How long would it take to do a painting?' I gave him an estimate. He asked me how much I made the year before and I told him. 'Divide that by 12 and I'll give you that much a month. Take all the time you need, and when the painting is finished, just bill me for it.'*

And that's the way it worked. It is certainly one of the more successful paintings I've done. The Chinese liked it: it was one of the first western paintings to be exhibited in China since the revolution.

It's the only painting where I had enough time to finish it—that is, where I didn't have something else pressing to do. Of course, as a perfectionist, if I waited until I got it 100 percent perfect, I'd probably still be working on it.

Coheleach was looking for simplicity and subdued, subtle colors, hence the grayish water which blends into the suggested mist of the background. The gray also complements the egret's pristine plumage, giving the painting a serenity which belies the egret's temperament as one of the most aggressive predators in the bird world.

Snowy Egrets, 30 X 40, Casein on Illustration Board

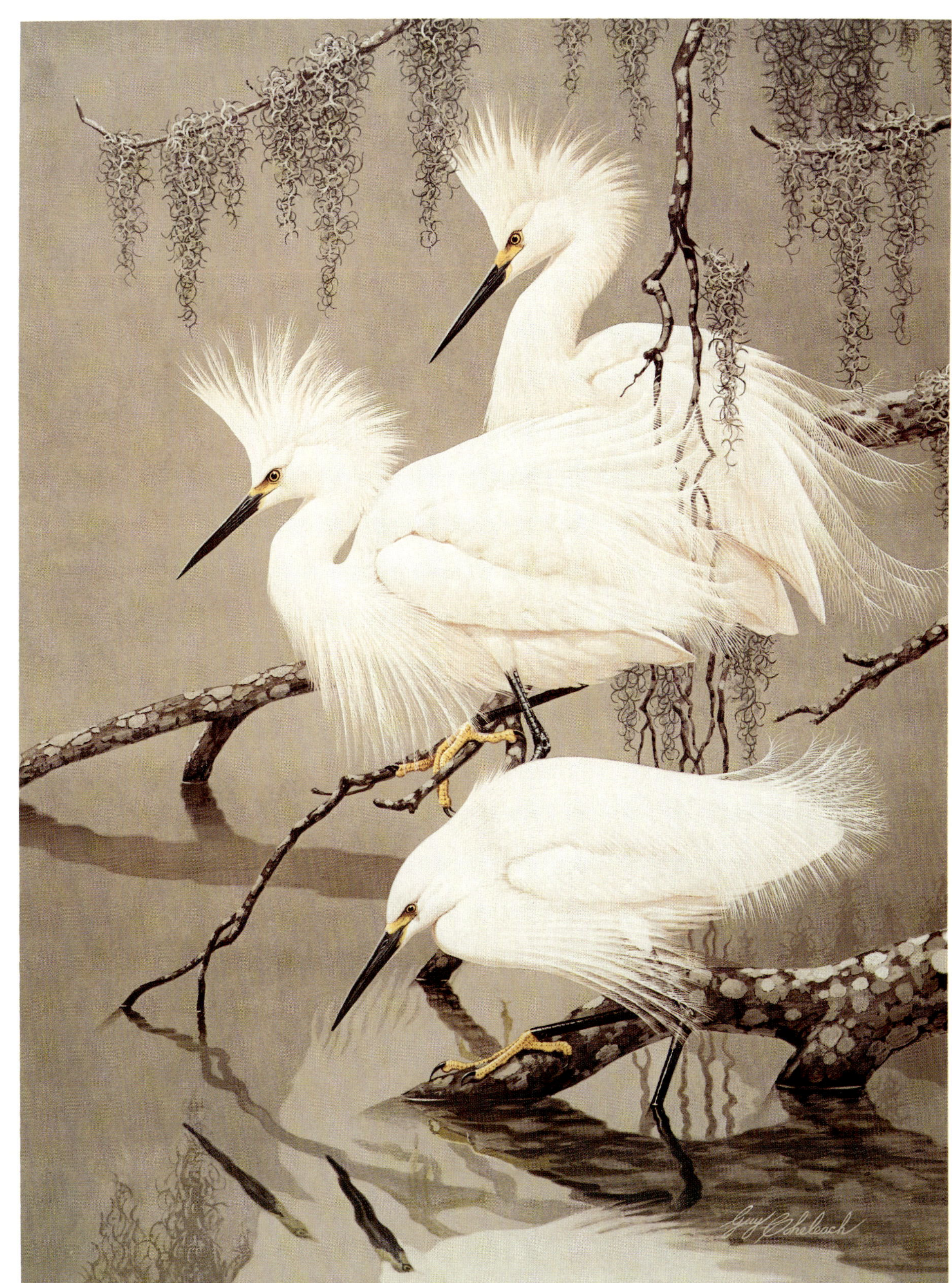

INDEX OF PRINTS & POSTERS